505

Great

Leaders, Scientists, Inventors, Sports People, Stage Performers

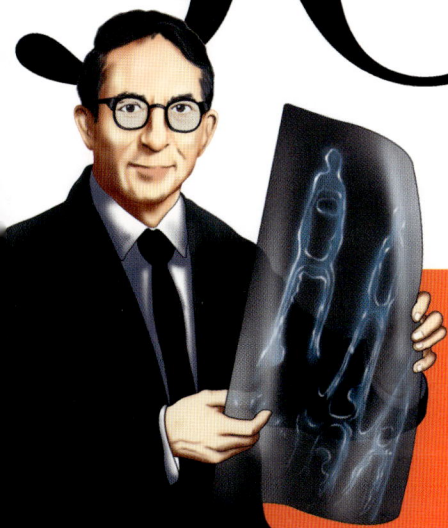

C O N T E N T S

Introduction

The famous author Mark Twain once said, "Great people are those who can make others feel that they too can become great." This book contains such inspirational stories about great personalities from various walks of life. What would the world be like if great leaders like Alexander the Great, Cleopatra, Julius Caesar, Queen Elizabeth I, Winston Churchill, Abraham Lincoln, Martin Luther King and Nelson Mandela had not existed? Can you imagine a life without cars, aeroplanes, telephones and all the other inventions that make our lives easier? What if there were no great sportsperson, musician or actor to look up to? It is impossible to think of a world without great people.

Some great people inspire others, while some teach us to learn from their mistakes and not follow in their footsteps. Read about the good deeds of certain leaders that changed the world for the better and the follies of others that nearly destroyed mankind.

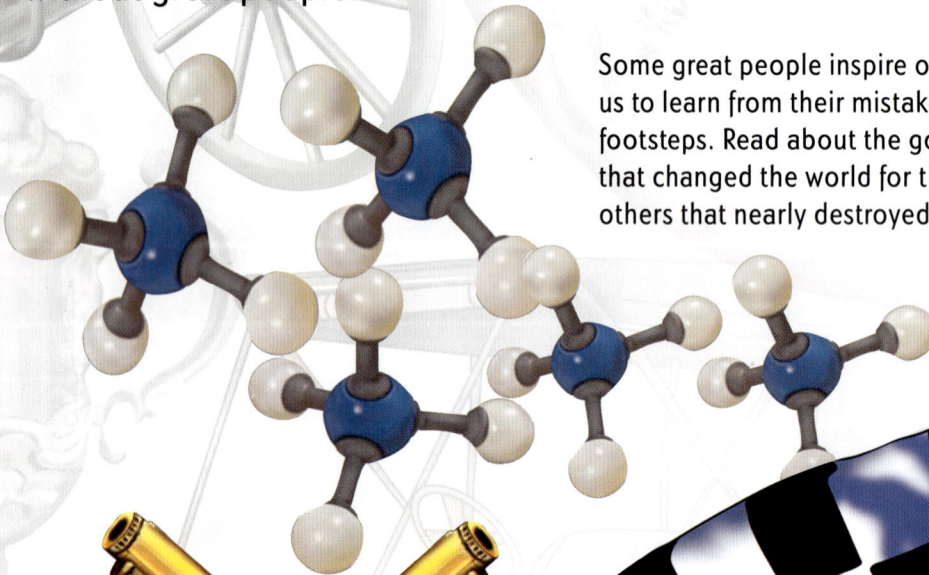

Learn how great sports people like Nadia Comaneci, Muhammad Ali and Pele rose to fame against all odds. Read about the fantastic records set in the field of sports and the men and women who sacrificed everything to follow their dreams. Their stories are incredible and truly inspiring. Enter the graceful world of figure skating and read about the extraordinary feats of some of the greatest names in the field. Discover the passion and determination of sporting legends like Sir Don Bradman, Martina Navratilova, George Best, Michel Platini and Michael Jordan. What is the story behind the invention of basketball? What makes some men risk their lives on the racetrack? Who holds the most number of championship titles in the world of chess? Find answers to all these questions and more in the section on great sporting personalities.

Flip through the pages to discover the story behind the invention of the safety pin. Find out how a musician composed some of the most heavenly strains of music ever heard, even though he could not hear his compositions himself. Discover how one great scientist's discovery triggered another scientist's imagination, and how one man's ambition changed the map of the whole world. Get an insight into the lives and character of great personalities and learn about the dreams that inspired them to greatness.

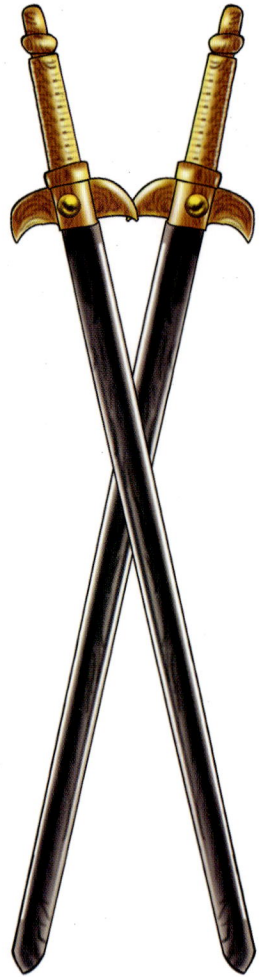

Great

Leaders

1 Ramses II
[1320 B.C. - 1224 B.C.]

1320 B.C.: Born to Seti 1 and Queen Tuya

1290 B.C.: Becomes pharaoh after his father's death

1224 B.C.: Dies at the age of 96

Ramses II the Great was the third king of Egypt's 19th dynasty. Soon after becoming the king, he began a series of wars, the most famous being the Battle of Kadesh. He expanded his empire as far as ancient Ethiopia (now Sudan). Egypt prospered under Ramses II, whose reign was the second longest in Egyptian history. According to legend, he was the pharaoh (Egyptian king) against whom Moses rebelled.

Ramses II

Cyrus the Great

2 Cyrus the Great
[c. 599 B.C. - c. 529 B.C.]

Cyrus the Great was king of Persia and the founder of the vast Persian Empire. In 550 B.C., he defeated the Median rulers and conquered Ecbatana. Subsequently, he extended his control to Lydia and Babylon, establishing the Persian Empire as the biggest power in the world. Cyrus was liked by all because of his generosity towards his people.

599 B.C.: Born to Cambyses, ruler of Anshan

559 B.C.: Succeeds his father to the throne

550 B.C.: Defeats Astyages, the last of the Median rulers

546 B.C.: Becomes the king of Persia and conquers Lydia

538 B.C.: Conquers Babylon

10

3 Pericles
[495 B.C. - 429 B.C.]

Pericles was one of the greatest democratic leaders of Athens. Under him Athens prospered and became very powerful. He built several monuments, including the Parthenon. The period between 461 and 379 B.C. is also known as the "Age of Pericles". However, the rise of Athens under Pericles was resented by neighbouring kingdoms and that led to the Peloponnesian War. During the war a plague spread through Athens, killing Pericles and most of his family.

495 B.C.: Born to Xanthippus and Agariste
458 B.C.: Elected strategos (general)
447 B.C.: Work on the Parthenon starts
429 B.C.: Dies

Pericles

Alexander

4 Demosthenes
[384 B.C. - 322 B.C.]

Known for his inspiring speeches, it is hard to believe that as a child Demosthenes stammered while speaking. The legend goes that Demosthenes, determined to overcome his problem, talked with pebbles in his mouth and recited verses while running! Indeed, by the age of 25 he could speak clearly. His powerful speeches against the invasion of Greece by King Philip of Macedonia, are famous.

384 B.C.: Born to a rich sword maker in Athens
377 B.C.: Orphaned at the tender age of seven
330 B.C.: Gives his greatest oration, "On the Crown"
322 B.C.: Swallows poison after failing in his efforts to free Greece from Macedonia

5 Alexander the Great
[356 B.C. - 323 B.C.]

356 B.C.: Born in Pella, to King Philip II of Macedonia
336 B.C.: Becomes king after Philip II is killed
333 B.C.: Defeats Darius III in the Battle of Issus
332 B.C.: Reaches Egypt, where he is accepted as the pharaoh; founds a city, later named Alexandria after him
July 331 B.C.: Defeats Darius again; becomes the "king of Asia"
327 B.C.: Defeats King Porus
June 13, 323 B.C.: Dies in Babylon

Alexander the Great was the king of Macedonia. He conquered most of the world, including the powerful Persian Empire. His victory against Darius III, king of Persia, won him the title, "king of Asia". Marching towards India, Alexander defeated King Porus at Hydaspes River (now Jhelum). Not satisfied, Alexander continued on his mission until his soldiers refused to go further. He, too, had grown weak from his wounds and long battles and died unable to fulfil his dream of conquering the world.

6 Pompey the Great
[106 B.C. - 48 B.C.]

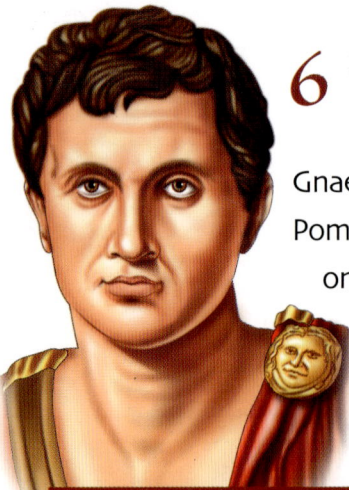

Gnaeus Pompeius Magnus, or Pompey the Great, is regarded as one of the greatest Roman generals of all times. The son of a Roman consul, Gnaeus Pompeius Strabo, Pompey was married to Julius Caesar's daughter. However, a desire to become more powerful turned Pompey against Caeser and he engaged in a long struggle with him. He was finally defeated by Caesar at the Battle of Pharsalus. Pompey escaped to Egypt seeking protection, only to be killed by one of King Ptolemy's councillors.

September 29, 106 B.C.: Born in Picenum

59 B.C.: Joins hands with Julius Caesar and marries his daughter Julia

54 B.C.: Friendship with Caesar ends after Julia's death

48 B.C.: Loses to Caesar (Battle of Pharsalus)

September 29, 48 B.C.: Killed in Egypt

Cleopatra

Julius Caesar

7 Julius Caesar
[100 B.C. - 44 B.C.]

Julius Caesar was a great Roman general and dictator. His greatest conquests included Gaul (present-day France and Belgium). In 47 B.C. Caesar defeated Pharnaces, king of the Cimmerian Bosporus, in five days. It was then that Caesar used the famous words, *veni, vidi, vici* ("I came, I saw, I conquered"), to describe the war. He returned to Rome as a dictator. On March 15, 44 B.C., a group of nobles, including his adopted son Brutus, murdered Caesar in the Senate House.

July 13, 100 B.C.: Born into a noble family in Rome

50 B.C.: Conquers Gaul; alliance with Pompey breaks, starting a civil war

48 B.C.: Defeats Pompey in Greece

46 B.C.: Returns to Rome; reforms the Roman calendar

45 B.C.: The month of Quintil is renamed July in his honour

March 15, 44 B.C.: Killed in Rome

8 Cleopatra - Queen of Egypt
[69 B.C. - 31 B.C.]

Cleopatra succeeded her father Ptolemy XII Auletes to the throne and was the last pharaoh of Egypt. Known for her beauty, ambition and intelligence, she could speak nine languages! When Julius Caesar captured Egypt, she sought his help to regain control from her brother Ptolemy XIII. Following Caesar's death, she married his general, Marcus Anthony. When Augustus Caesar defeated Anthony at the Battle of Actium and conquered Alexandria, Cleopatra killed herself using a snake.

69 B.C.: Born

51 B.C.: Succeeds to the throne along with her brother, Ptolemy XIII

47 B.C.: Becomes co-ruler with Ptolemy XIV, after having Ptolemy XIII killed with the help of Julius Caesar

36 B.C.: Marries Marcus Anthony

31 B.C.: Commits suicide after losing the Battle of Actium to Augustus

Augustus

9 Augustus Caesar
[63 B.C. - A.D. 14]

September 23, 63 B.C.: Born as Gaius Octavius

42 B.C.: Defeats Caesar's assassins, Brutus and Cassius, in the final battle at Philippi

September 2, 31 B.C.: Defeats Marcus Anthony in a naval battle near Actium

January 16, 27 B.C.: Roman Senate gives him the title of Augustus

12 B.C.: Becomes pontifex maximus (head of the Roman religion) after the death of Lepidus

August 19, A.D. 14: Dies in Nola, near Naples; succeeded by stepson Tiberius

Julius Caesar's great-nephew, Octavius, joined with Marcus Anthony and Marcus Aemilius Lepidus to kill his great-uncle's murderers. Later, though, Octavius fought Anthony for control of the empire and defeated him at the Battle of Actium. Octavius became the first emperor of Rome. In 27 B.C., the Roman Senate named him Augustus, meaning "the holy one".

10 Hadrianus
[76 - 138]

January 24, 76: Born in Spain

117: Succeeds his adoptive father, Trajan, as emperor

122: Orders the construction of Hadrian's Wall

132: Suppresses uprising of Jews

138: Adopts Antoninus Pius

July 10, 138: Dies

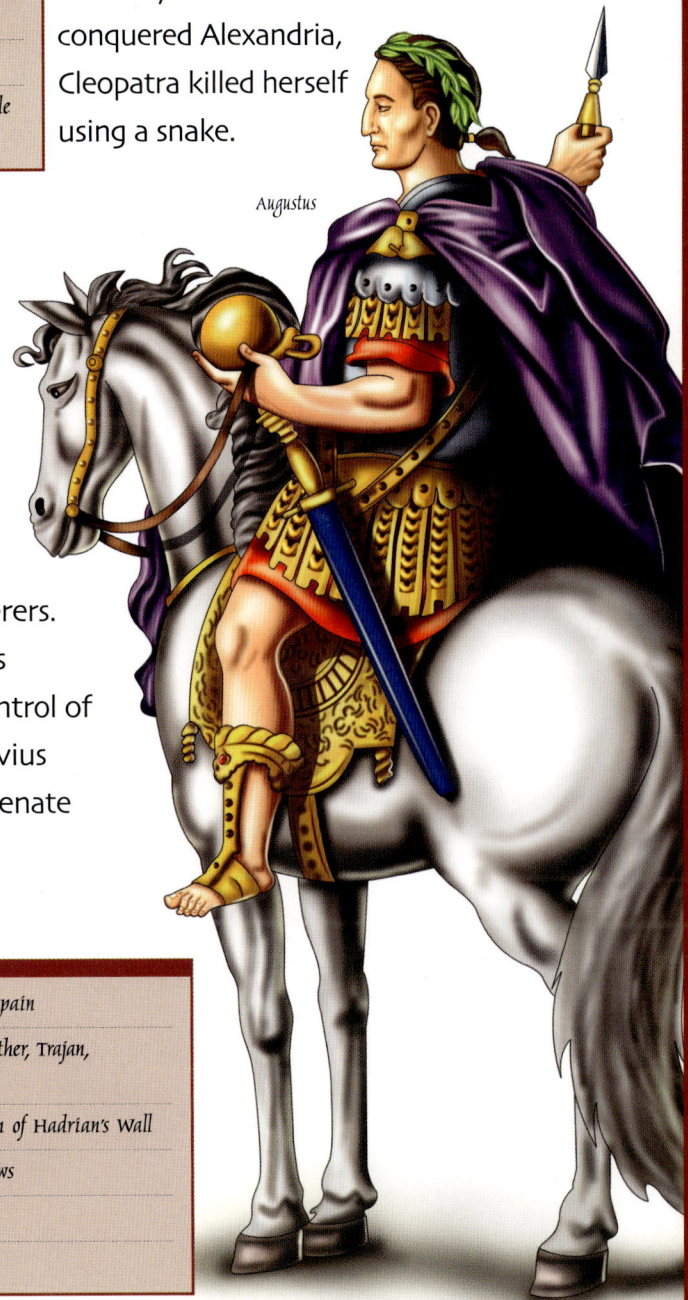

Publius Aelius Hadrianus, or Hadrian, was one of the "Five Good Emperors" of Rome. He brought stability and peace to his land. After suppressing a Jewish uprising, Hadrian declared Jerusalem a Roman city. He built the famous Hadrian's Wall, stretching 118 km (73 miles) across the north of Roman Britain, and the Arch of Hadrian in Athens. He also rebuilt the Pantheon in Rome. On his death, Hadrian was succeeded by Antoninus Pius.

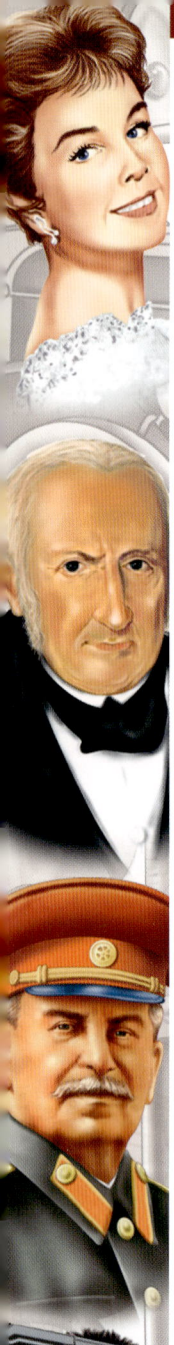

11 Marcus Aurelius
[121 - 180]

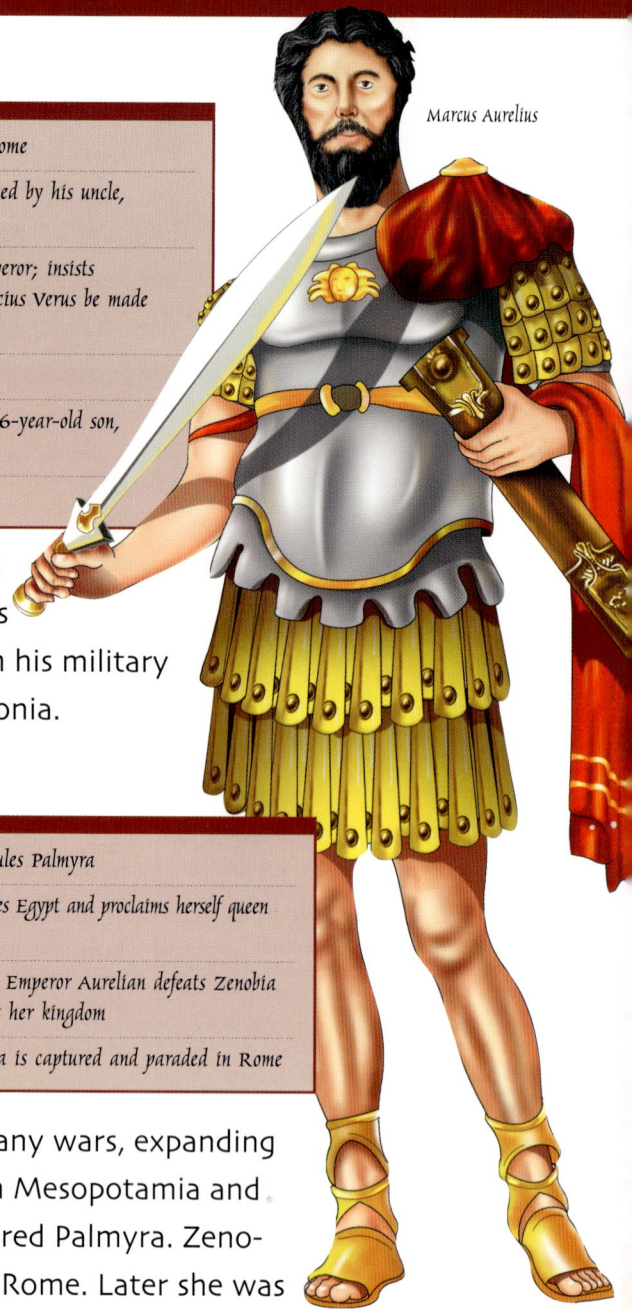

Marcus Aurelius belonged to the Nervan-Antonian dynasty of the Roman Empire. He was named Marcus Aurelius Antoninus when he was appointed heir to Emperor Antoninus Pius. A thoughtful and learned figure, Marcus is better known as a philosopher-king. The most famous of his works are the *Meditations*, written in Greek. He died in his military camp at Vindobona (Vienna) or Sirmium, Pannonia.

April 26, 121: Born in Rome

February 25, 138: Adopted by his uncle, Emperor Antoninus Pius

161: Becomes Roman emperor; insists that adoptive brother Lucius Verus be made co-emperor

169: Verus dies of stroke

177: Marcus makes his 16-year-old son, Commodus, co-emperor

March 17, 180: Dies

Marcus Aurelius

12 Zenobia
[Died after 274]

Zenobia reigned as queen of Palmyra in 267-272. She is believed to have murdered her husband Septimius Odenathus and obtained control of his lands for her son Vaballathus. She waged many wars, expanding her territory to East Asia Minor, Syria, northern Mesopotamia and Egypt. In 272, Roman Emperor Aurelian conquered Palmyra. Zenobia was captured and paraded on the streets of Rome. Later she was granted a villa in Tibur, where she spent the rest of her life.

267-272: Rules Palmyra

269: Captures Egypt and proclaims herself queen of Egypt

272: Roman Emperor Aurelian defeats Zenobia and conquers her kingdom

274: Zenobia is captured and paraded in Rome

13 Constantine the Great
[c. 280 - 337]

Constantine I was born to Roman Emperor Constantius I and Helena, an innkeeper's daughter. He reunited the Roman Empire after coming to power in 306. He was the first Roman emperor to support Christianity. He rebuilt the ancient Greek city of Byzantine, renamed it Nova Roma and made it his capital. It was renamed Constantinople after his death.

c. 280: Born in Naissus, Moesia

July 25, 306: His troops name him Augustus

315: Conquers Greece and the Balkans

May 11, 330: Makes Byzantine (now Istanbul, Turkey) the capital of the Roman Empire

May 22, 337: Dies in Ancyrona, Bithynia; before his death, divides the empire among his three sons

Constantine I

Attila

14 Attila the Hun
[406 - 453]

Attila and his brother Bleda succeeded their uncle as leaders of the Huns, a wandering tribe. It is believed that Attila killed his brother on a hunting trip to become the sole ruler. He then began terrorising Europe and Asia. His invasion of Gaul ended in defeat at the hands of the Romans and the Visigoths. Attila then invaded Italy. It is said that he did not capture Rome because of a request made by Pope Leo I.

406: Doubt still exists as to his exact year of birth

432: The Huns unite, for the first time, under Rua

434: Rua's nephews Attila and Bleda succeed him

445: Attila kills Bleda

447: Invades the Balkan provinces

September 20, 451: Defeated in the Battle of Chalons by the combined forces of Roman general Aetius and the Visigoths

452: Invades Italy, but does not capture Rome

453: Dies

Empress Theodora

15 Theodora
[c. 497 - 548]

c. 497: Born

525: Marries Justinian I

527: Becomes empress

532: Advises her husband on how to handle the Nika riots

548: Dies in Constantinople (now Istanbul, Turkey)

One of the greatest Byzantine rulers, Theodora was born to a bear keeper at the circus. She was an actress before she married Justinian I. When he succeeded to the throne, Theodora was proclaimed empress. An able leader, Theodora was responsible for crushing the Nika riots of 532. She also persuaded the emperor to change the laws to permit noblemen to marry lower-class women like her.

16 Maurice
[c. 539 - 602]

c. 539: Born in Cappadocia

582: Becomes emperor

591: Ends war with Persia

602: Killed by his soldiers on orders of Phocas

Maurice was a successful general who became the Byzantine emperor after the death of his father-in-law, Tiberius II. Maurice's rule was troubled by wars on all frontiers. Although he could not defeat the Lombards in Italy, he ended the war with Persia and restored Khusro II to the throne. Unfortunately, he failed to control the growing bitterness among his soldiers. He was overthrown and succeeded by a junior officer called Phocas.

Charlemagne

17 Charlemagne
[c.742 - 814]

April 2, c. 742: Born to the first Carolingian king, Pippin the Short

768: Becomes ruler with his brother Carloman

800: Crowned emperor by the Pope, in Rome

813: Makes son Louis I co-emperor

814: Dies; buried in the Aachen cathedral

Charlemagne ("Charles the Great") was the elder son of King Pippin III (the Short) of the Carolingian dynasty. On Pippin's death, Charlemagne and his brother Carloman became joint rulers. Carloman's death in 771 left Charlemagne the sole ruler of the Franks. In 800, on Christmas Day, Pope Leo III crowned him emperor. Literature, art and architecture flourished during his reign.

William I

18 William I
[c. 1027 - 1087]

Also called "William the Conqueror" and "William of Normandy", he was one of the greatest monarchs of England. At a very young age, he succeeded his father as the duke of Normandy. Later, William invaded England when Harold Godwinson, the earl of Wessex, succeeded King Edward to the throne. He defeated the earl at the Battle of Hastings to seize the throne.

c. 1027: Born in Falaise, Normandy, to Robert I, duke of Normandy and Arletta

1035: Becomes duke of Normandy

1047: Establishes power in Normandy by defeating rebel Norman barons with the help of King Henri I of France

October 14, 1066: At the famous Norman Conquest, William defeats King Harold

September 9, 1087: Dies after falling from a horse; buried at St. Stephen's Church, Caen

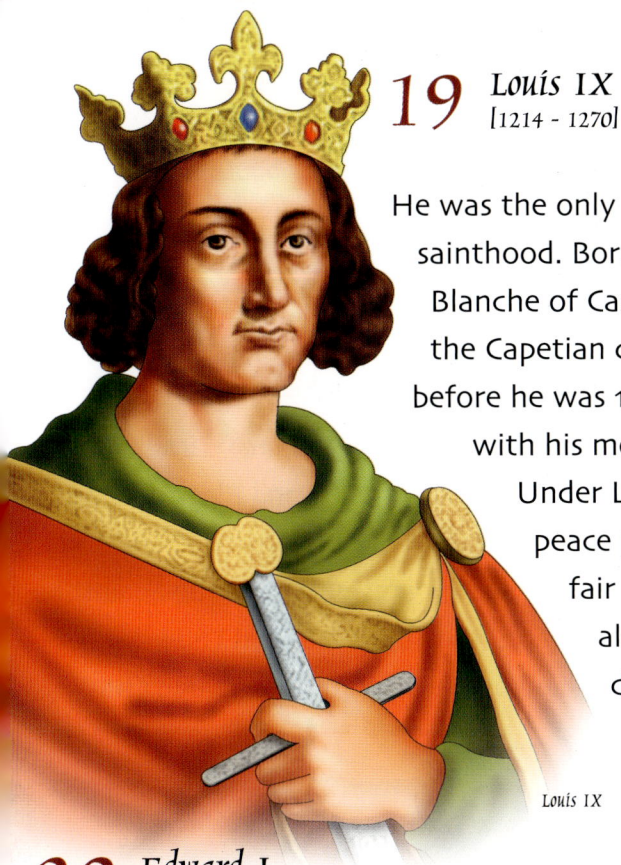

19 Louis IX
[1214 - 1270]

He was the only king of France to achieve sainthood. Born to King Louis VIII and Blanche of Castile, Louis IX belonged to the Capetian dynasty. His father died before he was 13 and he was made king, with his mother as acting ruler. Under Louis IX prosperity and peace prevailed in France. Known to be a just and fair ruler, he made running the government easier and also improved tax distribution. Pope Boniface VIII declared him a saint in 1297.

April 25, 1214: Born at Poissy, France

1226: Crowned the king of France after his father's death

May 27, 1234: Marries Marguerite de Provence

August 25, 1270: Dies near Tunis

August 11, 1297: Canonized by the Pope

Louis IX

20 Edward I
[1239 - 1307]

Soon after becoming the king of England, Edward I conquered Wales. He also crushed the Scottish uprising and killed their leader, Sir William Wallace, after defeating him in battle. Edward considered the Jews, most of whom were moneylenders, as a threat to the country and ordered them to wear yellow stars, so that they could be easily identified. Edward was also known for the various measures he introduced in administration.

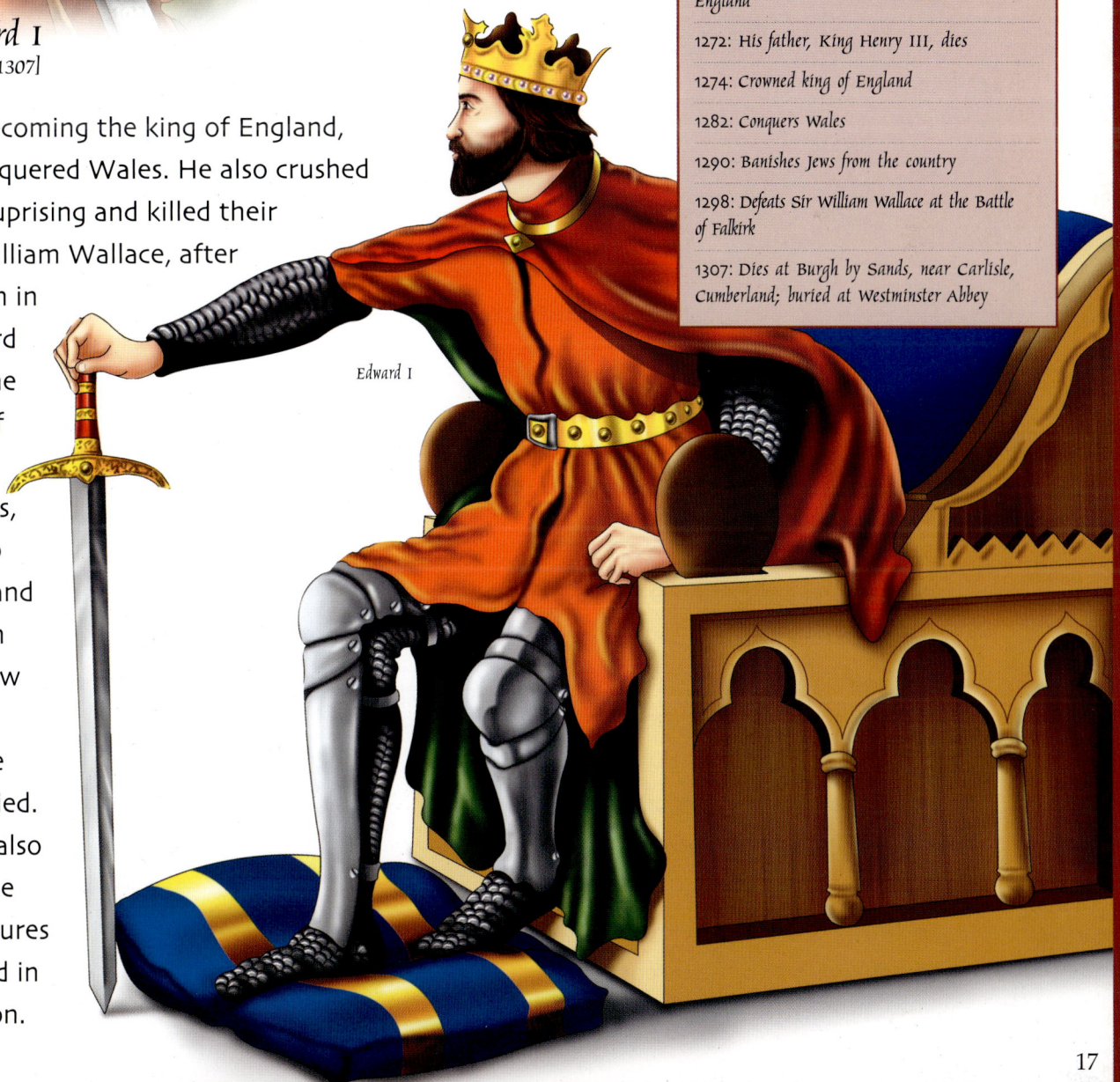

Edward I

1239: Born at the Palace of Westminster, England

1272: His father, King Henry III, dies

1274: Crowned king of England

1282: Conquers Wales

1290: Banishes Jews from the country

1298: Defeats Sir William Wallace at the Battle of Falkirk

1307: Dies at Burgh by Sands, near Carlisle, Cumberland; buried at Westminster Abbey

21 Timur
[1336 - 1405]

Timur

Timur, also called Timurlenk ("Timur the Lame"), was a Mongol conqueror known for his savage conquests. The son of a tribal leader, Timur claimed he was related to Genghis Khan (creator of the Mongolian Empire). Timur conquered the territory between the Caspian and Black seas and invaded several Russian states. He also captured Persia and invaded India. However, his greatest victory came against the Ottoman Turks, capturing Sultan Bayazid I and destroying his army. Timur died on an expedition to invade China.

1336: Born at Kesh near Samarkand, Uzbekistan

1369: Emerges as the supreme military leader of Turkistan

1398: Invades India and conquers Delhi

1402: Captures Sultan Bayazid I at Angora (now Ankara)

February 19, 1405: Dies of plague in Otrar

22 Ivan the Great
[1440 - 1505]

Ivan Vasilyevich, also called "Ivan the Great", was the grand prince of Moscow and the man responsible for uniting Russia. His greatest conquests included Tver and Novgorod. He freed Russia from the Tatars and put an end to threats of Mongol invasion. Ivan also formulated laws and promoted foreign artists. Monuments constructed in his time have a distinct Italian style.

January 22, 1440: Born in Moscow

1478: Captures Novgorod

1480: Frees Russia from the Tatars

October 27, 1505: Dies in Moscow; son Vasily III succeeds him

23 Isabella I
[1451 - 1504]

Isabella I

Isabella I, the queen of Castile, married King Ferdinand II of Aragon in 1469. She and her husband established the "Spanish Inquisition" against the Jews and Moors (Muslims) who, despite converting to Christianity, continued to practise their original religion. She was also responsible for throwing Jews out of Spain, the conquest of Granada and the forced conversion of the Moors. A great patron of art, the queen extended her support to the famous explorer Christopher Columbus.

April 22, 1451: Born to King John II and Queen Isabella of Portugal

1469: Marries King Ferdinand II

1478: Establishes the Spanish Inquisition

1479: Becomes queen of Castile after a four-year-long civil war following the death of her half-brother, King Henry IV

1492: Conquers Granada; expels Jews from Spain

November 26, 1504: Dies

24 *Maximilian I*
[1459 - 1519]

Maximilian I

Son of Emperor Frederick III, Maximilian I was the Holy Roman emperor and the king of Germany. As emperor, he introduced much-needed changes to the government and the army. He also joined the Holy League to counter the French and tried to expand his territory through the Italian Wars. Popular among his subjects, Maximilian promoted both science and the arts.

Mary I

March 22, 1459: *Born in Vienna, Austria*

1477: *Marries Mary, heiress of Burgundy*

1493: *Succeeds his father, Frederick III, as the Holy Roman emperor*

January 12, 1519: *Dies in Wels, Upper Austria; succeeded by his grandson Charles V*

25 *Mary I - Queen of England*
[1516 - 1558]

Queen Mary I of England was the only child of King Henry VIII and Queen Catherine. Unlike her father, Mary was a strong Catholic. Immediately after becoming the queen, she tried to establish Roman Catholicism in England. Several popular Protestant leaders were executed in the process, earning her the title "Bloody Mary". At the end, her attempts proved to be largely un-successful.

February 18, 1516: *Born in Greenwich, London*

July 19, 1553: *Becomes queen after half-brother Edward VI dies*

1554: *Marries Philip II of Spain*

November 17, 1558: *Dies in London; succeeded by half-sister Elizabeth I*

26 Philip II
[1527 - 1598]

King of Spain and of Portugal, Philip II was born to Holy Roman Emperor Charles V and Isabella of Portugal. He became king after his father stepped down in 1556. In 1580, he invaded Portugal and seized power. During his reign, Spanish colonies were established in the Americas and the 60-year war with France ended, but his rule was also marked by financial instability and conflicts with England and the Netherlands.

May 21, 1527: Born at Valladolid, Spain

1554: Marries Queen Mary I of England, after the death of his first wife

1556: Becomes king of Spain

1559: Signs the Peace of Cateau-Cambresis, ending the war with France

1598: His son Philip III succeeds him after his death

27 Elizabeth I
[1533 - 1603]

Elizabeth I was the last of the Tudors and succeeded Queen Mary I, who died childless. Several attempts were made to kill the Protestant queen, but Elizabeth survived and went on to become one of the most respected English monarchs. The arts, especially literature , flourished under her (Shakespeare lived during her time). Also called the "Virgin Queen", Elizabeth never married.

September 7, 1533: Born to King Henry VIII and his second wife, Anne Boleyn

1558: Succeeds Mary I as the queen of England

February 25, 1570: Excommunicated by the Pope Pius V; Ridolfo leads a Roman Catholic plot to kill the queen and replace her with Queen Mary I of Scotland

1587: Mary I of Scotland is executed

1588: Scores a decisive victory over the Spanish Armada, sent by King Philip II of Spain

March 24, 1603: Dies at Richmond Palace, Surrey, without naming her successor

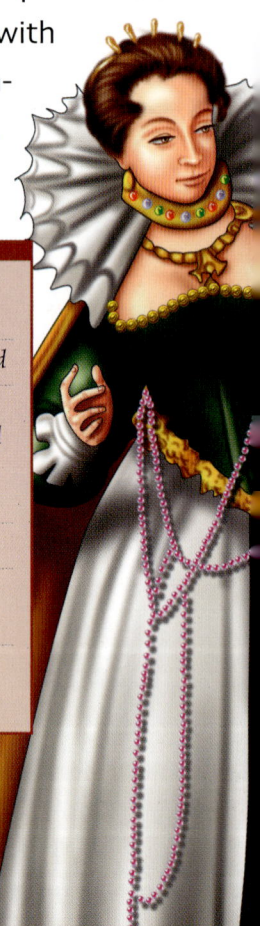

28 Henry IV
[1553 - 1610]

The first Bourbon king of France, King Henry IV was the son of Antoine de Bourbon and Jeanne d'Albret, the queen of Navarra. A man of vision and courage, Henry promoted agriculture and industry, built several roads, bridges and canals and expanded foreign trade. He also promoted colonization of Canada. One of the most popular rulers of all times, Henry IV was killed by a fanatical Roman Catholic.

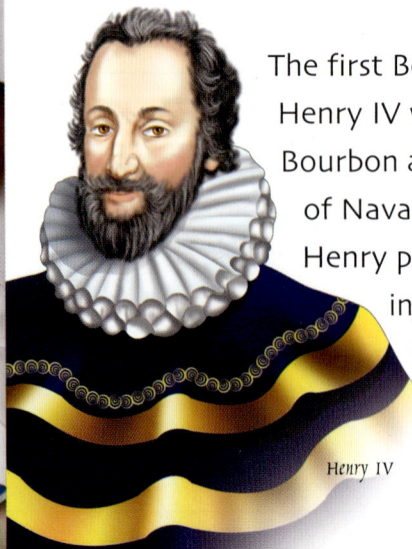

Henry IV

December 13, 1553: Born in Pau, Navarre

1584: Becomes legal heir to the French throne upon the death of the duke of Alencon

1589: After the death of King Henry III, the Catholic League prevents him from becoming king

July 25, 1593: Converts to Roman Catholicism

February 27, 1594: Crowned king of France

1578: Orders construction of Pont Neuf, the bridge across Seine River

May 14, 1610: Killed by Francois Ravaillac; buried at St. Denis Basilica

29 Oliver Cromwell [1599 - 1658]

Oliver Cromwell was a soldier and statesman who also served as lord protector of England for several years. He defeated King Charles I in the First Civil War and supported his removal from Parliament. Cromwell was involved in the king's trial and, finally, his execution after the Second Civil War. Cromwell is also infamously associated with the mass murder of over 3,000 Irishmen in Drogheda after its capture. This stirred up English-Irish hostilities, which were to last for over three centuries.

April 25, 1599: Born in Huntingdon, England, to Robert Cromwell and Elizabeth Stewart

1628: Elected to Parliament

1647: Supports removal of Charles I from Parliament

1649: Massacres over 3,000 people, including Irish Royalist soldiers and Catholic priests, in Drogheda

1651: Approves the Navigation Act, which led to the first of the Dutch Wars

1657: Declines the kingship offered by Parliament

September 3, 1658: Dies in London; within two years Charles II is restored as king

Sir Walter Raleigh lays down his cloak for Queen Elizabeth I

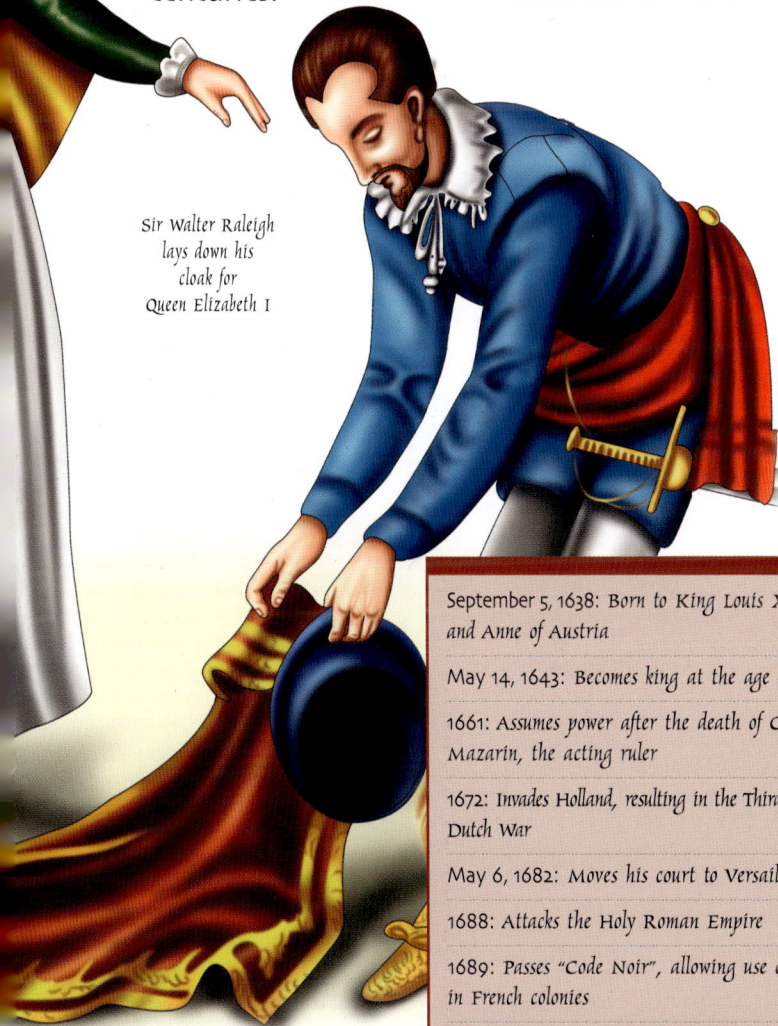

30 Louis XIV [1638 - 1715]

September 5, 1638: Born to King Louis XIII and Anne of Austria

May 14, 1643: Becomes king at the age of four

1661: Assumes power after the death of Cardinal Mazarin, the acting ruler

1672: Invades Holland, resulting in the Third Dutch War

May 6, 1682: Moves his court to Versailles

1688: Attacks the Holy Roman Empire

1689: Passes "Code Noir", allowing use of slaves in French colonies

September 1, 1715: Succeeded by his great-grandson Louis XV after his death

King Louis XIV ruled France from 1643 until his death in 1715. During his rule, France fought four major wars that expanded its boundaries and made it one of the most powerful states in Europe. Louis also promoted slavery in the French colonies and encouraged anti-Protestant activities. It is believed that his policies were largely responsible for the conditions leading to the French Revolution.

31 Peter I
[1672 - 1725]

Peter I

Peter the Great was the first emperor of Russia. He played a major role in the formation of modern Russia. As part of this exercise, he banned the traditional Russian dress, imposed taxes on beards and encouraged Russians to go abroad for education. During his rule, Russia was constantly at war – first with the Ottoman Empire and then with Charles XII of Sweden. He finally defeated Charles XII at Poltava, in 1709.

June 9, 1672: Born to Czar Alexis and his second wife, Natalya Naryshkina

1682: Made tsar with his brother Ivan V

1696: Becomes sole ruler after death of Ivan V

1700: Loses the Battle of Narva against Charles XII of Sweden

1703: Founds the city of St. Petersburg

1708: Defeated by Charles XII at Golovchin

June 27, 1709: Defeats Charles XII at Poltava, forcing him to flee

1721: Russian Senate proclaims him the emperor

February 8, 1725: Dies in St. Petersburg

32 Robert Walpole, 1st Earl of Orford
[1676 - 1745]

Regarded as the first British prime minister, Sir Robert Walpole served during the reigns of George I and George II. An able and shrewd statesman, Walpole adopted a policy of friendship even towards England's biggest rival, France. He introduced several economic reforms and promoted trade by encouraging the production of raw materials in the British colonies.

August 26, 1676: Born in Norfolk, England

1701: Becomes member of Parliament

1712: Convicted of corruption and imprisoned

1720: Returns to office

1721: Appointed lord of the treasury

1733: Proposal of excise tax on wine and tobacco is defeated in parliament

1742: Forced to resign on charges of rigging the Chippenham by-election; created earl of Orford

March 18, 1745: Dies in London; earlier, presents his residence for use by future prime ministers

33 Benjamin Franklin
[1706 - 1790]

January 17, 1706: Born to a soap-maker in Boston

1723: Runs away from home and goes to Philadelphia

1732: Starts writing Poor Richard's Almanack, famous for sayings like "A penny saved is a penny earned"

1751: Establishes the Pennsylvania Hospital, the first hospital in independent United States

1775: Becomes the first U.S. postmaster general

1787: Participates in the Federal Constitutional Convention to formulate the U.S. Constitution

April 17, 1790: Dies; buried in the Christ Church burial grounds in Philadelphia

A statesman of great standing, Franklin spent his early days writing and publishing. Later, pursuing his interest in science, he demonstrated that lightning is electrical and also invented the lightning rod. However, Franklin is most remembered for his role in the American Revolution. He negotiated the Treaty of Paris in 1783 and worked to put an end to slavery.

34 William Pitt, the Elder (1st Earl of Chatham)
[1708 - 1778]

William Pitt was the secretary of state of England and also nominal prime minister twice, during the reigns of George II and George III. As head of the government from 1757, Pitt directed the defeat of France in India and Canada. However, he was forced to resign when King George III came to power in 1761. Pitt opposed the Treaty of Paris and criticised the government's policies towards the American colonies. At the same time, though, he was not in favour of granting them independence.

William Pitt

Frederick II

November 15, 1708: Born in London

1746: Paymaster general of the forces in Henry Pelham's government

1755: Dismissed for criticising the government's war policies

1756: Recalled by George II; made secretary of State

1757: Becomes the prime minister of a coalition government

1761: Resigns from office

1766: Returns as prime minister; accepts title of earl of Chatham

1768: Resigns on account of ill health

May 11, 1778: Dies in Hayes, Kent; buried in Westminster Abbey

The U.S. dollar with Benjamin Franklin potrait

35 Frederick II
[1712 - 1786]

January 24, 1712: Born to King Frederick William I

1740: Succeeds his father as king of Prussia

1740-48: Involved in the War of the Austrian Succession

August 17, 1786: Friedrich Wilhelm II succeeds him upon his death

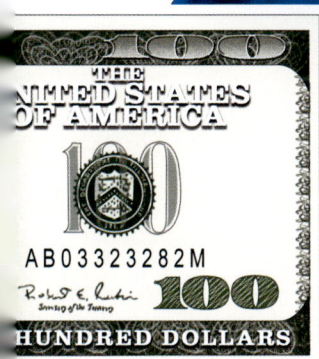

Frederick the Great was the king of Prussia. Under him, Prussia flourished as a great European power. His dream of an independent Germany, however, did not come true until a century later. Often referred to as the "enlightened monarch", Frederick II brought about important changes to the law, promoted trade and encouraged education. He loved art and music. Being a flutist himself, he wrote many pieces of flute music.

36 Catherine II
[1729 - 1796]

Married to Tsar Peter III, Catherine II was more popular than her husband. She conspired to declare herself the ruler and, shortly afterwards, had the tsar killed. As empress of Russia, Catherine increased the power of the centre over rural areas and freed the nobles from taxes and state service. She was a keen supporter of the arts and literature and even wrote several comedies and stories.

May 2, 1729: Born in Stettin, Prussia, to Prince Christian Augustus of Germany

1744: Marries the future tsar, Peter III

1762: Peter is killed six months after he becomes tsar; Catherine succeeds him

1778: Mediates between Prussia and Austria in the War of the Bavarian Succession

1780: Creates a group to defend neutral ships from attacks by Great Britain during the American Revolution

1783: Conquers Crimea after first war with the Ottoman Empire

1785: Issues charter freeing nobles from state service and taxes

November 17, 1796: Dies near St. Petersburg, Russia; succeeded by Paul I

George Washington

37 George Washington
[1732 - 1799]

Called the "father of his country", George Washington was the first president of the United States. He played a major role in America's attainment of freedom. As president, he made several administrative reforms and was also involved in the creation of the US capital, District of Columbia (Washington, D.C.). He also crushed the Whisky Rebellion (1794) caused by the imposing of excise tax on whisky.

February 22, 1732: Born to Augustine Washington and Mary Ball, in Westmoreland, Virginia

1775: Assumes command of the Continental Army during the American Revolutionary War

1781: Defeats British troops under General Cornwallis at the Battle of Yorkham, putting an end to British hold over America

February 4, 1789: Elected president

1792: Elected president for the second term

February 25, 1793: Holds the first cabinet meeting

December 14, 1799: Dies; buried on his estate at Mount Vernon, Virginia

John Adams

38 John Adams
[1735 - 1826]

The second president of the United States, John Adams also played a key role in the drafting of the Massachusetts Constitution. In 1789-97, he had served as vice-president under George Washington. Adams became the president in 1797, after Washington refused to run for elections a third time. The term was marked by the unpopular Alien and Sedition Act, by which foreigners were forced out of the country and the freedom of the press was limited. This largely resulted in Adams's defeat in the next elections.

October 30, 1735: Born in Braintree, Massachusetts

1780: Frames the Massachusetts Constitution

April 21, 1789: Becomes the first vice-president of independent America

1797: Becomes president after defeating Thomas Jefferson

1798: Alien and Sedition Act passed

July 4, 1826: Dies in Quincy, Massachusetts, on the 50th anniversary of American independence

39 Thomas Jefferson
[1743 - 1826]

Horatio Nelson

The third president of the United States, Thomas Jefferson wrote the Declaration of Independence, announcing America's separation from Britain. He was the first president to work from the White House. The founder of the Democratic Party, he also developed the theory of states' rights, with lesser authority given to the federal government. In 1803, he helped in the purchase of Louisiana from France ("Louisiana Purchase").

April 13, 1743: Born in Shadwell, Virginia

1779: Becomes the governor of Virginia

1790: Becomes the secretary of state

1800: Takes office as president

1803: Launches the Lewis and Clarke Expedition to the U.S. Pacific coast

1809: Retires from public life

July 4, 1826: Dies in Monticello, Virginia

40 Horatio Nelson, Viscount
[1758 - 1805]

British commander Horatio Nelson is known for his victories over the French general Napoleon. One such was in the Battle of the Nile in 1798. By trapping Napoleon's fleets in Egypt, he ended Napoleon's attempts to attack the British in India. The greatest victory, however, was undoubtedly the Battle of Trafalgar. Nelson died in this battle, but not before defeating the joined forces of France and Spain.

September 29, 1758: Born in Norfolk, England

1777: Becomes lieutenant; assigned to West Indies during the American Revolution

1794: Loses sight in one eye after getting shot in a battle at Calvi, Corsica

1797: Loses his right arm during a battle to capture the town of Santa Cruz in Spain

1801: Appointed commander-in-chief of the British navy

October 21, 1805: Dies in action at the Battle of Trafalgar, Spain

41 Andrew Jackson
[1767 - 1845]

Andrew Jackson

The seventh president of the United States, he is known for his notorious decisions, especially the Indian Removal Act of 1830. Under this act, Native American tribes living east of the Mississippi River were driven out of their lands. Ignoring the Supreme Court ruling, Jackson sent military support to expel the native population. This eventually led to the infamous "Trail of Tears", in which about 4,000 Cherokees were killed enroute to Oklahoma.

March 15, 1767: Born to Andrew Jackson, sr. and Elizabeth Hutchinson, in Waxhaws region, South Carolina

1815: Defeats British troops at the Battle of New Orleans

1829: Elected president

1830: Passes the Indian Removal Act

1832: Dismantles the Bank of the United States

1835: Sends military support to remove the natives from their lands .

January 30, 1835: The first-ever attempt to kill an American president

June 8, 1845: Dies in Tennessee

42 Napoleon Bonaparte
[1769 - 1821]

Military dictator and the emperor of France, Napoleon was nicknamed "Little Corporal". His military ambitions cost the lives of millions. This made him unpopular, despite the fact that he introduced several lasting changes for the betterment of education, economy and laws. He conquered most of Western and Central Europe. However, his attempts to conquer Great Britain were foiled by Admiral Nelson. Napoleon was finally defeated by the duke of Wellington at the Battle of Waterloo.

Napoleon Bonaparte

August 15, 1769: Born in Ajaccio, Corsica.

1798: His fleets are defeated at the Battle of the Nile

1804: Crowns himself emperor of France

May 26, 1805: Crowned king of Italy

1812: Invades Russia, but forced to retreat

1813: Suffers defeat at the Battle of the Nations against the Allied forces of Britain, Russia, Sweden, Spain, Portugal, Prussia, Austria and a few German states

March 31, 1814: Paris is occupied; in April Napoleon is forced to step down from the throne and is exiled to the island of Elba

February 26, 1815: Escapes from Elba and returns to Paris

June 18, 1815: Defeated at the Battle of Waterloo

May 5, 1821: Dies in exile on the island of St. Helena

43 Alexander I of Russia
[1777 - 1825]

To start with, Alexander I was a very broad-minded leader. He suppressed the secret police, lifted the ban on foreign travel and books, reformed education and improved the lives of slaves. Later, disillusioned by a farmers' revolt and betrayed by Napoleon, Alexander gave up his liberal views. Instead, he adopted a stricter approach and withdrew most of the reforms. He died mysteriously and was succeeded by his brother Nicholas I.

December 23, 1777: Born to Tsar Paul I and Maria Fedorovna

1801: Succeeds his father after the latter is killed

1807: Allies with Napoleon by the Treaty of Tilsit

1812: Napoleon invades Russia after a spate of political conflicts

1813: Participates in the Battle of the Nations against Napoleon

December 1, 1825: Dies at Taganrog

Alexander I

44 Jose de San Martin
[1778 - 1850]

This famous South American freedom fighter returned home from serving in the Spanish army, only to join the freedom struggle against Spain. San Martin first defeated the Spanish troops in Chacabuco in 1817. In 1818, he freed Chile by defeating the royalists at Maipu. He became the protector of Peru after capturing Lima in 1821, but soon retired from public life. He went to Europe in 1824, spending the rest of his life in poverty.

February 25, 1778: Born in Yapeyu, Argentina

1812: Joins revolution against Spain

1817: Defeats Spanish troops at Chacabuco

1818: Frees Chile

1821: Conquers Lima

1822: Meets Simon Bolivar, leaving him the task of completing the conquest of Peru

1850: Dies in self-imposed exile in France

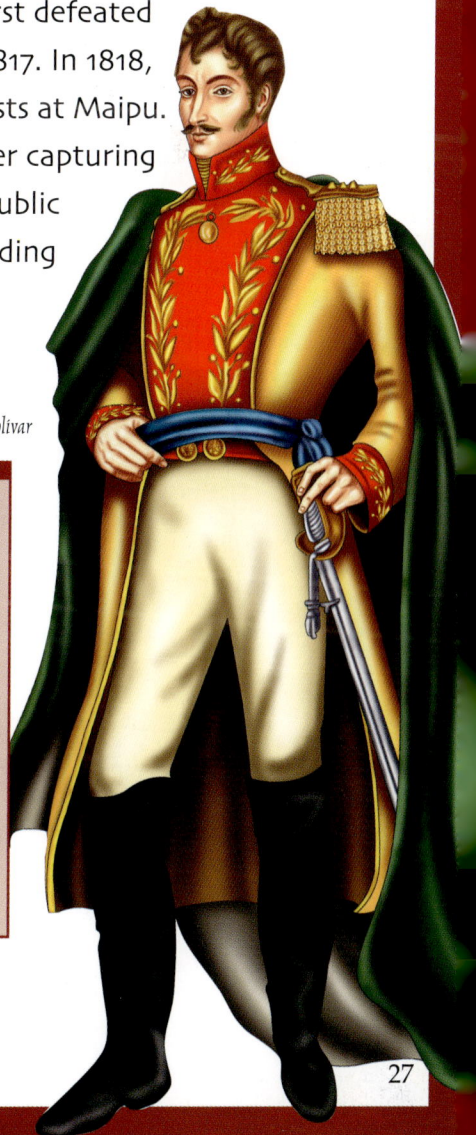

Simon Bolivar

45 Simon Bolivar
[1783 - 1830]

Simon Bolivar led independence struggles in Venezuela, Colombia, Panama, Ecuador, Peru and Bolivia. After serving under Napoleon for a while, Bolivar returned to Venezuela in 1807 and took active part in the revolution there. In 1819, he created Gran Colombia – consisting of countries free of Spanish control – and became its president.
In 1822, he added Peru to the group. Bolivar resigned when the Gran Columbia collapsed in 1828.

July 24, 1783: Born in Caracas, New Granada (now Colombia, Venezuela and Ecuador)

1808: Joins the "resistance juntas"

1819: Creates Gran Colombia consisting of Venezuela, Colombia, Panama and Ecuador.

January 17, 1819: Proclaims the Republic of Colombia

1824: Decisively defeats the Spanish at Junin

1825: Bolivia is created in his honour

December 17, 1830: Dies of tuberculosis, near Santa Maria, Colombia

46 Abraham Lincoln
[1809 - 1865]

February 12, 1809: *Born in Kentucky*

1856: *Joins the Republican Party*

1860: *Elected president*

April 12, 1861: *The American Civil War begins*

January 1, 1863: *Issues Emancipation Proclamation*

July 1-3, 1863: *Battle of Gettysburg takes place; over 7,000 soldiers are killed*

November 19, 1863: *Delivers the Gettysburg Address at the dedication of a cemetery to soldiers killed in the battle*

1864: *Re-elected as president*

April 15, 1865: *Dies in Washington, D.C.*

Abraham Lincoln was the 16th American president, whose anti-slavery views resulted in the four-year-long American Civil War. To suppress the revolt, Lincoln issued the Emancipation Proclamation under which slaves in the rebel states (southern states like Georgia) were freed. In his famous Gettysburg Address, he described democracy as "government of the people, by the people and for the people." On April 15, 1865, during a performance at Ford's Theatre, Lincoln was shot dead by actor John Wilkes-Booth.

Abraham Lincoln

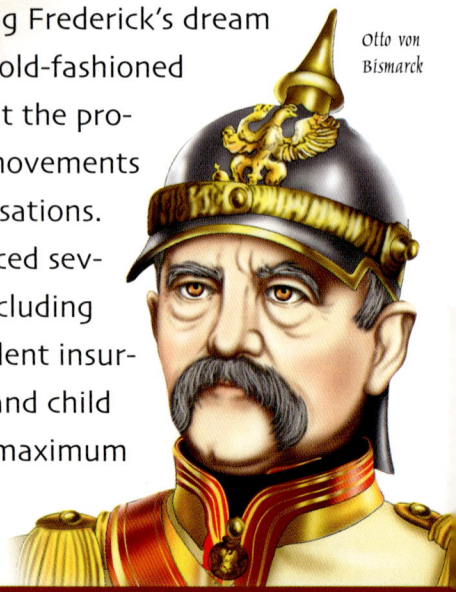

47 Otto von Bismarck
[1815 - 1898]

Otto von Bismarck was prime minister of the Kingdom of Prussia and the first chancellor of the German Empire. Through a series of wars, he fulfilled King Frederick's dream of a unified Germany. An old-fashioned politician, Bismarck fought the pro-working class (socialist) movements by banning several organisations. However, he also introduced several economic reforms, including pensions, health and accident insurance, limiting of women and child labour and setting down maximum working hours.

Otto von Bismarck

April 1, 1815: *Born in Altmark, Prussia*

1862: *Appointed prime minister of Prussia*

1871: *Establishes the German Empire; becomes chancellor*

1878: *Passes laws to suppress the socialist movement*

1890: *Dismissed from office by the new king, Wilhelm II*

1898: *Dies in Friedrichsruh, near Hamburg*

48 Victoria - Queen Of England
[1819 - 1901]

Queen Victoria ruled Great Britain for a record 63 years! Her rule saw a huge expansion of the British Empire. Devoted to her husband, Prince Albert, she withdrew from public life for three years after his death. This earned her the nickname "Widow of Windsor". At the persuasion of Prime Minister Benjamin Disraeli, she finally made a comeback and accepted the title of Empress of India. She was succeeded by her eldest son Edward VII.

May 24, 1819: Born to Edward Augustus, duke of Kent and Princess Victoria of Saxe-Coburg-Saalfield

June 20, 1837: Succeeds William IV at the age of 18

February 10, 1840: Marries her cousin, Prince Albert

1861: Withdraws from public life after Prince Albert's death

January 1, 1877: Becomes Empress of India

January 22, 1901: Dies at Osborne House on the Isle of Wight

Queen Victoria

49 Harriet Tubman
[1820 - 1913]

She played a major role in ending slavery in America. Born into slavery in Maryland, Tubman escaped in 1849 to become a defender of slaves. She led more than three hundred slaves to freedom through the 'Underground Railroad', forcing the weaker ones with a loaded revolver. During the civil war, Tubman served as a nurse and a spy for the Union forces in South Carolina.

1820: Born in Dorchester.

1849: Escapes slavery.

1861: Serves in the Union forces as a nurse during the civil war.

March 10, 1913: Dies in the home for needy blacks founded by her in Auburn, New York

Henri Marie La Fontaine

50 Henri Marie La Fontaine
[1854 - 1943]

La Fontaine was a Belgian senator for 36 years and was devoted to international peace. As a senator, he was responsible for various ground-breaking efforts to improve education, labour and foreign affairs. He supported the adoption of an eight hour day and forty hour working week. He also supported the League of Nations and disarmament. A part of the organized peace movement since the early 1880s, he won the Nobel Peace Prize in 1913.

April 11, 1854: Born in Brussels.

1895: Becomes a senator for the first time.

1897: Submits a bill on mine inspection.

1907: Becomes President of the International Peace bureau.

1913: Receives Nobel Peace Prize.

1926: Supports eight hour a day work programme.

1920: Attends the First Assembly of League of Nations.

May 14, 1943: Dies before Belgium is liberated.

51 Woodrow Wilson
[1856 - 1924]

Woodrow Wilson

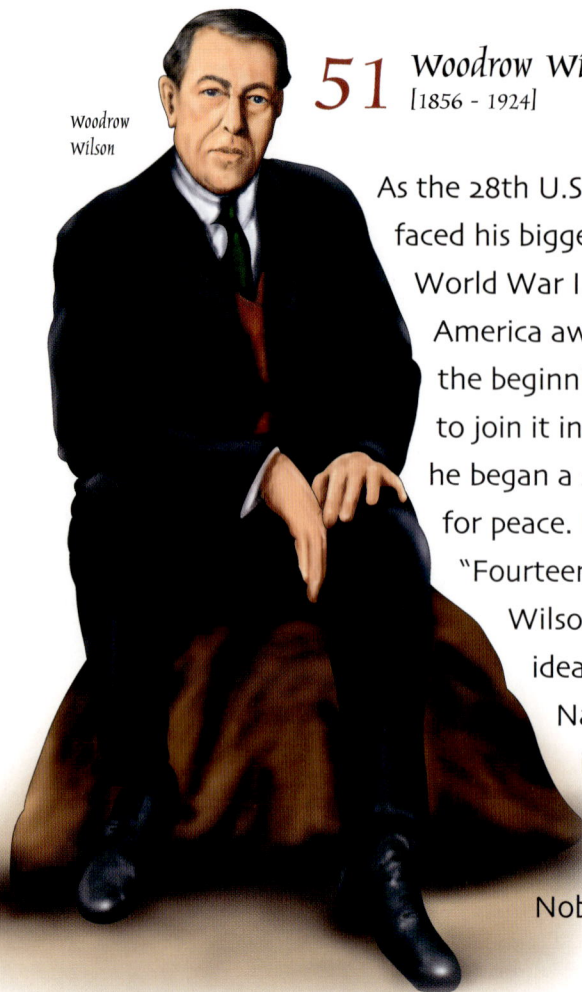

As the 28th U.S. president, Wilson faced his biggest challenge during World War I. Although he kept America away from the war in the beginning, he was forced to join it in 1916. After the war, he began a strong movement for peace. In his famous "Fourteen Points" address, Wilson came up with the idea of the League of Nations. This was implemented during the Paris Peace Conference in 1919 and Wilson was awarded the Nobel Prize for Peace.

December 28, 1856: *Born in Staunton, Virginia, U.S.*

1913: *Becomes president*

1914: *Decides not to participate in World War I*

1916: *Re-elected as president*

April 6, 1917: *Joins World War I by declaring war on Germany*

January 8, 1918: *Makes his Fourteen Points speech*

1919: *His idea of a League of Nations included in the Treaty of Versailles; awarded the Nobel Prize for Peace*

October 2, 1919: *A stroke leaves him partially paralysed*

1921: *Retires from the White House*

February 3, 1924: *Dies in Washington, D.C.*

52 Theodore Roosevelt
[1858 - 1919]

Theodore Roosevelt became the U.S. president in 1901, when President William McKinley was killed. Considered to be the first "conservation" president, Roosevelt established the United States Forest Service, 51 bird reserves, 150 national forests and 5 national parks. Fondly called Teddy, he once refused to kill a bear cub during a hunting trip, after which, toy manufacturers started naming teddy bears after him!

Theodore Roosevelt

October 27, 1858: *Born in New York City*

September 14, 1901: *Becomes president*

1904: *Re-elected as president*

1906: *Wins Nobel Prize for Peace for the Russo-Japanese peace treaty*

October 14, 1912: *Escapes an attempt to kill him; doctors refuse to remove the bullet in his chest since it can prove fatal*

January 6, 1919: *Dies at Oyster Bay, Nassau county, New York*

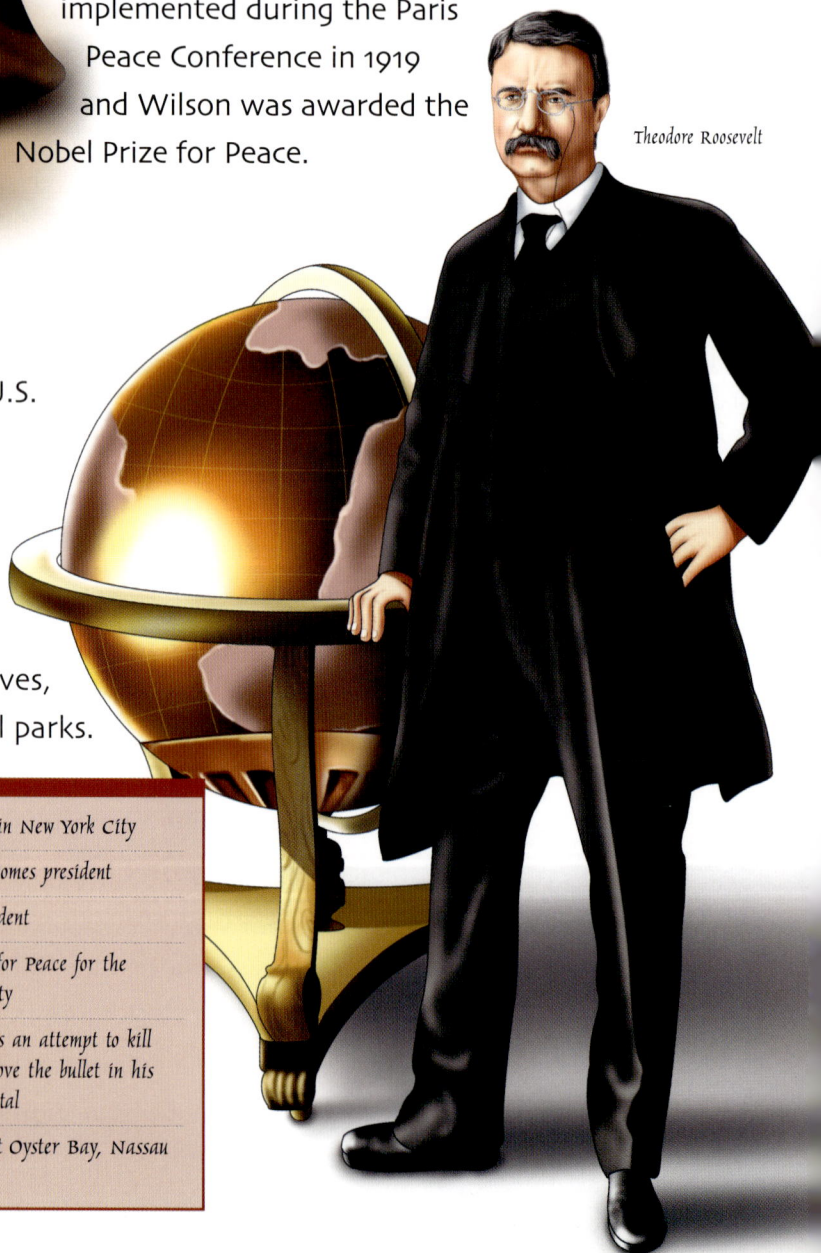

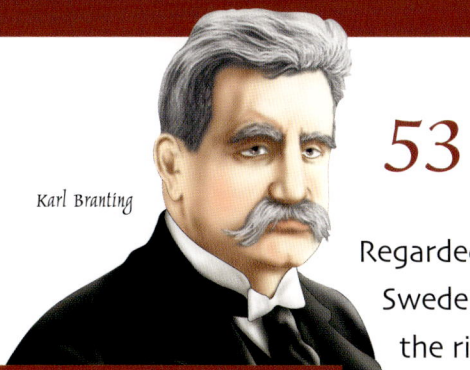
Karl Branting

53 Karl Hjalmar Branting
[1860 - 1925]

Regarded as the father of socialism (movement for workers' rights) in Sweden, Branting was also the nation's prime minister. He upheld the rights of workers and criticised laws against unions. Although he insisted on Sweden staying out of World War I, he participated in the Paris Peace Conference and got his country into the League of Nations. He was also involved in drafting the Geneva Protocol to settle international disputes legally. In 1921, he shared the Nobel Prize for Peace with Christian Louis Lange.

November 23, 1860: *Born in Stockholm*

1889: *Forms the Social Democratic Labour Party*

1920: *Becomes prime minister*

October 1920: *Dissolves parliament; loses the elections*

1921: *Returns as prime minister; wins Nobel Prize for Peace*

1924: *Becomes prime minister for the third time*

January 1925: *Resigns from office due to illness*

February 24, 1925: *Dies in Stockholm*

Douglas Hyde

54 Douglas Hyde
[1860 - 1949]

Douglas Hyde was an Irish scholar and politician. He helped revive Irish language and literature by setting up the Gaelic League in 1893.

January 17, 1860: *Born in Frenchpark, in County Roscommon, Ireland*

1909-32: *Teaches modern Irish*

1938: *Becomes the first president of Ireland*

April 1940: *Suffers stroke and is confined to the wheelchair*

June 24, 1945: *Retires due to ill health*

July 12, 1949: *Dies in Dublin, Ireland*

The league went on to produce great leaders like Eamon de Valera and Michael Collins. In 1938, Hyde became the first president of Ireland and held office until 1945. He wrote several books, the most famous being *A Literary History of Ireland* and *The Love Songs of Connacht*.

55 Aristide Briand
[1862 - 1932]

March 28, 1862: *Born in Nantes, France*

1905: *Passes the law of separation of church and state*

1906: *Becomes minister of education and religion*

1909: *Becomes premier for the first of 11 times*

1925: *Co-authors the Locarno Pact*

1926: *Shares the Nobel Prize for Peace with Stresemann*

1928: *Drafts the Kellog-Briand pact banning war*

March 7, 1932: *Dies in Paris, France*

Briand became the French premier in 1909. He participated in the movement for labour-union formation and also in drafting the law of separation of church and state. A tireless supporter of international peace, Briand was criticised for trying to make peace with Germany. However, it was Briand who played a leading role in formulating the Locarno Pact – a treaty intended to establish peace in western Europe and ease relations with Germany.

56 Sir Austen Chamberlain
[1863 - 1937]

Sir Chamberlain was a British politician, most remembered for his contributions to world peace. Although he opposed the League of Nations' Geneva Protocol (1924), Chamberlain was actively involved in the formulation of the Locarno Pact. He also had the foresight to predict that Hitler would be the greatest threat to world peace. Although he did not hold a cabinet position after 1931,

Austen Chamberlain

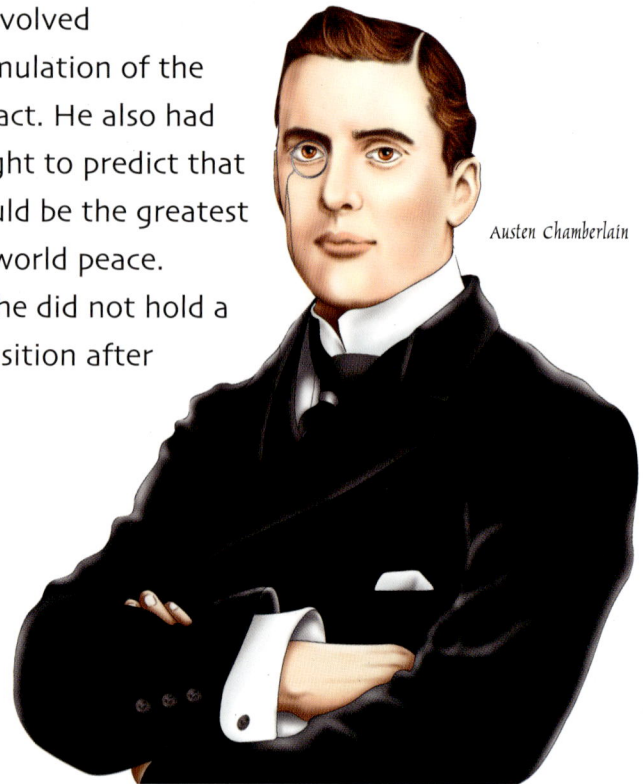

October 16, 1863: Born in Birmingham, Warwickshire, England

1915: Becomes Secretary of State for India.

1921: Becomes leader of the Conservative Party

1924: Becomes secretary of state for foreign affairs

1925: Awarded the Nobel Peace Prize for his role in the Locarno Pact

March 17, 1937: Dies of apoplexy in London

Mahatma Gandhi

57 Mohandas Karamchand Gandhi
[1869 - 1948]

Also known as "Mahatma" ("Great Soul"), Gandhi was the key figure in India's freedom struggle. His principles of satyagraha and non-violence have influenced leaders like Martin Luther King and Nelson Mandela. Gandhi led such simple and non-violent – yet effective – movements as the Dandi March and Quit India. He was an ardent supporter of Hindu-Muslim unity. Ironically, he was killed by a fanatic who was angered by his concern for the Muslims.

October 2, 1869: Born in Porbandar, Gujarat, India

April 5, 1930: Leads thousands to the sea to collect salt, in the famous Dandi March

1942: Starts the Quit India movement; imprisoned for two years.

August 15, 1947: India becomes independent; Pakistan splits from India to form a separate Muslim country

January 30, 1948: Killed by Nathuram Godse in New Delhi, India

58 *Vladimir Ilyich Lenin*
[1870 - 1924]

Vladimir Ilyich Lenin

A Russian revolutionary, Lenin was the founder of Bolshevism (later the Russian Communist Party). After returning from exile, Lenin organised the Socialist Revolution of October 1917 and subsequently established a Soviet government. The new government took control of banks and industry. It also put an end to private ownership of land and gave farmers and workers more rights. After his death, Lenin was succeeded by Stalin.

1870: *Born Vladimir Ilyich Ulyanov at Simbirsk, Russia*

1895: *Exiled to Siberia*

1900: *Leaves Russia*

October 1917: *Lenin returns to Russia to overthrow Aleksandr Kerensky's government*

1921: *Launches the New Economic Policy allowing private companies to operate*

January 21, 1924: *Dies of a stroke, in Gorki, near Moscow, Russia*

59 *Arthur Griffith*
[1871 - 1922]

March 31, 1871: *Born in Dublin*

1899: *Founds a newspaper, the United Irishman*

1905: *Founds Sinn Fein*

August 12, 1922: *Dies in Dublin, at the beginning of the civil war*

Griffith was the founder of Sinn Fein, the famous political wing of the Irish Republican Army. He fought for the creation of two different governments for England and Ireland, to be headed by one common monarch – namely, the king of England. Elected to the parliament in 1918, he was also responsible for the Anglo-Irish Treaty (1921) establishing the Irish Free State.

60 *Cordell Hull*
[1871 - 1955]

Cordell Hull

The U.S. secretary of state for 12 years, Cordell Hull worked for the improvement of international relations. He helped in signing peace and trade agreements with several countries. He also promoted the Good Neighbor Policy towards Latin America, giving it financial help. During World War II, he backed the establishment of a world organisation to maintain peace. In 1913 Hull introduced the first Federal Income Tax bill.

October 2, 1871: *Born in Overton county, Tennessee*

1930: *Elected to the U.S. Senate*

1933: *Appointed secretary of state*

1944: *Resigns from his post*

1945: *Wins the Nobel Prize for Peace; serves as senior adviser to the American delegation to the United Nations conference in San Francisco*

July 23, 1955: *Dies in Bethesda, Maryland, U.S.*

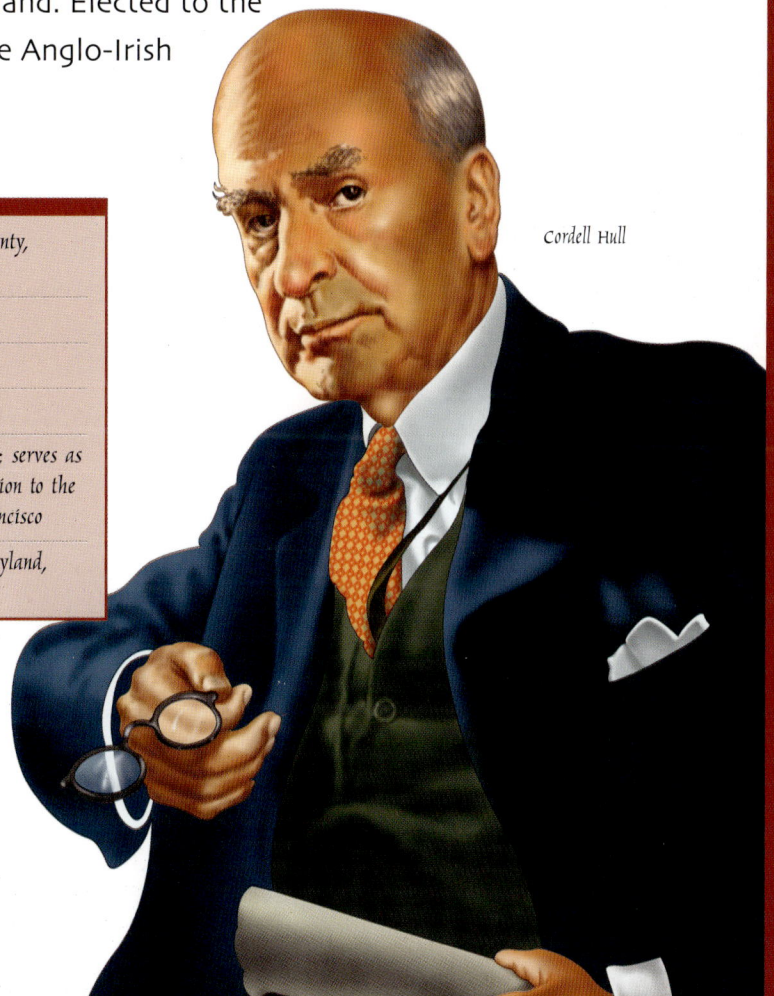

61 Winston Churchill
[1874 - 1965]

Winston Churchill

As the British prime minister during World War II, Churchill took an aggressive stand against Hitler. He also opposed the Indian independence struggle and viewed the Soviet Union as a threat. He put an end to the government's control over steel and auto industries introduced by the Labour Party. One of the greatest public figures of recent times, Churchill was also a great writer and received the Nobel Prize for Literature in 1953.

1874: *Born in Oxfordshire, England*

May 1940: *Becomes the prime minister after Neville Chamberlain resigns*

1945: *Loses the elections to Labour Party*

1951: *Returns as the prime minister*

1953: *Receives knighthood*

1955: *Resigns, but remains member of parliament*

1963: *President Kennedy offers him honorary citizenship of the United States*

1965: *Dies in London*

62 Gustav Stresemann
[1878 - 1929]

Founder of the German People's Party, Stresemann, was also chancellor and foreign minister in the Weimar Republic (German government). Although he supported the monarchy during World War I, Stresemann realised the need to improve relations between Germany and its enemy nations and actively campaigned to achieve this. He renewed the Rapallo Treaty with Russia and got Germany admitted into the League of Nations as a great power. He won the 1926 Nobel Prize for Peace for his contribution to the Locarno Pact.

May 10, 1878: *Born in Berlin, Germany*

1907: *Enters the Reichstag*

1918: *Founds the German People's Party*

1923: *Becomes chancellor*

1924: *Becomes foreign minister*

1926: *Germany is admitted into the League of Nations*

October 3, 1929: *Dies in Berlin after suffering a stroke*

63 Leon Trotsky
[1879 - 1940]

1879: *Born to Jewish parents in Yanovka, Ukraine*

October 1917: *Organises the socialist revolution*

1922: *Stalin succeeds Lenin as leader of the party*

1928: *Expelled from the party by Stalin*

1929: *Banished from Russia; given asylum by Turkey*

1935: *Moves to Norway*

December 1936: *Soviet government gets him expelled from Norway; moves to Mexico*

August 20, 1940: *Killed in Coyoacan, Mexico*

Trotsky was a Russian leader who played a prominent role in the 1917 Russian Revolution that brought the Bolsheviks into power. He was also the founder of the Red Army. Trotsky opposed Stalin's plan for "socialism in one country", meant to make the Soviet Union the only world power. This led to his exile from the country. In 1940 he was killed in Mexico by Ramon Mercader, a Spanish communist believed to be Stalin's agent.

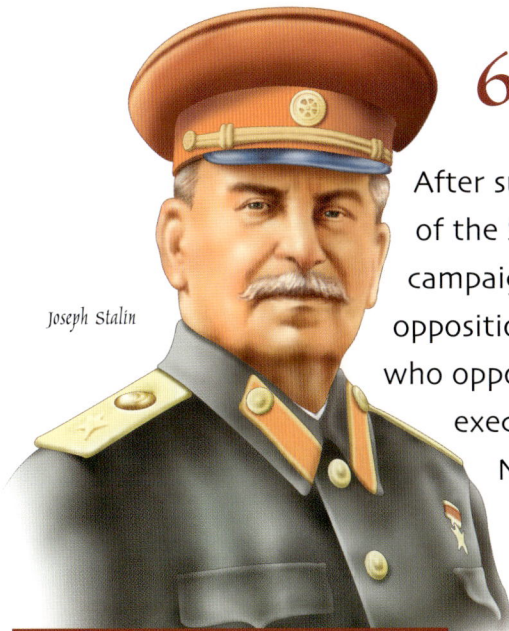

Joseph Stalin

64 Joseph Stalin
[1879 - 1953]

After succeeding Lenin as leader of the Soviet Union, Stalin launched a campaign of terror to end all opposition. Old Bolshevik leaders, who opposed Stalin, were tried and executed in the 1930s. The failed Nazi invasion in 1941 further strengthened Stalin's position. After defeating Hitler, he continued his brutalities. Although Stalin is best remembered for his reign of terror and dictatorship, his economic reforms like the Five-Year Plan improved the financial condition of the country.

1879: Born to a shoemaker in Gori, Georgia

1922: Succeeds Lenin as leader of the Bolsheviks

1934: Joins League of Nations

1939: Signs non-aggression pact with Germany

1941: Hitler invades Russia

March 5, 1953: Dies of cerebral haemorrhage, in Moscow

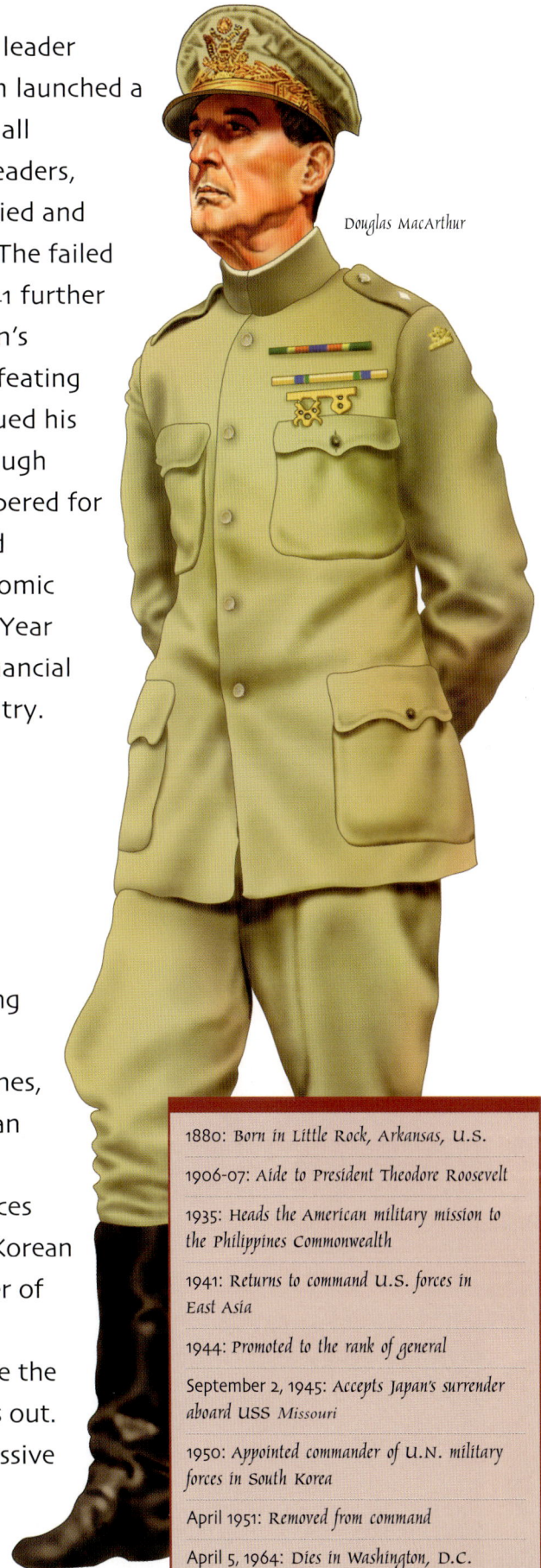

Douglas MacArthur

65 Douglas MacArthur
[1880 - 1964]

One of the greatest American generals, Douglas MacArthur played an important role during World War II and the Korean War. He liberated the Philippines, accepted the surrender of Japan on September 2, 1945 and commanded the Allied forces positioned there. In the Korean War, as the commander of U.N. military forces in South Korea, he drove the North Korean forces out. However, his aggressive methods forced President Truman to recall him.

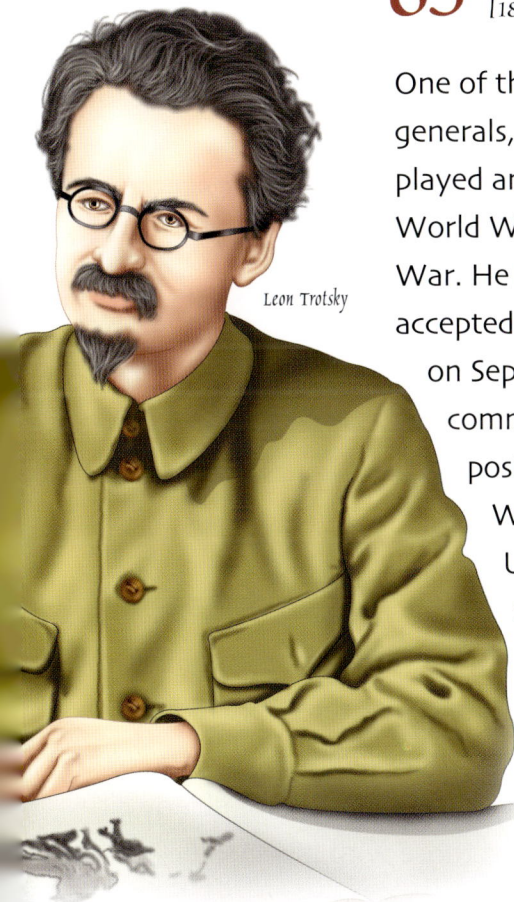

Leon Trotsky

1880: Born in Little Rock, Arkansas, U.S.

1906-07: Aide to President Theodore Roosevelt

1935: Heads the American military mission to the Philippines Commonwealth

1941: Returns to command U.S. forces in East Asia

1944: Promoted to the rank of general

September 2, 1945: Accepts Japan's surrender aboard USS *Missouri*

1950: Appointed commander of U.N. military forces in South Korea

April 1951: Removed from command

April 5, 1964: Dies in Washington, D.C.

66 George Catlett Marshall
[1880 - 1959]

George Marshall

An American general and cabinet member, George Marshall made valuable contributions during times of both war and peace. During World War II, he directed the conquest of Germany. After the war he was appointed special ambassador to China. He promoted the "Marshall Plan" to improve post-war European economy. This plan also led to the formation of the North Atlantic Treaty Organisation (NATO).

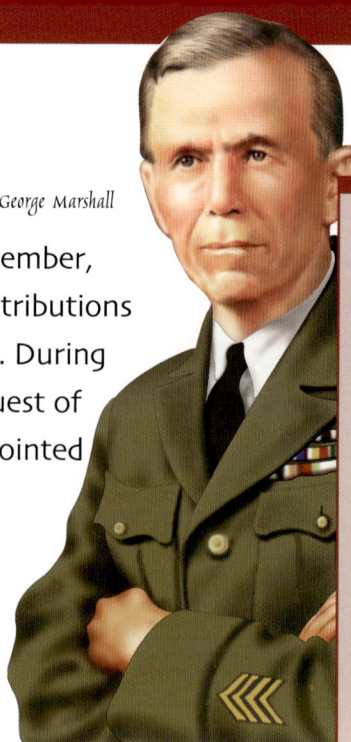

December 31, 1880: Born in Uniontown, Pennsylvania

1919-24: Serves in the army during World War I

September 1939: Becomes chief of army staff

1944: Promoted to the rank of general

January 1947: Made secretary of state

July 1947: Marshall Plan is proposed

January 1949: Resigns due to ill health

September 1950: Returns as secretary of defense

September 1951: Resigns from the post

1953: Wins the Nobel Prize for Peace

October 16, 1959: Dies in Washington, D.C.

67 Kemal Atatürk
[1881 - 1938]

March 12, 1881: Born in Salonika, Greece

1919: Forms the Turkish Nationalist Republican Party

October 29, 1923: Turkish Republic is founded; Atatürk is elected president

1924: Abolishes the caliphate

November 10, 1938: Dies in Istanbul, Turkey

Atatürk ("father of Turks") was the founder and the first president of the Republic of Turkey. He formed the Turkish Nationalist Republican Party, which overthrew the Ottoman Empire and defeated the Greeks. After coming to power in 1923, Atatürk launched a variety of reforms. He replaced the Law of Islam with the Swiss Civil Code, thus separating religion and the state. He also simplified the Turkish script, helping to increase literacy.

68 Franklin D. Roosevelt
[1882 - 1945]

Franklin Roosevelt

Franklin Roosevelt was the only U.S. president to be elected four times. This led to a change in the Constitution, limiting further presidencies to 2 terms. Roosevelt balanced the country's economy during the Great Depression (a period of great financial difficulty after World War I) providing support for elderly citizens and those with low incomes.

January 30, 1882: Born in Hyde Park, New York

1933: Becomes the president

1935: Introduces the Social Security system, providing support for elderly citizens and for those who earn less

January 6, 1941: Makes his famous State of the Union Address, also called the 'Four Freedoms' Speech.

December 7, 1941: Japanese attack Pearl Harbor.

April 12, 1945: Dies in Warm Springs, Georgia

69 *Eamon de Valera*
[1882 - 1975]

Eamon de Valera was the Prime Minister and President of Ireland. He is famous for his role in the Easter Rising of 1916. He was very passionate about his cause and refused to accept the Anglo-Irish Treaty and the Irish Free State since it excluded Northern Ireland and demanded loyalty to the British Monarchy. During his term, a new constitution declaring Ireland a fully independent state was introduced. He also kept Ireland neutral during World War II.

Benito Mussolini

Eamon de Valera

October 14, 1882: Born in New York City

1913: Joins the newly founded group called Irish Volunteers

1916: Leads a Volunteer unit in the Easter Rising

1917: Elected Member of Parliament and becomes the President of Sinn Fein

June 1922: Start of the Irish Civil War

1926: Forms a new party called Fianna Fail or Soldiers of Destiny

1932: Becomes the Prime Minister following his party's win in elections

1959: Becomes President of Ireland

1973: Retires at the age of 91

1975: Dies in a Dublin nursing home soon after his wife's death

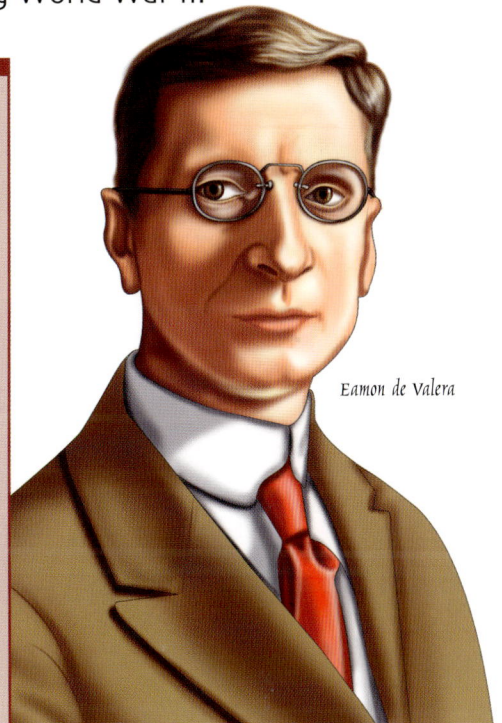

70 *Benito Mussolini*
[1883 - 1945]

Mussolini was an Italian dictator and the founder of fascism (a kind of dictatorship) which he believed would strengthen the nation. He kept an iron control over the press and suppressed opposition using force. He replaced the parliamentary system with absolute dictatorship and encouraged terrorism.
He glorified war and later joined hands with Hitler, calling the alliance "Axis Powers". But, following Italy's defeat in World War II and Germany's collapse in 1945, Mussolini was captured by anti-fascists and shot dead.

July 29, 1883: Born in Predappio, Romagna

November 1914: Founds the newspaper called The Italian People

1919: Fascism emerges as an organized political movement

1922: Becomes the Premier of Italy

1928: Ends the Parliamentary system of government

1935: Allies with Germany

1936: Aids Francisco Franco in the Spanish Civil War

1939: Rome-Berlin Axis is formed

1940: Italy enters World War II

1943: Allies invasion turns Mussolini's colleagues against him and he loses power

April 28, 1945: After the German collapse he is caught and shot

71 Adolf Hitler
[1889 - 1945]

Hitler was a German dictator and the founder of Nazism. He was responsible for World War II and the Holocaust, a period when over 6 million Jews were killed. Hitler believed that the Germans belonged to the superior Aryan race and were meant to rule the world. Those who opposed him were tortured and killed in concentration camps. He killed himself in his Berlin mansion on April 30, 1945, to avoid capture by the Russians.

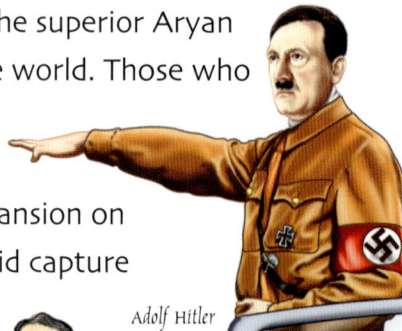

Adolf Hitler

Michael Collins

| April 20, 1889: Born in a small town near Linz, Upper Austria |
| 1919: Joins German's Workers' Party and renames it National Socialist German Workers' Party or the Nazi Party |
| 1934: Proclaims himself Fuhrer (Leader) |
| September 1, 1939: Invades Poland starting World War II |
| June 1941: Attacks USSR disregarding the non-aggression pact between the two nations |
| 1943: Defeated at the Battle of Stalingrad |
| April 29, 1945: Marries Eva Braun |
| April 30, 1945: Both commit suicide in Hitler's Berlin bunker |

72 Michael Collins
[1890 - 1922]

Considered a legend in Irish History, Michael Collins' contribution to the creation of the present Republic of Ireland is invaluable. Like most great Irish leaders, Collins became famous during the Easter Rising. After a prolonged struggle, Collins, along with Arthur Griffiths negotiated and signed the Anglo-Irish Treaty that set up the Irish Free State. He served as the Minister for Finance in the new government for a short while. He was killed by Republicans during the Civil War.

| October 16, 1890: Born in Sam's Cross, West Cork |
| November 1909: Joins the Irish Republican Brotherhood |
| 1916: Participates in the Easter Rising |
| 1918: Becomes a Member of Parliament |
| January 1919: Organises the Irish Republican Army and leads it in the Irish War of Independence |
| December 1921: Negotiates and signs the Anglo-Irish Treaty |
| June 1922: Irish Civil War begins |
| August 22, 1922: Killed in an ambush in County Cork. He was barely 32 years old |

73 Ho Chi Minh
[1890 - 1969]

Ho Chi Minh was a famous Vietnamese freedom fighter who fought to free North Vietnam from France and other foreign forces. He led the Viet Minh independence movement of 1941, successfully driving the Japanese and the French out. He became the President of the Democratic Republic of Vietnam in 1954. However, he continued to fight to re-unite North and South Vietnam until his death in 1969.

Ho Chi Minh

May 19, 1890: *Born in Vietnam*

1911: *Leaves Vietnam working on a French ship*

1920: *Founds the French Communist Party*

September 1945: *Proclaims the republic of Vietnam but agrees it will remain an autonomous state in the French Union*

1954: *After defeating France becomes President of North Vietnam and soon after engages in battle to re-unite North and South Vietnam*

74 Dwight D. Eisenhower
[1890 - 1969]

Nicknamed 'Ike', Dwight Eisenhower was an American President and the General of the United States Army. As the President, Eisenhower enforced 'desegregation' in schools to allow the admission of black students. He spent very little money on the military and ended the Korean War by signing agreements with Korea and China. Though the US was not involved in any major military activity during his term, there was an increase in the nuclear arms race.

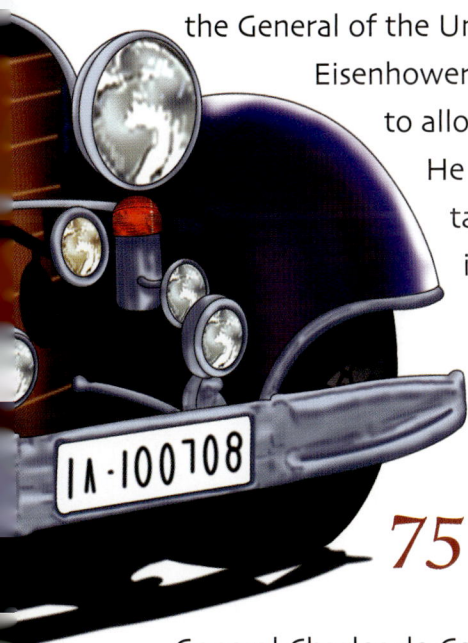

October 14, 1890: *Born in Denison, Texas*

December 1943: *Made Supreme Commander of the Allied forces in World War II*

1952: *Elected as President*

1953: *Helps achieve ceasefire in the Korean War*

1956: *Passes the Interstate Highway Act*

1957: *Enforces desegregation by sending troops to Little Rock Arkansas when its Governor refused entry of black students into Little Rock Central High School*

March 28, 1969: *Dies in Washington D. C.*

IA-100708

75 Charles de Gaulle
[1890 - 1970]

Charles de Gaulle

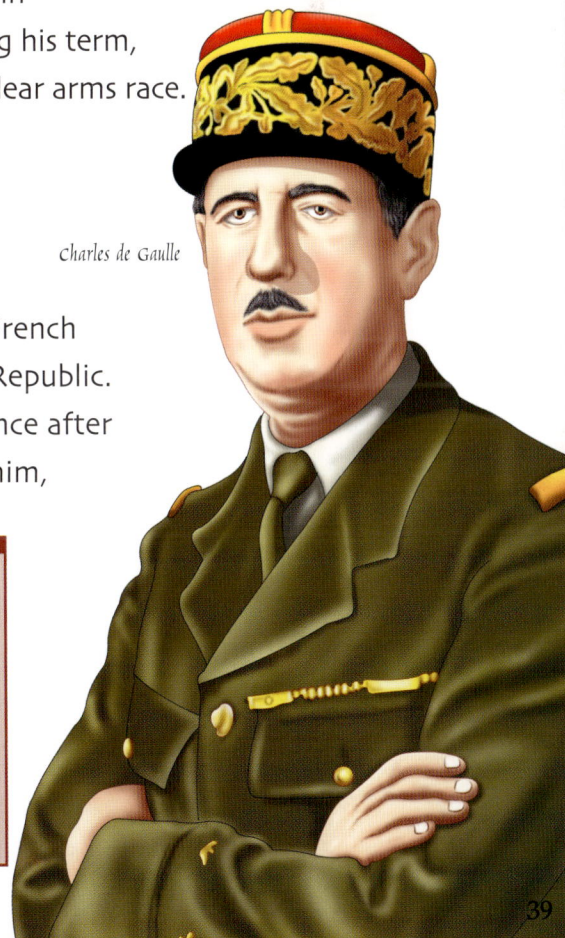

General Charles de Gaulle was the leader of the Free French forces during World War II and the first President of the Fifth Republic. He introduced tough measures to improve the economy of France after the war and ordered the making of a new constitution. Under him, France became politically stable and gained importance in the international stage. He also improved relations with China and Germany. He retired in 1969 following the defeat of his motion to change the constitution.

November 22, 1890: *Born in Lille, France*

1940: *Founds the Free French Forces*

1958: *Formation of the Fifth Republic*

January 1959: *Becomes the President of the Fifth Republic*

April 28, 1969: *Retires to Colombey-les-deux-Églises, where he dies a year later*

76 Khan Abdul Ghaffar Khan
[1890 - 1988]

Known as 'Badshah Khan' (Khan of Khans), Ghaffar Khan was a Pathan leader famous for his non-violent opposition of British rule. His goal was a united and independent India. To achieve this, he founded the 'Khudai Khidmatgar' (meaning 'Servants of God') in 1929. He was inspired by Gandhi and viewed his own struggle as a Jihad (religious war) with only the enemy holding swords. He died in Peshawar in 1988.

1890: Born into a Pathan family in Charsadda, Afghanistan

September 1929: Founds the 'Khudai Khidmatgar'

1987: Awarded Bharat Ratna – India's highest civilian award

January 18, 1988: Dies at Peshawar, and is buried in Jalalabad, Afghanistan

77 Francisco Franco
[1892 - 1975]

This Spanish military dictator rose to power in the 1930's by winning the Spanish Civil War. He did so with the help of Hitler and Mussolini. However, Franco kept Spain out of World War II. After the war, Franco befriended the U.S. by allowing it to set up military bases in Spain during the Cold War. Franco remained in power until his death despite growing hatred towards him.

December 4, 1892: Born in El Ferrol, Spain

1926: Becomes the youngest General ever in a European Army

July 17, 1936: Leads a military uprising starting the Spanish Civil War

March 28, 1939: Conquers Madrid ending the Civil War

1947: Declares Spain a Monarchy but does not name a King until later in 1969

1955: Spain enters the United Nations

November 20, 1975: Dies in Madrid

Francisco Franco

78 Mao Tse-Tung
[1893 - 1976]

Mao Tse-Tung was the founder of the People's Republic of China. He led the Communist Party to power after winning the Chinese Civil War. He also built the Red Army and was responsible for uniting China. He has, however, been criticized for his terrible economic and political decisions taken while in power, one of which was the 'Great Leap Forward' programme that resulted in widespread starvation. Despite his faults, Mao continues to be worshipped in China.

December 26, 1893: Born in Shaoshan, Hunan Province, China

1926: Chinese Civil War between the Communists and Kuomintang begins

1927: Leads the Autumn Harvest Uprising at Changsha, Hunan and barely escapes death

1931-34: Establishes the Chinese Soviet Republic

1934-35: Leads the Red Army on the famous Long March, emerging as a Communist leader

1937-1945: Sino-Japanese War

1949: Establishes the People's Republic of China after defeating the Kuomintang in the Civil War

1958: Launches the 'Great Leap Forward' programme

1966: Starts the Cultural Revolution to re-establish himself

September 9, 1976: Dies in Beijing, China

Mao Tse-Tung

79 *Nikita Sergeyevich Khrushchev*
[1894 - 1971]

Leader of the Soviet Union, Nikita Khrushchev condemned Stalin saying he was responsible for mass murders. On becoming the Premier, Khrushchev crushed the Hungarian revolution. He also started the space program that launched Sputnik I and Yuri Gagarin into space. He is said to have demanded an apology from the U.S. President Eisenhower for flying U-2 spy planes over USSR. He was removed from office after the Cuban missile crisis, following his decision to place nuclear missiles in Cuba to threaten America.

Nikita Sergeyevich Khrushchev

April 17, 1894: *Born in Kalinovka, Kursk Province, Russia*

March 27, 1958: *Becomes the Premier of the Soviet Union*

May 16, 1960: *Demands apology from US ending the Big Four summit in Paris*

May 1962: *Decides to place nuclear missiles in Cuba following similar acts by US in Turkey, threatening the USSR*

October 15, 1962: *The thirteen days Cuban Missile Crisis begins. Soviet Union agrees to pull out after US agrees to do the same in Turkey*

1964: *Removed from office and placed under house arrest*

September 11, 1971: *Dies at his home in Moscow after seven years of house arrest*

80 *Ayatollah Ruhollah Khomeini*
[1900 - 1989]

Khomeini was an Iranian religious leader. He came to power by overthrowing Mohammed Reza Pahlavi, the then Shah of Iran. Khomeini's rule ended western influence in Iran. Shia Islamic Law was instituted with strict dress codes, press was suppressed and women lost their rights as equal citizens. Iraqi leader Saddam Hussein felt threatened by the spread of Khomeini's ideology and invaded Iran, thus beginning the decade-long Iran-Iraq War.

Ayatollah Ruhollah Khomeini

May 17, 1900: *Born as Ruhollah Mousavi in Khomeyn, Iraq*

1964: *Exiled from Iran for criticizing the Shah*

February 1, 1979: *Returns to Iran to join the Iranian Revolution*

February 11, 1979: *Seizes power*

September 22, 1980: *Start of the Iran-Iraq War.*

June 3, 1989: *Dies in Tehran, Iran*

81 Leonid Ilich Brezhnev
[1906 - 1982]

Leonid Ilich
Brezhnev

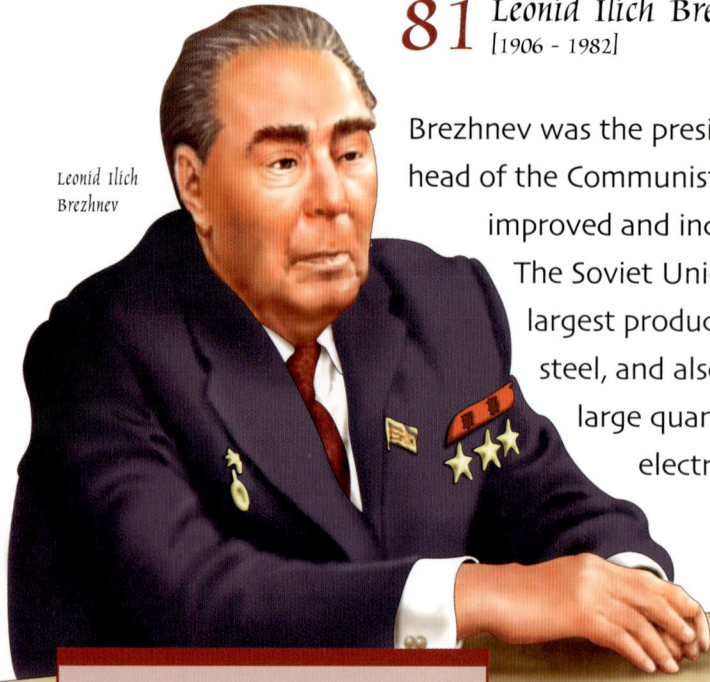

Brezhnev was the president of the Soviet Union and the head of the Communist Party. Under him, living standards improved and industrial production increased. The Soviet Union became the largest producer of oil and steel, and also manufactured large quantities of electronic goods.

Ronald Reagan

December 19, 1906: *Born in Kamenskoye, Ukraine*

1964: *Becomes head of the Communist Party*

1968: *Introduces the Brezhnev Doctrine to support the invasion of Czechoslovakia*

1977: *Becomes president of the Soviet Union*

1979: *Invades Afghanistan*

November 10, 1982: *Yuri Andropov succeeds him on his death*

82 Ronald Reagan
[1911 - 2004]

The 40th American president, Ronald Reagan was also a popular Hollywood actor. He was a supporter of Franklin Roosevelt and a strong anti-communist. As president, Reagan reduced taxes, stabilised the economy and built up the military. He also proposed the expensive space-based defense system, popularly called "Star Wars".

February 6, 1911: *Born in Tampico, Illinois*

1966: *Elected governor of California*

1980: *Wins the presidential elections*

March 30, 1981: *Survives an attempt to kill him*

August 5, 1981: *Dismisses over 11,000 striking air traffic controllers for not obeying his orders to return to work*

1986: *The Iran-Contra Affair comes out in public; the Reagan government is accused of selling arms to Iran*

June 5, 2004: *Dies in Los Angeles, California*

83 *Sirimavo Bandaranaike*
[1916 - 2000]

1916: *Born Sirimavo Ratwatte*

1959: *Succeeds her husband as prime minister of Ceylon*

1972: *Promotes the new Constitution and changes the name of the country to Sri Lanka*

1977: *Her party is defeated in elections*

1980: *Expelled from the parliament*

1988: *Loses presidential elections*

1994: *Returns as prime minister*

2000: *Dies in Colombo, Sri Lanka*

Sirimavo Bandaranaike was the world's first woman prime minister. She succeeded her husband as the prime minister of Ceylon (now Sri Lanka) after he was killed in 1959. During her term, she promoted a new constitution that declared the country a republic. She lost power in 1977, but returned as prime minister when her daughter, Chandrika Kumaratunga, became president in 1994. Six years later she resigned due to ill health.

84 *John F. Kennedy*
[1917 - 1963]

One of the most popular presidents in American history, JFK's 1,000 days in office were marked by the increased role of America in the space race and by the Vietnam War. His term also saw the Cuban missile crisis and the Bay of Pigs invasion of Cuba. These events worsened the Cold War with the Soviet Union. He also cut taxes and extended federal aid to education and medical care for the aged under Social Security.

John F. Kennedy

May 29, 1917: *Born in Brookline, Massachusetts*

1953: *Marries Jacqueline Lee Bouvier*

1956: *Writes Profiles in Courage, for which he later won the Pulitzer Prize*

1961: *Becomes the 35th President of the United States; establishes the Alliance for Progress to provide financial aid to the Latin American countries*

April 1961: *Approves the Bay of Pigs invasion of Cuba by Cuban exiles trained by the Central Intelligence Agency*

October 1963: *Active involvement in the Vietnam War*

November 22, 1963: *Shot and killed in Dallas, Texas, by Lee Harvey Oswald*

85 *Nelson Mandela*
[1918 -]

July 18, 1918: *Born in Qunu, Transkei*

1952: *Becomes the deputy national president of the African National Congress (ANC)*

1960: *Launches guerilla warfare against the government*

1964: *Sentenced to life in prison on charges of sabotage*

1990: *President Frederik Willem de Klerk releases him*

July 1991: *Elected president of ANC*

1993: *Shares Nobel Peace Prize with de Klerk*

1994: *Becomes president of South Africa after winning first multiracial elections*

Nelson Mandela

Nelson Mandela was the first black president of South Africa. He helped to end apartheid in his country. Initially, he conducted his fight in a non-violent manner. However, after a group of peaceful demonstrators were killed in Sharpeville, he declared war on the government. Mandela was sentenced to life imprisonment in 1964, though he continued to inspire the fight against apartheid. Finally, in 1990, President de Klerk released Mandela, who went on to win the first multiracial elections in South Africa.

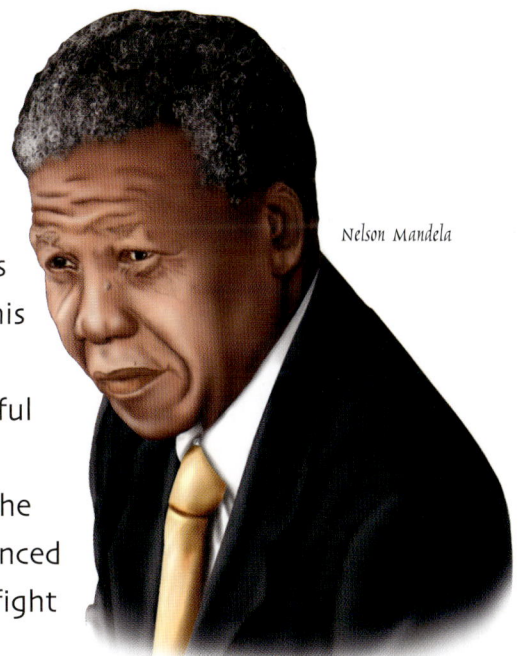

86 Yitzhak Rabin
[1922 - 1995]

Rabin was the prime minister of Israel. He is famous for ordering "Operation Entebbe", in which the Israel Defence Forces rescued passengers of a hijacked plane. He also played a major role in the 1993 Oslo Peace Accords, which created the Palestinian Authority and gave it partial control over parts of Gaza Strip and the West Bank. The accord won Rabin the 1994 Nobel Peace Prize, which he shared with Yasser Arafat and Shimon Peres.

March 1, 1922: Born in Jerusalem

1968: Becomes ambassador to the U.S.

1974: Succeeds Golda Meir as the prime minister of Israel

July 3, 1976: Orders Operation Entebbe

1993: Signs the Oslo Peace Accords with Palestine Liberation Organization (PLO)

1994: Signs peace treaty with Jordan

November 5, 1995: Killed by Yigal Amir, an Israeli law student and activist, in Tel Aviv-Yafo, Israel

Jimmy Carter

87 Jimmy Carter
[1924 -]

Jimmy Carter is one of three American presidents to be awarded the Nobel Peace Prize. While in office, he faced his toughest challenge when 52 Americans were taken hostage by Iranian terrorists. Although the rescue attempt failed, he managed to negotiate their release. Carter is also renowned for his service to society after retirement, and was conferred with the Nobel Peace Prize in 2002.

October 1, 1924: Born in Plains, Georgia

1977: Becomes the 39th U.S. President

September 7, 1977: Turns control of Panama Canal over to Panama

1979: Allows ousted Iranian leader Mohammad Reza Shah Pahlavi into the country, leading to the hostage crisis in Iran

1980: Boycotts the Summer Olympics in Moscow, following Soviet invasion of Afghanistan

May 12, 2002: First American president to visit Cuba during Fidel Castro's rule

2002: Wins the Nobel Peace Prize

88 Margaret Thatcher
[1925 -]

Margaret Thatcher

The first female prime minister of Britain, she is also popularly known as the "Iron Lady". The only British prime minister of the 20th century to serve in three consecutive terms, Margaret Thatcher is both admired and hated for her economic reforms. She strongly supported the handing over of national industries to private companies. Differences within her party over political and economic issues eventually forced her to resign.

October 13, 1925: Born in Grantham, Lincolnshire, England

May 4, 1979: Becomes prime minister

1983: Gets re-elected as prime minister

1986: Allows the United States to bomb Libya from air bases in Britain

November 22, 1990: Resigns from office

89 *Kim Dae Jung*
[1925 -]

Kim Dae Jung became the president of South Korea in 1997. He immediately began efforts to befriend North Korea and promote democracy and human rights. In 2000 he travelled to North Korea for a historic meeting with its leader, Kim Jong II. In the same year, Kim Dae Jung was awarded the Nobel Peace Prize for his efforts. However, implications that he might have bribed Kim Jong II for the meeting have harmed his reputation.

January 6, 1924: *Born in Hayi-do, Korea*

1997: *Becomes the president of South Korea*

June 2000: *Meets Kim Jong II; wins the Nobel Peace Prize for his efforts to make peace with North Korea*

Kim Dae Jung

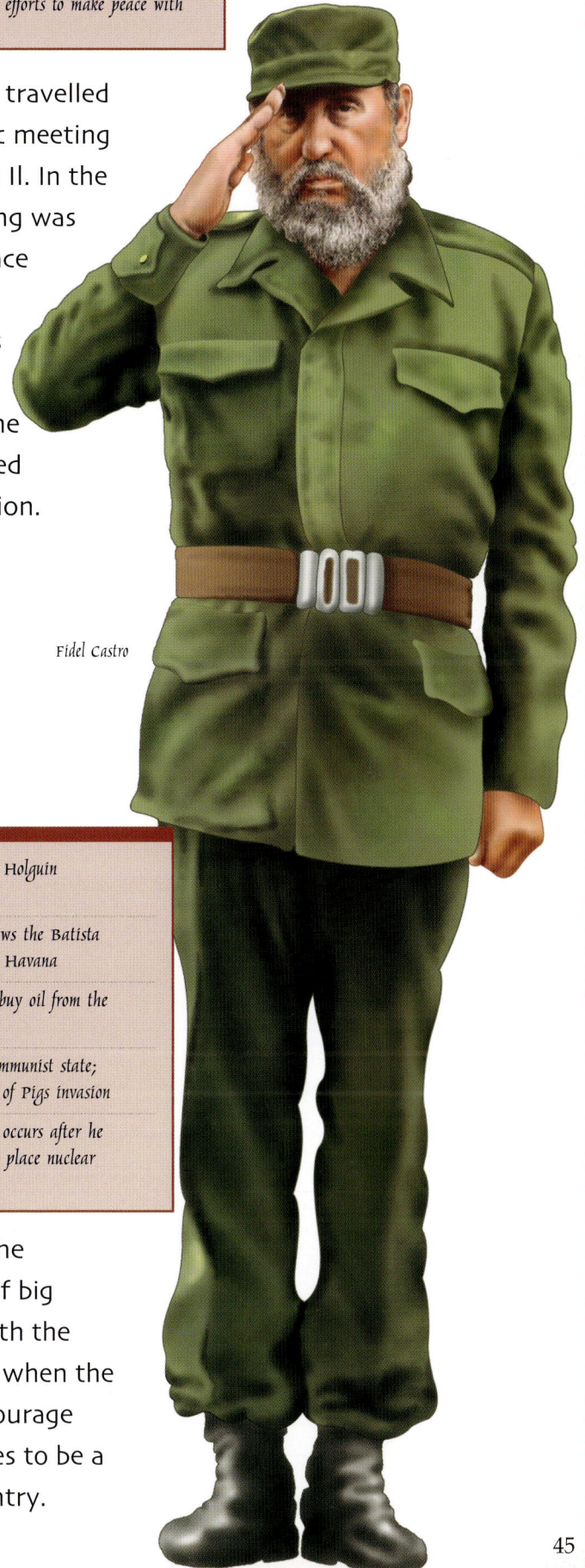

Fidel Castro

90 *Fidel Castro*
[1926 -]

President Fidel Castro of the Cuban Republic is credited with improving health facilities and living conditions of the poor, and also with promoting education. His problems with the United States started when he seized the property of big American companies in Cuba, and began to trade with the Soviet Union. Cuba faced major financial problems when the Soviet Union collapsed. Castro then began to encourage foreign companies to come to Cuba. He continues to be a symbol of social justice and progress in his country.

August 13, 1926: *Born in Holguin Province, Cuba*

January 1, 1959: *Overthrows the Batista government and takes over Havana*

1960: *Signs agreement to buy oil from the Soviet Union*

1961: *Declares Cuba a Communist state; America sponsors the Bay of Pigs invasion*

1962: *Cuban missile crisis occurs after he allows the Soviet Union to place nuclear weapons in Cuba*

91 Che Guevara
[1928 - 1967]

June 14, 1928: *Born in Argentina*

1954: *Meets Fidel Castro in Mexico*

1959: *Helps Castro overthrow Batista and take control of Cuba*

1961-65: *Serves as minister of industry in Castro's government*

1965: *Leaves for Congo*

October 1967: *Killed in Bolivia*

Che Guevara was a Cuban revolutionary who also served in Fidel Castro's government. Apart from helping Castro to overthrow the Cuban dictator Batista, Guevara was also responsible for cutting ties with the United States and directing Cuba towards the Soviet Union. He left Cuba in 1965 to support freedom struggles in Congo and, subsequently, Bolivia. During a guerilla attack in Bolivia, he was captured and killed by government troops.

92 Henry Kissinger
[1923 -]

Henry Kissinger

As U.S. foreign-policy adviser, Kissinger accomplished several important tasks. He helped begin the Strategic Arms Limitation Talks (SALT) with the Soviet Union to control the production of nuclear weapons.

May 27, 1923: *Born in Furth, Germany*

1938: *Flees with his family to the United States to escape Hitler's anti-Jewish activities*

1943: *Becomes a U.S. citizen*

1968: *Appointed advisor to Richard Nixon*

May 26, 1972: *SALT I Treaty between the United States and the Soviet Union is signed*

1972: *Arranges President Nixon's visit to China*

1973: *Becomes secretary of state; American troops are withdrawn from Vietnam; Kissinger is awarded the Nobel Prize for Peace*

He also arranged President Nixon's visit to China in 1972. He supported the withdrawal of U.S. troops from Vietnam and later won the Nobel Peace Prize for negotiating the end of fighting with North Vietnam.

93 Yasser Arafat
[1929 - 2004]

Leader of the Palestine Liberation Organization (PLO), Arafat is known for his efforts to maintain peace between Israel and Palestine. Under him, the PLO not only gave up terrorism,

Yasser Arafat

but also signed a peace agreement with Israel, for which he won the 1994 Nobel Peace Prize. However, the peace process has not been smooth and terrorist activities still continue.

August 24, 1929: *Born in Cairo, Egypt*

1969: *Becomes chairman of PLO*

November 15, 1988: *Proclaims the State of Palestine and controls operations from Tunisia*

December 15, 1988: *Gives up terrorism and promises to recognise Israel*

1993: *Signs the Oslo Peace Accord with Isreal*

1994: *Wins the Nobel Peace Prize*

January 20, 1996: *Becomes president of the Palestinian Authority*

November 11, 2004: *Dies in a French hospital near Paris*

94 Helmut Kohl
[1930 -]

Helmut Kohl was the chancellor of West Germany and, later, of re-unified Germany as well. Under him, West Germany prospered and became a major power in the world. He launched his efforts to re-unify East and West Germany in 1989, when East Germany began to collapse. Shortly after the fall of the Berlin Wall, Kohl became the first chancellor of a unified Germany.

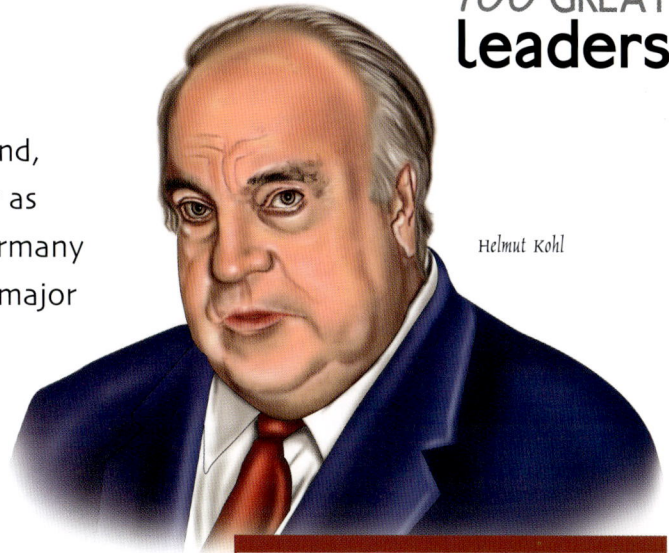

Helmut Kohl

Mikhail Gorbachev

April 3, 1930: *Born in Ludwigshafen am Rhein*

1973: *Becomes chairman of the Christian Democratic Union*

October 1, 1982: *Becomes chancellor of West Germany*

November 9, 1989: *The Berlin Wall falls*

December 1990: *Becomes chancellor of re-unified Germany*

1998: *Loses the elections to the Social Democrats led by Gerhard Schroder*

95 Mikhail Gorbachev
[1931 -]

Former president of the Soviet Union, Gorbachev is famous for his social and economic reforms – among them, glasnost (openness) and perestroika (economic restructuring). He also ended the Cold War, for which he won the Nobel Peace Prize. In 1988 he allowed Soviet bloc nations like Czechoslovakia to return to democracy. This led to the collapse of Communism in Eastern Europe and resulted in the ultimate break-up of the Soviet Union.

March 2, 1931: *Born in Privolye, Stavropol region, Russia*

March 11, 1985: *Takes over the leadership of the Soviet Union on the death of Konstantin Chernenko*

February 1986: *Launches glasnost and perestroika*

1990: *Wins the Nobel Peace Prize for his contribution towards ending the Cold War*

1991: *Attempt to overthrow him fails; returns to power after spending three days under house arrest, only to find Yeltsin in command*

December 25, 1991: *Resigns as president*

December 26, 1991: *The Supreme Soviet officially dissolves the Soviet Union*

96 Desmond Tutu
[1931 -]

Tutu was a South African religious leader who fought against apartheid (racial discrimination). He was also the first black Anglican archbishop of Cape Town, South Africa. Winner of the 1984 Nobel Peace Prize, Tutu headed the Truth and Reconcilia-tion Commission that looked into the abuse of human rights during the apartheid era.

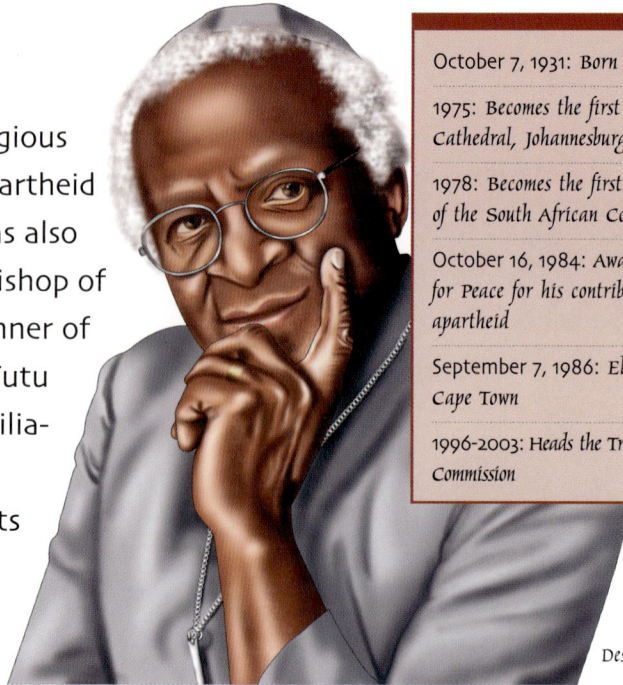

October 7, 1931: Born in Klerksdorp Transvaal

1975: Becomes the first black dean of St. Mary's Cathedral, Johannesburg

1978: Becomes the first black general secretary of the South African Council of Churches

October 16, 1984: Awarded the Nobel Prize for Peace for his contribution to the fight against apartheid

September 7, 1986: Elected archbishop of Cape Town

1996-2003: Heads the Truth and Reconciliation Commission

Desmond Tutu

97 King Hussein
[1935 - 1999]

King Hussein

Hailed as a peacemaker, King Hussein of Jordan was known for his pro-Western stand. This was, however, resented by the other Arab nations, especially the Palestinians. Hussein's relations with Palestine worsened when Israel captured the West Bank (earlier a Palestinian territory) during the Arab-Israeli War. Later, though, he played a major role in encouraging peace talks between the Arabs and the Israelis. In 1994, he signed a peace treaty with Israel.

November 14, 1935: Born Prince Talal of Jordan

1953: Becomes king of Jordan after his grandfather, King Abdullah I, is killed

1967: Loses West Bank to Israel in the Arab-Israeli War

1970: Civil war begins in Jordan

1991: Refuses to join anti-Iraqi forces during the Gulf War

February 7, 1999: Dies in Amman, Jordan

98 F.W. de Klerk
[1936 -]

March 18, 1936: Born in Johannesburg

1989: Takes over as president after P.W. Botha resigns

1990: Releases Nelson Mandela from prison

1991: Calls for drafting a new constitution, leading to the formation of the first multiracial government in South Africa

1994: Becomes the vice-president under Mandela's presidency

1997: Retires from politics

As president of South Africa, de Klerk played a big role in ending apartheid in the country. Soon after coming to power, he lifted the ban on anti-racist parties and released Nelson Mandela from prison. In 1991 he abolished all the remaining apartheid laws and set in motion the process for the first multiracial government in South Africa. He received the 1993 Nobel Peace Prize along with Mandela.

99 John Hume
[1937 -]

One of the most important political figures of Northern Ireland, Hume was the founder-member of the Credit Union Party (later the Social Democratic and Labour Party, or SDLP) and a member of the Northern Ireland parliament. He was awarded the 1999 Nobel Peace Prize with David Trimble, the Ulster Unionist party leader, for their efforts to find a peaceful solution to the Northern Ireland conflict.

January 18, 1937: Born in Londonderry, Northern Ireland

1969: Becomes a member of parliament

1979: Succeeds Gerry Fitt as the leader of the SDLP

1983: Becomes a member of parliament of Britain

1999: Wins the Nobel Peace Prize

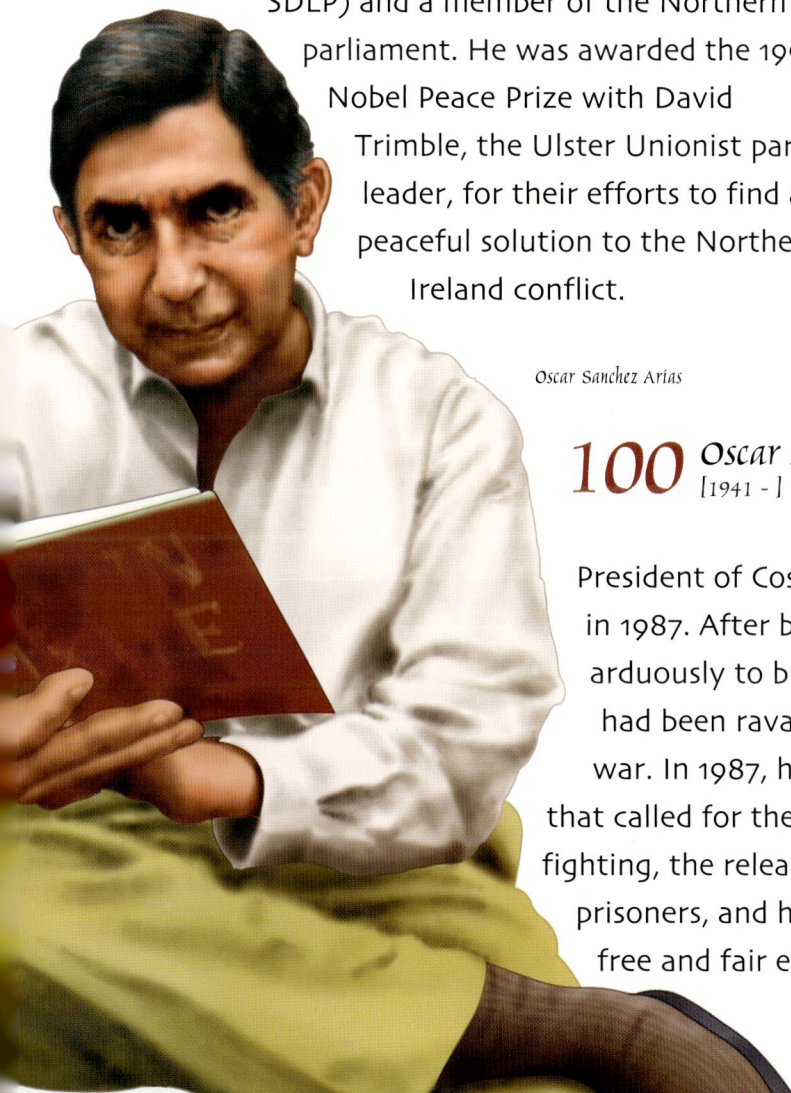

Oscar Sanchez Arias

John Hume

100 Oscar Arias Sanchez
[1941 -]

President of Costa Rica, Arias won the Nobel Peace Prize in 1987. After becoming the president, he worked arduously to bring back peace to Central America, which had been ravaged by civil war. In 1987, he led efforts that called for the end of fighting, the release of political prisoners, and holding of free and fair elections.

September 13, 1941: Born in Costa Rica

1970: Becomes financial adviser to the president

1972: Becomes minister of planning

1986: Becomes president of Costa Rica

1987: Wins the Nobel Peace Prize for his efforts to maintain peace in Central America

Great

Scientists

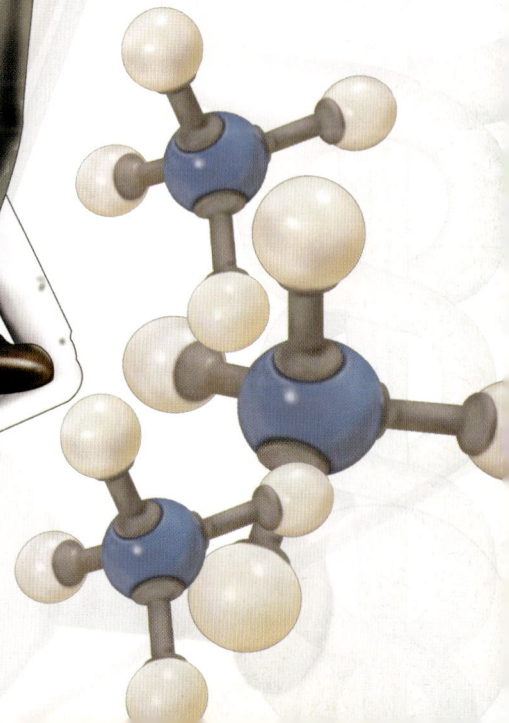

101 Pythagoras
[c. 580 B.C. - c. 500 B.C.]

c. 580 B.C.: Born on the island of Samos, Ionia, Greece

c. 500 B.C.: Dies at Metapontum, Lucania

Pythagoras was a Greek mathematician and philosopher who formulated the Pythagorean theorem. He believed that the universe could not exist without numbers. He started a school to impart these ideas and his followers came to be known as Pythagoreans. Considered the founder of modern mathematics, his teachings have influenced great thinkers like Plato and Aristotle.

Pythagoras

102 Hippocrates
[c. 460 B.C. - c. 377 B.C.]

Hippocrates was an ancient Greek physician and is widely regarded as the father of medicine. He freed medicine from the superstitions of his time and established it as a science. He is also associated with the Hippocratic oath taken by medical students on their graduation. Although he did not write the oath, it contains his ideas and principles regarding medicine and doctors.

c. 460 B.C.: Born on the island of Cos, Greece

c. 450-350 B.C.: Writes on various topics such as surgery, epidemics and ulcers, all of which along with the *Aphorisms* (short medical truths) were compiled as the *Corpus Hippocraticum* (Hippocratic Corpus)

c. 377 B.C.: Dies in Larissa, Thessaly, Greece

Aristotle

103 Aristotle
[384 B.C. - 322 B.C.]

384 B.C.: Born in Stagira, Chalcidice, Greece

367 B.C.: Enters the Academy of Plato in Athens

342 B.C.: Becomes tutor to Alexander the Great

335 B.C.: Establishes his school, the Lyceum, in Athens

322 B.C.: Dies in Chalcis, Euboea

Aristotle was an ancient Greek scientist and philosopher. He made valuable contributions to various branches of science. He was a student of Plato and teacher to Alexander the Great. Aristotle dissected and studied over 500 animal species and laid the foundation for the modern classification of animals. He believed in a spherical Earth and promoted the theory of an unchanging universe with Earth at its centre.

104 Euclid
[c. 325 B.C. - c. 265 B.C.]

c. 325 B.C.: Born

c. 265 B.C.: Dies in Alexandria, Egypt

Euclid was a very famous mathematician of Greco-Roman origin. He wrote the *Elements*, a treatise containing his work on geometry and other branches of mathematics. The first six of the 13 volumes deal with plane geometry, while the rest deal with the theory of numbers, solid geometry and other arithmetic problems. Although not much is known about his life, Euclid's contribution to mathematics is unquestionable.

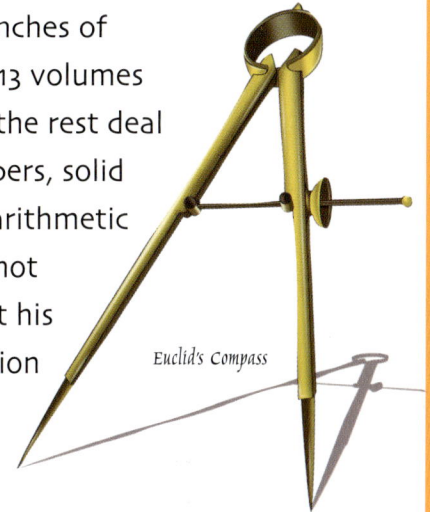

Euclid's Compass

Euclid

105 Archimedes
[c. 287 B.C. - c. 212 B.C.]

This famous Greek mathematician and inventor has to his credit many inventions and discoveries that helped shape modern science. According to a well-known legend, he came up with the principles of density and buoyancy upon observing that water overflowed from his bath when he sat in it. He ran home without remembering to wear his clothes, shouting "Eureka!" ("I have found it!"). The discovery was later named Archimedes' principle. He also invented the Archimedes' screw, calculated the value of pi and made several other contributions to mathematics.

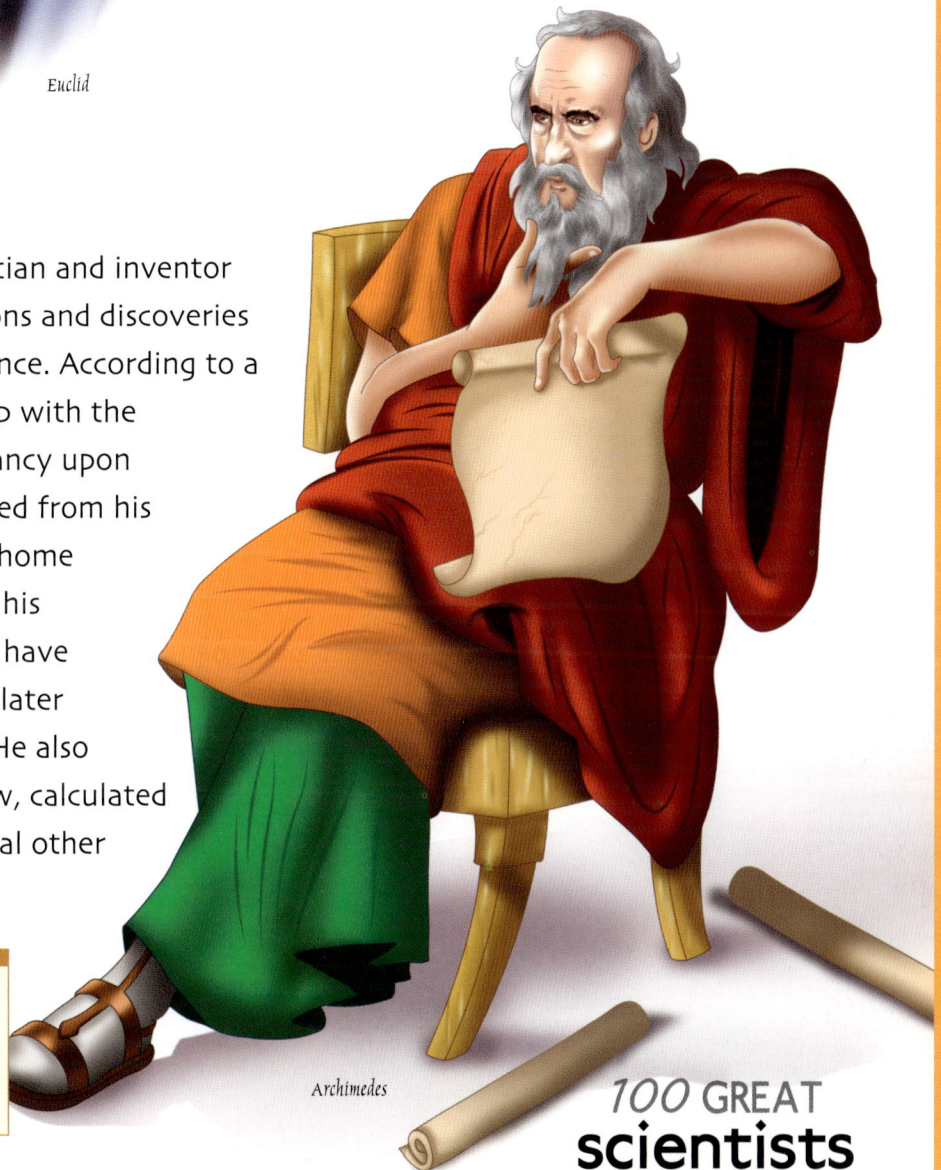

c. 287 B.C.: Born in Syracuse, Sicily (now part of Italy)

c. 212 B.C.: Killed by Roman soldiers during the siege of Syracuse in the Second Punic War, after he held them at bay for three years with his war engines

Archimedes

100 GREAT
scientists

106 Eratosthenes
[c. 276 B.C. - c. 194 B.C.]

He was a Greek scientist and astronomer, considered to be the first to calculate the Earth's circumference. He did so using arithmetic calculations and information on the varying altitudes of the Sun at noon over Alexandria and Syene (now Aswan, Egypt). Eratosthenes also formulated a system of latitude and longitude and made a map of the world as known at the time. He adopted the word "geography", and also measured the distances of the Sun and the Moon from the Earth.

c. 276 B.C.: Born in Cyrene, North Africa (now Shahhat, Libya)

c. 240 B.C.: Becomes head of the library at Alexandria, Egypt

c. 195 B.C.: Goes blind

c. 194 B.C.: Starves himself to death in Alexandria

Eratosthenes' Earth

107 Lucretius
[c. 99 B.C. - c. 55 B.C.]

c. 99 B.C.: Born as Titus Lucretius Carus

c. 50 B.C.: Writes De rerum natura (On the Nature of Things)

c. 55 B.C.: Commits suicide

Lucretius was a Latin poet and philosopher, best known for his epic poem *De rerum natura (On the Nature of Things)*. In this masterpiece, Lucretius holds up the theory of the Greek philosopher Epicurus – that everything, including the soul, is made up of atoms and that there is no need to fear God or death. These views are thought to have laid the foundations for later scientific discoveries such as Dalton's atomic theory and Darwin's theory of evolution.

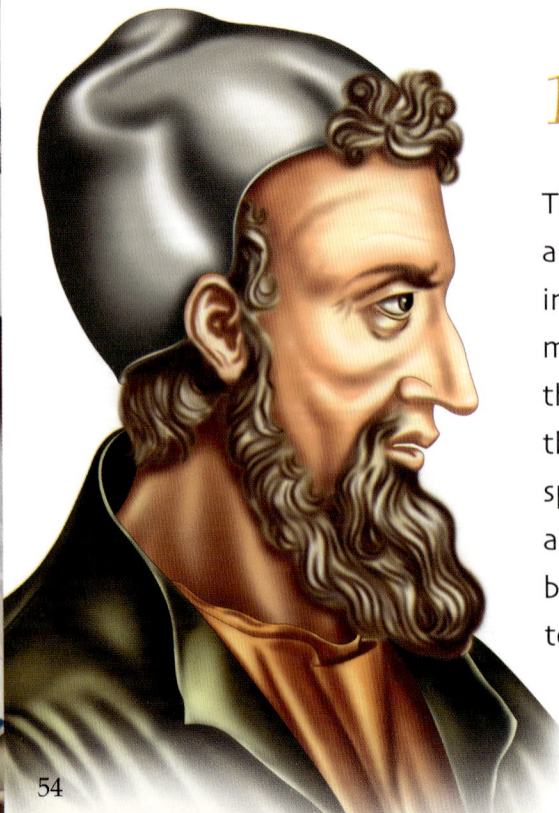

108 Galen
[A.D. 129 - c. 216]

A.D. 129: Born in Pergamum, Mysia, Anatolia (now Bergama, Turkey)

157: Works as physician in a gladiator school

162: Lives in Rome and becomes court physician to Emperor Marcus Aurelius

c. 216: Dies

This Greek physician and philosopher greatly influenced European medicine for over a thousand years. By dissecting animals, he demonstrated the functions of kidneys and proved that cutting the spinal cord causes paralysis. He also showed that arteries carried blood – not air – and promoted bloodletting (withdrawal of a good amount of blood to cure or prevent diseases).

Galen

109 *Susruta* [c. 380 - c. 450]

Susruta was a surgeon in ancient India. He lived at the court of the Gupta rulers in their capital, Pataliputra (modern Patna). According to legend, Susruta mended a man's nose by inserting two pipes in it and covering it with flesh from the man's cheek! He also operated on ears, lips and eyes and delivered a baby through operation (Caesarean section).

It is believed that he gave wine to his patients to make them numb to pain. Susruta recorded his surgical methods in a book entitled *Susrutasamhita*. In this work he also listed various kinds of surgical instruments.

c. 380: Born in India

c. 450: Dies

Susruta performing ear surgery

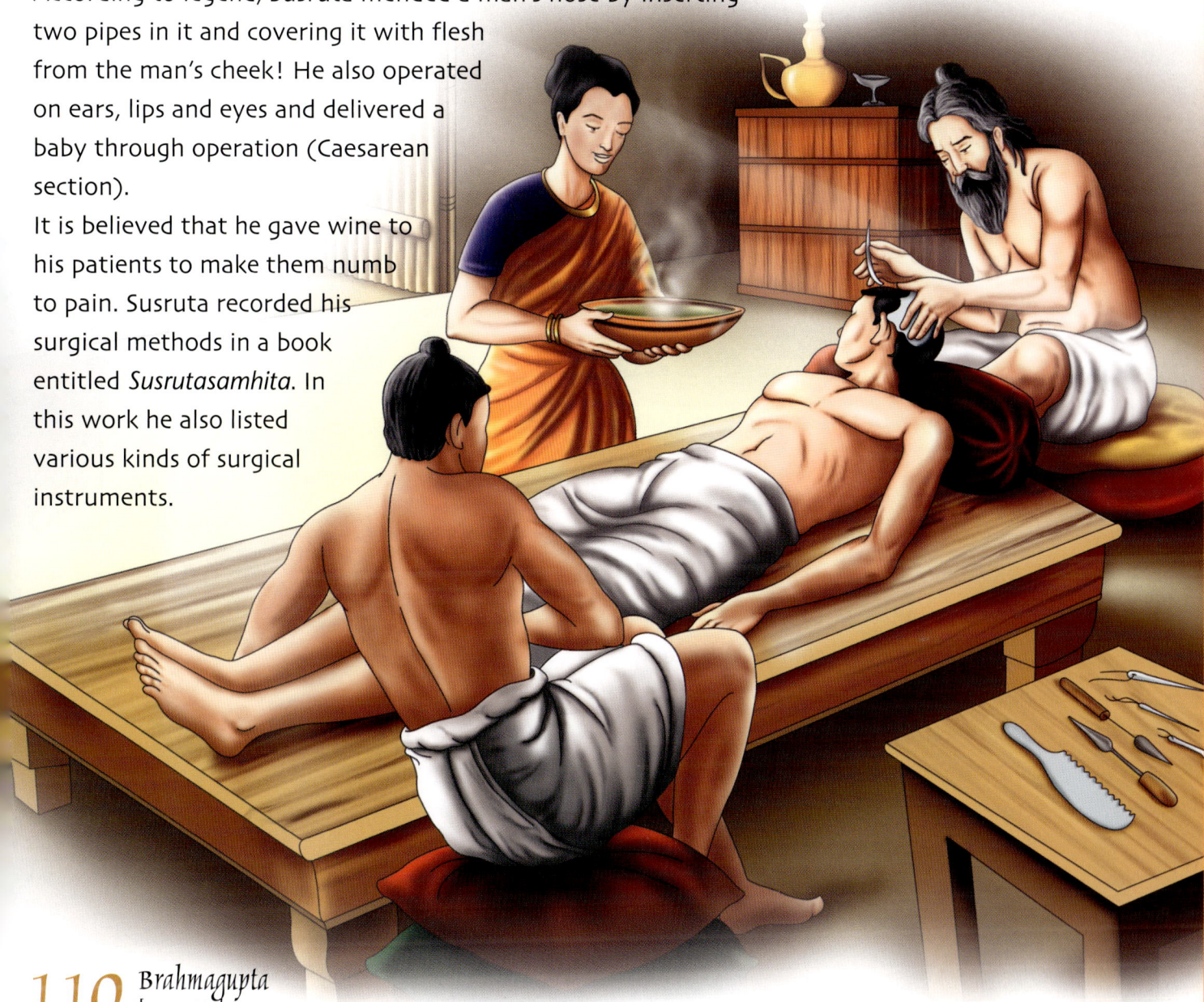

110 *Brahmagupta* [598 - 668]

He was a great Indian mathematician who is believed to have discovered zero and its functions. He explained that addition or subtraction of zero with any number gave the same number (e.g., $1+0 = 1$; $1-0 = 1$). He also declared that multiplying a number with zero would result in zero ($1 \times 0 = 0$). However, he was wrong in saying that division of zero by zero was zero. Brahmagupta also made many other mathematical discoveries and proposed the law of gravitation even before Newton proved it.

598: Born in Madhya Pradesh, India

628: Defines zero in Brahma-sphuta-siddhanta (The Opening of the Universe)

c. 668: Dies in (possibly) Bhillamala (modern Bhinmal), Rajasthan, India, after writing his second work, Khandakhadyaka (A Piece Eatable)

100 GREAT
scientists

111 Alhazen
[c. 965 - c. 1040]

c. 965: Born as Ibn al-Haytham, in Basra, Iraq

c. 1040: Dies in Cairo, Egypt

An Arab mathematician and astronomer, Alhazen was the
first to suggest that light was reflected into the eye from the objects one saw. His tests were
held in a dark room with a small hole in one of the walls. Outside, five lanterns were placed
facing the wall with the hole. He noticed that there were five different lights in the room,
although all of them travelled through one hole. Also, the light disappeared when an object
was placed in its path. Thus, he proved that light travels in a straight line.

112 Nicolaus Copernicus
[1473 - 1543]

February 19, 1473: Born in Torun, Poland

1514: Records his findings, for the first time, in a
handwritten book called Commentariolus (Little
Commentary) and distributes it among his friends

May 24, 1543: Dies in Frauenburg, East Prussia
(now Frombork, Poland)

Nicolaus Copernicus

Nicolaus Copernicus was
a Polish astronomer who
proposed that the Sun is
at the centre of the universe, with the Earth and
other planets revolving around it. The
Copernican system also states that the Earth
rotates on its own axis. Although Copernicus
arrived at this theory early in his life, it was
not made public until his death. The first printed
copy of his theory, called *De Revolutionibus
Orbium Coelestium libri vi (Six Books Concerning
the Revolutions of the Heavenly Orbs)*, was given
to him on his deathbed. According to legend,
Copernicus awoke from his coma, looked at his
book and died peacefully.

113 Andreas Vesalius
[1514 - 1564]

Andreas Vesalius

December 1514: Born in Brussels (now in Belgium)

1543: Records his findings in the book De humani
corporis fabrica libri septem (The Seven Books on
the Structure of the Human Body)

June 1564: Dies on the Island of Zacynthus,
Republic of Venice (now in Greece)

He was the first to
describe the structure of
a human body (anatomy)
correctly. He recorded his
findings after careful dissection of dead human bodies.
His description proved Galen wrong in many ways.
Vesalius showed that Galen's anatomy was based
on animal dissections and that he had no actual
knowledge of the human body.

114 Tycho Brahe
[1546 - 1601]

Tycho Brahe was a great Danish astronomer, famous for his discovery of a new star. He did so without the help of a telescope! He also coined the word *nova* (for "new" star) and correctly estimated the position of over 777 fixed stars. However, he did not accept the Copernican theory. Instead, he believed that the Sun revolved around the Earth, while the other planets moved around the Sun. Many great scientists, including Kepler and Newton, based their discoveries on his observations.

December 14, 1546: *Born in Knudstrup, Denmark*

1572: *Discovers a new star*

1573: *Publishes his discovery in the book,* De nova stella

October 24, 1601: *Dies in Prague*

Tycho Brahe

115 Johannes Kepler
[1571 - 1630]

German astronomer Johannes Kepler assisted Tycho Brahe in his scientific investigations. Kepler is famous for his laws of planetary motion, also called Kepler's Laws. Through these laws, he first established that the planets moved around the Sun in ellipses and not in circles and that they move faster as they come closer to the Sun.

Johannes Kepler

December 27, 1571: *Born in Wurttemberg, Germany*

1604: *Observes a new star, which becomes famous as Kepler's Supernova*

1609: *Records two laws of planetary motion in a book,* Commentaries on the Motions of Mars

1611: *Presents the principles of the Keplerian telescope, popularly called the astronomical telescope*

1619: *Publishes his third law of planetary motion in* Harmony of the Worlds

November 15, 1630: *Dies in Regensburg*

100 GREAT
scientists

116 William Harvey
[1578 - 1657]

William Harvey was the first to discover that the heart pumped blood to all parts of the body. He also correctly explained blood circulation, stating that the blood returned to the heart and then pumped out again. This clashed with Galen's idea that blood was carried by veins from the liver and by arteries from the heart to the rest of the body, where it was used up. Harvey's theory was not accepted until years after his death.

April 1, 1578: *Born in Folkestone, Kent, England*

1616: *Announces his discovery of the circulatory system*

1628: *Publishes his work*

June 3, 1657: *Dies in London*

117 Blaise Pascal
[1623 - 1662]

June 19, 1623: *Born in Clermont-Ferrand, France*

1654: *Devotes himself to religious preaching and helping the poor*

August 19, 1662: *Dies in Paris*

1974: *The computer programme Pascal is named after him*

One of the greatest mathematicians and physicists ever, Pascal was a child genius. He wrote a paper on conic sections at the age of 16 and invented the mechanical calculator at 19! He also formulated what became known as Pascal's law – that pressure applied on a fluid (like water) in a container is distributed equally and without loss to all parts of the fluid as well as to the walls of the container. Pascal also invented the hydraulic press and the syringe. His last years were dedicated to religious activities.

Blaise Pascal

118 Robert Boyle
[1627 - 1691]

Also called the father of chemistry, Robert Boyle was the first to precisely define chemical elements and chemical reaction. He also invented a vacuum pump, which he used to demonstrate that air is necessary in combustion (burning), breathing and the carrying of sound.

Robert Boyle

January 25, 1627: *Born in County Waterford, Ireland*

1661: *Publishes his book* The Sceptical Chymist

December 31, 1691: *Dies in London*

119 Marcello Malpighi
[1628 - 1694]

Malpighi made valuable observations on the structure of body organs (including the skin, brain and kidneys) and the development of the chick inside the egg. He was the first to use a microscope for such complicated investigations. He also discovered the capillary network, thus establishing William Harvey's theory of blood circulation. Through his experiments with the silkworm, he discovered that insects use small holes in their skin called tracheae, instead of lungs, to breathe. Several body parts, including a human skin layer, have been named after him.

March 10, 1628: Born in Crevalcore, near Bologna, Italy

1653: Becomes a doctor of medicine

1691: Becomes chief physician to Pope Innocent XII

November 30, 1694: Dies in Rome

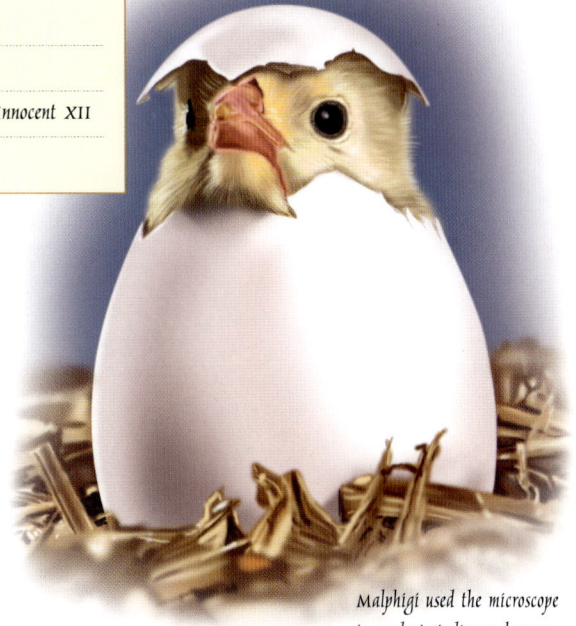

Malphigi used the microscope to conduct studies on how a chick developed inside the egg

120 Christiaan Huygens
[1629 - 1695]

A Dutch mathematician and physicist, Huygens founded the theory that light consists of waves. He also discovered Titan, the largest moon of Saturn and found that the rings around the planet are made of rocks. He was one of the first scientists to talk about life on other planets, a theory that later led to the mission to Mars!

April 14, 1629: Born at The Hague

1655: Discovers Saturn's moon, Titan

1656: Makes the first pendulum clock

1659: Publishes his Saturn ring theory in Systema Saturnium

July 8, 1695: Dies at The Hague after suffering from a serious illness

Christiaan Huygens

100 GREAT
scientists

121 Anton van Leeuwenhoek
[1632 - 1723]

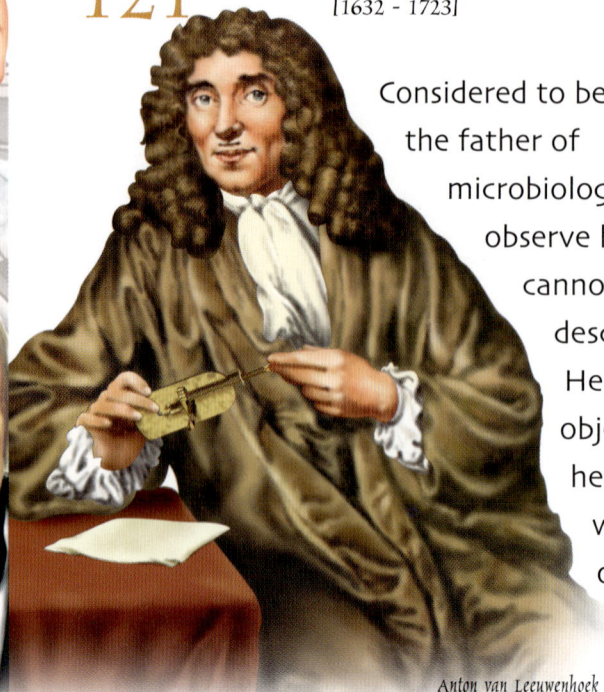

October 24, 1632: *Born in Delft, The Netherlands*

1677: *Describes the sperms of insects, dogs and humans*

August 26, 1723: *Dies in Delft*

Considered to be the father of microbiology, Leeuwenhoek was the first to observe bacteria, protozoa and sperm, which cannot be seen with the naked eye. The first correct description of red blood cells also came from him. He also developed a simple microscope that magnified objects 270 times their size! Using this microscope, he observed protozoa in ponds, rainwater and well water. It is said that Leeuwenhoek made over 400 lenses for the microscope.

Anton van Leeuwenhoek

122 Isaac Newton
[1642 - 1727]

December 25, 1642: *Born in Woolsthorpe, Lincolnshire, England*

1687: *Publishes the Principia, containing his laws of motion and universal gravitation*

1704: *Publishes his theory on light and colour in the book Opticks*

1705: *Becomes the first scientist to be knighted by the Queen*

March 20, 1727: *Dies in London*

Sir Isaac Newton was a British physicist, celebrated for his law of universal gravitation. Legend has it that the idea struck Newton when he saw an apple fall from a tree. He concluded that a force (gravity) on Earth attracted the apple towards the ground. He went on to prove that the same gravitational force holds the Moon in its orbit around the Earth. He also demonstrated that white light is made up of all the colours visible to the human eye and that these colours are the primary constituents of white light.

123 Edmond Halley
[1656-1742]

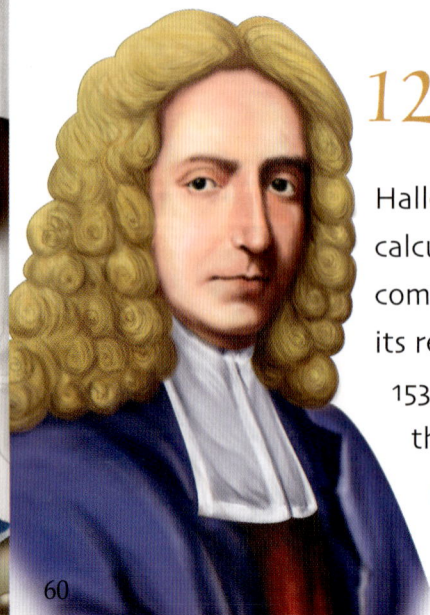

November 8, 1656: *Born near London*

1705: *Predicts the return of his comet*

1720: *Becomes astronomer royal at Greenwich Observatory*

January 14, 1742: *Dies in Greenwich, near London*

Halley was the first to calculate the orbit of a comet and also predict its return. From his observations, he deduced that the comets of 1531, 1607 and 1682 were one and the same. He also claimed that the comet had appeared earlier in 1305, 1380 and 1456, further predicting that it would return after 76 years, in December 1758. Indeed, Halley's Comet was seen on December 25, 1758!

Edmond Halley

124 Carolus Linnaeus
[1707 - 1778]

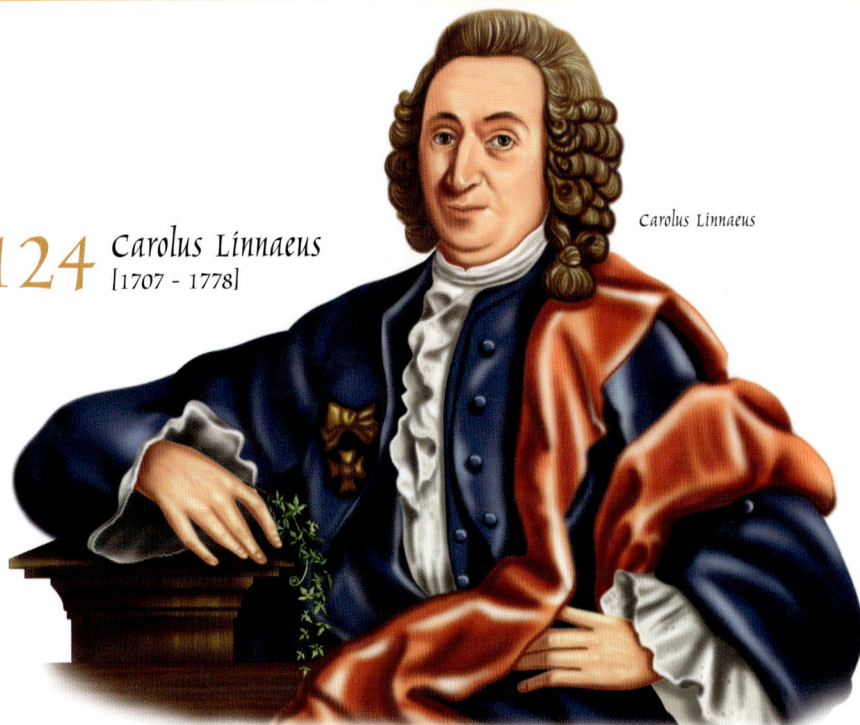

Carolus Linnaeus

Isaac Newton

Linnaeus was responsible for the modern scientific classification of plants and animals. He classified the plant kingdom mainly on the basis of flower parts (stamens and pistils).

May 23, 1707: Born in Rashult, Smaland, Sweden
1737: Publishes the Genera Plantarum, classifying plants based on the number of stamens and pistils
1753: Writes the Species Plantarum, describing plants in terms of genus and species
1758: Publishes the 10th edition of Systema Naturae, applying the binomial system of naming animals
January 10, 1778: Dies in Uppsala, Sweden

The Linnaeus system divides the two main groups – plant and animal kingdoms – into phylum, class, order, family, genus and species. He also promoted the binomial system of naming organisms, in which the genus and species names are combined. For instance, in Homo sapiens, the name given to man, Homo is the genus and sapiens is the species.

125 Comte de Buffon
[1707 - 1788]

September 7, 1707: Born in Montbard, France
1739: Appointed keeper of the royal botanical garden (Jardin du Roi, now Jardin des Plantes)
1773: Created a count (comte)
April 16, 1788: Dies in Paris

Georges-Louis Leclerc, Comte (Count) de Buffon, was a French naturalist, best remembered for his work on natural history. As keeper of the royal botanical garden in Paris, Buffon made an account of all the known plants and animals in the region. This was to become the 44 volumes of his great book called *Histoire naturelle, generale et particulière*. However, only 36 of these were published during his lifetime.

100 GREAT
scientists

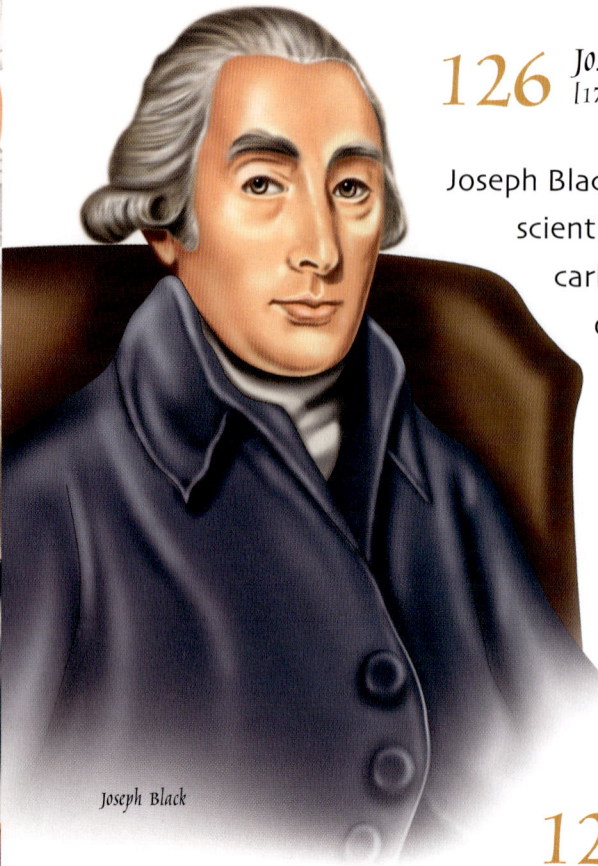

126 Joseph Black
[1728 - 1799]

Joseph Black was a Scottish scientist who discovered carbon dioxide. He observed in his experiments that when subjected to strong heat, calcium carbonate was converted into calcium oxide, giving off a gas. He termed this unknown gas "fixed air". Further experiments showed that candles did not burn in it, nor did it support animal life. Black thus concluded that this "fixed air" is a product of respiration.

April 16, 1728: Born in Bordeaux, France

1756: Becomes professor of chemistry at Glasgow University, Scotland

1766: Becomes professor of chemistry at University of Edinburgh, Scotland

November 10, 1799: Dies in Edinburgh

Joseph Black

127 Henry Cavendish
[1731 - 1810]

October 10, 1731: Born in Nice, France

1766: Isolates hydrogen and observes its properties

February 24, 1810: Dies in London

An English physicist and chemist, Cavendish is famous for his discovery of the nature and properties of hydrogen, which he named "inflammable gas". He also discovered that burning this "inflammable gas" produced water. He measured the density and the mass of the Earth by a method now popularly called the Cavendish experiment.

Joseph Priestley

128 Joseph Priestley
[1733 - 1804]

March 13, 1733: Born in Birstall Fieldhead, Yorkshire (now West Yorkshire), England

June 23, 1762: Marries Mary Wilkinson

1774: Discovers oxygen

1794: Moves to Pennsylvania, U.S.

February 6, 1804: Dies in Northumberland, Pennsylvania

Priestley discovered several gases, including oxygen and nitrogen. He generated oxygen by heating red mercuric oxide. By dissolving "fixed air" (carbon dioxide) in water, he also produced carbonated water (soda water). Apart from this, Priestley was deeply involved with the political developments of the time. His support of the French Revolution (began in 1789) led to his house, library and laboratory being destroyed in the Priestley Riots of 1791. Later, he moved to the United States and spent the rest of his life there.

129 William Herschel
[1738 - 1822]

English astronomer Sir William (Frederick) Herschel, originally Friedrich Wilhelm Herschel, discovered Uranus (the first planet to be discovered since prehistoric times) and infrared radiation. He also discovered Oberon and Titania, the satellites of Saturn and constructed a map of the galaxy based on the known stars. Knighted in 1816, Herschel was a skilled musician too.

William Herschel

November 15, 1738: Born in Hanover, Germany

1757: Moves to England

1781: Discovers Uranus

1782: Appointed private astronomer to King George III

August 25, 1822: Dies in Slough, Buckinghamshire, England

130 Antone-Laurent Lavoisier
[1743 - 1794]

Regarded as the father of modern chemistry, Lavoisier gave oxygen its name and was responsible for the system of naming chemical substances. Many of the names that are still used – like sulphuric acid, sulphates and sulphites – were created by him. He demonstrated the role of oxygen in animal and plant respiration, as well as in metal rusting. He also named the "inflammable gas" discovered by Henry Cavendish as hydrogen. Lavoisier reproduced Cavendish's experiment by combining hydrogen with oxygen to produce water.

Antone-Laurent Lavoisier

August 26, 1743: Born in Paris, France

1779: Gives oxygen its name

1787: Describes a method for naming chemicals in his Methode de nomenclature chimique

May 8, 1794: Beheaded in Paris during the French Revolution

100 GREAT
scientists

131 Jean-Baptiste Lamarck
[1744 - 1829]

August 1, 1744: Born in Picardy, France

1802: Coins the term "biology"

1809: Records his theory of evolution, Lamarckism, in Zoological Philosophy

December 18, 1829: Dies in Paris

He coined the terms "biology" and "invertebrate" (animals without a backbone). He also suggested that man belongs to the animal kingdom. According to one of Lamarck's theories, animals acquire characteristics during their lifetime and pass these on to their offspring. He also stated that repeated use of an organ improves it, while disuse weakens it. Thus, he proposed that the giraffe developed a long neck by stretching up to reach tall trees and passing on the trait to its young. This theory, called Lamarckism, was later proved wrong by Darwin's theory of evolution.

Jean-Baptiste Lamarck

132 Pierre-Simon Laplace, Marquis de
[1749 - 1827]

May 17, 1749: Born in Berkeley, Gloucestershire, England

1796: Discovers smallpox vaccine

January 26, 1823: Dies in Berkeley

He was a French mathematician and astronomer, known for his inquiries into the stability of the solar system. Using Newton's theory of gravitation, Laplace was able to explain why the planets moved away from their orbits at times. He also discovered that the solar system was formed when gaseous nebula (cloud of gas and dust found among the stars) cooled and became compressed. This theory formed the basis of future work on the origin of planets.

March 23, 1749: Born in Normandy, France

1773: Explains the deviations of planets from their orbits

1796: Publishes his theory about the origin of the solar system

March 5, 1827: Dies in Paris

133 Edward Jenner
[1749 - 1823]

As a young boy, Jenner noticed that people suffering from cowpox did not catch smallpox. Deciding to test this theory, he infected a young boy named James Phipps with cowpox. After the boy had recovered, Jenner injected him with smallpox. As expected, the boy was unaffected, proving that cowpox made people immune to smallpox. Jenner called his method "vaccination" and the organism causing the disease, "virus". Jenner came to be widely regarded as the father of vaccination. Smallpox was wiped out from the world in the late 1970s.

134 John Dalton
[1766 - 1844]

Dalton was a pioneer in the development of the atomic theory. According to this theory, all matter is composed of small particles that cannot be divided. He called these particles atoms. He also explained that the atom of a certain element will have its own unique qualities and weight. Dalton, who suffered from colour blindness, also investigated and published the first scientific paper on this condition, to be called Daltonism after him.

September 5/6, 1766: Born in Cumberland, England

1794: Records his findings on colour blindness in the book, *Extraordinary facts relating to the visions of colours*

1803: Introduces his atomic theory

July 27, 1844: Dies after a stroke, in Manchester, England

John Dalton

January 22, 1775: Born in Lyon, France

1820: Explains electromagnetism

June 10, 1836: Dies in Marseille, France

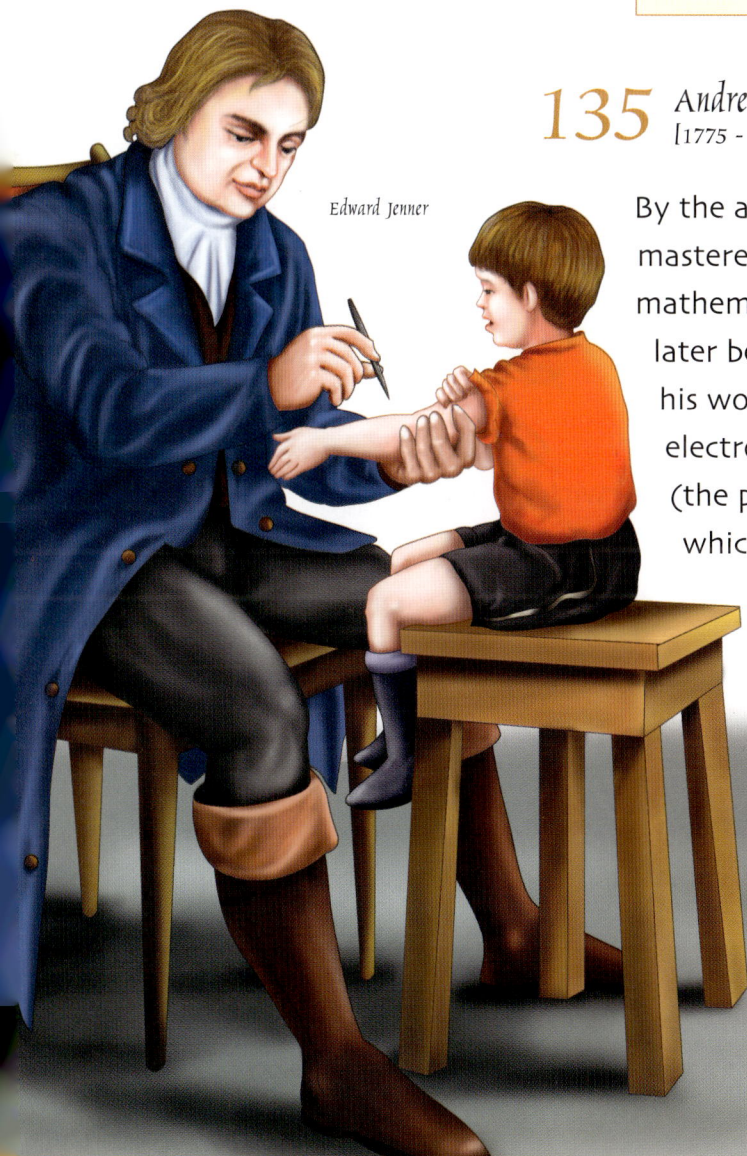

Edward Jenner

135 Andre-Marie Ampere
[1775 - 1836]

By the age of 12, Ampere had mastered the field of mathematics. However, he later became famous for his work in electromagnetism (the property by which a magnetic needle moves when electricity is passed through a nearby wire). Ampere formulated a law that described the magnetic force between electric currents. He also invented an instrument to measure the flow of electricity. It was later improved upon and came to be called the galvanometer. The unit of electricity called ampere was named after the great scientist.

Andre-Marie Ampere

100 GREAT
scientists

136 Friedrich Wohler
[1800 - 1882]

July 31, 1800:	Born in Eschersheim, Germany
1827:	Develops a method of isolating aluminium
1828:	Produces urea
September 23, 1882:	Dies in Gottingen, Germany

German chemist Wohler was the first to produce urea in a laboratory. While trying to make ammonium cyanate from silver cyanide and ammonium chloride, he made urea, an organic compound used as a fertilizer. The discovery proved that a substance like urea – normally produced by living organisms during metabolism – could also be produced from non-living matter. Wohler also developed a method to prepare metallic aluminium.

Justus Liebig, Freiherr von

137 Justus Liebig, Freiherr von
[1803 - 1873]

May 12, 1803:	Born in Darmstadt, Germany
1852:	Becomes professor at the University of Munich
April 18, 1873:	Dies in Munich, Bavaria

Liebig is known for his contributions to the development of biochemistry and agricultural chemistry. He discovered that plants feed on nitrogen and carbon dioxide, as well as on minerals in the soil. Thereupon, he developed nitrogen-based fertilisers. Liebig also formulated the Law of the Minimum, according to which increasing a nutrient that is already easily available to the plant does not increase its growth. Growth can be improved only by increasing the nutrient that is insufficient.

138 Charles Robert Darwin
[1809 - 1882]

February 12, 1809:	Born in Shrewsbury, Shropshire, England
1831-36:	Undertakes the scientific trip aboard HMS Beagle
1859:	Publishes On the Origin of Species by Means of Natural Selection
1871:	Explains the evolution of man in The Descent of Man
April 19, 1882:	Dies in Downe, Kent

Famous for his theory of evolution, Charles Darwin collected his data while on a scientific trip aboard HMS *Beagle*. According to the theory, organisms with an advantage over others will compete better in the struggle for existence ("survival of the fittest") and produce more young ones. Moreover, the trait that helps them survive will be passed on to the next generation. He explained that this system of "natural selection" causes the gradual disappearance of the weaker organism and lies at the root of evolution of species.

Charles Robert Darwin

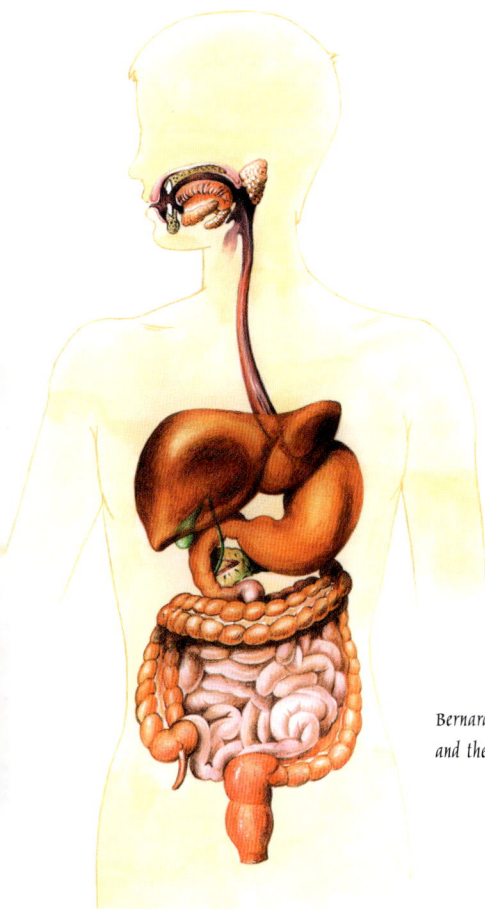

139 Claude Bernard
[1813 - 1878]

He was a French physiologist who gave up literature to study medicine. He discovered the mechanisms involved in digestion, including the role of the pancreas. He also described the function of the liver in breaking down carbohydrates and explained that some of the digestion takes place inside the intestines. He was thrice awarded by the Academie Des Sciences.

July 12, 1813: *Born in Saint- Julien, France*

1865: *Publishes An Introduction to the Study of Experimental Medicine*

February 10, 1878: *Dies in Paris*

Bernard explained the functions of the pancreas and the liver in the human digestive system

140 Hermann von Helmholtz
[1821 - 1894]

Considered one of the greatest scientists of the 19th century, Helmholtz made valuable contributions to various scientific fields. However, he is most famous for his law of conservation of energy, which states that energy is not lost but only changed from one form to another. He also invented the ophthalmoscope and used it to explain the structure of the eye.

August 31, 1821: *Born in Potsdam, Prussia (now Germany)*

1847: *Formulates the law of conservation of energy*

1851: *Invents the ophthalmoscope*

September 8, 1894: *Dies in Charlottenburg, Berlin, Germany*

Hermann von Helmholtz

100 GREAT
scientists

141 Rudolf (Carl) Virchow
[1821 - 1902]

October 13, 1821: Born in Pomerania, Prussia

1849: Becomes professor at the University of Wurzberg

1856: Becomes director of the Pathological Institute, Berlin

1858: Publishes Die Cellularpathologie

September 5, 1902: Dies in Berlin

Rudolf Virchow was a German pathologist and the founder of cellular pathology. According to him, only a cell or a group of cells fall sick and not the whole organism. He further established that a cell divides itself to form a new cell. Virchow also founded the fields of comparative pathology (comparison of diseases common to human beings and animals) and a branch of anthropology called ethnology (study and comparison of the characteristics of various human societies).

Rudolf (Carl) Virchow

142 Francis Galton
[1822 - 1911]

February 16, 1822: Born in Birmingham, Warwickshire, England

1883: Coins the term "eugenics"

1909: Attains knighthood

1869: Publishes Hereditary Genius, in which he proposes that talent is inherited

January 17, 1911: Dies in Haslemere, Surrey, England

Sir Francis Galton was a British scientist and a cousin of Charles Darwin. He is well-known for his theory of eugenics, which deals with selective mating to produce superior beings. Thus, when two intelligent and healthy people are mated, their child would be a gifted one in every manner. Galton also established the modern system of classifying fingerprints, which is still used to trace criminals.

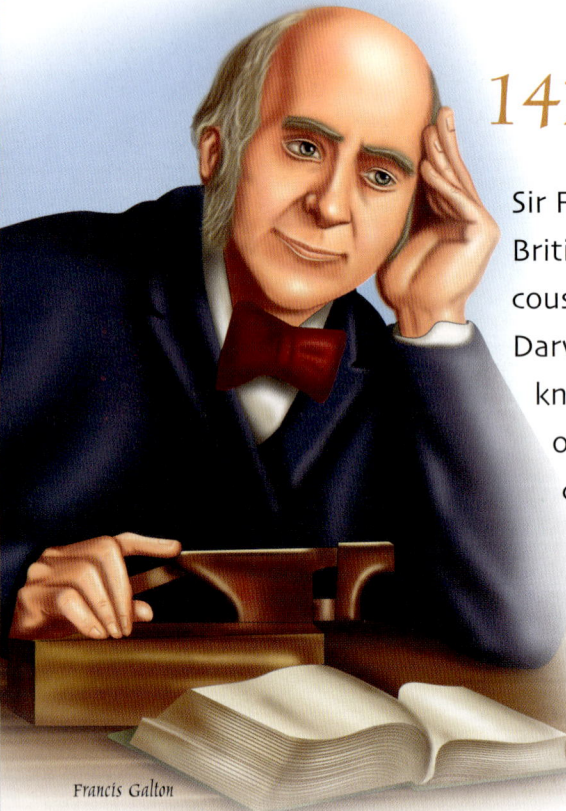

Francis Galton

143 Gregor (Johann) Mendel
[1822 - 1884]

July 22, 1822: Born in Heinzendorf, Austria

1843: Becomes a monk

1856: Begins experiments with the garden pea

January 6, 1884: Dies in Brunn, Austria-Hungary (now Brno, Czech Republic)

Widely regarded as the father of genetics, Mendel was an Austrian monk and botanist. His experiments on heredity using the garden pea are legendary. For over seven years, he cultivated and tested around 28,000 pea plants. He established that character, or traits, are inherited. He established the theory that parents pass on their characteristics to their offspring through a carrier called genes.

144 Louis Pasteur
[1822 - 1895]

One of the greatest microbiologists, Pasteur made ground-breaking discoveries in medical science. He described the role of micro-organisms (like bacteria) in causing diseases and in souring of food. This led to the discovery of pasteurisation, a method which uses heat to kill micro-organisms. Pasteur later developed vaccines for chicken cholera and anthrax (the word "vaccine" was coined by him). He also produced the first rabies vaccine, used to treat a boy bitten by a rabid dog.

Gregor (Johann) Mendel

Louis Pasteur

December 27, 1822: *Born in Dole, France*

1885: *Administers the first rabies vaccine*

1888: *The Pasteur Institute is founded*

September 28, 1895: *Dies in Saint-Cloud, near Paris*

145 Gustav Robert Kirchhoff
[1824 - 1887]

German physicist Kirchhoff was the first to show that current flows through a conductor (substance that carries electric current – copper and water, for instance) at the speed of light. He joined with Robert Bunsen to prove that every element produces a certain light when heated by a current passing through it. Together they used this theory to find out the composition of the Sun. In the process, they also discovered the new elements, caesium and rubidium.

March 12, 1824: *Born in Konigsberg, Prussia (now Kaliningrad, Russia)*

1860: *Discovers caesium*

1861: *Discovers rubidium*

October 17, 1887: *Dies in Berlin*

100 GREAT
scientists

146 Joseph Lister
[1827 - 1912]

Joseph Lister

Joseph Lister is regarded as the father of antiseptic medicine. While working at the Glasgow Royal Infirmary, Lister noticed that almost 50 percent of the patients operated upon died from infection (sepsis). At first he thought these infections were caused by dust, until he learnt about Pasteur's theory that micro-organisms cause infections. Using phenol (carbolic acid) as an antiseptic, he controlled these infections and reduced the number of deaths. Lister's principle that bacteria must be kept away from surgical wounds remains at the heart of modern-day surgery.

April 5, 1827: Born in Upton, Essex, England

1861: Becomes surgeon at the Glasgow Royal Infirmary

1867: Publishes a series of articles on antisepsis

1893: Retires from practice

February 10, 1912: Dies in Walmer, Kent, England

James Clerk Maxwell

147 James Clerk Maxwell
[1831 - 1879]

Scottish physicist Maxwell's ideas formed the basis for quantum physics and the theory of the structure of atoms. His most important achievement was his demonstration that light is an electromagnetic wave. He showed that electric and magnetic energy travel through space as waves, at the speed of light.

Maxwell's theories also paved the way for Albert Einstein's theory of relativity.

June 13, 1831: Born in Edinburgh, Scotland

1873: Publishes the *Treatise on Electricity and Magnetism*

November 5, 1879: Dies in Cambridge, England

August 16, 1832: Born in Neckarau, near Mannheim, Baden (Germany)
1858: Becomes assistant to Helmholtz
1862: Publishes his biggest work, *Contributions to the Theory of Sense Perception*
1873-74: Writes the path-breaking book, *Principles of Physiological Psychology*
1879: Establishes the first psychological laboratory
1881: Founds the first psychology journal
August 31, 1920: Dies in Grossbothen, Germany

148 Wilhelm Wundt
[1832 - 1920]

A German physiologist and psychologist, Wilhelm Max Wundt is widely regarded as the father of experimental psychology. While working with Hermann von Helmholtz, Wundt wrote his book *Contributions to the Theory of Sense Perception*. During this period Wundt also took up lecturing in psychology. He emphasised the need for using experimental methods, which became the basis of modern psychology.

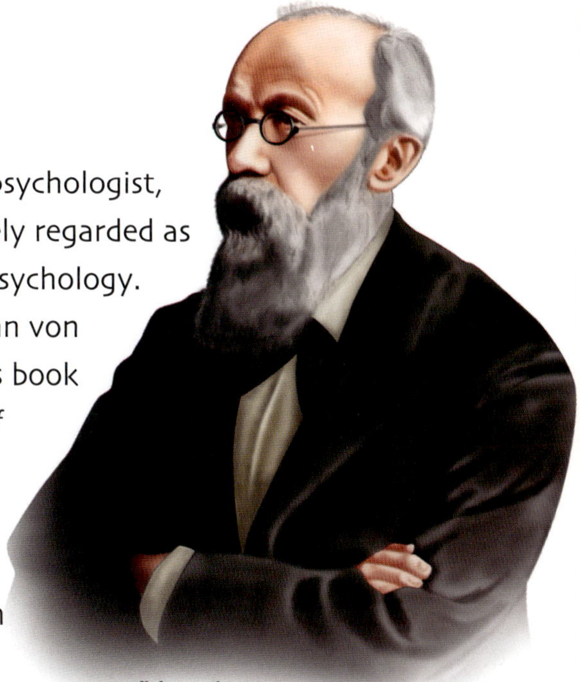

Wilhelm Wundt

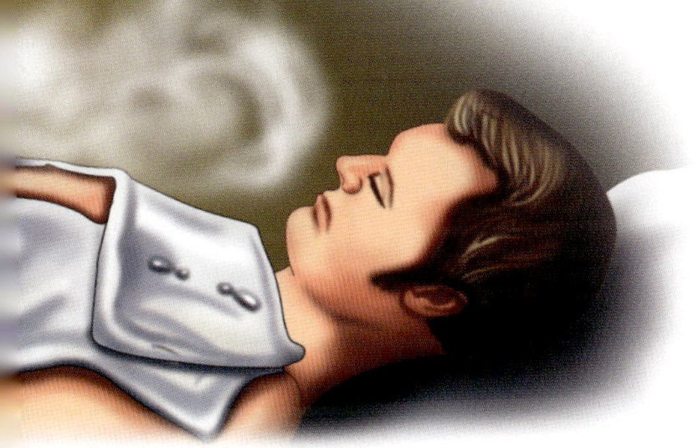

	IA	IIA	IIIB	IVB	VB	VIB	VIIB	— VIIB —			IB	IIB	IIIA	IVA	VA	VIA	VIIA	O
1	1 H																	2 He
2	3 Li	4 Be											5 B	6 C	7 N	8 O	9 F	10 Ne
3	11 Na	12 Mg											13 Al	14 Si	15 P	16 S	17 Cl	18 Ar
4	19 K	20 Ca	21 Sc	22 Ti	23 V	24 Cr	25 Mn	26 Fe	27 Co	28 Ni	29 Cu	30 Zn	31 Ga	32 Ge	33 As	34 Se	35 Br	36 Kr
5	37 Rb	38 Sr	39 Y	40 Zr	41 Nb	42 Mo	43 Tc	44 Ru	45 Rh	46 Pd	47 Ag	48 Cd	49 In	50 Sn	51 Sb	52 Te	53 I	54 Xe
6	55 Cs	56 Ba	57 *La	72 Hf	73 Ta	74 W	75 Re	76 Os	77 Ir	78 Pt	79 Au	80 Hg	81 Tl	82 Pb	83 Bi	84 Po	85 At	86 Rn
7	87 Fr	88 Ra	89 +Ac	104 104	105 105	106 106	107 107	108 108	109 109	110 110	111 111	112 112		114 114		116 116		118 118

*Lanthanide Series	58 Ce	59 Pr	60 Nd	61 Pm	62 Sm	63 Eu	64 Gd	65 Tb	66 Dy	67 Ho	68 Er	69 Tm	70 Yb	71 Lu
+Actinide Series	90 Th	91 Pa	92 U	93 Np	94 Pu	95 Am	96 Cm	97 Bk	98 Cf	99 Es	100 Fm	101 Md	102 No	103 Lr

The modern periodic table containing all the known elements

149 Dmitri Ivanovich Mendeleyev
[1834 - 1907]

Mendeleyev (also spelt Mendeleev) was a Russian chemist who created the periodic table of chemical elements. He arranged the known elements according to their properties and the weight of their atoms. All elements with similar properties were put under one group and then arranged according to the increase in their atomic weights.

February 8, 1834: Born in Tobolsk, Siberia, Russia
1869: Formulates the periodic law
1871: Presents his final form of the periodic table
February 2, 1907: Dies at St. Petersburg, Russia

150 Joseph Norman Lockyer
[1836 - 1920]

May 17, 1836: Born in Rugby, Warwickshire, England
1869: Starts the famous science journal, *Nature*
1897: Attains knighthood
August 16, 1920: Dies in Salcombe Regis, Devon, England

Sir Lockyer was an English astronomer who, in 1868, discovered helium in the Sun's atmosphere. He did so while examining the Sun and the stars through a spectroscope. He named this previously unknown element as "helium" (Greek for "Sun"). Lockyer also named the layer of gas around the Sun as chromosphere.

151 Robert Koch
[1843 - 1910]

One of the founders of bacteriology, Koch won the 1905 Nobel Prize for his findings on tuberculosis. He discovered the micro-organisms that cause tuberculosis, cholera and conjunctivitis and also studied the disease cycle of anthrax. He devised methods, still in use, to grow micro-organisms in laboratories and developed a vaccination for rinderpest.

December 11, 1843: Born in Clausthal, Hanover, Germany

1876: Publishes his work on the anthrax disease and its micro-organism

1878: Publishes his discoveries on diseases caused by infection of wounds

1882: Records his discovery of mycobacterium tuberculosis – the bacterium that causes tuberculosis

1883: Goes to Egypt, where he discovers vibrio cholerae – the bacterium that causes cholera

1896: Develops vaccination for rinderpest in farm animals

1905: Awarded the Nobel Prize in Physiology or Medicine

May 27, 1910: Dies in Baden-Baden, Germany

152 Wilhelm Conrad Roentgen
[1845 - 1923]

A German physicist, Roentgen discovered X-rays. Also called Roentgen rays, he first discovered these short-wave rays in 1895. Thinking that these rays were not related to light, Roentgen named them X-rays. He also produced the first X-ray photographs, showing the bones in his wife's hands.

March 27, 1845: Born in Lenney, Prussia (now Remscheid, Germany)

1901: Becomes the first to receive the Nobel Prize in Physics

February 10, 1923: Dies in Munich, Germany

Robert Koch

153 Hugo de Vries
[1848 - 1935]

Dutch botanist and geneticist de Vries discovered and named the phenomenon of mutation. In his experiments on the evening primrose plant, he rediscovered Mendel's laws of heredity and developed his own theory. He explained mutations as sudden, unpredictable changes in an organism that can be passed on to the offspring. He proposed that this is how new species develop and evolve. His discovery helped in establishing Darwin's theory universally.

February 16, 1848: Born in Haarlem, The Netherlands

1900: Rediscovers Mendel's laws of heredity

1901: Publishes his findings on mutation in the book The Mutation Theory

May 21, 1935: Dies near Amsterdam, The Netherlands

154 Ivan Petrovich Pavlov
[1849 - 1936]

Ivan Petrovich Pavlov

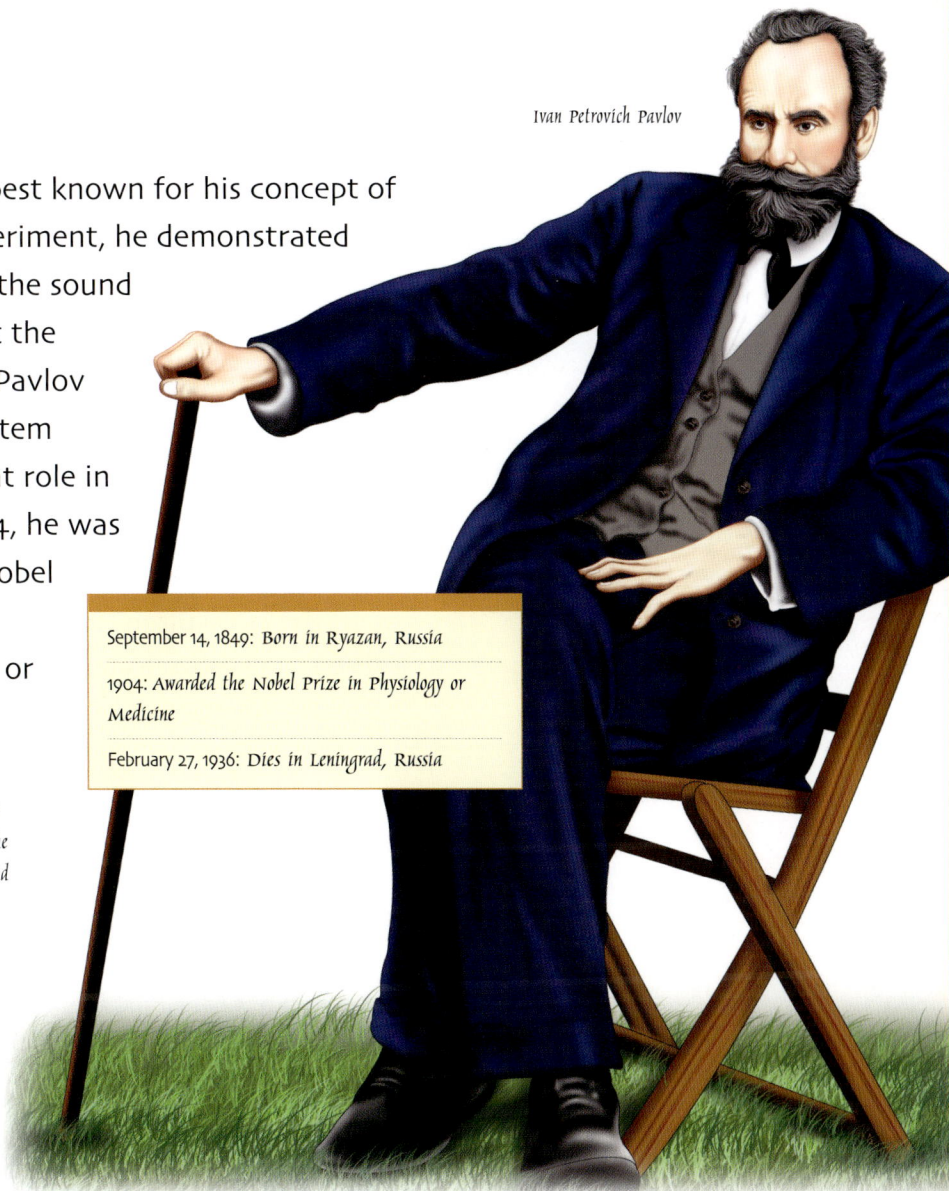

Pavlov was a Russian physiologist, best known for his concept of conditioned reflex. In a famous experiment, he demonstrated that a hungry dog trained to relate the sound of a bell with food would salivate at the sound even in the absence of food. Pavlov also proved that the nervous system played an important role in digestion. In 1904, he was awarded the Nobel Prize in Physiology or Medicine.

Roentgen's first X-ray photograph showing the bones in his wife's hand

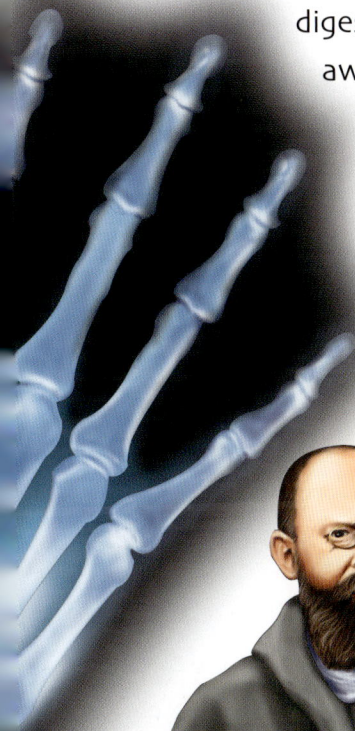

September 14, 1849: Born in Ryazan, Russia

1904: Awarded the Nobel Prize in Physiology or Medicine

February 27, 1936: Dies in Leningrad, Russia

Emil Fischer

155 Emil Fischer
[1852 - 1919]

October 9, 1852: Born in Euskirchen, Prussia (Germany)

1902: Wins the Nobel Prize in Chemistry

July 15, 1919: Dies in Berlin, Germany

Emil Hermann Fischer was a German organic chemist who determined the structures of uric acid, caffeine and other related compounds. He proved that all these can be derived from a single compound, which he called purine. He also determined the structures of various sugars like glucose and fructose. His research has proved to be of utmost importance in the field of organic chemistry.

100 GREAT
scientists

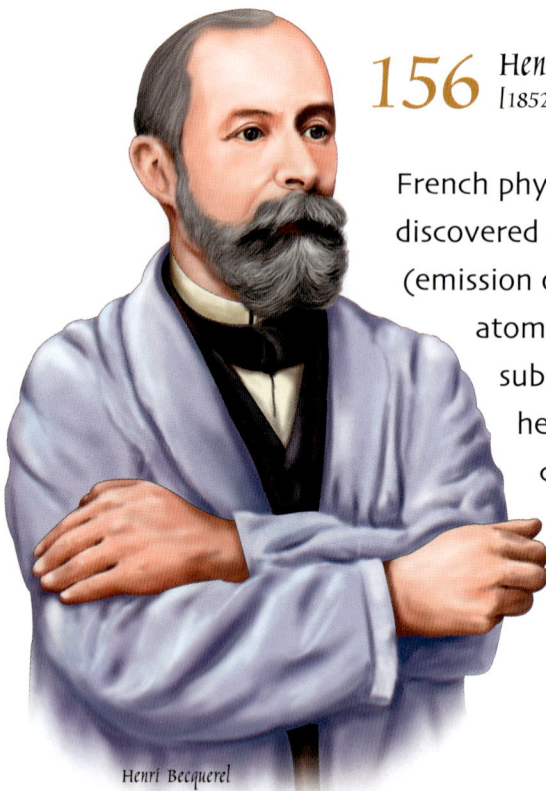

156 Henri Becquerel
[1852 - 1908]

French physicist Henri Becquerel discovered radioactivity (emission of rays or waves by atoms of radioactive substances like uranium). He made this discovery when he noticed that the element uranium gave out rays that could not be seen. He demonstrated these rays by using them to darken a photographic plate. The breakthrough led to similar experiments that resulted in the discovery of radium. The unit of radioactivity is named Becquerel (Bq) in his honour.

December 15, 1852: Born in Paris

1896: Discovers radioactivity in uranium

1903: Receives Nobel Prize in Physics along with the Curies

August 25, 1908: Dies in Le Croisic, Brittany, France

Henri Becquerel

157 Albert Michelson
[1852 - 1931]

December 19, 1852: Born in Strelno, Prussia (now in Poland)

1902: Publishes his book Velocity of Light

1907: Receives the Nobel Prize in Physics

May 9, 1931: Dies in Pasadena, California, U.S.

Albert Abraham Michelson was an American physicist who calculated the speed of light, using instruments (like the interferometer) he invented. In 1887, he joined with Edward W. Morley to conduct the Michelson-Morley experiment. They found that the speed of light was unaffected by the motion of the Earth, thus proving that this speed is constant. Michelson was the first to measure the diameter of a distant star. In 1907, he became the first American scientist to win the Nobel Prize.

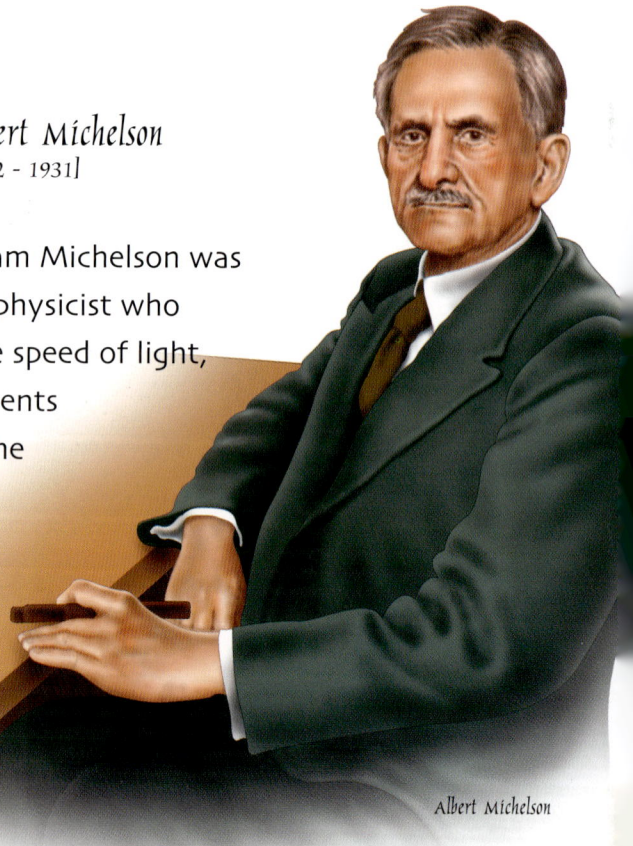

Albert Michelson

158 Heike Kamerlingh Onnes
[1853 - 1926]

Dutch physicist Onnes was the first to produce liquid helium. He also produced a temperature near absolute zero and discovered that metals like lead and mercury lost all electrical resistance when cooled to such temperatures – a phenomenon also known as superconductivity.

September 21, 1853: Born in Groningen, The Netherlands

1884: Establishes the Cryogenic Laboratory at Leiden University

1908: Produces liquid helium

1911: Discovers superconductivity

1913: Awarded the Nobel Prize in Physics

February 21, 1926: Dies in Leiden, The Netherlands

159 Paul Ehrlich
[1854 - 1915]

Ehrlich is famous for his ground-breaking work in the field of immunology (science of the body's immune system that prevents diseases) and chemotherapy (treatment of diseases like cancer using chemical drugs). He discovered the medicine Salvarsan, the first effective cure for syphilis. He also described methods of staining tissue and micro-organisms with dyes, to help diagnose and treat diseases. He won the Nobel Prize in Physiology or Medicine in 1908.

Paul Ehrlich

160 Sigmund Freud
[1856 - 1939]

Sigmund Freud

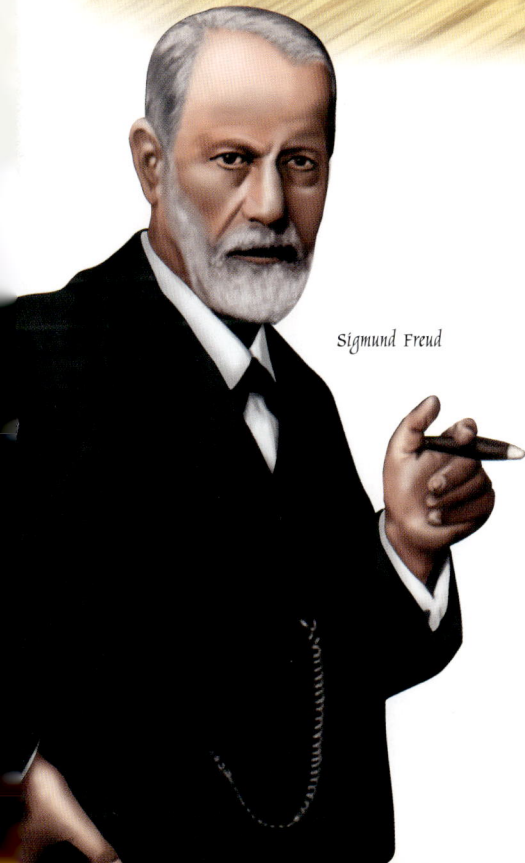

The founder of psychoanalysis, Austrian psychiatrist Freud enquired into unconscious mental processes to help the mentally ill. He believed that most people suppressed unpleasant memories, which in turn caused mental disturbances. According to Freud, such mental illness was caused by unexpressed emotions (anger, fear). He hypnotised (put into semi-conscious state) his patients to find out the cause for their pain. Apart from hypnosis, Freud also studied dreams to help his patients.

100 GREAT
scientists

161 Joseph John Thomson
[1856 - 1940]

Sir Joseph John Thomson revolutionised the study of atomic structure by discovering the electron, a sub-atomic particle (found inside the atom) with negative charge. He also discovered the isotopes of various chemical elements. In 1906, he was awarded the Nobel Prize for Physics for his work on discharge (conduction) of electricity through gases.

December 18, 1856: Born in Cheetham Hill, near Manchester, England

1897: Discovers electron

1908: Attains knighthood

August 30, 1940: Dies in Cambridge, England

Joseph John Thomson

162 Heinrich Rudolf Hertz
[1857 - 1894]

Heinrich Rudolf Hertz

A student of Hermann von Helmholtz, Heinrich Hertz was the first to send out and receive radio waves. His breakthrough led to the invention of the radio. The frequency of radio waves was named Hertz in his honour. He also proved that, like light, radio waves are electromagnetic in nature. Later, he explained that even heat is an electromagnetic radiation.

February 22, 1857: Born in Hamburg, Germany

1888: Demonstrates electromagnetic radiation by producing radio waves

January 1, 1894: Dies in Bonn, Germany

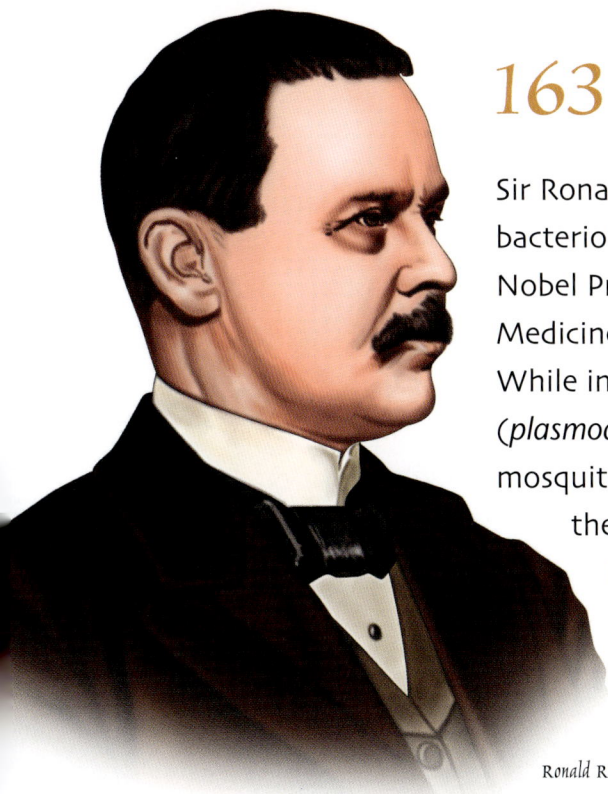

163 Ronald Ross
[1857 - 1932]

Sir Ronald Ross was a bacteriologist who won the 1902 Nobel Prize in Physiology or Medicine for his work on malaria. While in India, he observed the disease-causing organism (*plasmodium vivax*) in the stomach of a particular type of mosquito (called *Anopheles*). On studying the life cycle of the organism, he realised that it can also be found in the mosquito's saliva. He thus proved that malaria is spread by a mosquito bite.

May 13, 1857: *Born in Almora, India*
1897: *Discovers the organism that causes malaria in mosquitoes*
1902: *Receives the Nobel Prize*
1911: *Attains knighthood*
September 16, 1932: *Dies in London*

Ronald Ross

164 Alfred Binet
[1857 - 1911]

Alfred Binet was a French psychologist who devised the popular intelligence test. It is said that he created the test to identify students who needed extra help with their studies. At the time, Binet thought that lower IQ (intelligence quotient) pointed to a need for more teaching, instead of showing an inability to learn. The system that he devised is widely used in schools, industries and even in the army.

July 8, 1857: *Born in Nice, France*
1905-11: *Works on developing the intelligence test*
1915: *Publishes A Method of Measuring the Development of the Intelligence of Young Children*
October 18, 1911: *Dies in Paris*

165 Charles Sherrington
[1857 - 1952]

November 27, 1857: *Born in London*
1906: *Publishes his famous book, The Integrative Action of the Nervous System*
1922: *Knighted*
March 4, 1952: *Dies in Eastbourne, Sussex, England*

Charles Sherrington

Sir Sherrington is famous for his contributions to the development of brain surgery and the treatment of nervous disorders. According to Sherrington's law, when one muscle is stimulated, the opposing muscles are repressed. He also coined the terms "neuron" and "synapse" and explained their functions. In 1932, he shared the Nobel Prize in Physiology or Medicine with Edgar Douglas Adrian, for their discoveries regarding the functions of neurons.

166 Max Planck
[1858 - 1947]

Max Karl Ernst Ludwig Planck was a German physicist and widely recognised as the father of modern physics. He developed the quantum theory (dealing with the behaviour of material particles as well as with the property by which matter gives out and takes in energy). This theory is based on the principle that matter and energy can both behave like either particles or waves. Planck was awarded the Nobel Prize in Physics in 1918.

April 23, 1858: *Born in Kiel, Germany*

1900: *Introduces the quantum theory*

October 4, 1947: *Dies in Gottingen, West Germany*

Max Planck

167 Franz Boas
[1858 - 1942]

Franz Boas

Franz Boas was mainly responsible for establishing modern cultural anthropology. He was part of an expedition to Baffin Island, where he conducted detailed studies on Eskimo culture. He also directed the Jesup North Pacific Expedition, which investigated the relationship between the aborigines of Siberia and North America. Boas rejected the theory that some communities are naturally more civilised or developed than others. Instead, he proposed that all human groups developed equally but in different ways, depending on historic and cultural factors.

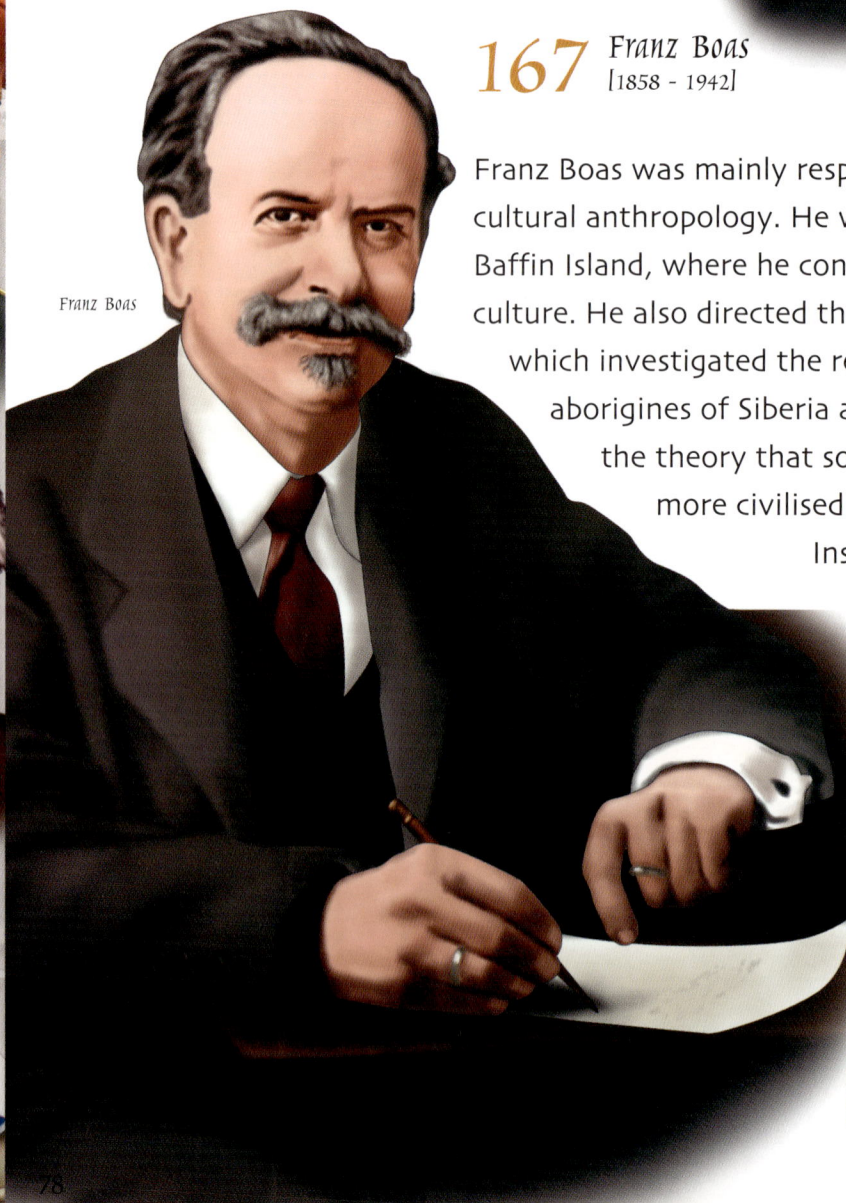

July 9, 1858: *Born in Minden, Westphalia, Prussia (Germany)*

1896-1905: *Directs the Jesup North Pacific Expedition*

1911: *Publishes The Mind of Primitive Man*

1940: *His revolutionary book, Race, Language and Culture is published*

December 22, 1942: *Dies in New York, U.S.*

168 Jagdish Chandra Bose
[1858 - 1937]

November 30, 1858: Born in Mymensingh (now in Bangladesh), Bengal, India

1920: Becomes Fellow of the Royal Society, London

November 23, 1937: Dies in Giridih, Bihar

He was an Indian physicist and plant physiologist who proved that plants have life. Dipping a plant up to its stem in poison, he observed the spot on a screen that indicated the pulse of the plant. Gradually, the to-and-fro movement of the spot became shaky and came to a sudden stop. This indicated that the plant had died. Bose further explained that plants, like animals, responded to stimuli, but took a longer time to do so. He also invented an instrument called crescograph to measure plant growth.

169 Frederick Gowland Hopkins
[1861 - 1947]

June 20, 1861: Born in Eastbourne, England

1901: Discovers tryptophan

1925: Knighted

1929: Wins the Nobel Prize in Physiology or Medicine with Christiaan Eijkman

May 16, 1947: Dies in Cambridge

Sir Hopkins was a biochemist, famous for his discovery of vitamins. During his feeding experiments with laboratory animals, Hopkins realised that the nutrient factors were vital to the animals' health. He named these "accessory food factors" (later renamed "vitamins"). Hopkins also isolated tryptophan, an important amino acid, from protein and demonstrated that working muscles produce lactic acid.

Frederick Gowland Hopkins

170 Thomas Hunt Morgan
[1866 - 1945]

Chromosome

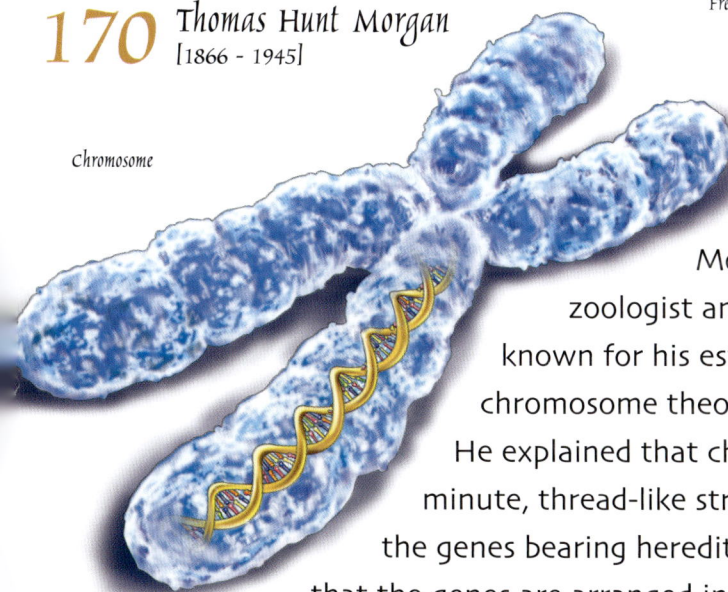

Thomas Hunt Morgan was a zoologist and geneticist, best known for his establishment of the chromosome theory of heredity. He explained that chromosomes are minute, thread-like structures that carry the genes bearing hereditary traits (characters). Further, he also found that the genes are arranged in a straight line on the chromosome. Although Morgan did not initially believe in the Mendelian theory of heredity, he changed his mind after his experiments with the fruit fly (Drosophila). Morgan was awarded the Nobel Prize for Physiology or Medicine in 1933.

September 25, 1866: Born in Lexington, Kentucky, U.S.

1909: Begins experimenting with the fruit fly

1915: Publishes his findings in his book Mechanism of Mendelian Heredity

December 4, 1945: Dies in Pasadena, California, U.S.

100 GREAT
scientists

171 Marie Curie
[1867 - 1934]

Marie Curie was the first scientist to win two Nobel Prizes. With her husband, Pierre Curie, she discovered the elements polonium and radium. The Curies received the 1903 Nobel Prize in Physics for their work on radiation (which was first discovered by Henri Becquerel). Madame Curie won the Nobel Prize again in 1911, this time in Chemistry, in recognition of her work in radioactivity (a word coined by her).

Marie Curie

November 7, 1867: *Born as Maria Sklodowska in Warsaw, Poland*

1895: *Marries Pierre Curie*

1903: *Shares the Nobel Prize in Physics with Pierre and Henri Becquerel*

1911: *Awarded the Nobel Prize in Chemistry*

July 4, 1934: *Dies due to blood cancer caused by exposure to radioactivity*

172 Karl Landsteiner
[1868 - 1943]

He was an Austrian-American pathologist, best remembered for his discovery of major blood groups (A, B and O). Later, along with A.S. Weiner, he also identified the Rhesus, or Rh, factor. This factor determines whether the blood group is positive or negative, as in whether it is A+ or A-. In 1930, Landsteiner received the Nobel Prize in Physiology or Medicine.

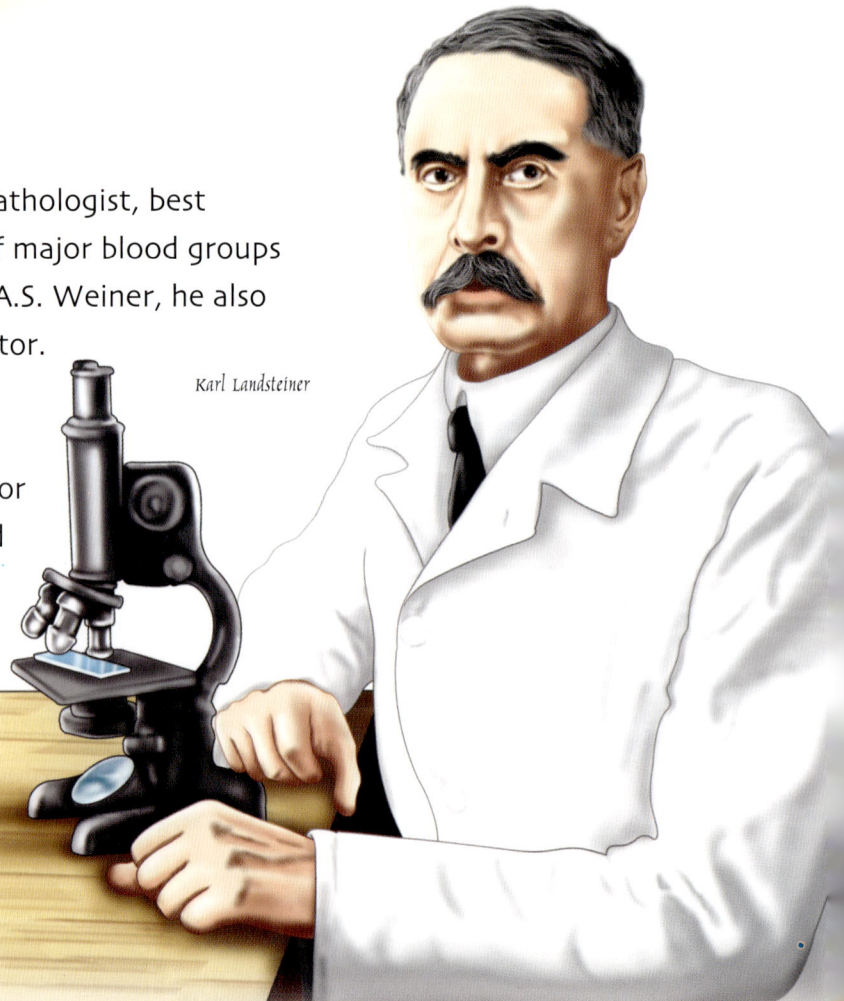

Karl Landsteiner

June 14, 1868: *Born in Vienna, Austria*

1909: *Discovers the major blood groups and develops a system to classify them*

1940: *Identifies the Rh factor*

June 26, 1943: *Dies in New York, U.S.*

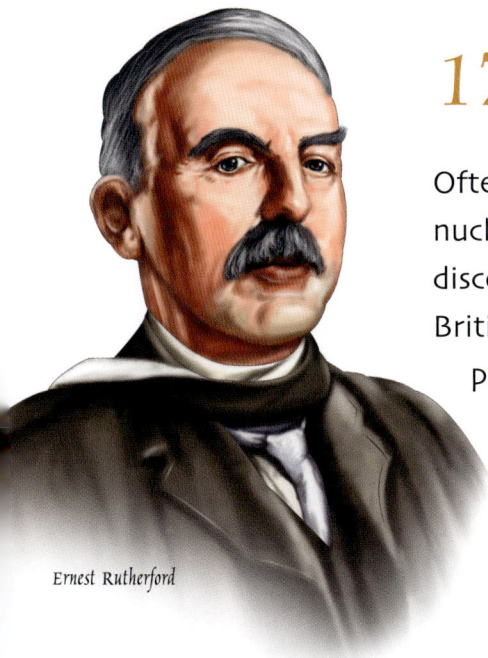

173 Ernest Rutherford
[1871 - 1937]

Often referred to as the father of nuclear physics, Sir Rutherford discovered the atomic nucleus. The British physicist proposed that the positive charge and the mass of the atom are concentrated at its centre (nucleus), surrounded by negative orbiting electrons. He was awarded the Nobel Prize in Chemistry in 1908 for his work on radioactive substances, specifically on the breaking down of the radioactive elements.

August 30, 1871: Born in Spring Grove, New Zealand

1910: Discovers the atomic nucleus

1914: Attains knighthood

October 19, 1937: Dies in Cambridge, England

Ernest Rutherford

174 Oswald Theodore Avery
[1877 - 1955]

October 21, 1877: Born in Halifax, Canada

1944: Discovers that gene is made up of DNA

February 20, 1955: Dies in Nashville, Tennessee, U.S.

He proved that genes are made up of DNA (deoxyribonucleic acid). He did so by following up on an experiment conducted by the English bacteriologist, Frederick Griffith, on the pneumonia-causing bacteria. It was noticed that when two different strains of bacteria (the dangerous and the harmless) were mixed, the harmless one gained the ability to infect. Obviously, some substance in one bacterium made the harmless one deadly. Avery realised that a pure sample of this substance (later identified as gene) was destroyed by a substance that digested DNA, thus proving that DNA is a unit of genes.

175 Albert Einstein
[1879 - 1955]

March 14, 1879: Born in Wurttemberg, Germany

1905: Publishes papers on photoelectric effect and special theory of relativity

1915: Publishes general theory of relativity

1921: Awarded the Nobel Prize in Physics

1939: Persuades President Franklin D. Roosevelt to start the Manhattan Project

April 18, 1955: Dies in Princeton, New Jersey, U.S.

Albert Einstein

Einstein's special and general theories of relativity are the cornerstones of modern science. In his special theory of relativity, Einstein established that $E=mc^2$ (where E is the energy, m is the mass of a body and c the speed of light). This formula proposes that mass can be converted into energy, a theory that was mostly rejected at that time. This was why he was awarded the Nobel Prize for his work on photoelectric effect, instead of the relativity theory! Einstein also turned down an offer to become the first prime minister of Israel.

176 Alfred Lothar Wegener
[1880 - 1930]

German meteorologist and geophysicist Wegener put forth the famous continental drift theory. According to him, the present continents existed as a large mass of land (he called it Pangaea) over 200 million years ago. This mass gradually separated into various land masses which drifted to their present positions. To prove his theory, Wegener showed that South America and Africa could be fitted together as in a jigsaw puzzle. The theory was, however, not accepted until the 1960s.

November 1, 1880: *Born in Berlin, Germany*

1915: *Publishes his book,* The Origin of Continents and Oceans

November 1930: *Dies during his fourth expedition to Greenland*

Alfred Lothar Wegener

177 Alexander Fleming
[1881-1955]

He was a Scottish bacteriologist who discovered the antibiotic called penicillin. Fleming was conducting research on antibacterial substances, when he noticed that a fungus (called *penicillium notatum*) had accidentally developed in a dish containing staphylococcus bacteria.
He was surprised to see that this fungus had prevented the growth of bacteria around it.
He named it "penicillin". Fleming also discovered lysozyme, a substance found in body secretions like saliva and tears, which kill bacteria.

Alexander Fleming

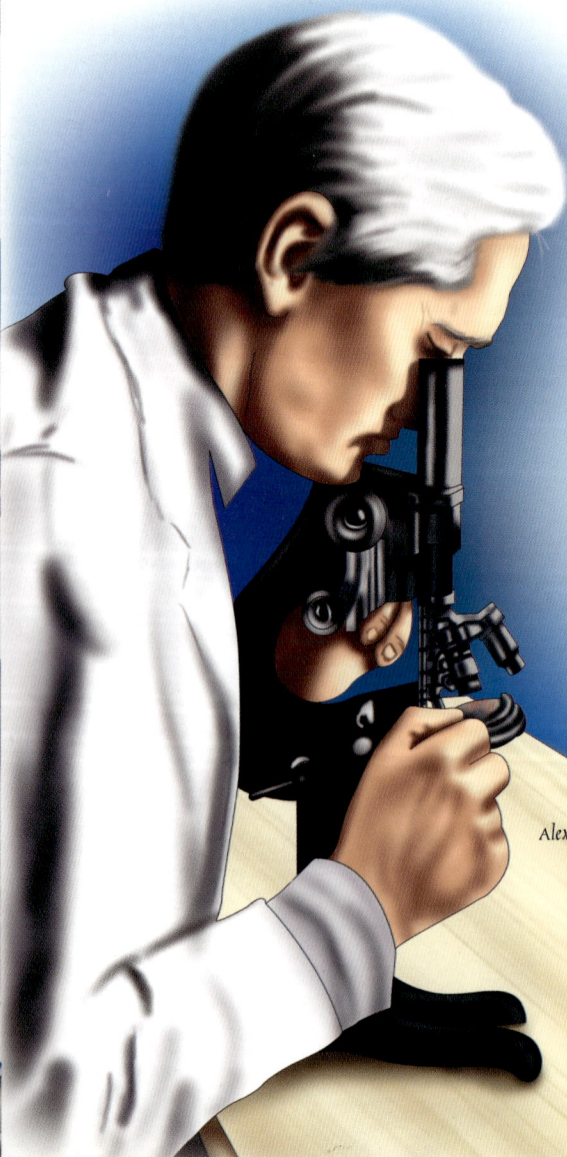

August 6, 1881: *Born in Lochfield, Scotland*

1921: *Discovers lysozyme*

1928: *Discovers penicillin*

1945: *Receives the Nobel Prize in Physiology or Medicine for discovering penicillin*

March 11, 1955: *Dies in London*

178 Arthur Stanley Eddington
[1882 - 1944]

Renowned for his work in the field of astrophysics, Eddington investigated the interior structure of stars and formulated theories of their evolution. He was the first to suggest that stars derive their energy from the nuclear fusion of hydrogen to helium. Eddington also popularised Einstein's general theory of relativity by being the first to explain it in the English language.

December 28, 1882: Born in Westmorland, England
1926: Publishes his most famous work, The Internal Constitution of the Stars
1930: Attains knighthood
November 22, 1944: Dies in Cambridge

179 Neils Bohr
[1885 - 1962]

October 7, 1885: Born in Copenhagen, Denmark
1913: Puts forth his model of atomic structure
1922: Awarded the Nobel Prize in Physics
1957: Receives the first U.S. Atoms for Peace Award
November 18, 1962: Dies in Copenhagen

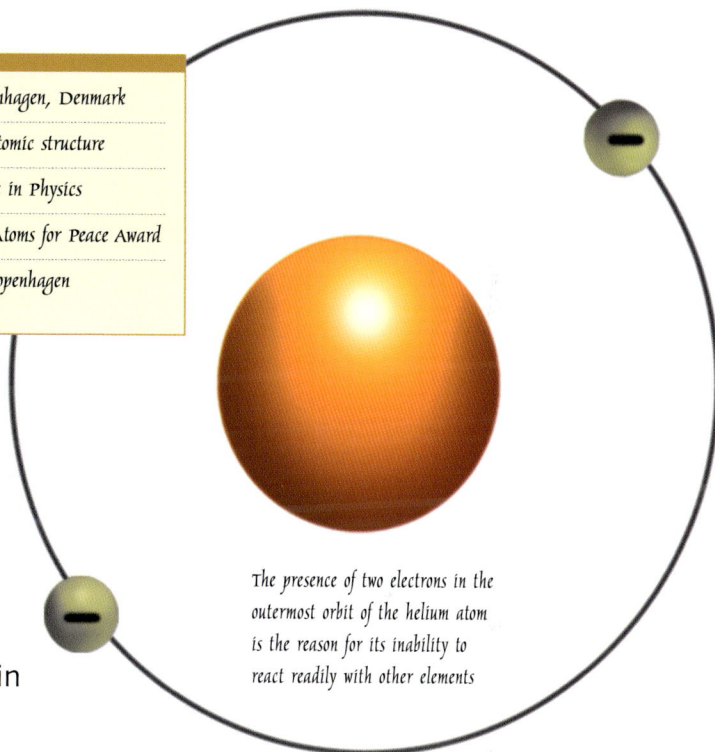

He was the first to apply the quantum theory to atomic structure. According to the Bohr model of the atom, the electron moves in a circle around the nucleus at a fixed distance from it. He also suggested that the outer orbits hold more electrons, thus fixing the chemical properties of the atom. He maintained that as long as an electron remains in one place, no energy is given off. His discovery earned him the 1922 Nobel Prize in Physics. The element Bohrium is named after him.

The presence of two electrons in the outermost orbit of the helium atom is the reason for its inability to react readily with other elements

180 Srinivasa Ramanujan
[1887 - 1920]

December 22, 1887: Born in Erode, Tamil Nadu, India
1914: Goes to London
1918: Elected to the Royal Society of London
1919: Returns to India due to health problems
April 26, 1920: Dies of tuberculosis in Kumbakonam, Tamil Nadu

A mathematical genius, Ramanujan made significant contributions to the theory and partition of numbers. Largely self-taught, Ramanujan never attended university. It is said that he had mastered trigonometry by the age of 12 and was even inventing his own complicated theorems! He sent a list of his theorems to the famous mathematician Godfrey Hardy, who invited him to England. Ramanujan was the first Indian, as well as the first Asian, to be elected to the Royal Society.

Srinivasa Ramanujan

100 GREAT
scientists

181 Chandrasekhara Venkata Raman
[1888 - 1970]

He is famous for his work on the scattering of light. When he first learned about the Compton effect of X-rays (producing an increase in the wavelength), Raman became convinced that this effect could also hold true for light. After several experiments, he discovered that when passed through a transparent medium, some of the light that is scattered has different wavelengths. Popularly called the Raman effect, it won him the 1930 Nobel Prize in Physics.

November 7, 1888: *Born in Tiruchinapalli, Tamil Nadu, India*

1924: *Elected Fellow of the Royal Society*

1929: *Knighted*

1943: *Establishes the Raman Research Institute in Bangalore, Karnataka, India*

November 21, 1970: *Dies in Bangalore*

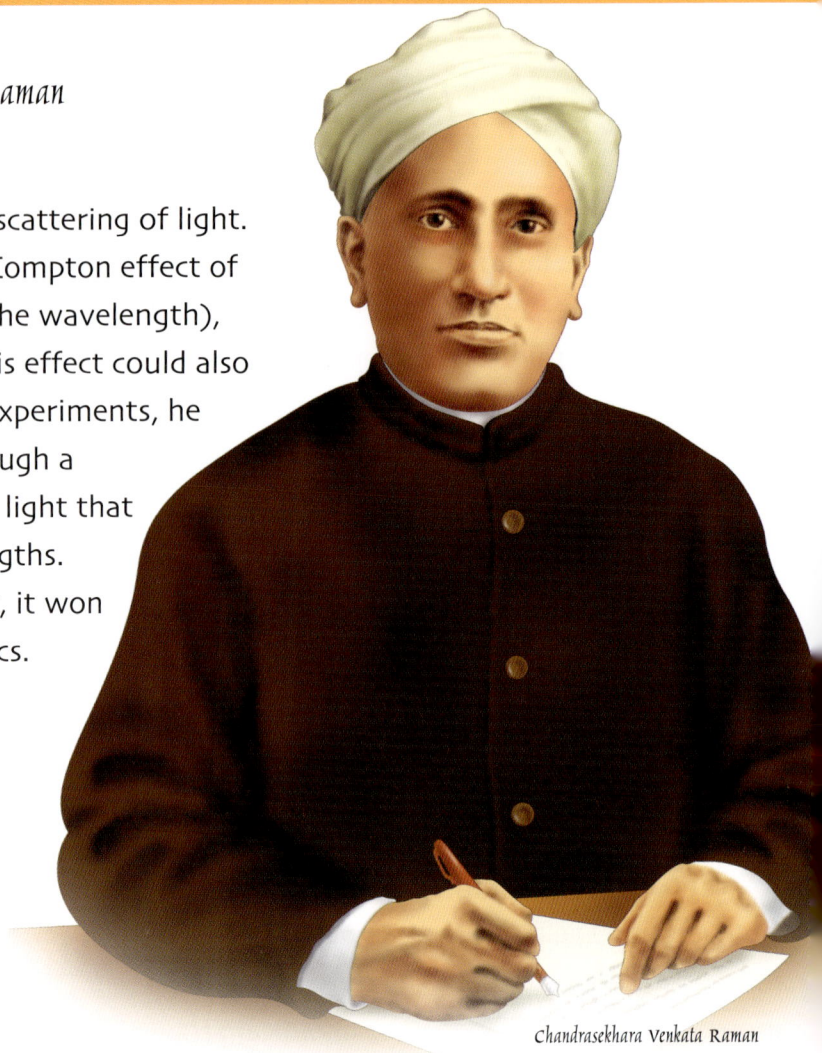

Chandrasekhara Venkata Raman

182 Edwin Hubble
[1889 - 1953]

Edwin Hubble

He was a noted American astronomer who proved that the universe is expanding. In 1924, Hubble observed that the nebulae seen earlier were not a part of our galaxy. In fact, they were galaxies outside the Milky Way. Later, he also formulated what became known as the Hubble law – stating that the distances between the galaxies or cluster of galaxies are continuously increasing, thus expanding the universe.

November 20, 1889: *Born in Marshfield, Missouri, U.S.*

December 30, 1924: *Announces his discovery of an expanding universe*

September 28, 1953: *Dies of a stroke in San Marino, California, U.S.*

183 Joseph Hermann Muller
[1890 - 1967]

December 1, 1890: Born in New York, U.S.

1926: Induces mutation by using X-rays

April 5, 1967: Dies in Indianapolis, U.S.

The American geneticist is best remembered for his demonstration that X-rays can bring about mutations. He also explained that mutations are caused by the breaking up of chromosomes and by changes in individual genes. In 1946, Muller was awarded the Nobel Prize in Physiology or Medicine. He dedicated most of his life to increasing public awareness about the genetic dangers of radiation. He pointed out that constant exposure to radiation or similar industrial processes could result in severe genetic mutations, often causing incurable diseases.

184 James Chadwick
[1891 - 1974]

October 20, 1891: Born in Manchester, England

1932: Discovers the neutron

1935: Wins the Nobel Prize in Physics for his discovery

1945: Knighted

July 24, 1974: Dies in Cambridge

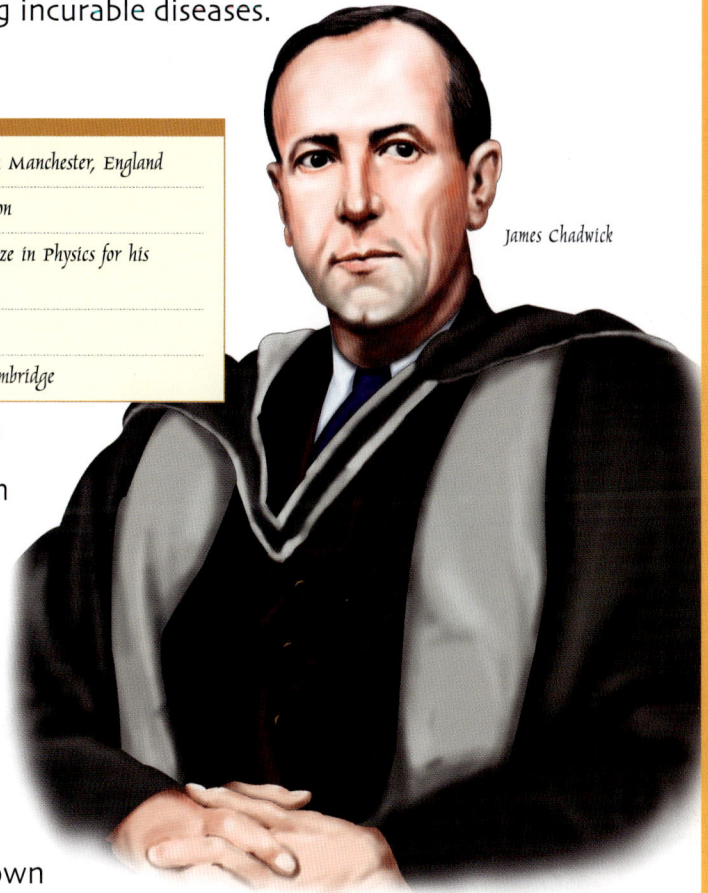

Sir Chadwick discovered the neutron, a subatomic particle with no electric charge. He observed that alpha particles (nuclei of helium) are charged and, hence, repelled by positive charges in the nuclei of heavy atoms. A neutron, though, has no charge and can enter and split the nuclei of the heaviest elements. The discovery paved the way for nuclear fission of uranium and, thereby, the creation of the atom bomb.

James Chadwick

185 John Burdon Sanderson Haldane
[1892 - 1964]

He was a British geneticist, known for experimenting upon himself. Haldane contributed greatly to the development of population genetics and enzyme chemistry. He calculated that, on average, mutation occurs once for every 50,000 people per generation.

November 5, 1892: Born in Oxford, England

1932: Publishes his famous book, The Causes of Evolution

1963: Coins the term "clone", from the Greek word for "twig"

December 1, 1964: Dies of cancer in Bhubaneswar, Orissa, India

Thus, he re-established Darwin's theory of evolution. Haldane also discovered a cure for tetanus and convulsions.

John Burdon Sanderson Haldane

100 GREAT
scientists

186 Jean Piaget
[1896 - 1980]

August 9, 1896: Born in Neuchatel, Switzerland

1929: Becomes professor of child psychology at the University of Geneva, Switzerland

September 17, 1980: Dies in Geneva

A leading development psychologist of the 20th century, Piaget was originally a marine biologist. His interest in psychology was aroused as he observed the process of mental development in his own children. Later, working with Alfred Binet, Piaget became fascinated with the kinds of mistakes children of different ages could make while taking intelligence tests. Analysing the reasoning processes of children, Piaget proposed his theory that the development of a child's mind happens in four genetically determined stages, which always follow the same order. Today, Piaget's theory forms the basis of child psychology.

Jean Piaget

187 Linus Carl Pauling
[1901 - 1994]

February 28, 1901: Born in Portland, Oregon, U.S.

1931: Awarded the American Chemical Society's Langmuir Prize

1951: Wins the Lewis Medal

August 19, 1994: Dies in California

One of the greatest chemists ever, Pauling was the first to receive two unshared Nobel Prizes. He was also among the first scientists to apply the quantum theory to the study of molecular structures, especially chemical bonding. His book, *The Nature of the Chemical Bond and the Structure of Molecules and Crystals*, is considered to be one of the most popular chemistry texts. In 1954 he was awarded the Nobel Prize in Chemistry and in 1962 his campaign for nuclear disarmament earned him the Nobel Peace Prize.

188 Enrico Fermi
[1901 - 1954]

He was one of the main founders of nuclear physics. He discovered artificial radioactivity produced by neutrons - work for which he won the 1938 Nobel Prize in Physics. The Italian-born American scientist is also renowned for his invention of the atomic pile (nuclear reactor). He played an important role in the development of the atomic and hydrogen bombs. Element number 100 in the periodic table is named "fermium" in his honour.

September 29, 1901: Born in Rome, Italy

1938: Receives the Nobel Prize; leaves for the United States

1942: Creates the first controlled nuclear chain-reaction in uranium

1946: Receives the Congressional Medal of Merit

1954: Becomes the first recipient of a special U.S. government award, which was later renamed the Enrico Fermi Award

November 28, 1954: Dies in Chicago, Illinois, U.S.

189 Werner Heisenberg
[1901 - 1976]

Werner Karl Heisenberg was one of the founders of quantum mechanics (quantum physics). He is best known for his uncertainty principle, which states that it is impossible to correctly determine the position and speed of a subatomic particle like the electron. Heisenberg also led Germany's unsuccessful attempts to develop an atomic bomb during World War II.

Werner Heisenberg

December 5, 1901: *Born in Wurzburg, Germany*

1927: *Publishes his uncertainty principle*

1932: *Receives the Nobel Prize in Physics for his work on quantum mechanics*

February 1, 1976: *Dies in Munich, Germany*

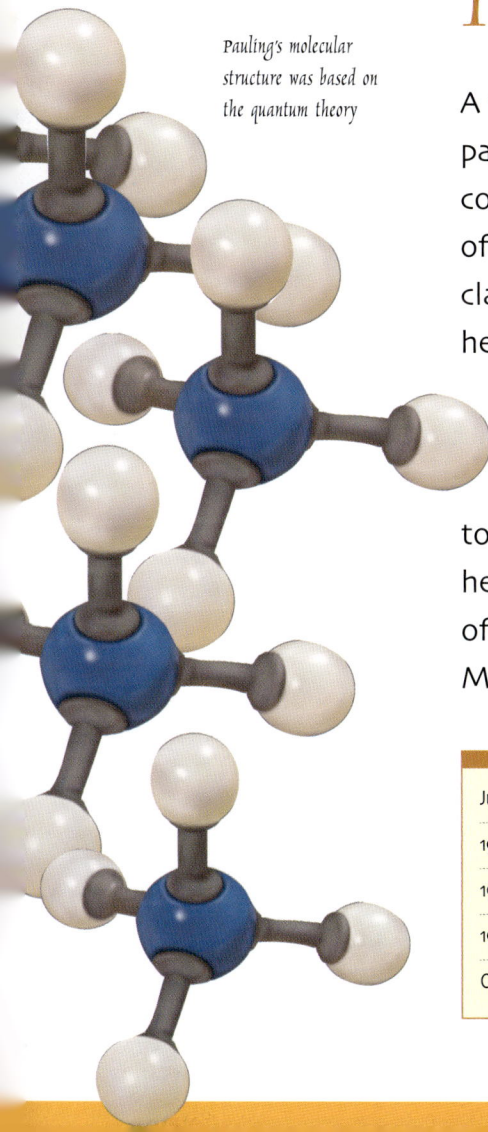

190 George Gaylord Simpson
[1902 - 1984]

Pauling's molecular structure was based on the quantum theory

A well-known American palaeontologist, Simpson's contributions to the theory of evolution include a detailed classification of mammals. However, he is best remembered for his studies of intercontinental migration of prehistoric mammals. Using the fossils he gathered on his trips to the United States and Argentina, he traced the migration patterns of animals during the Mesozoic Era.

June 16, 1902: *Born in Chicago, U.S.*

1949: *Publishes Tempo and Mode in Evolution*

1953: *Publishes Major Features of Evolution*

1965: *Publishes The Geography of Evolution*

October 6, 1984: *Dies in Tucson, Arizona*

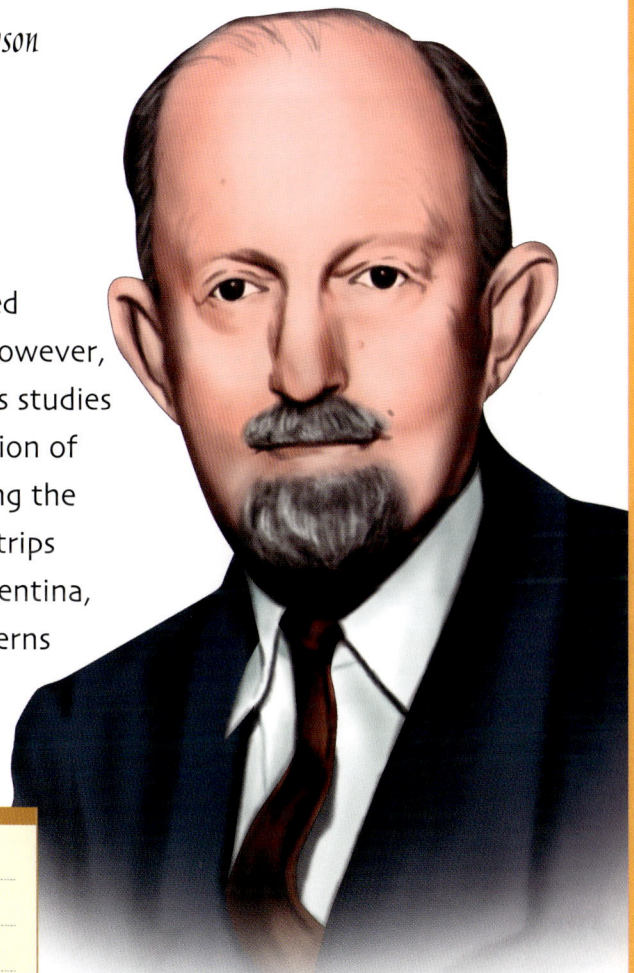

George Gaylord Simpson

100 GREAT
scientists

191 George Gamow
[1904 - 1968]

A renowned Russian nuclear physicist and cosmologist, Gamow proposed the "liquid drop" model of the atomic nucleus. According to him, the nucleus is like a drop of fluid, held together by a strong nuclear force. His premise laid the basis for modern theories of nuclear fission and fusion. In addition to developing theories of star formation, Gamow also put forth a theory of radioactive decay in which alpha particles are given out by a nucleus.

March 4, 1904: Born in Odessa, Russian Empire (now in Ukraine)

1928: Formulates a theory of radioactive decay

1948: Develops the big-bang theory of the origin of the universe

1954: Presents a theory of genetic code (later proved correct)

August 19, 1968: Dies in Colorado, U.S.

192 Albert Bruce Sabin
[1892 - 1975]

He developed the oral polio vaccine that is widely used against polio. Sabin grew the polio virus in human nerve tissue outside the body, to prove that the organism did not enter the body through respiratory organs. Having also established that it mainly infected the digestive system, he proposed that an oral vaccine of live, but weak, virus would work longer than a killed virus. Moreover, the latter only prevents paralysis, while Sabin's vaccine checks both paralysis and infection.

August 26, 1906: Born in Bialystok, Poland, Russian Empire (now in Poland)

1930: Becomes a U.S. citizen

c. 1959: Develops live oral vaccine for polio

1960: His vaccine is approved for use in the United States

March 3, 1993: Dies in Washington D.C., U.S.

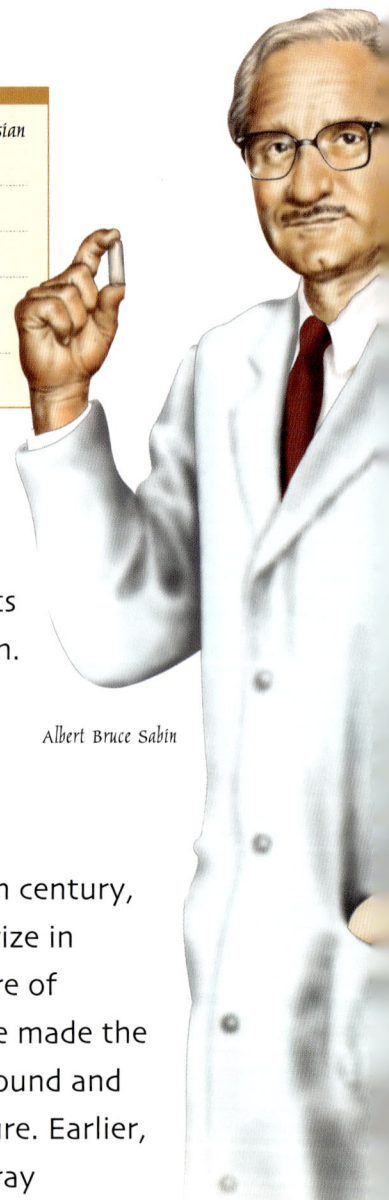

Albert Bruce Sabin

193 Dorothy Crowfoot Hodgkin
[1910 - 1994]

One of the most notable chemists of the 20th century, Dorothy Hodgkin received the 1964 Nobel Prize in Chemistry for determining the structure of vitamin B_{12} (vitamin B complex). She made the first X-ray photograph of the compound and also determined its atomic structure. Earlier, in 1933, she also made the first X-ray photograph of a protein (pepsin). In 1965, Hodgkin became the second woman ever to receive the Order of Merit.

Dorothy Crowfoot Hodgkin

May 12, 1910: Born in Cairo, Egypt

1933: Makes the first X-ray photograph of a protein

1948: Makes the first X-ray photograph of vitamin B_{12}

July 29, 1994: Dies in Shipston-on-Stour, Warwickshire, England

194 Melvin Calvin
[1911 - 1997]

Calvin is famous for his discovery of the chemical pathways of photosynthesis. It is said that at the end of World War II, Earnest Lawrence, inventor of the cyclotron, told Calvin to "do something useful" with all the radioactive carbon-14 made during the war. After much thought, Calvin decided to use the radioactive properties of the element to trace the path of carbon dioxide during photosynthesis in plants. After years of observation, Calvin and his team noticed that the carbon dioxide was converted into carbohydrates and other organic compounds. He also demonstrated that this process of conversion is part of the "dark reactions" that happen in the night. This discovery, named Calvin Cycle, won him the 1961 Nobel Prize in Chemistry.

Calvin cycle

CARBON DIOXIDE

FOOD SUGAR WATER ACID HYDROGEN SUGAR STORAGE OXYGEN

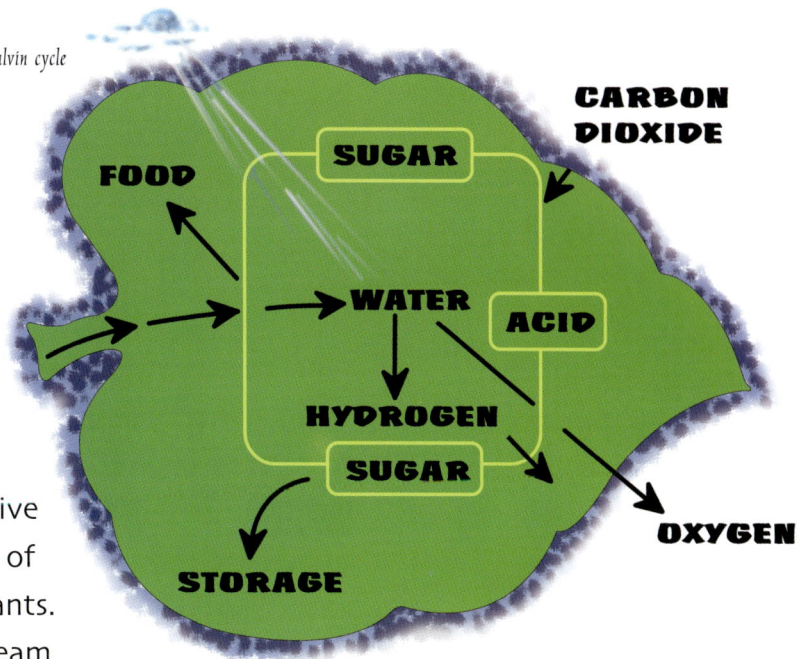

April 8, 1911: Born in St. Paul, Minnesota, U.S.

January 8, 1997: Dies in Berkeley, California.

195 Jonas Edward Salk
[1914 - 1995]

A physician and medical researcher, Salk was the first to develop a safe and effective vaccine for polio. Salk first confirmed that three strains of the polio virus exist. He then showed that the killed virus from these strains can produce antibodies against the disease without actually causing infection. In 1955, Salk's vaccine was released for use in the United States. It has since played a vital role in the near eradication of the dreaded disease.

Jonas Edward Salk

October 28, 1914: Born in New York, U.S.

1954: Discovers the polio vaccine

1977: Awarded the Presidential Medal of Freedom

June 23, 1995: Dies in La Jolla, California

100 GREAT
scientists

196 Francis Crick
[1916 - 2004]

June 8, 1916: *Born in Northampton, England*

1953: *Announces the discovery of the DNA molecular structure*

1966: *Publishes his book* Of Molecules and Men

July 28, 2004: *Dies in San Diego, California, U.S.*

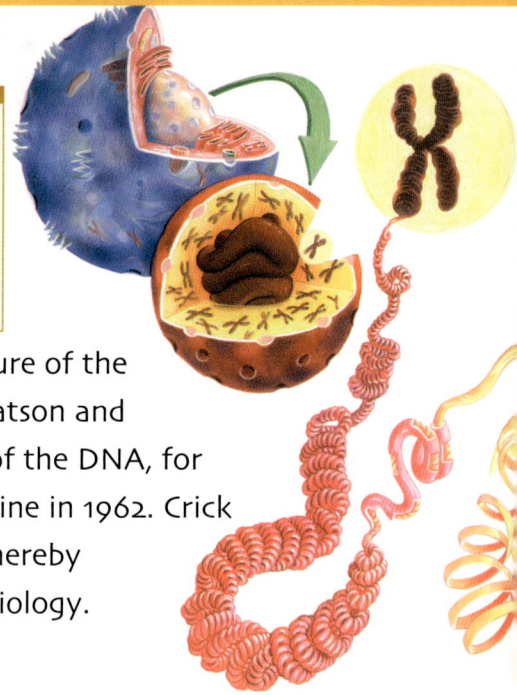

One of the best-known scientists in modern times, Francis Harry Compton Crick was one of the discoverers of the structure of the DNA molecule. In 1951, he joined with James Dewey Watson and Maurice Wilkins to develop the double-helix structure of the DNA, for which they won the Nobel Prize in Physiology or Medicine in 1962. Crick also explained the way DNA is used to build proteins, thereby contributing greatly to the development of molecular biology.

197 Gertrude Belle Elion
[1918 - 1999]

Being female in her age, Elion was unable to find a research position. Hence she started her career as a lab assistant. In 1944, she joined the Burroughs Wellcome Laboratories as assistant to George Herbert Hitchings, a pharmacologist. Together they discovered new drug treatments for malaria, bacterial infections, organ transplantation and even such dreaded diseases as leukaemia (blood cancer) and AIDS. They were awarded the 1988 Nobel Prize in Physiology or Medicine, together with James Black.

January 23, 1918: *Born in New York, U.S.*

February 21, 1999: *Dies in Chapel Hill, New Connecticut, U.S.*

Gertrude Belle Elion

198 Frederick Sanger
[1918-]

August 13, 1918: *Born in Gloucestershire, England*

1955: *Determines the structure of insulin*

1958: *Receives his first Nobel Prize*

1980: *Shares his second Nobel Prize with Paul Berg and Walter Gilbert*

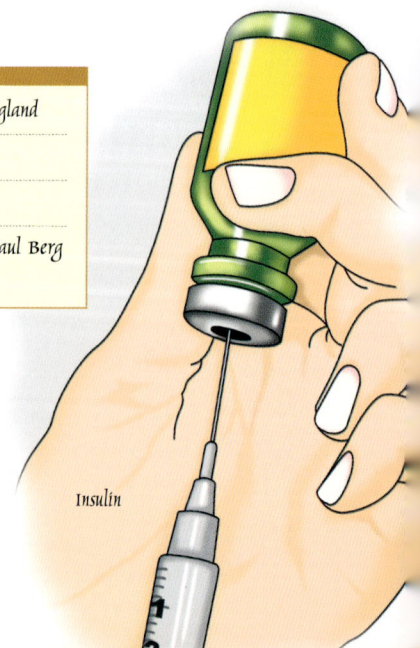

Famous for determining the structure of insulin, Sanger is one of the few scientists who have won the Nobel Prize twice. He received the first in 1958 for his work on the structure of proteins, especially insulin. The techniques he used in his 10-year-long experiment have helped in discovering the structure of many other complex proteins. In 1980, he received his second Nobel Prize, this time in Chemistry.

Insulin

199 James Dewey Watson
[1928-]

April 6, 1928: Born in Chicago, Illinois, U.S.

1953: Announces the discovery of the molecular structure of DNA

1968: Publishes his best-selling book, The Double Helix

American geneticist Watson was co-discoverer of the molecular structure of DNA. For this achievement, he shared the 1962 Nobel Prize in Physiology or Medicine with Francis Crick and Maurice Wilkins. Watson has given a very entertaining account of the discovery in his book, *The Double Helix*. From 1988 to 1992, he headed the Human Genome Project that aimed to map the entire human DNA. He was last serving as the president of the Cold Spring Harbour Laboratory in New York.

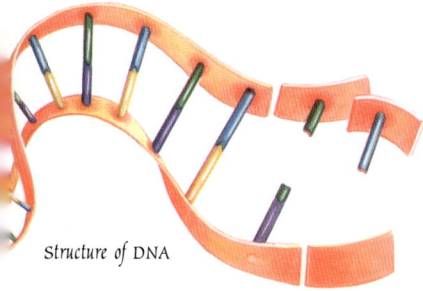

Structure of DNA

200 Stephen Hawking
[1942-]

January 8, 1942: Born in Oxford, England

1962: Diagnosed with the muscular disease called amyotrophic lateral sclerosis

1971: Provides mathematical support for the big-bang theory

1974: Suggests that black holes do not exist forever

1988: His best-seller, A Brief History of Time, is published

2001: Publishes his book, The Universe in a Nutshell

Considered one of the best theoretical physicists of recent times, Hawking is famous for his theory that black holes are not permanent. He showed that black holes evaporate by what is now called "Hawking radiation". He also provided mathematical support for the big-bang theory. Despite being confined to a wheelchair due to an incurable muscular disease, Hawking is highly active. His disease has also forced him to use a computer-generated voice synthesiser to speak, yet he continues to teach and lecture. Widely admired for his courage, Hawking also made a guest appearance in *Star Trek: The Next Generation*, a popular television series.

Stephen Hawking

100 GREAT
scientists

Great

Inventors

201 Johannes Gutenberg
[c. 1390 - c. 1468]

Regarded as the father of modern printing, Johannes Gutenberg invented movable type printing for letters and symbols. Although not much is known about his life, it is believed that Gutenberg entered into a partnership with a German businessman, Johann Fust, to set up a press. It is said that Gutenberg printed the Latin Bible, which is popularly called the Gutenberg Bible in his honour. His hand-operated press used a series of blocks, each bearing a single letter on its face. The invention made copying manuscripts faster and simpler.

c.1390: Born in Mainz, Germany
c.1450: Joins with Johann Fust to set up a printing press
c.1456: Completes printing the 42-line Gutenberg Bible
February 3, 1468: Dies in Mainz, Germany

Gutenberg set up a printing press in 1450

202 Galileo Galilei
[1564 - 1642]

Born to a musician, Galileo first studied medicine. Soon, however, he turned his attention to mathematics, and it was in this field that Galileo left his mark. He invented the telescope and made some important discoveries. He observed that the Earth's moon had an irregular surface, and that Jupiter, too, had moons (satellites). However, his strong support for the Copernican system made him unpopular with the Church; he was placed under house arrest until his death.

Galileo Galilei

February 15, 1564: Born in Pisa, Italy
1609-10: Discovers that the surface of the moon is irregular
January 7, 1610: Discovers Jupiter's satellites
1632: Writes the famous book, Dialogue Concerning the Two Chief World Systems
January 8, 1642: Dies in Arcetri, near Florence, Italy

203 Cornelis Jacobszoon Drebble
[1572 - 1633]

A Dutch inventor and physicist, Drebbel is credited with many inventions such as the thermostat and a clock that could rewind constantly according to changes in the atmospheric pressure and temperature. However, Drebbel is best known for building the first navigable submarine. It consisted of a wooden frame covered with waterproof leather. The oars on its sides helped move the vessel both on the surface and underwater. Air tubes with floats provided the crew with oxygen.

1572: Born in Alkmaar, The Netherlands
1598: Receives patent for his "perpetual motion clock"
1620: First submarine voyage undertaken in the Thames River, at a depth of about 5 m (15 feet)
November 7, 1633: Dies in London, England

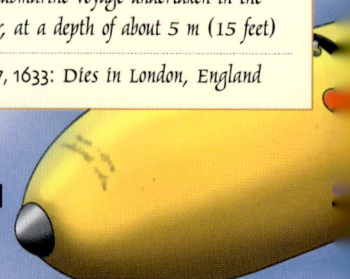

204 Evangelista Torricelli
[1608 - 1647]

Evangelista Torricelli invented the barometer

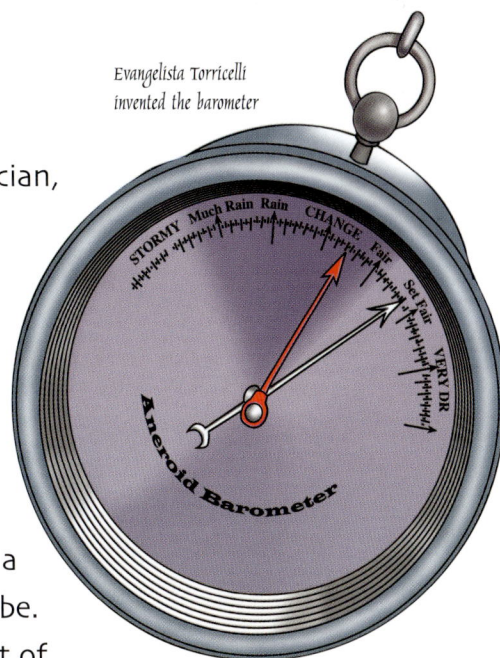

An Italian physicist and mathematician, Torricelli invented the barometer. Following a suggestion made by Galileo, he conducted an experiment using a glass tube filled with mercury. He observed that some of the mercury did not flow out when the tube was inverted into a dish. He also noticed a vacuum above the mercury in the tube. He realised that the height of mercury changed according to the atmospheric pressure. The barometer was thus invented. The torr, a unit of pressure, is named after him.

October 15, 1608: Born in Faenza, Italy

1641: Becomes Galileo's assistant

1643: Invents the barometer

October 25, 1647: Dies in Florence, Italy

205 Robert Hooke
[1635 - 1703]

July 18, 1635: Born in Freshwater, Isle of Wight, England

1655: Assists Robert Boyle, the famous chemist

1660: Discovers the law of elasticity

1665: Publishes his book, Micrographia

March 3, 1703: Dies in London

Best known for the law of elasticity - named after him - English physicist Hooke is also responsible for inventions like the iris diaphragm in cameras and the universal joint used in motor vehicles. He also invented the modern air pump, the hygrometer and the reflecting telescope. He made important contributions to the fields of microbiology and geology as well.

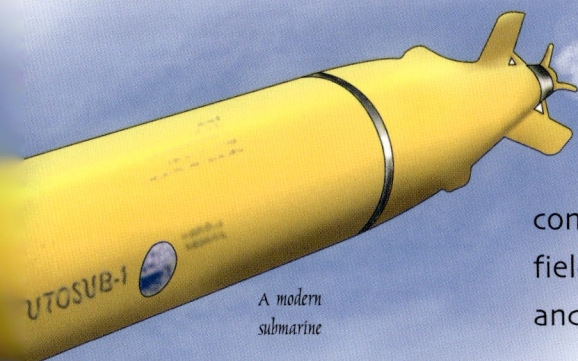

A modern submarine

Robert Hooke

100 GREAT
Inventors

206 Bartholomew Cristofori
[1655 - 1731]

He was an Italian harpsichord maker who is credited with the invention of the piano. Cristofori's piano was called gravicembalo col piano e forte ("harpsichord that plays soft and loud"). The instrument was given this name because of its ability to change loudness according to the pressure applied on the keys, a property not seen in the harpsichord. Some of Cristofori's original pianofortes exist even today.

The piano was invented by Cristofori in 1709

May 4, 1655: Born in Venice

1711: Publishes diagrams of how a piano works

January 27, 1731: Dies in Florence, Italy

207 Daniel Gabriel Fahrenheit
[1686 - 1736]

May 24, 1686: Born in Gdansk, Poland

1709: Invents the alcohol thermometer

1714: Develops the mercury thermometer

September 16, 1736: Dies in Hague, Dutch Republic (now The Netherlands)

Fahrenheit was a Polish physicist who invented the alcohol thermometer. Although the first thermometers were made by Galileo, they were not reliable. Fahrenheit made the first successful thermometer using alcohol. He later developed the mercury thermometer, which gave better results. The Fahrenheit scale of temperature is named after him and is commonly used even today.

208 James Watt
[1736 - 1819]

Watt invented the modern steam engine. Largely self-taught, Watt was working as an engineer on the Forth and Clyde Canal, when he was introduced to Thomas Newcomen's steam engine. Using a separate condenser, he reduced the loss of heat and increased the engine's efficiency. He improved it further by adding a pressure gauge and rods to guide the piston up and down. Watt also introduced the concept of horsepower. The watt, a unit of power, is named after him.

January 19, 1736: Born in Greenock, Scotland

1769: Improves the Newcomen steam engine by adding a separate condenser

1775: Starts to manufacture his new engine

1782: Patents his double-acting engine in which the piston pushed and pulled

1784: Adds rods to guide the up-and-down movements of the piston

1790: Invents the pressure gauge

August 25, 1819: Dies near Birmingham, England

209 Joseph Michel Montgolfier
[1740 - 1810]

Joseph Michel and his brother Jacques Etienne invented the hot-air balloon. While watching wood chips rise over a fire, they concluded that the burning created a gas that caused any light material over it to rise. In 1783, they made the first public demonstration of their invention. The balloon rose to a height of about 1,829 m (6,000 feet) and was airborne for 10 minutes. Following several test flights, the brothers launched the first successful manned flight over Paris.

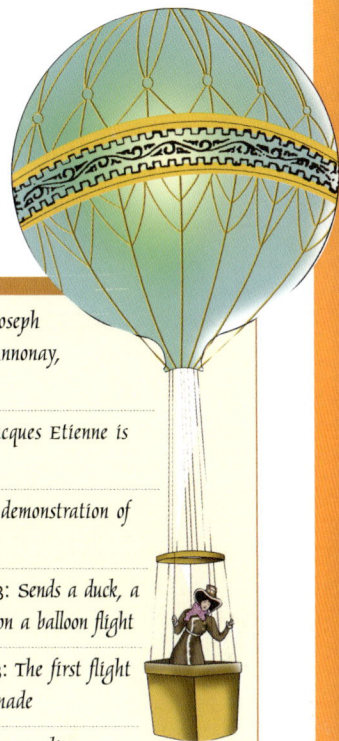

Joseph Montgolfier

August 26, 1740: Joseph Michel is born in Annonay, France

January 6, 1745: Jacques Etienne is born in Annonay

June 5, 1783: First demonstration of the hot-air balloon

September 19, 1783: Sends a duck, a sheep and a rooster on a balloon flight

November 21, 1783: The first flight carrying people is made

August 2, 1799: Jacques dies on a balloon flight from Lyon to Annonay

June 26, 1810: Joseph Michel dies in Balaruc-les-Baines, France

210 Edmund Cartwright
[1743 - 1823]

April 24, 1743: Born in Marnharm, Nottinghamshire, England

1785: Patents his invention

1789: Obtains patent for a wool-combing machine

October 30, 1823: Dies in Hastings, Sussex, England

The steam engine

This British inventor built the power loom. In the summer of 1784, after a visit to Richard Arkwright's cotton-spinning mills, Cartwright was inspired to invent a power-driven machine for weaving. The first patented machine was crude. It was strapped vertically with an overpowered shuttle and needed two men to manage it. After further improvements, the loom could be strung horizontally with decreased power. It also had devices that automatically rolled the cloth off the loom and even detected broken threads.

Edmund Cartwright

Alessandro Volta

211 Alessandro Volta
[1745 - 1827]

An Italian physicist, Alessandro Volta formulated a practical method to generate continuous electric current by inventing the electric battery. He built the voltaic pile in an attempt to disprove Luigi Galvani's theory that animal tissues contained electricity. Volta held that electricity was produced by the contact of different metals in a moist environment and that it did not require animal tissue. In 1800, he publicly demonstrated the first electric battery. In 1881, the volt, a unit of electricity, was named in his honour.

February 18, 1745: Born in Como, Lombardy, Italy

1775: Invents the electrophorus to generate static electricity

1800: Demonstrates the battery's ability to generate continuous electricity

March 5, 1827: Dies in Como, Lombardy, Italy

212 Nicolas Conte
[1755 - 1805]

A self-taught chemist and inventor, Nicolas-Jacques Conte was initially a painter. In 1794, there was a shortage of English graphite due to the Anglo-French war. The Committee for Public Well-Being asked Conte to produce a pencil with raw materials available in France. He did so by mixing graphite with clay. He also realised that by varying the amount of clay and graphite, it was possible to make the pencil harder or dryer. Conte's method is still used in the wood-cased pencil industry.

August 4, 1755: Born in Aunou-sur-Orne, near Sees, France

1794: Invents the modern graphite pencil

January 1795: Obtains a French patent and starts production of the Conte pencil

December 6, 1805: Dies in Paris, France

Louis-Sebastien Lenormand coined the word "parachute"

213 Louis-Sebastien Lenormand
[1757 - 1839]

Widely regarded as the first person to jump using a parachute, there is very little information about Louis-Sebastien Lenormand. Although the Chinese are believed to have invented the parachute, Lenormand is credited with demonstrating the principle and also with the coining of the word "parachute". In 1783, he made a safe jump from a tower, using a parachute of 4.3-m (14-foot) diameter.

1757: Born in France

1783: Demonstrates the principle of the parachute

1839: Dies in France

214 Robert Fulton
[1765 - 1815]

Robert Fulton

He was an American inventor who built the first commercially successful steamboat. Fulton showed an interest in engineering at a very young age. His first works included a system of inland waterways and various models of submarines and torpedoes. In 1801, American leader Robert R. Livingston asked him to build a steamboat. In 1807, Fulton's "Clermont" made the 240-km (150-mile) journey between New York City and Albany in 32 hours, one-third of the usual sailing time!

November 14, 1765: Born in Lancaster County, Pennsylvania, U.S.

1800: Builds a submarine, the "Nautilus"

August 7, 1807: Fulton's steamboat "Clermont" is launched

1812: Builds the first steam warship

February 24, 1815: Dies in New York City

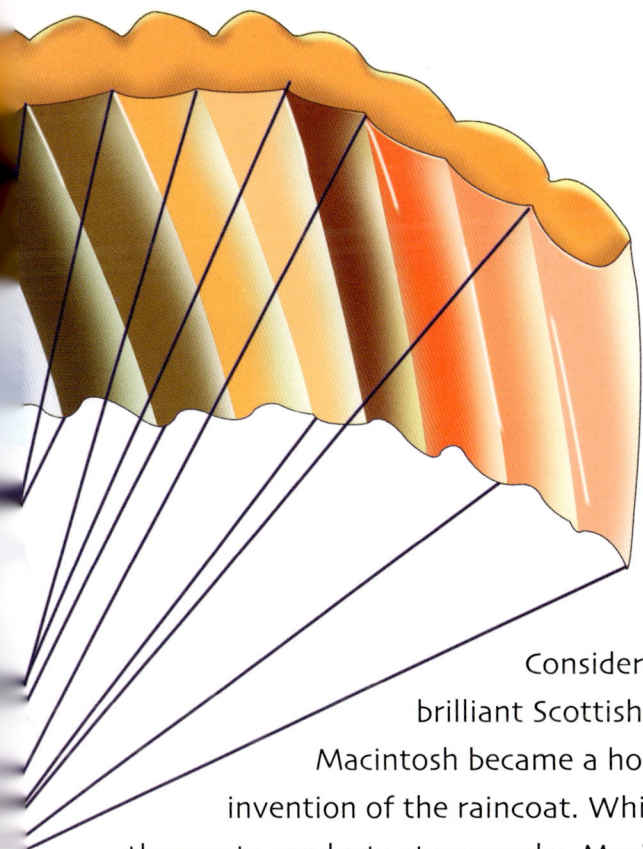

Charles Macintosh invented the first waterproof garment

215 Charles Macintosh
[1766 - 1843]

Considered one of the most brilliant Scottish chemists of all times, Macintosh became a household name with his invention of the raincoat. While trying to find uses for the waste products at gasworks, Macintosh observed that naphtha obtained from coal tar could dissolve natural rubber. Encouraged by this discovery, he used the dissolved rubber to join two pieces of cloth together to produce the first waterproof garment! The material was introduced in 1824 as "Mackintosh".

December 29, 1766: Born in Glasgow, Scotland

1823: Invents the raincoat and obtains a patent for it

1834: Starts his own factory of waterproof garments

July 25, 1843: Dies near Glasgow, Scotland

100 GREAT
Inventors

216 Humphry Davy
[1778 - 1829]

Sir Humphry Davy established his reputation as a brilliant scientist early in his life. Though he made many valuable discoveries, his greatest contribution was the invention of the miner's safety lamp (also called Davy lamp). In 1815, Davy learnt about the dangers of the methane gas that filled the mines. The candles used by miners to light their way could spark off a fire, putting their lives in danger. So Davy replaced the candles with a flameless lamp, thus increasing safety in the mines.

December 17, 1778: Born in Penzance, Cornwall, England

1799: Discovers that nitrous oxide (laughing gas) has a numbing power, ideal for use during surgery

1812: Attains knighthood

1815: Invents the miner's safety lamp

May 29, 1829: Dies in Geneva, Switzerland

217 Rene Laennec
[1781 - 1826]

Rene-Theophile-Hyacinthe Laennec was a French doctor who invented the stethoscope. One day, while examining a patient, Laennec rolled up sheets of paper and placed them on his patient's chest. He was thrilled to discover that not only could he hear the sounds of the lungs and heart through the roll, but they were louder and clearer. Laennec then created the first stethoscope from a hollow piece of wood. The instrument had a hole in one end and a cone in the other.

February 17, 1781: Born in Quimper, Brittany, France

1816: Invents the stethoscope

August 13, 1826: Dies in Kerlouanec

The modern stethoscope

218 William Sturgeon
[1783 - 1850]

Son of a shoemaker, Sturgeon received very little formal education. Not wanting to become a cobbler, he ran away from home to join the army. Due to his scientific skills, he was soon made a lecturer in the Royal Military College at Addiscombe, Surrey. In 1825 he demonstrated his first electromagnet. The seven-ounce magnet could support nearly 4 kg (9 pounds) of iron when current was passed through it. His electromagnet led to the invention of the telegraph and the electric motor.

The first electromagnet was a horseshoe-shaped piece of iron that wrapped with a loosely wound coil of several turns

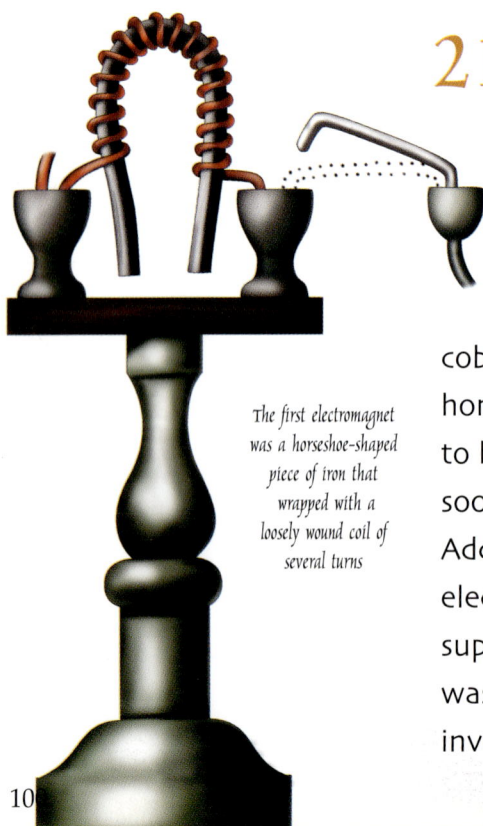

May 22, 1783: Born in Whittington, Lancashire, England

1825: Invents the first electromagnet capable of supporting more than its own weight

1832: Builds an electric motor and also invents the commutator used in it

1836: Invents the first suspended coil galvanometer to measure current

December 4, 1850: Dies in Prestwich, Lancashire

219 Samuel Morse
[1791 - 1872]

Samuel Finley Breese Morse initially chose painting as a career. However, in 1832, while travelling on the ship Sully, Morse learnt about the electromagnet. He immediately thought of making an electric telegraph. Unaware that such attempts were being made elsewhere in the world, he pursued his experiments with enthusiasm. He developed a system of using dots and dashes that became popular as the Morse Code. Upon the completion of the first American telegraph line in 1844, between Baltimore and Washington, he sent the message, "What hath God wrought!"

April 27, 1791: Born in Charlestown, Massachusetts, U.S.

1832-35: Starts work on his electric telegraph

1838: Develops the Morse code

1844: Sends the first telegraphic message

April 2, 1872: Dies in New York, U.S.

Michael Faraday apart from inventing the electric motor also built the first generator and transformer

Telegraph machine

220 Michael Faraday
[1791 - 1867]

English physicist and chemist Michael Faraday was born into a humble family. As a boy, he worked with a bookbinder, during which time he developed an interest in science. This eventually led him to become an assistant to Sir Humphry Davy, under whom he learned chemistry. However, Faraday's major contributions were to be in the fields of electricity and magnetism. He invented the dynamo and the electric motor. His observations also laid the foundations for modern electromagnetic technology.

September 22, 1791: Born in Newington, Surrey, England

1812: Becomes an assistant to Sir Humphry Davy

1821: Invents the electric motor

August 25, 1867: Dies in Hampton Court, England

100 GREAT
Inventors

221 Charles Babbage
[1791 - 1871]

Known as the father of computing, Charles Babbage is said to be the inventor of the first automatic digital computing machine. In an attempt to develop machines capable of complex mathematical calculations, he developed plans for the Analytical Engine. The Analytical Engine was designed to perform all kinds of arithmetical operations and was to contain a memory unit to store the numbers, along with all the other basic elements of a computer. Considered a forerunner of the modern computer, the project was, however, never completed.

December 26, 1791: Born in London

1812: Starts work on mathematical calculators

c.1821: Presents a model of the first Difference Engine, but fails to complete it

c.1833: Starts work on the Analytical Engine

October 18, 1871: Dies in London

1991: British scientists build a functional Difference Engine based on the original plans of Babbage, thus proving him correct

222 Mary Kies
[19th century]

Mary Kies

May 5, 1809: Receives patent

1836: Patent file is destroyed in the great Patent Office fire

In the early 19th century, women in the United States could not patent their inventions despite a law allowing them to do so. This was mainly because in many states women could not legally own property independently. Finally, a hat-maker from Connecticut, Mary Dixon Kies, broke this pattern. She became the first woman to receive a U.S. patent, having invented a process for weaving straw with silk or thread.

February 6, 1802: Born in Gloucester, England

June 19, 1829: Patents the concertina

1837: Patents his electric telegraph

1841: Obtains a patent for the type-printing telegraph, the first apparatus that printed telegrams in type

1868: Receives knighthood

October 19, 1875: Dies in Paris

223 Charles Wheatstone
[1802 - 1875]

He was a British physicist with many innovations to his credit. However, his most famous invention is the concertina, a wind instrument with keys. Born to a musician, Wheatstone's interest in musical instruments was only natural.

He created an instrument consisting of 24 buttons (keys), metal reeds and bellows, providing wind power when operated by hand. Wheatstone also invented an early form of the microphone and made several improvements to the telegraph.

Charles Wheatstone

Charles Babbage

224 Louis Braille
[1809 - 1852]

He was a French educator who developed the Braille system of printing and writing for the blind. Braille himself was blinded in an accident when he was three years old. While studying at the Royal Institute for Blind Youth, in Paris, he met a former soldier named Charles Barbier. Through him, Braille learnt about "night writing", a code used by French soldiers, made up of a series of 12 dots. Braille simplified it by reducing the number of dots to six. Later, in 1837, he also added symbols for maths and music in the script.

The Braille system uses a series of dots

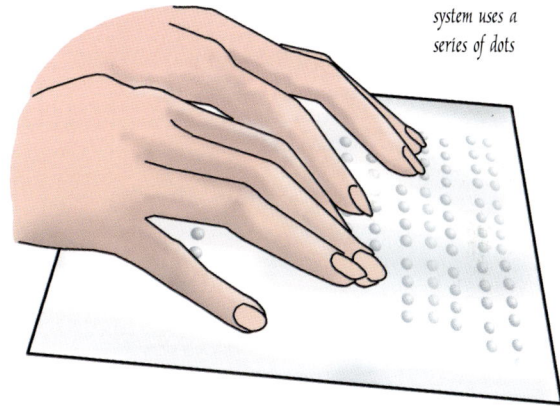

225 Cyrus Hall McCormick
[1809 - 1884]

McCormick drew his passion for invention from his father, a Virginian farmer who had patented farming equipment. The talented son developed a mechanical reaper that combined all the steps of harvesting. After obtaining a patent for his invention, McCormick started to manufacture and sell the machine himself. Finally in 1847, he set up a factory in Chicago to mass-produce the reaper.

100 GREAT
Inventors

226 Elisha Greaves Otis
[1811 - 1861]

Even though it is commonly believed that Otis invented the elevator, he was, infact, only responsible for the brakes! However, Otis was not to know that his seemingly simple invention would help make skyscrapers a reality. His safety device constituted of a steel spring catch that held the elevator even if the rope broke. At his first demonstration of this device, he had the rope cut while he was halfway up in an elevator. The platform did not fall, making his brakes a roaring success.

Elisha Greaves Otis

August 3, 1811: *Born in Halifax, Vermont, U.S.*

1852: *Invents elevator brakes*

1853: *Sets up his own manufacturing unit*

1854: *Demonstrates his safety device at the American Institute Fair at the Crystal Palace, New York City*

March 23, 1857: *Installs world's first passenger safety elevator in the E.V. Haughwout and Company departmental store in New York*

April 8, 1861: *Dies in Yonkers, New York, U.S.*

227 Samuel Colt
[1814 - 1862]

Samuel Colt invented the Colt revolver

July 19, 1814: *Born in Hartford, Connecticut, U.S.*

1830: *Leaves for India by sea*

1835: *Patents the revolver in England and France*

1836: *Patents the revolver in the U.S. and establishes the Patent Arms Manufacturing Company in Paterson, New Jersey*

1842: *Forced to shut his factory due to poor sales*

1843: *Invents the first remote-controlled explosive device*

1847: *Resumes manufacturing guns; introduces the six-shot, .44-calibre Walker revolver*

January 10, 1862: *Dies in Hartford*

Famous for inventing the Colt revolver, the American firearms manufacturer hit on the idea during a voyage to India. Inspired by the wheel of the ship he was on, Colt carved a wooden model of a handgun with a revolving chamber. He then spent years improving it, before first patenting the working model in 1835. He set up a company that manufactured firearms, including the famous Colt .45. His revolvers were widely used in the Mexican War and the American Civil War.

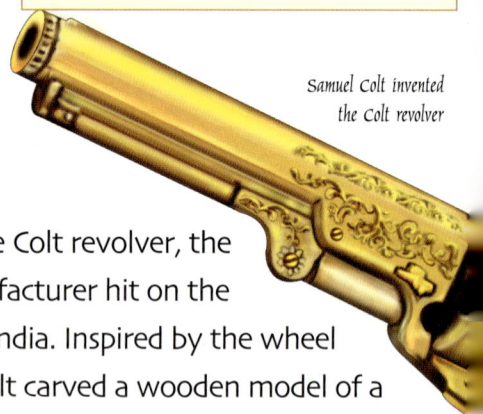

228 Thomas Adams
[1818 - 1905]

1818: *Born in Staten Island, New York City*

1869: *Creates chicle-based chewing gum*

1871: *Patents the first machine for manufacturing gum*

1872: *Creates the famous Black Jack chewing gum*

1888: *The Tutti-Frutti chewing gum becomes the first gum to be sold in a vending machine*

1905: *Dies*

The modern chewing gum came about rather accidentally. The famous Mexican general Antonio Lopez de Santa Anna had asked Adams to make rubber from chicle (the milky latex of the sapodilla tree). After an unsuccessful first attempt, Adams suddenly remembered that Mexicans chewed the chicle latex. Inspired by this, he sweetened the latex and sold it as chewing gum!

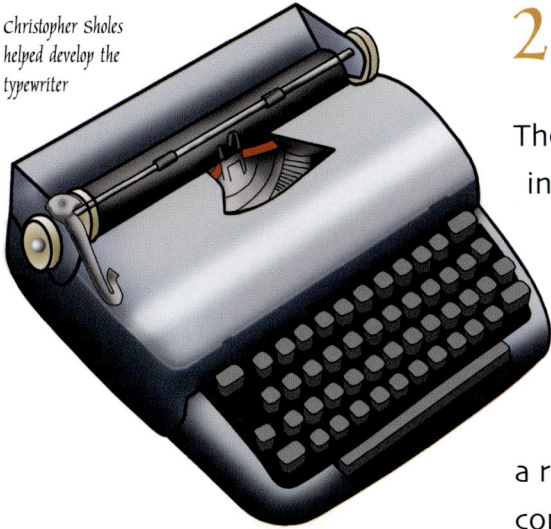
Christopher Sholes helped develop the typewriter

229 Christopher Latham Sholes
[1819 - 1890]

The first practical typewriter was developed by American inventor Christopher Latham Sholes. He was experimenting with a page-numbering machine, when the idea of a letter-printing machine was born. In 1868, Sholes – along with Carlos Glidden and Samuel W. Soule – obtained a patent for the typewriter. However, the keys, which were alphabetically arranged, used to get jammed when struck at a rapid pace. Sholes suggested separating the letters that most commonly appeared together, so the speed of typing could be increased. His new keyboard (called QWERTY, after the re-ordered keys in the uppermost row) is still in use.

February 14, 1819: *Born near Mooresburg, Pennsylvania, U.S.*

1867: *Develops the typewriter*

1873: *Sells his patent rights to the Remington Arms Company for $12,000*

1874: *The Remington company starts manufacture of the "Remington typewriter"*

February 17, 1890: *Dies in Milwaukee, U.S.*

230 Elias Howe
[1819 - 1867]

Howe first came up with the idea of his sewing machine while working at a textile mill. A needle with an eye at its sharp point pushes the thread through the fabric to form a loop. The loop is caught by a mechanism below the fabric. The next loop from the needle is then pulled through the first loop to form a lock stitch. The speed of the machine completely changed the way clothes were manufactured. However, despite having patented his machine, Howe had to fight a legal battle with co-inventors Issac Singer and Allen Wilson, before he was given due credit.

The sewing machine model as shown at Philadelphia in 1867

July 9, 1819: *Born in Spencer, Massachusetts, U.S.*

September 10, 1846: *Obtains a patent for his lock-stitch sewing machine*

1854: *Wins the legal battle to establish his patent rights*

October 3, 1867: *Dies in Brooklyn, New York, U.S.*

100 GREAT
Inventors

231 Levi Strauss
[1829 - 1902]

Levi Strauss moved to San Francisco to set up a dry-goods business. His customers included a tailor named Jacob Davis. Davis had invented a unique method to make sturdy work pants, by putting metal rivets on the pocket corners and at the base of the zipper. Not having enough money for a patent application, Davis approached Levi. Together, they patented this innovation that marked the birth of jeans. It is believed that their pants were made from a material from France called "serge de Nimes", now famous as denim!

The old name for "jeans" was "waist overalls"

February 26, 1829: *Born in Buttenheim, Bavaria*

1847: *Goes to New York, U.S.*

1853: *Becomes an American citizen; sets up business in San Francisco*

May 20, 1873: *Receives patent for an "improvement in fastening pocket openings"; starts making copper-riveted "waist overalls" (old name for "jeans")*

September 27, 1902: *Dies in San Francisco, U.S.*

232 George Pullman
[1831 - 1897]

George Mortimer Pullman was an American inventor who designed the sleeping car for trains. The first Pullman sleeping car, the "Pioneer", was invented with Ben Field and introduced in 1865. It included folding upper berths, a feature still in use. Pullman's car received nationwide publicity when it carried the departed president Abraham Lincoln's body across the country.

George Pullman's sleeping cars

March 3, 1831: *Born in Brocton, New York, U.S.*

1867: *Establishes the Pullman Palace Car Company to build sleeping cars*

1868: *Introduces dining cars*

1880: *Establishes the town of Pullman near Chicago*

October 19, 1897: *Dies in Pullman Town, Chicago*

233 Nikolaus August Otto
[1832 - 1891]

He was a German engineer who developed the four-stroke internal-combustion engine in 1876. This engine's piston moves up and down four times, giving the engine its name. The piston movements draw in fuel and air and compress the mixture in a cylinder, thereby causing an internal explosion. Because of its dependability, efficiency and quietness, over 30,000 Otto cycle engines were built within a decade.

June 10, 1832: *Born in Holzhausen, Nassau, Germany*

1861: *Builds his first gasoline engine*

January 26, 1891: *Dies in Cologne, Germany*

234 Alfred Nobel
[1833 - 1896]

Alfred Bernhard Nobel is famous for inventing dynamite. Aware of the dangers of liquid nitroglycerine (an explosive), Nobel devised a method of solidifying the substance. He patented what he called "dynamite" in 1867. Besides explosives, Nobel made several chemical inventions and held 355 patents in various countries. He left a huge part of his wealth to establish the Nobel Prize, reflecting his keen interest in the sciences, literature and world peace.

Nobel invented dynamite in 1866

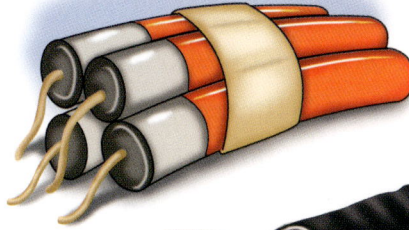

October 21, 1833: Born in Stockholm, Sweden

1863: Receives patent for a detonator that used electrical shock, rather than heat, to cause explosion

1866: Invents dynamite

1867: Granted patent for dynamite

1875: Invents blasting gelatine

1887: Obtains patent for a smokeless blasting powder, "ballistite"

November 27, 1895: Signs his final will at the Swedish-Norwegian club in Paris, leaving his wealth to constitute the Nobel Prize

December 10, 1896: Dies in San Remo, Italy

Alfred Nobel

235 Gottlieb Wilhelm Daimler
[1834 - 1900]

Daimler was one of the pioneers of the automotive industry. Attempting to improve the Otto cycle engine, Daimler and his friend Wilhelm Maybach came up with an improved version of the engine. It was lightweight, fast and more efficient. Later, the twosome created what is believed to be the world's first motorcycle, by attaching the engine to a bicycle! They also developed the first four-wheeled motor car by adapting an engine to a horse-carriage. It is said that Daimler – a person who revolutionised the car industry – did not like to drive!

The first motorcycle was a bicycle fitted with an engine!

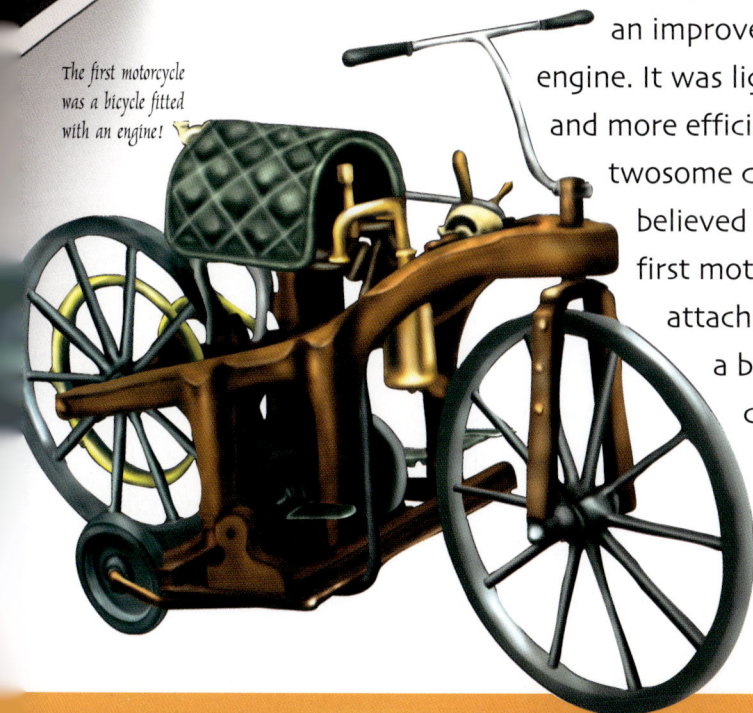

March 17, 1834: Born in Schorndorf, Wurttemberg, Germany

1872: Works as technical director at Nikolaus Otto's company

1882: Starts his own company with Wilhelm Maybach

1885: Patents the Daimler engine and invents the motorcycle

1886: Creates the first four-wheeled motor car

1890: Establishes the Daimler Company in Cannstatt

1899: Designs the first Mercedes car, named after his partner Emil Jellinek's daughter

March 6, 1900: Dies in Cannstatt, near Stuttgart

100 GREAT
Inventors

236 Lewis Edson Waterman
[1837 - 1901]

1837: Born in Decatur, Otsego County, New York

1899: Opens a pen factory at Montreal

1901: Dies, leaving the business to his nephew, Frank D. Waterman

Waterman was an insurance agent who invented the capillary feed in fountain pens. In 1883, he had bought a new fountain pen on the occasion of the signing of a big contract. However, just as the client was about to sign, the ink leaked on to the document! Waterman lost the contract to his competitor. Unhappy with the turn of events, he began making his own fountain pens. He used the capillary principle, by which the ink flow was controlled and made steady. He called his pen "the Regular" and patented it in 1884.

237 John Dunlop
[1840 - 1921]

February 5, 1840: Born in Dreghorn, North Ayrshire, Scotland

1867: Moves to Belfast, Ireland

1888: Patents the "pneumatic" tyre

October 24, 1921: Dies in Dublin, Ireland

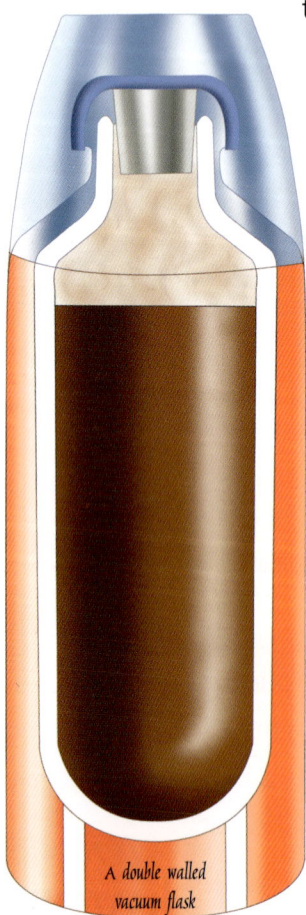

Scottish veterinarian John Boyd Dunlop developed the famous pneumatic (air-filled) tyre quite by accident. One day, while watching his son ride a tricycle, Dunlop noticed the boy's discomfort whenever he rode over stones. He realised that this was because of the tyres. So he wrapped the wheels in thin rubber sheets and glued them together. He then inflated them for a cushioning effect, thus making the first pneumatic tyre. Ten years later, his tyre had almost wiped out the solid tyres.

238 James Dewar
[1842 - 1923]

A double walled vacuum flask

September 20, 1842: Born in Kincardine-on-Forth, Scotland

1889: Co-invents cordite, an explosive used extensively in World War I

1892: Invents the vacuum flask

1899: Succeeds in liquefying hydrogen

1904: Receives knighthood

1921: Measures solar radiation using instruments cooled with liquid oxygen

March 27, 1923: Dies in London

He was a British chemist and inventor, best known for creating the thermos flask. While studying gasses at low temperature, Sir Dewar built a double-walled vacuum flask made of glass. Later, he realised that using metal would make it stronger. However, the surface of the metal absorbed the gas, making the vacuum ineffective. In 1905, he found that placing a piece of charcoal into the flask and cooling it, solved the problem. He also painted the inside of the flask with silver to reduce radiation.

239 Karl Friedrich Benz
[1844 - 1929]

He is considered to be one of the inventors of the gasoline-powered motor car. In 1885, Karl Benz built his first three-wheeler with a four-stroke engine. However, it drew little public interest initially. So, his wife Bertha Benz embarked on a secret trip from Mannheim to Pforzheim – the first long-distance trip in motor-car history! When news about Bertha's adventurous journey spread, demand for the car started pouring in.

Inflated tyres are extensively used today

November 25, 1844: Born in Karlsruhe, Baden, Germany

1872: Marries Bertha Ringer

1879: Invents a two-stroke engine

1883: Establishes the Benz & Co. company with Max Rose and Friedrich Wilhelm Esslinger, in Mannheim

1886: Introduces the "Benz Patent Motor Car"

1903: Resigns from the company

1926: Benz & Co. merges with Daimler-Motoren-Gesellschaft (DMG)

April 4, 1929: Dies in Ladenburg, near Mannheim, Germany

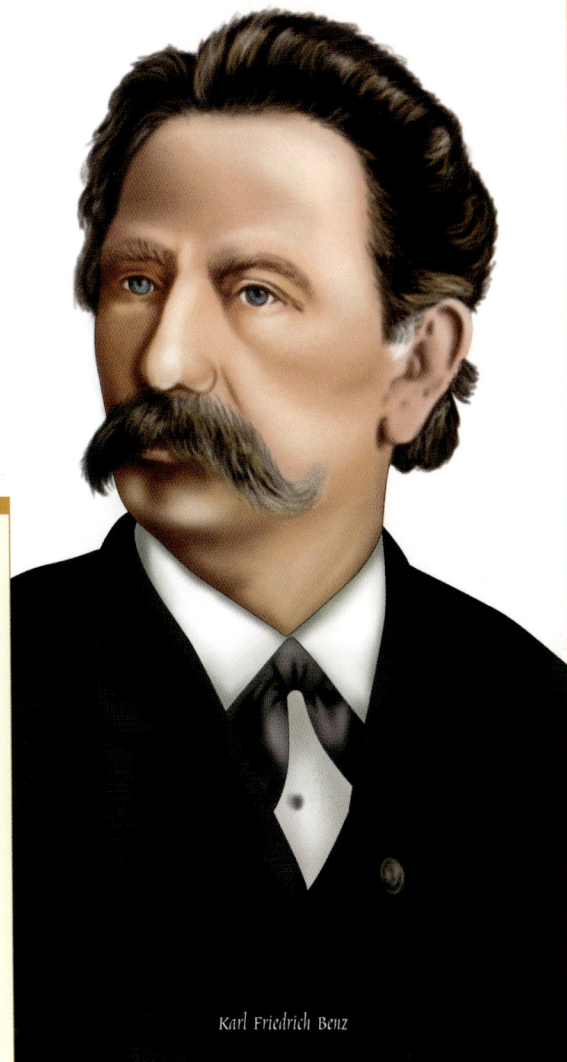

Karl Friedrich Benz

240 George Westinghouse
[1846 - 1914]

One of the most famous American inventors of the 19th century, Westinghouse made invaluable contributions to the railway industry. His inventions included a rotary steam engine and a switch that enabled a train to pass over intersecting rails at junctions. However, he is best remembered for developing the first successful brake system that used compressed air. This system proved more effective than the existing manual brake in preventing accidents.

George Westinghouse

October 6, 1846: Born in Central Bridge, New York, U.S.

1865: Receives patent for the rotary steam engine

1868: Invents the air brake system; obtains patent in 1869

March 12, 1914: Dies in New York City

100 GREAT
Inventors

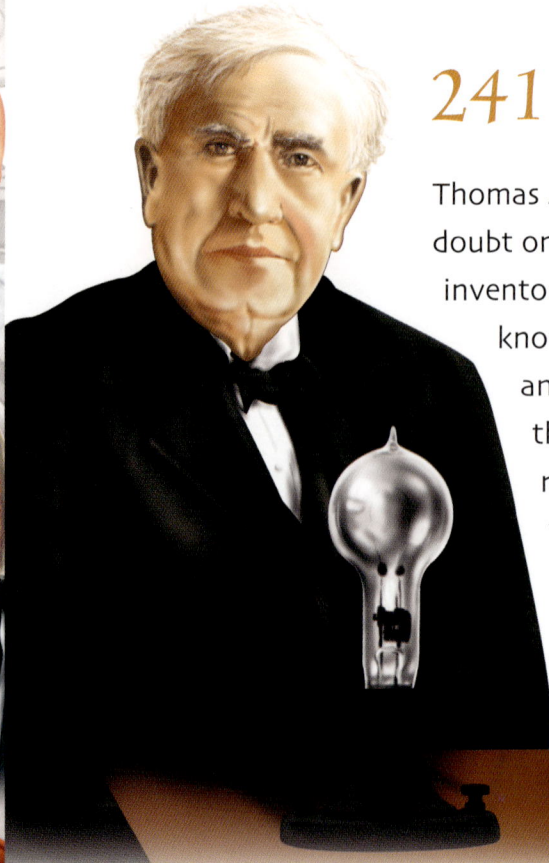

241 Thomas Alva Edison
[1847 - 1931]

Thomas Alva Edison is without doubt one of the greatest inventors the world has ever known. Edison's genius as an inventor is clear from the fact that he held a record 1,093 patents, of which almost 400 were for the electric light! Among his most famous inventions were the carbon-button transmitter (1877), the phonograph (1877), the incandescent light bulb (1879) and the motion-picture camera (1891). Edison also established the first-ever industrial-research laboratory.

Thomas Alva Edison

February 11, 1847: Born in Milan, Ohio, U.S.

1862-68: Works as a telegrapher

1868: Patents the electrical vote recorder

1871: Helps Sholes to make the first working model of the typewriter

1877: Invents the carbon-button transmitter that is still used in telephones and microphones

1914: Invents the Telescribe, thus making it possible to record both sides of a telephone conversation for the first time

October 18, 1931: Dies in New Jersey, U.S.

242 Alexander Graham Bell
[1847 - 1922]

By inventing the telephone, Bell revolutionised communication as we see it today. His invention gave the words "a small world" a whole new meaning. Bell had been toying with the idea of transmitting voice from a very young age. While working on improving the telegraph, he came up with the idea of a telephone. He started to work tirelessly with his assistant Thomas Watson. Finally, on March 10, 1876, Bell transmitted the first complete sentence. He also invented the photophone and the graphophone.

March 3, 1847: Born in Edinburgh, Scotland

1871: Moves to the United States

1872: Establishes a school for training teachers of the deaf, in Boston, Massachusetts

1882: Becomes a U.S. citizen

1876: Invents and patents the telephone

1877: Co-founds the Bell Telephone Company

August 2, 1922: Dies in Beinn Bhreagh, Cape Breton Island, Nova Scotia, Canada

243 Walter Hunt
[1796 - 1859]

Though pins had been in use years before Hunt's safety pin, they did not have a protective clasp. Hunt's safety pin not only had a clasp, but also a spring that held the two ends together. Apparently, Hunt was twisting a piece of wire and trying to think of a way to settle a $15 debt, when he accidentally invented the safety pin. Upon realising that he had created something of great use, Hunt patented what he called the "dress pin". However, he sold the rights for a paltry sum of $400 to pay off his debt.

244 Karl Braun
[1850 - 1918]

Karl Ferdinand Braun was a German inventor who won the 1909 Nobel Prize in Physics for his contributions to wireless telegraphy. However, he is best known as the inventor of the cathode-ray tube, or "Braun tube". Braun developed his idea from the premise that when two electrodes are subjected to high voltage, the electrons from the cathode (negative electrode) travel to the anode (positive electrode). He built what he called the "cathode-ray indicator tube", which is an integral part of the modern television.

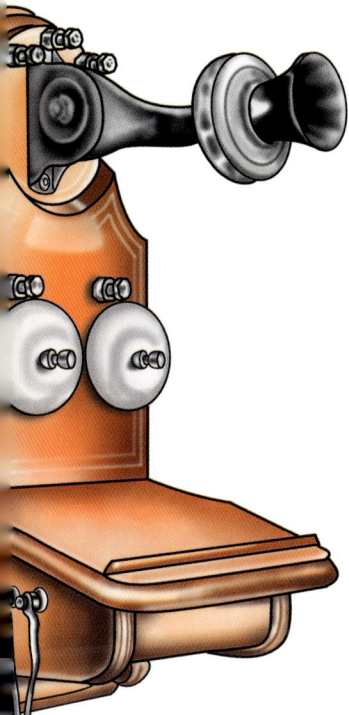

June 6, 1850: Born in Fulda, Hesse-Kassel (now in Germany)

1897: Invents the cathode-ray tube, but does not patent his invention

1898: Starts work on improving wireless telegraphy

1909: Shares the Nobel Prize in Physics with Guglielmo Marconi

April 20, 1918: Dies in Brooklyn, New York

Karl Braun

An early wall-hung telephone

The safety pin was first created by Walter Hunt

July 29, 1796: Born in Martinsburg, New York

c. 1834: Invents the modern sewing machine before Elias Howe, but does not patent it, fearing it would cause unemployment

April 10, 1849: Patents the safety pin

June 8, 1859: Dies

245 John Milne
[1850 - 1913]

Widely accepted as the father of seismology, John Milne invented the seismograph, an instrument used to study earthquakes. The word comes from the Greek words *seismos* - meaning earthquake - and *metero* - meaning measure. A geologist and mining engineer, Milne became interested in the study of earthquakes while in Japan. He set up the world's first seismological society and conducted extensive research on Japanese earthquakes.

December 30, 1850: Born in Liverpool, England

1880: Invents the horizontal pendulum seismograph; establishes the Seismological Society of Japan with colleagues Sir James Alfred Ewing and Thomas Gray

February 17, 1895: A fire destroys his home, observatory and library

1895: Returns to England; settles on the Isle of Wight and promotes establishment of earthquake observatories across the world

July 30, 1913: Dies in Shide, Isle of Wight

100 GREAT
Inventors

246 Emil Berliner
[1851 - 1929]

Emil (also spelt Emile) Berliner improved Bell's telephone with a "loose-contact" transmitter. It was a type of microphone that increased the volume of the transmitted voice. Even more significantly, Emil invented the disc record gramophone. Unlike Edison's cylinder gramophone, Berliner's used a flat disc. This enabled inexpensive, mass production of gramophones. Berliner also experimented with an early version of the helicopter, which was demonstrated to the US Army in 1922.

Emil Berliner

May 20, 1851: Born in Hannover, Hanover, Germany
1870: Moves to the United States
1876: Invents the "loose-contact" transmitter
1887: Patents his gramophone
1893: Forms the United States Gramophone Company of Washington, D.C.
1895: Establishes the Berliner Gramophone Company of Philadelphia
1898: Opens the Berliner Gramophone Company of London
August 3, 1929: Dies in Washington D.C., U.S.

247 George Eastman
[1854 - 1932]

An American inventor, George Eastman developed the dry roll film and the hand-held camera. After working briefly for a bank, Eastman turned his attention to making photographic film rolls. Having made the first film roll, Eastman invented a small hand-held camera he named Kodak. The success of his inventions spurred him on to establish the Eastman Kodak Company, the first of its kind to mass-produce photography equipment.

July 12, 1854: Born in Waterville, New York
1880: Patents a dry-plate formula and a machine for making it
1885: Introduces the first transparent photographic film
1888: Introduces the Kodak camera
1889: Invents the first transparent roll film, leading to Edison's invention of the motion-picture camera
March 14, 1932: Dies in Rochester, New York

248 King Camp Gillette
[1855 - 1932]

Gillette played an important role in making razors popular

King Camp Gillette is incorrectly known as the inventor of the safety razor. However, his disposable steel blade certainly played a vital role in the razor's popularity. Gillette was forced to work at a young age, after his family lost everything in the Great Chicago Fire of 1871. As a travelling salesman, Gillette came up with an idea of an inexpensive safety razor blade that could be replaced easily. He started the American Safety Razor Company, later re-named Gillette Safety Razor Company.

January 5, 1855: Born in Wisconsin, U.S.
September 28, 1901: Establishes the American Safety Razor company
1903: First razors are produced; sells 51 razors and 168 blades
1904: Sells some 90,884 razors and 123,648 blades
July 9, 1932: Dies in Los Angeles, California, U.S.

249 Nikola Tesla
[1856 - 1943]

July 9/10, 1856: Born in Smiljan, Croatia

1884: Arrives in New York and briefly works under Thomas Alva Edison

1891: Invents the Tesla coil

1899-1900: Proves that earth can be used as a conductor

January 7, 1943: Dies in New York City

Serbian by birth, Tesla arrived in the United States in 1884. The very next year, he sold the patent rights to his system of alternating-current dynamos and transformers to George Westinghouse. Tesla's electric transformers revolutionised the power industry by helping the production of alternating current. Westinghouse used the system to light the World's Columbian Exposition at Chicago in 1893. As a result, Tesla won the contract to install a power station at Niagara Falls. However, his biggest contribution was in the form of the induction coil (named Tesla coil in his honour), which continues to be used in radios and televisions.

250 Rudolf Diesel
[1858 - 1913]

Famous for developing a pressure-ignited heat engine named after him, Diesel's invention was inspired by a cigarette lighter. He noted with fascination that the piston in a lighter compressed the air in a glass tube, causing the tinder in it to glow. He immediately began his 13-year-long labour to create and perfect an economical – yet highly efficient – alternative to the steam engine. His engine soon became popular and was used extensively in ships, electric power plants, oil drills and, eventually, automobiles.

Rudolf Diesel

George Eastman was a pioneer in the photography industry. He invented the first hand-held camera.

March 18, 1858: Born in Paris, France

1898: Patents the diesel engine

September 29, 1913: Dies by drowning in the English Channel

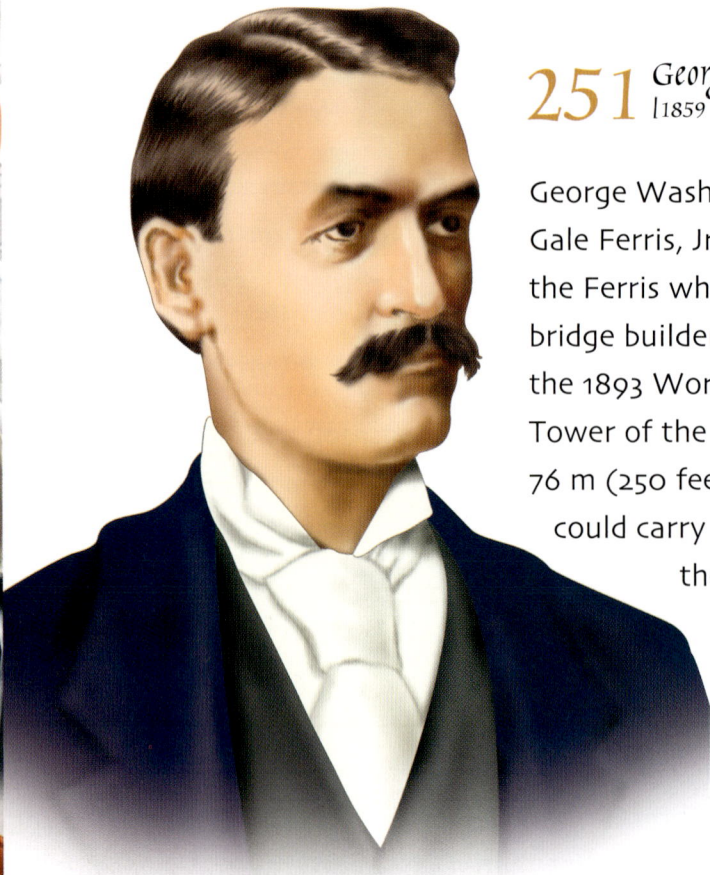

251 George Ferris
[1859 - 1896]

George Washington Gale Ferris, Jr., invented the Ferris wheel. A bridge builder by profession, Ferris built the wheel for the 1893 World's Columbian Fair, to rival the Eiffel Tower of the 1889 Paris World's Fair. Ferris' wheel was 76 m (250 feet) in diameter and had 36 cars. Each car could carry around 40 passengers. A huge success then, the Ferris wheel continues to be a major part of the American carnivals.

George Ferris

252 Schuyler Wheeler
[1860 - 1923]

1882: Develops the electric fan

Dr. Schuyler Skaats Wheeler invented the electric fan. The story goes that the idea occurred to him while he watched a ferry on the Hudson River. He observed that the propeller of the ferry created waves on the water. Realising that the same mechanism can produce cool air, Wheeler created the first electric fan using two metal blades. His model consisted of a propeller attached to a shaft that was operated by an electric motor.

Schuyler Wheeler's electric fan had only two blades

253 Jesse Wilford Reno
[1861 - unknown]

Inventor of the escalator, Jesse Reno thought of the idea at the young age of 16. While in Georgia, Reno first gave shape to his idea and obtained a patent for his "endless conveyor". Reno first installed his moving stairway as an amusement ride in Coney Island, Brooklyn. The popularity of the ride brought Reno's invention into the limelight and soon he was swamped by orders from all over the world. Reno's escalator had stationary handrails that were later replaced with moving handrails.

1861: Born in Fort Leavenworth, Kansas, U.S.

1891: Invents the escalator

March 15, 1892: Patents his invention

1895: Installs the escalator in Coney Island

1902: Establishes the Reno Electric Stairways and Conveyors Limited in London

1911: Sells his patent rights to Otis Elevator Company

254 Henry Ford
[1863 - 1947]

His biggest contribution to the automotive industry was the assembly-line production method. In this system, the workers stood in one place and added a part to each vehicle as it moved past them. This made the manufacturing and assembling process much easier and also increased the number of cars produced. Not only did it mark the beginning of a revolution in the car industry, it also made Ford's company a giant in its field.

The Model-T was the first car to be made using the assembly line

July 30, 1863: Born in Wayne County, Michigan, U.S.

1896: Constructs a four-wheeled car

1903: Establishes the Ford Motor Company

1908: Introduces the famous Model T car

1913: Introduces the assembly-line production method

April 7, 1947: Dies in Dearborn, Michigan, U.S.

255 Leo Baekeland
[1863 - 1944]

Baekeland's invention of bakelite, an inexpensive, nonflammable and versatile plastic, helped establish the plastic industry. His first invention was Velox, a photographic paper that could be developed under artificial light. He, however, sold the patent rights to George Eastman for a million dollars and set up a laboratory. Later, while attempting to make a synthetic alternative for shellac, he created bakelite. Today, bakelite is used in cars, electronics and even jewellery.

Leo Baekeland

November 14, 1863: Born in Ghent, Belgium

1889: Arrives in U.S.

1893: Invents Velox

1899: Sells his patent rights to George Eastman

1909: Invents bakelite

1910: Establishes the Bakelite Corporation

February 23, 1944: Dies in Beacon, New York

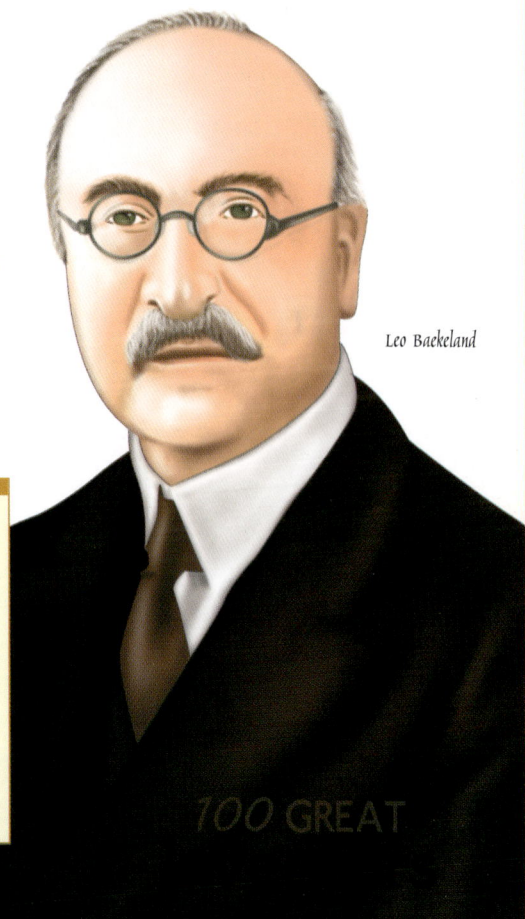

256 Wilbur and Orville Wright
[1867 - 1912] [1871 - 1948]

April 16, 1867: Wilbur is born in Millville, Indianapolis, U.S

August 19, 1871: Orville is born in Dayton, Ohio, U.S.

1889: Open a printing business

1892: Start their bicycle business

December 17, 1903: Orville flies the first Wright flyer at Kitty Hawk, North Carolina; lasts 12 seconds over a distance of 36.6 m (120 feet). Wilbur's flight lasts for 59 seconds and covers 260 m (852 feet)

1906: Obtain patent for their flyer

May 1908: The brothers carry a passenger on the plane for the first time

August 1908: The first public exhibition flight takes place at Le Mans in France

1910: Make their first and only flight together

May 30, 1912: Wilbur dies of typhoid fever in Dayton, Ohio

January 30, 1948: Orville dies in Dayton

December 17, 1903, is the most memorable day in the history of aviation. This was the day when Wilbur Wright and his brother Orville accomplished the first-ever powered and controlled aeroplane flight. Born into a humble family, the Wright brothers worked towards their dream by making bicycles. Inspired by the German glider Otto Lilienthal, the brothers constructed the Wright flyer. Among other ground-breaking features, the plane had the first lightweight engine and movable wing tips that helped control it.

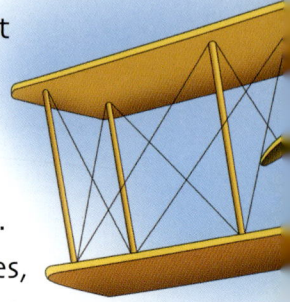

257 Valdemar Poulsen
[1869 - 1942]

November 23, 1869: Born in Copenhagen, Denmark

1898: Patents the telegraphone

1903: Patents the Poulsen arc transmitter

July 1942: Dies in Copenhagen

Poulsen took to engineering early on in his life. Working at the technical department at the Copenhagen Telephone Company, he invented the telegraphone, a forerunner of the modern tape recorder. Using his "telegrafoon", Poulsen demonstrated that it was possible to record and play back voices on a magnetised steel wire. He also invented the Poulsen arc transmitter for producing continuous radio waves, contributing to the development of radio broadcasting.

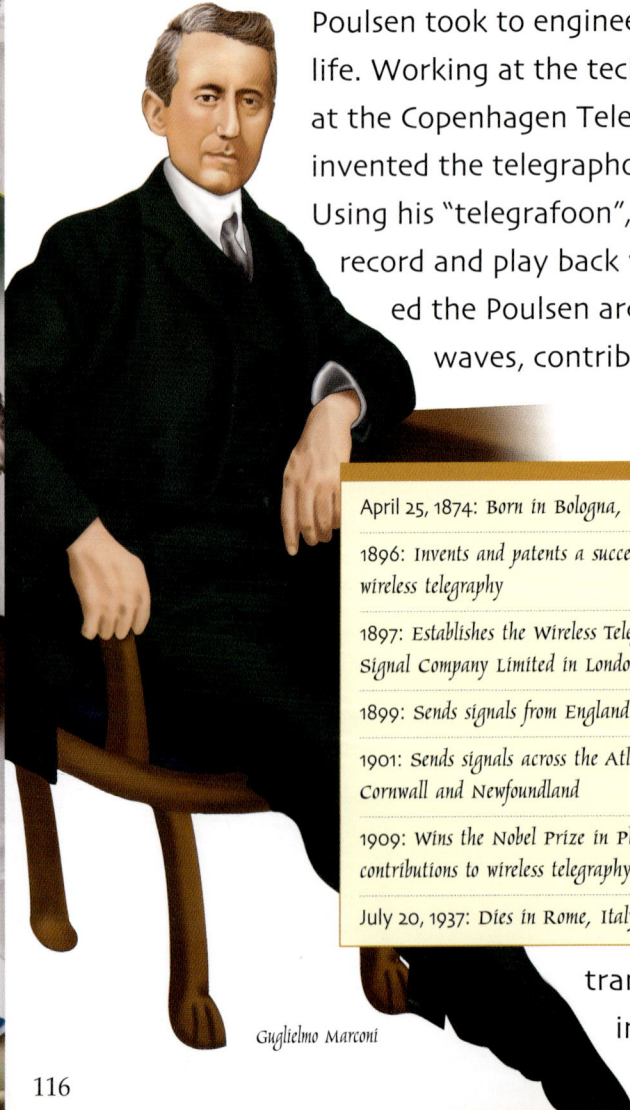

258 Guglielmo Marconi
[1874 - 1937]

April 25, 1874: Born in Bologna, Italy

1896: Invents and patents a successful system of wireless telegraphy

1897: Establishes the Wireless Telegraphy & Signal Company Limited in London

1899: Sends signals from England to France

1901: Sends signals across the Atlantic, between Cornwall and Newfoundland

1909: Wins the Nobel Prize in Physics for his contributions to wireless telegraphy

July 20, 1937: Dies in Rome, Italy

At the age of 21, Marconi invented the first practical system of wireless telegraphy. He continued to improve his device and succeeded in sending signals across the English Channel to France. In 1901, he proved that the wireless waves are not affected by the Earth's curvature. He did this by transmitting signals across the Atlantic Ocean covering a distance of about 3,380 km (2,100 miles).

Guglielmo Marconi

The Wright brothers fly the first ever controllable powered aeroplane in 1903

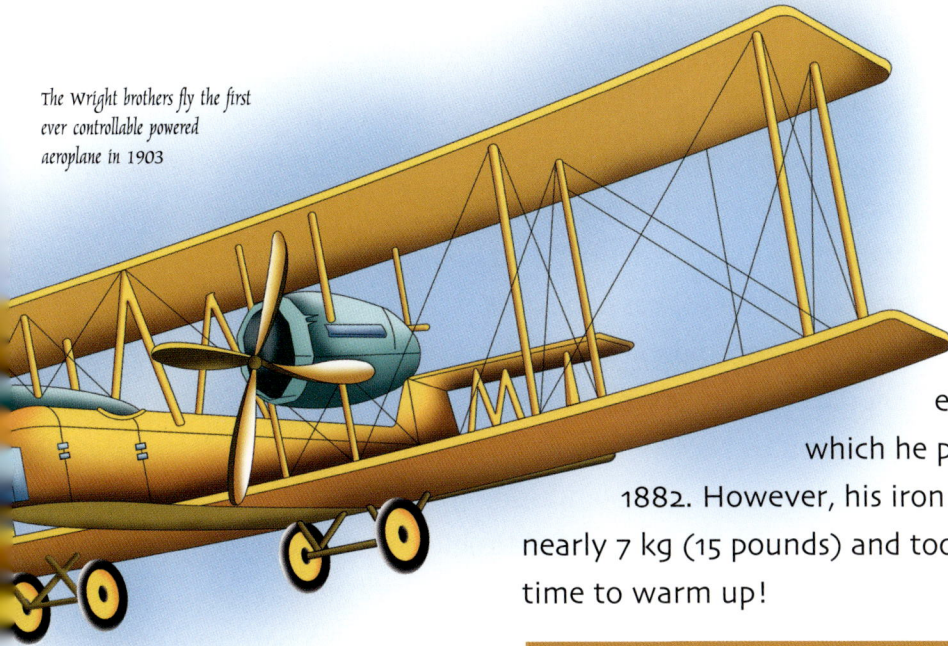

259 Henry W Seeley
[unknown]

Not much is known about this American inventor, except that his contribution to our daily lives has been enduring and much valued. Seeley invented the electric iron, which he patented in 1882. However, his iron weighed nearly 7 kg (15 pounds) and took a long time to warm up!

June 6, 1882: Invents and patents his "electric flatiron"

A modern version of Seeley's "electric flatiron"

260 Willis Carrier
[1876 - 1950]

Rightfully called the "father of cool", Willis Haviland Carrier's name is inseparably connected with air conditioners. Even as a youngster, Carrier exhibited the genius that was to later make him a household name. The very fact that Carrier's air conditioner was inspired by fog is a proof of his brilliant mind. One foggy evening in Pittsburgh, Carrier was waiting for his train when he came up with the idea of creating artificial fog with air and a spray of water. This led to the first-ever spray-type air conditioner that could control humidity and temperature. Carrier named his invention an "apparatus for treating air".

Willis Carrier

November 26, 1876: Born in Angola, New York

1902: Installs his first air conditioner in a printing press in Brooklyn

1906: Develops the "apparatus for treating air", which is much more efficient than the first version

1915: The Carrier Engineering Corporation is established

October 7, 1950: Dies in New York City

100 GREAT
Inventors

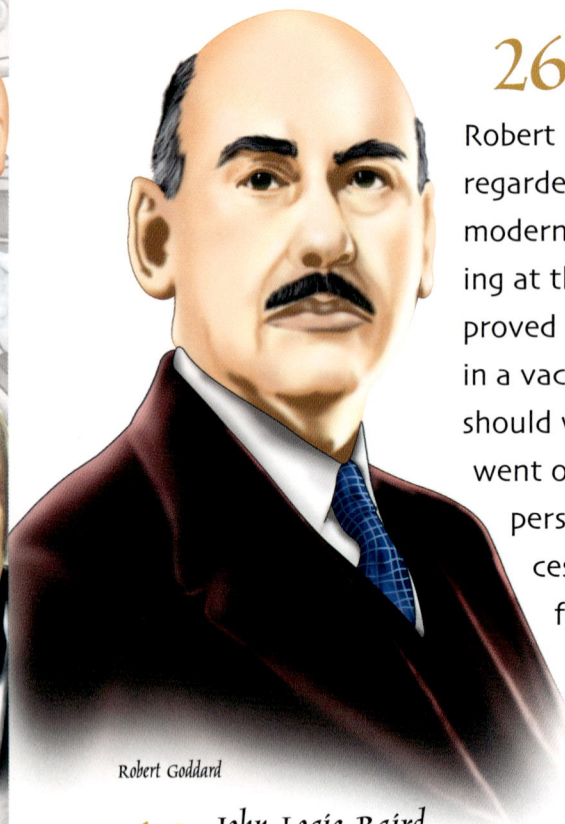

261 Robert Goddard
[1882 - 1945]

Robert Hutchings Goddard is regarded as the father of modern rocketry. While working at the Clark University, he proved that a rocket can work in a vacuum (meaning that it should work in space). He went on to become the first person to develop and successfully launch a liquid-fuelled rocket engine. Apart from this, Goddard developed rocket-fuel pumps and self-cooling rocket engines. He also patented the automatic steering apparatus for rockets.

October 5, 1882: Born in Worcester, Massachusetts, U.S.

1914: Receives a patent for his liquid-fuelled rocket

1918: Develops the "bazooka"

1919: Publishes his famous book, A Method of Reaching Extreme Altitudes

March 16, 1926: Launches the world's first liquid-fuelled rocket from a farm in Auburn, Massachusetts

August 10, 1945: Dies in Baltimore, U.S.

Robert Goddard

262 John Logie Baird
[1888 - 1946]

John Logie Baird earlier tried his hand at selling medicated socks and also set up jam and soap factories in Trinidad. The mixed response forced him to wind up his business and return to Britain. Baird then created a crude version of the television. The apparatus consisted of a motor on a tea chest. A biscuit tin held the projection lamp, while round pieces of cardboard served as scanning discs!

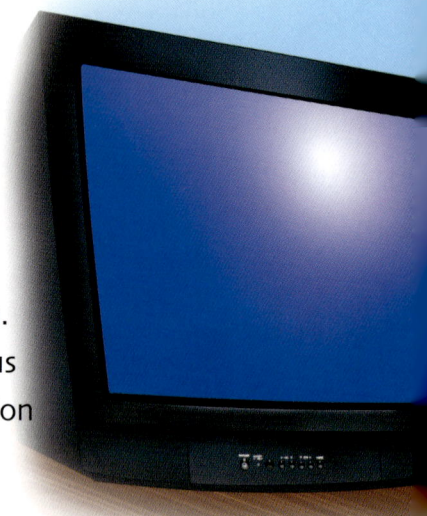

Igor Sikorsky

263 Igor Sikorsky
[1889 - 1972]

Igor Sikorsky designed the first multi-motor aeroplane as well as the modern helicopter. Forced to leave Russia after the 1917 Revolution, Sikorsky first moved to France and eventually to the United States. At Long Island, New York, he established the Sikorsky Aero Engineering Corporation. Afterwards, he designed a twin-engine amphibian aircraft and a successful model of the helicopter. Sikorsky's single-rotor design continues to be used in helicopters.

May 25, 1889: Born in Kiev, Russia

1913: Builds the first four-engine aeroplane with an enclosed cabin

1919: Goes to the U.S.

1923: Establishes his company

1931: Designs the two-engine amphibian aircraft

1939: Designs the modern helicopter

October 26, 1972: Dies in Connecticut, U.S.

264 Sir Robert Alexander Watson-Watt
[1892 - 1973]

He started his career as a meteorologist, using his knowledge of radio to locate thunderstorms. During this period he realised the need for a method to locate aircraft. In 1919, he patented a device that used short-wave radio waves to locate aeroplanes. He continued to improve this device and soon came up with the radar concept – sending out radio waves to aeroplanes, receiving their reflections and using the intervening time to calculate the distance. His radar system played an important role in the defeat of Germany during World War II.

April 13, 1892: Born in Brechin, Angus, Scotland

1919: Patents his radio-location device

1940: His radars help Britain counter German air raids

1942: Receives knighthood

December 5, 1973: Dies in Inverness, Inverness-shire, Scotland

John Logie Baird

Radar is used to locate aircrafts

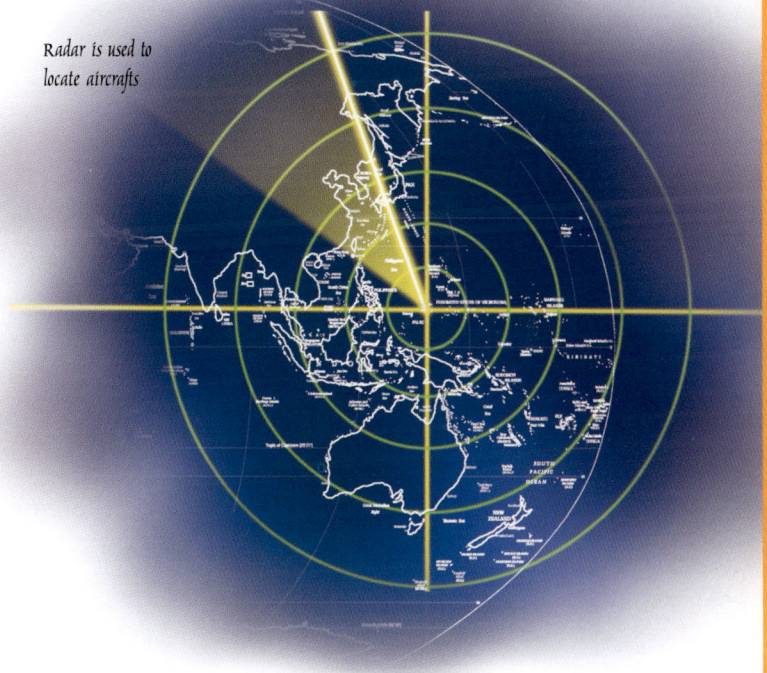

August 13, 1888: Born in Helensburgh, Dunbarton, Scotland

1924: Becomes the first to transmit a moving image

1926: Demonstrates his television to scientists from the Royal Institution, London

1927: Establishes the Baird Television Development Company

1928: Transmits images across the Atlantic to New York

1931: Achieves the first live transmission of the Epsom Derby

June 14, 1946: Dies in Sussex, England

265 John Larson
[c. 1892 - c. 1983]

John Larson invented the polygraph, popularly called the lie-detector test. A police officer, Larson was fascinated by the possibility of being able to determine whether a person was telling the truth or not. Although the concept of a lie detector was not new, Larson built a unique machine that could record changes in blood pressure, pulse and respiration. His system was adopted by the police in 1924. Later, his student Leonarde Keeler replaced it with a more effective version.

c.1892: Born in the United States

1921: Develops the polygraph test

c.1983: Dies

100 GREAT
Inventors

266 Percy Spencer
[1849 - 1970]

Percy Lebaron Spencer invented the microwave oven while working for Raytheon, a company that produced radars for the American defence forces. One day as he stood near a magnetron, Spencer observed that the chocolate bar in his pocket melted. This aroused his curiosity. He then placed some popcorn in front of the magnetron and watched in wonder as the kernels popped. This simple experiment eventually led him to invent the microwave oven.

Percy Spencer

July 19, 1849: *Born in Howland, Maine, U.S.*
1945: *Invents the microwave oven*
September 8, 1970: *Dies*

267 Wallace Hume Carothers
[1896 - 1937]

After receiving his PhD in chemistry from the University of Illinois, Carothers began research on polymers at Harvard University. When DuPont opened a research laboratory for the development of artificial material, Carothers was chosen to lead its research team. Extensive research on the compounds of high molecular weight led to the creation of the first synthetic polymer fibre, later named "nylon" and a synthetic rubber, neoprene.

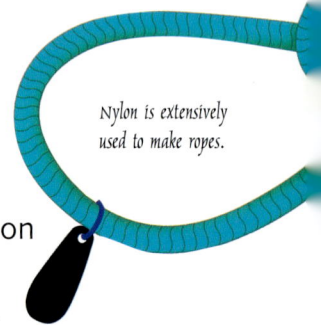

Nylon is extensively used to make ropes.

268 Mary Anderson
[unknown]

Until 1903, car drivers had their own way of coping with the rainwater that fell on the windshields. Usually the annoyed driver would stop the car and manually wipe the windshield. Mary Anderson was to change all that by inventing the windshield wiper. The idea occurred to her when she saw drivers in New York City constantly stopping their cars to remove snow and moisture from their windshields. Anderson's wiper consisted of a lever that could be operated from inside the car. When switched on, the lever activated an arm equipped with a rubber blade.

1903: *Thinks of the idea for the windshield wiper*
1905: *Obtains patent*
1913: *Mechanical windshield wipers become a regular feature of cars*

269 Ernest Lawrence
[1901 - 1958]

Ernest Orlando Lawrence invented the cyclotron, a device that can cause nuclear particles to move at very high speed without the use of high voltages. These fast-moving particles can be used to strike atoms and split them. Lawrence's first model of the cyclotron was made of wire and sealing wax. Its successful demonstration not only made Lawrence famous, but also contributed to the making of the atom bomb.

August 8, 1901: Born in Canton, South Dakota, U.S.

1929: Develops the cyclotron

1939: Receives the Nobel Prize in Physics

1957: Receives the Enrico Fermi Award

August 27, 1958: Dies in Palo Alto, California

Ernest Lawrence

April 27, 1896: Born in Burlington, Iowa, U.S.

1928: Joins DuPont and starts research on artificial materials

April 1930: His assistant, Arnold M. Collins, isolates neoprene

1934: Develops nylon

April 29, 1937: Takes his own life

1939: Mass production of nylon begins

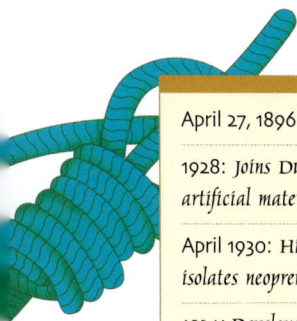

William Lear set up a company to produce small private planes

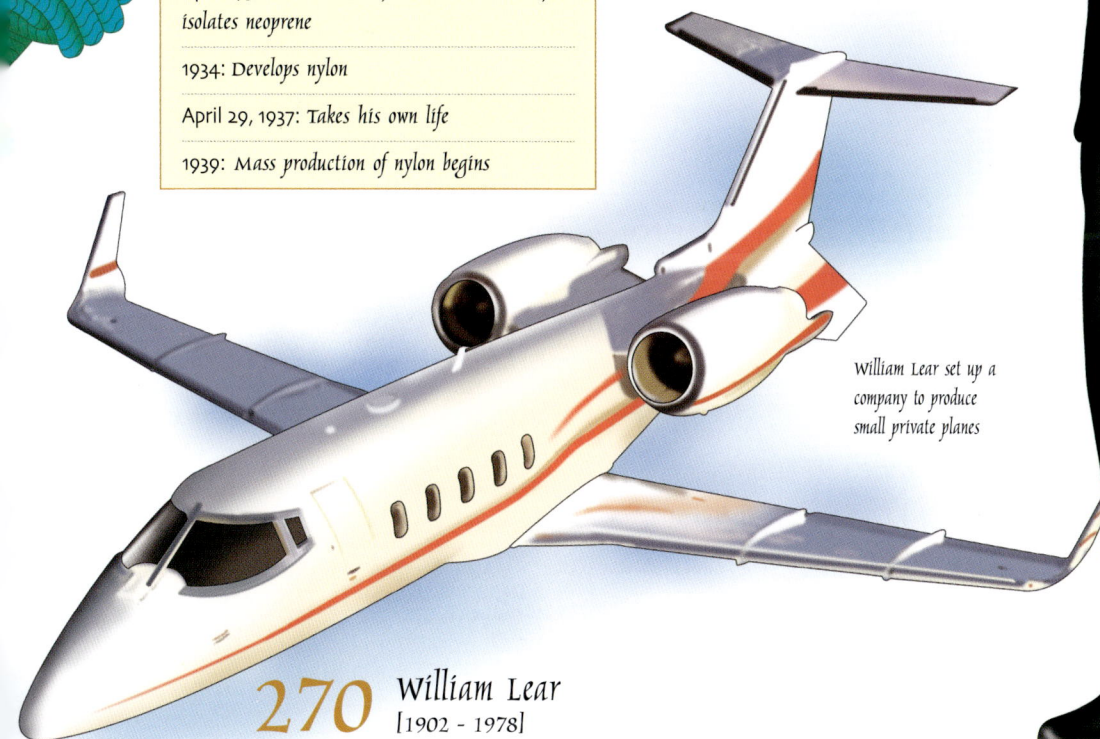

270 William Lear
[1902 - 1978]

An American inventor of great repute, William Lear's name is usually associated with the jet plane named after him. His most significant invention, though, was the car radio. Having developed the car radio, Lear sold it to Galvin Manufacturing Company, to be marketed under the brand name Motorola. In 1963, he established Lear Jet Incorporated to produce small private aircraft, which soon became popular with big companies. The following year, he invented the eight-track stereo that laid the foundations for the car-stereo industry.

June 26, 1902: Born in Hannibal, Missouri, U.S.

1930: Designs the car radio

1964: Develops the eight-track car stereo

May 14, 1978: Dies in Reno, Nevada, U.S.

100 GREAT
Inventors

271 Chester Carlson
[1906 - 1968]

Chester Floyd Carlson was an American physicist and the inventor of xerography (photocopy). An employee at the patent department, Carlson was required to make copies of patent drawings and other documents. While most people then depended on chemical solutions to produce copies, Carlson investigated ways to obtain "dry copies". In 1938, he succeeded in producing copies using a photoconduction process.

Chester Carlson

February 8, 1906: Born in Seattle, Washington, U.S.
1938: Develops the photocopying process
1940: Obtains patent for his invention
1944: Signs an agreement with Battelle Development Corporation for further research on the process
1947: Sells his rights to the Haloid Company (later renamed Xerox Corporation)
1958: Xerox launches its first office copier
September 19, 1968: Dies in New York City

272 Frank Whittle
[1907 - 1996]

While serving as a pilot with the Royal Air Force (RAF), Whittle realised the potential of developing a plane that could fly at high speed and altitude. He started working on an engine that used a "jet" of air for movement. Although the air ministry rejected the idea in the beginning, Whittle patented it and established Power Jets Limited to continue his research. After several modifications, the jet engine was finally ready to take flight on May 15, 1941.

June 1, 1907: Born in Coventry, Warwickshire, England
1928: Qualifies as a pilot in the RAF
1930: Patents his jet engine
1936: Establishes Power Jets Limited
1948: Retires from the RAF as air commodore
1948: Attains knighthood; moves to the United States
1976: Becomes a research professor at the U.S. Naval Academy, Maryland
1986: Awarded the Order of Merit
August 9, 1996: Dies in Baltimore, Maryland, U.S.

273 George de Mestral
[1907 - 1990]

Like many other inventions, velcro was invented accidentally. Returning from his walk one day, George de Mestral found cockleburs (weeds with hooks) stuck to his clothes. Fascinated, Mestral examined one of them under a microscope and found the tiny hooks that helped the cocklebur to attach itself to cloth or fur. After eight years of experiment, Mestral developed and perfected what he named "velcro".

June 19, 1907: Born near Lausanne, Switzerland
1948: Conceives the idea of velcro
1955: Obtains patent for his invention
February 8, 1990: Dies

274 John Bardeen
[1908 - 1991]

The transistor was co-invented by John Bardeen

American physicist and co-inventor of the transistor, John Bardeen is the only scientist to have won the Nobel Prize in Physics twice. After World War II, Bardeen joined Bell Telephone Laboratories Incorporated, where he carried out research on semi-conductors. His work eventually led to the invention of the transistor, for which he shared the 1956 Nobel Prize with William B. Shockley and Walter Brattain. He once again shared the Nobel Prize in 1972, with Leon Cooper and J. Robert Schrieffer, for his work on superconductivity.

Sir Frank Whittle

May 23, 1908: Born in Wisconsin, U.S.

1936: Receives his doctorate from Princeton University

1938-45: Works at the Naval Ordnance Laboratory, Washington, D.C.

1957: Develops the theory of superconductivity

1977: Receives the Presidential Medal of Freedom, the highest honour awarded to a U.S. civilian

January 30, 1991: Dies in Boston, Massachusetts

Willem Kolff

February 14, 1911: Born in Leiden, Holland

1945: His device saves the life of an old woman, who then lived for another seven years

1950: Goes to the U.S., where he conducts research on artificial hearts at the Cleveland Clinic Foundation

1957: An artificial heart is implanted in an animal for the first time

1982: Supervises artificial heart implant in a human patient

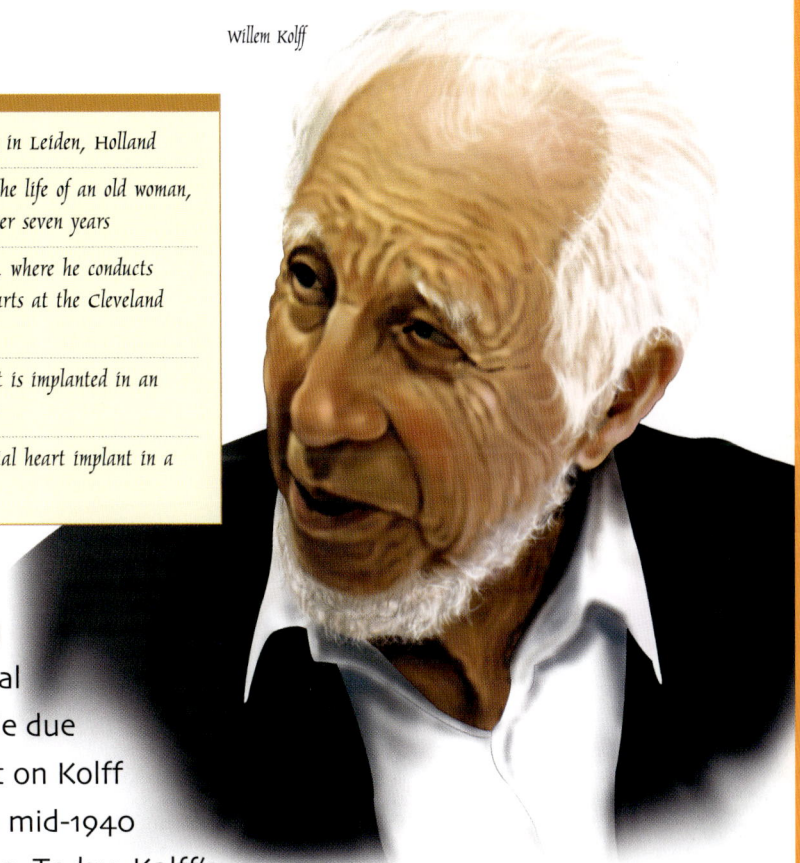

275 Willem Kolff
[1911 -]

Willem Kolff spent most of his childhood learning medicine from his father, Jacob Kolff. As a medical student, Willem witnessed a 22-year-old man die due to kidney failure. The incident had a deep effect on Kolff and he devoted himself to finding a solution. In mid-1940 he invented the artificial kidney dialysis machine. Today, Kolff's machine makes it possible for patients with kidney failure to live longer.

100 GREAT
Inventors

276 Luis Walter Alvarez
[1911 - 1988]

Luis Walter Alvarez's landing system helped planes land in bad weather

Dr. Luis Walter Alvarez held patents for more than 30 inventions and made ground-breaking discoveries in nuclear physics, but his most valuable contribution came during World War II, when he developed three vital radar systems: the microwave early-warning system; the Eagle high-altitude bombing system; and, most importantly, a landing system that assisted aircraft to land even in bad weather. The landing system is used even today on civilian aircraft.

June 13, 1911: Born in San Francisco, California

1944-45: Involved in the Manhattan Project for the development of the atomic bomb, at the Los Alamos Laboratory; develops a detonator for setting off the plutonium bomb

August 6, 1945: Witnesses the bombing of Hiroshima, Japan

1968: Awarded the Nobel Prize in Physics for developing the hydrogen bubble chamber and using it in the discovery of unknown subatomic particles like the Y-particle

1963: Assists the Warren Commission in its investigation into President John F. Kennedy's assassination

1980: Joins his son Walter Alvarez in publishing the theory that a meteor caused the extinction of dinosaurs on Earth

September 1, 1988: Dies of cancer in Berkeley, U.S.

277 Ruth Handler
[1916 - 2002]

Mattel, the toy company that manufactures Barbie, originally made picture frames. One of the founders, Elliot Handler, soon started to make doll-house furniture too. After his partner, Harold Matson, left the company, Elliot and his wife Ruth took over the reins. One day while watching her daughter, Barbara, play with dolls, it struck Ruth that little girls lived their dreams through dolls. This led to her creating "Barbie", named so after her daughter's nickname.

278 Al Gross
[1918 - 2000]

Regarded as the founding father of wireless communication, Al Gross invented the walkie-talkie. His interest in radio communication began when he was just nine years old, when during a boat trip on Lake Erie, he first listened to a wireless. Apart from the walkie-talkie, Gross also invented the telephone pager and made important contributions to the invention of cordless and cellular telephones.

Al Gross

279 Gordon Gould
[1920 - 2005]

Gordon Gould did not just invent the laser, he also coined the word. A great admirer of Thomas Alva Edison, he dreamt of being an inventor as a young boy and later graduated in physics. During World War II, he worked on the Manhattan Project. According to Gould himself, the idea of the laser was born one night in 1957. He defined his concept as Light Amplification by Stimulated Emission of Radiation, or LASER. However, he did not apply for a patent until 1959.

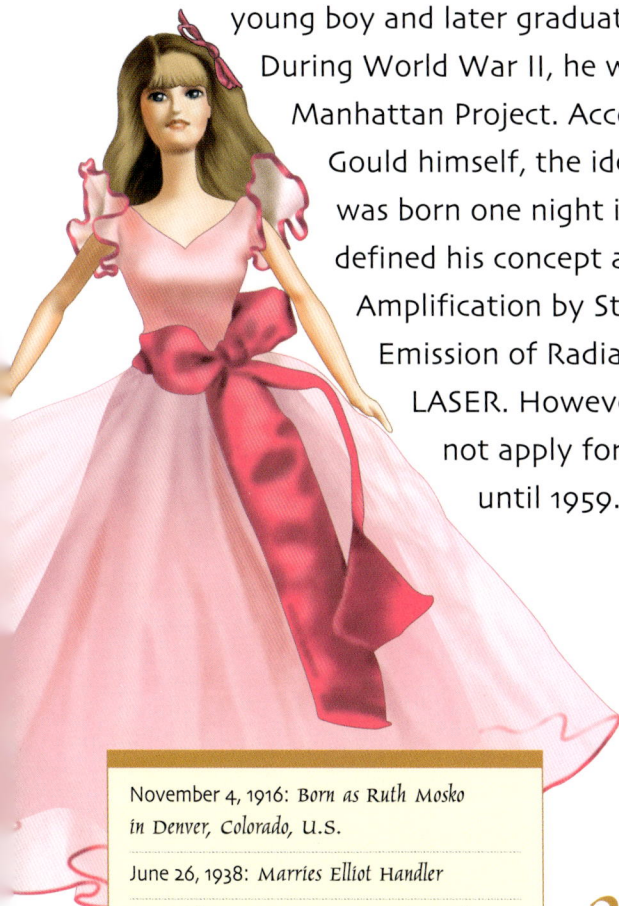

Gordon Gould

July 17, 1920: *Born in New York City*

1960: *Starts legal battle over the patenting of the laser*

1977: *Receives his first laser patent*

2005: *Dies*

Ruth Handler thought of creating the Barbie doll while watching her daughter play

November 4, 1916: *Born as Ruth Mosko in Denver, Colorado, U.S.*

June 26, 1938: *Marries Elliot Handler*

1945: *Elliot enters into a partnership with Harold Matson to establish Mattel Creations (later Mattel, Inc.)*

1959: *Introduces "Barbie" at a toy fair in New York City*

1961: *Introduces "Ken", named after her son*

1967: *Becomes the president of Mattel*

1975: *Resigns from Mattel Inc.*

April 27, 2002: *Dies in Los Angeles, California*

280 Charles P. Ginsburg
[1920 - 1992]

Known as the father of the video cassette recorder, Charles Paulson Ginsburg started his career as an engineer in a local radio station. As head of the research team at Ampex Corporation, Ginsburg developed the first videotape recorder (VTR). It marked a turning point in television broadcasting. The Ampex VRX-1000 (also Mark IV) saw the beginning of a multi-million-dollar industry. The VTR eventually led to the development of the video cassette recorder, or the VCR.

July 27, 1920: *Born in San Francisco, California*

1952: *Joins Ampex Corporation; starts working on developing the VTR*

1956: *CBS becomes the first television network to use the VTR technology*

1958: *Granted patent for his invention*

April 9, 1992: *Dies in Eugene, Oregon, U.S.*

1918: *Born in Toronto, Canada*

1934: *Receives his amateur radio licence at the age of 16*

1938: *Invents the walkie-talkie*

1949: *Develops the telephone pager*

December 21, 2000: *Dies in Sun City, Arizona, U.S.*

100 GREAT
Inventors

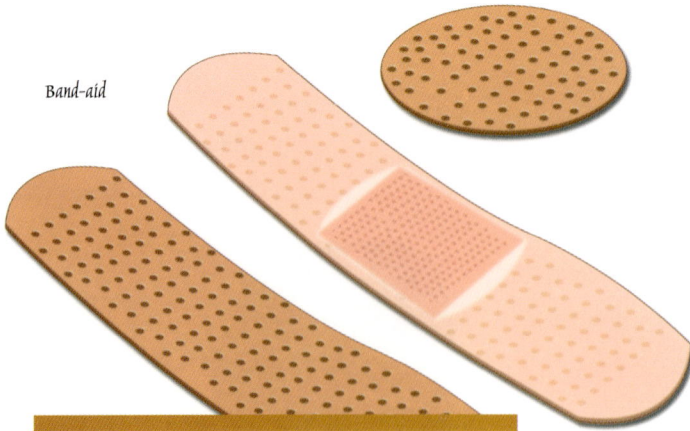

Band-aid

281 Earle Dickson
[1892 - 1961]

Earle Dickson invented the band-aid for his wife, who was always injuring herself while preparing food. Upon realising that the big bandages came off easily, he started to think of a better alternative. He attached square pieces of gauze to the centre of a surgical tape. He then placed crinoline to make the tape germ-free. Now, all that was required was to cut a piece of the tape to bandage the wound. Dickson presented the idea to his employers at Johnson & Johnson, who in turn sold it under the brand name Band-Aid.

October 10, 1892: Born

1917: Marries Josephine Francis Knight

1920: Invents band-aid

1921: Handmade band-aids are introduced to the public

1924: The first machine-made and sterilised band-aids are introduced

September 21, 1961: Dies

282 Jerome Lemelson
(1923 - 1997)

One of the most prolific American inventors, it is said that Lemelson received at least one patent every month, for 40 years! In all, he owned more than 500 patents. His inventions led to the development of automatic teller machines (ATM), cordless phones, fax machines and even robotics. His innovations also led him to fight several court cases regarding patent rights. The loss of most of these cases made Lemelson determined to protect the rights of independent inventors like himself. He established the Lemelson foundation with this purpose in mind.

July 18, 1923: Born in Staten Island, New York, U.S.

1953: Obtains his first patent for a toy cap

1954: Marries Dorothy Ginsberg

1958: Resigns from his job to devote himself completely to inventing

1996: Diagnosed with liver cancer, inspiring him to improve cancer-treatment devices

October 1, 1997: Dies at the age of 74

283 Jack St. Clair Kilby
[1923 - 2000]

Jack Kilby was only an average student. However, that did not stop him from inventing the integrated circuit (microchip). Kilby had just started his career with Texas Instruments, when he developed his ground-breaking device. Although it is the "planar IC" created by Robert Noyce that is widely used, Kilby is credited with starting the information age. He also invented the pocket calculator, which was the first popular device to use the integrated circuit.

November 8, 1923: Born in Jefferson City, Montreal, U.S.

July 1958: Starts working on the integrated circuit

September 12, 1958: Demonstrates his chip for the first time

2000: Awarded the Nobel Prize in Physics for his work on the integrated circuit

A microchip

284 Rufus Stokes
[1924 - 1986]

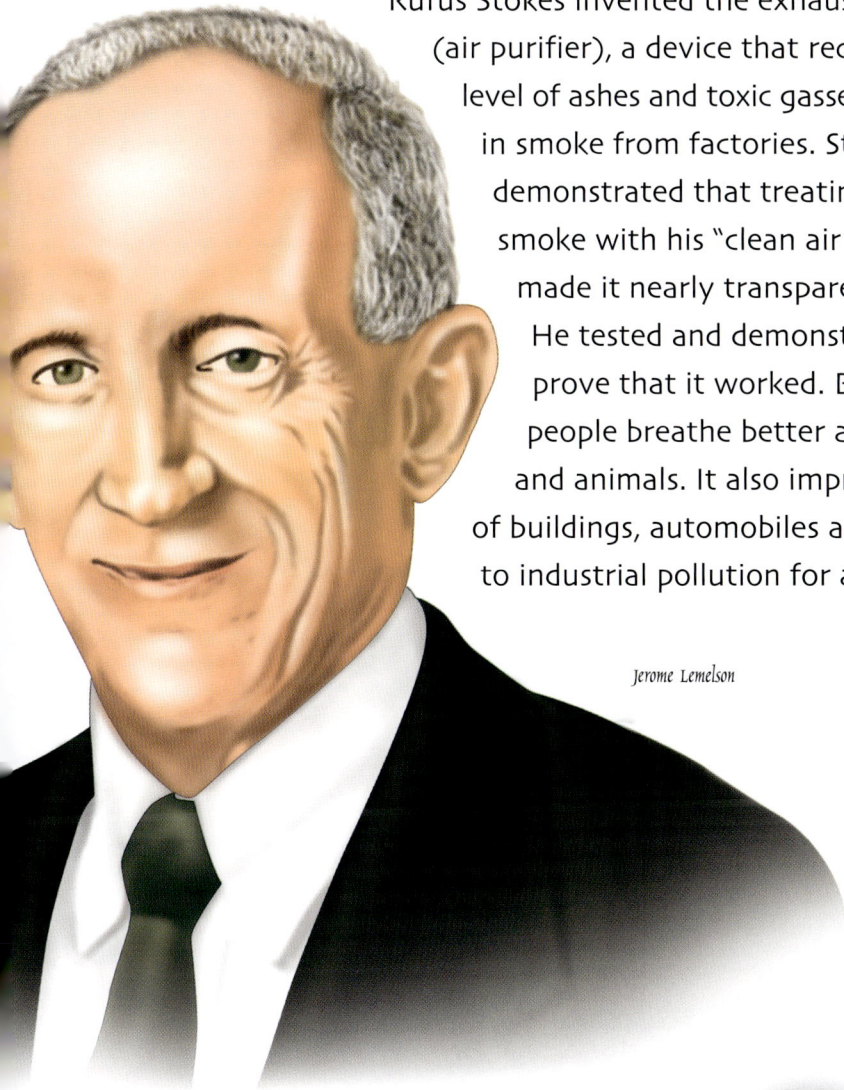

Rufus Stokes invented the exhaust purifier (air purifier), a device that reduces the level of ashes and toxic gasses emitted in smoke from factories. Stokes demonstrated that treating the smoke with his "clean air machine" made it nearly transparent, making it much less poisonous. He tested and demonstrated several models of the filters to prove that it worked. By reducing pollution, the filters helped people breathe better and also improved the health of plants and animals. It also improved the appearance and the durability of buildings, automobiles and other such objects exposed to industrial pollution for a long time.

Jerome Lemelson

1924: Born in Alabama

January 17, 1966: Invents the exhaust purifier and files for patent

April 16, 1968: Obtains patent for his invention

1986: Dies

285 Douglas Engelbart
[1925 -]

Although Douglas Engelbart invented a number of computer-related devices, his most important contribution has been the "mouse". Engelbart's aim was always to simplify computer usage and thereby increase its popularity as an office tool. With this in mind, he developed a system called the NLS (oNLine System). Through this system he introduced the mouse, hypermedia and video teleconferencing.

January 30, 1925: Born in Portland, Oregon

1962: Starts work on the NLS

December 9, 1968: Demonstrates the NLS and the mouse in public

1989: Retires and establishes the Bootstrap Institute

The mouse is an important component of a computer today

100 GREAT
Inventors

286 Seymour Cray
[1925 - 1996]

An American electronics engineer, Seymour Roger Cray is best known for the supercomputers he designed. He established Cray Research Incorporated to build the world's fastest supercomputers. In 1976 he introduced his Cray-1 system, which took supercomputing to new levels. The Cray-2 followed in 1985. Cray also designed the world's first transistor-based computer called the CDC 1604.

September 28, 1925: Born in Chippewa Falls, Wisconsin, U.S.

1957: Co-founds Control Data Corporation (CDC)

1972: Establishes Cray Research Incorporated

1976: Introduces the Cray-1 supercomputer

1985: Demonstrates the Cray-2

October 5, 1996: Dies in Colorado Springs, Colorado

287 David Warren
[1925 -]

Dr. David Warren invented the flight data recorder, popularly called the "black box". While working at the Aeronautical Research Laboratories, Dr. Warren was involved in investigations into an aircraft crash. He saw that recording the conversations of the crew would provide clues to the reasons for unexplained crashes. He then invented the first "ARL Flight Memory Recorder" built to record four hours of cockpit conversations and instrument readings.

March 20, 1925: Born in Groote Eylandt, Northern Territory, Australia

1950: Becomes a rocket-fuel chemist

1953: Joins the Aeronautical Research Laboratories in Melbourne

1957-58: Builds and demonstrates the Flight Memory Recorder, but fails to arouse interest

1958: Secretary of the U.K. Air Registration Board invites Warren to demonstrate the device in Britain

1960: A mysterious crash in Australia leads to a court order making flight recorders compulsory

1962: Warren improves his original device and builds a crash- and fire-proof container for it

1967: Australia becomes the first country in the world to make flight-recording compulsory

288 Robert S. Ledley
[1926 -]

Robert Ledley is best known for inventing the ACTA (Automatic Computerised Transverse Axial) diagnostic X-ray scanner – the forerunner of the modern CAT scanner. Ledley's invention made a major breakthrough in diagnosing diseases and revolutionised medical research. With the whole-body scanner, it was now possible to do medical imaging and three-dimensional reconstructions of the body. Ledley was also the first to use the scanner for planning radiation therapy for cancer patients and to detect bone diseases.

June 28, 1926: Born in New York City

November 25, 1975: Granted patent for his invention

1997: Awarded the National Medal of Technology

Robert S. Ledley

Seymour Cray

289 James T. Russell
[1931 -]

A music lover, Russell was often annoyed by the low quality of his phonograph records. The desire for a better recording system inspired him to invent the compact disc (CD). Russell thought of a system that would work without any contact between its parts. Familiar with digital data recording, Russell went on to apply the same principle to the compact disc that he developed. He then continued to improve his CD to include not just music, but any kind of data.

1931: Born in Bremerton, Washington

1965: Joins Battelle Memorial Institute as a senior scientist

1970: Obtains patent for the CD-ROM (compact disc read-only memory), the first of 26 such patents in the field

James T. Russel invented the compact disc with the view to improving recording quality

290 Robert Dennard
[1932 -]

Robert Heath Dennard invented the one-transistor dynamic random-access memory (DRAM). Dennard's device not only increased computer memory, but also made the personal computer (PC) a reality. After receiving his PhD in electrical engineering, Dennard joined IBM's research division, working on integrated-circuit designs and memory cells. It was there that Dennard came up with his revolutionary idea of reducing RAM to a single transistor, thus also making it feasible to reduce the size of the computer.

September 5, 1932: Born in Terrell, Texas

1958: Joins the research centre at IBM

1966: Invents RAM

1968: Granted patent for his invention

1988: Awarded the National Medal of Technology

The "black box" helps determine reasons for an aircraft crash

100 GREAT
Inventors

129

291 Martin Cooper
[1928 -]

Regarded as the father of mobile phones, Cooper made the first-ever call from a portable handheld cellular phone. After AT&T had introduced the first car telephone, Cooper launched his efforts to develop a "real" cellular phone. At the time, he was the general manager of Motorola's Communications Systems Division. On April 3, 1973, Cooper placed the historical call to his counterpart at AT&T Bell Labs, from the streets of New York City!

Martin Cooper

1928: Born in Chicago, Illinois, U.S.

1983: Motorola introduces the Dyna-Tac model

April 1992: Establishes ArrayComm, a wireless technology company

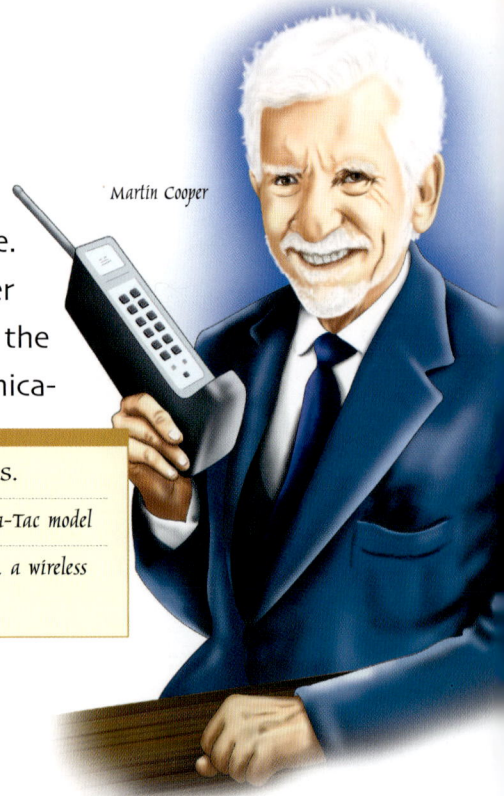

292 James Fergason
[1934 -]

James Fergason is responsible for improving and popularising liquid crystal display (LCD) technology. The earlier LCDs used a huge amount of power and were of poor quality. Fergason changed all that with his new device. His discoveries relating to the properties of liquid crystals led to the mass production of digital watches. LCD technology is now used in calculators, computer displays and other such electronic devices. Fergason holds more than a hundred U.S. patents, most of which are for his work on LCD technology.

January 12, 1934: Born in Wakenda, Missouri, U.S.

1970: Improves the LCD and makes it commercially successful

1971: Starts manufacturing LCD at his company, International Liquid Crystal Company (ILIXCO).

293 Raymond V. Damadian
[1936 -]

March 16, 1936: Born in Forest Hills, New York

1970: Discovers the medical use of magnetic resonance

March 1971: Publishes his results in the journal Science

1974: Obtains the patent for his scanning method

1977: Builds the first MRI scanner and obtains the first image of a human body

1978: Establishes his own company, FONAR

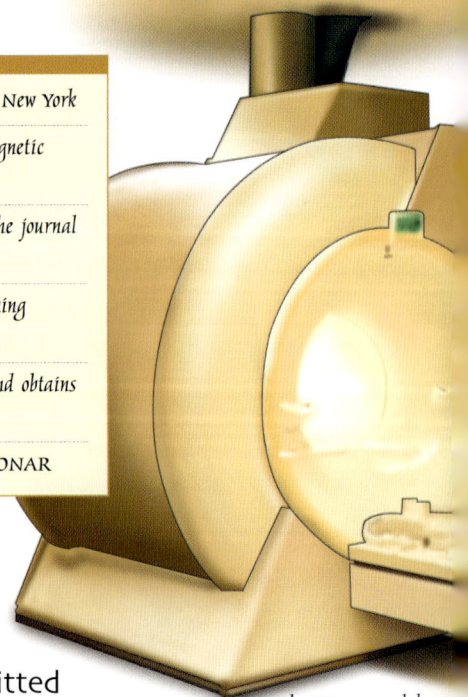

Dr. Damadian is famous for developing magnetic resonance imaging (MRI). A talented tennis player and violinist, Damadian chose a career in medicine, showing particular interest in cancer, possibly influenced by the painful death of his grandmother due to cancer. While working at the SUNY Downstate Medical Center in Brooklyn, Damadian discovered that he could easily distinguish healthy tissues from the cancerous ones, with the help of radio signals emitted by them. He went on to construct the world's first MRI scanner.

The MRI scanner helps detect cancer tissues

294 Phil Knight
[1938 -]

A sports enthusiast, Phil Knight was a middle-distance runner and trained under the famous Bill Bowerman. The competitive spirit of Bowerman had a deep influence on young Knight, who came up with an idea to end German domination of the American sports-shoes industry. Bowerman and Knight established Blue Ribbon Sports (BRS), a company that imported Japanese sports shoes and sold them in the United States. Later, the twosome took to making shoes on their own. Thus it was that BRS gave way to Nike and a new revolution in the form of sneakers began!

February 24, 1938: Born in Portland, Oregon

1962: Establishes Blue Ribbon Sports

1964: Bowerman and Knight start distributing their shoes to athletes at local meets

1966: Opens their first retail outlet

1970: Bowerman pours liquid rubber into his wife's waffle iron, thus creating the famous waffle sole

1971: Renames the company as Nike, after the Greek goddess of victory. A graphic design student, Carolyn Davidson, creates the famous "swoosh" trademark for a fee of just 35 dollars!

1974: The Waffle Trainer featuring Bowerman's waffle sole is introduced

2004: Steps down as CEO and President of Nike; his 35% stake in the company is estimated at $7.9 billion, making him the 30th richest man in America!

Phil Knight

295 Ray Tomlinson
[1941 -]

Tomlinson was working on a programme called SNDMSG (short for "send message") at BBN Technologies, when he created the email. The SNDMSG programme allowed users of the same computer to leave messages for one another. He was also working on another program, CYPNET, that allowed files to be transferred between computers within the ARPANET network (later to become the Internet). Tomlinson decided to combine the two to create the email!

1941: Tomlinson is born

1971: Creates the email, choosing the symbol @ to separate the name of the person and the machine in the address; sends the first message to himself, on the computer next to him. The message simply read QWERTYUIOP

Tomlinson chose this symbol to separate the person's name and the machine name when he created the email

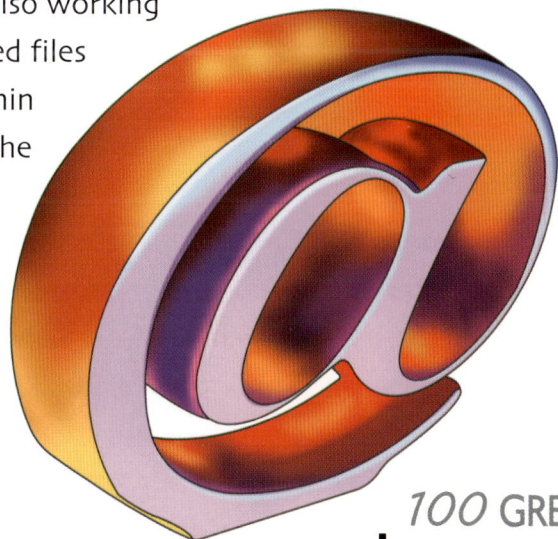

100 GREAT
Inventors

296 Nolan Bushnell
[1943 -]

The founder of Atari, Nolan Bushnell is often referred to as the father of the video-arcade industry. Although video games were already reality by then, Bushnell is credited with turning it into a profitable industry. While still in college, Bushnell became a fan of the famous Spacewar game. Later, he created the Computer Space on the same lines. Despite its failure to arouse public interest, Bushnell went on to create the most popular game in history – the Pong. A true businessman, Bushnell had it installed in a tavern in Sunnyvale, California, thus beginning the age of video arcades.

Nolan Bushnell

February 5, 1943: Born in Clearfield, Utah

1970: Designs and builds the Computer Space video game

1972: Establishes Atari Corporation, a video-game company and releases Pong, the first successful video-arcade game

1976: Sells Atari to Warner Communications (now AOL Time-Warner)

1977: Establishes the famous Pizza Time Theatres restaurant chain

1978: Resigns from Atari

1984: Resigns from Pizza Time Theatres

1999: Establishes another video-game company, uWink

297 Erno Rubik
[1944 -]

July 13, 1944: Born in Budapest, Hungary

1974: Invents the cube and names it Magic Cube

1975: Applies for Hungarian patent

1977: Production of the cube begins

1980: The Magic Cube is renamed Rubik's Cube after its creator

The Rubik's cube

The famous Rubik's Cube was the brainchild of Erno Rubik, an interior-design professor. Rubik, who had a passion for geometry, liked to teach using models made from paper, wood and cardboard. Always looking for new ways to challenge his students, Rubik thought of creating a puzzle that was simple yet required immense patience and creativity. The final inspiration came one afternoon as he watched the Danube river flow. The smooth pebbles under the water became the basis of the cube's interiors. The rounded interior made it easy to twist the cube.

298 Tim Berners-Lee
[1955 -]

Tim Berners-Lee's genius is evident from a story about his college days. It is said that he built his first computer while still a student at Queen's College at Oxford University. He made it possible with just a soldering iron, a processor and an old television. Not hard for a person who went on to create the World Wide Web (www), an effective way of distributing information globally. Berners-Lee also created such well-known web concepts as http://, HTML and URL.

June 8, 1955: Born in London

1989: Presents the concept of World Wide Web to his employers at CERN

1990: Puts the first website, info.cern.ch, online

1991: Makes the World Wide Web available on the Internet

1994: Establishes the World Wide Web Consortium (W3C) for the development of the web

299 Robert Patch
[1957 -]

While most inventors show early signs of genius, they usually make a name for themselves much later in life. Not so in the case of Robert Patch. A child genius beyond doubt, Patch was granted a patent for his toy truck when he was only six years old! His truck could be easily assembled and disassembled by a child. It could also be changed from a closed-van style truck to an open pick-up type.

1957: Robert Patch is born

June 4, 1963: Granted patent for his toy truck

300 Don Wetzel
[unknown]

1968: The idea of an ATM is born

1969: Develops the first ATM and ATM card with magnetic strip; Chemical Bank installs the first-ever ATM at its Rockville branch

Don Wetzel invented one of the most widely used machines of all time — the automatic teller machine, popularly called ATM. Wetzel got the idea when he was waiting in a line at a bank. At the time, he was working with a company that developed automatic baggage-handling equipment. He got two of his colleagues interested in the concept and together they developed the ATM and the first ATM card. Wetzel's ATM, however, did only basic functions like giving out cash. Today an ATM can perform a range of tasks, including help you deposit money in the bank!

Don Wetze invented the ATM that simplified banking

100 GREAT
Inventors

Great

in Sports

Baseball

301 Ty Cobb
[1886 - 1961]

December 18, 1886: *Born in Narrows, Georgia, U.S.*

1905: *Joins the Detroit Tigers as outfielder; remains with them until 1926*

May 5, 1925: *Sets an American League record of 16 total bases in a single game that remains unbroken*

1927-28: *Plays with the Philadelphia Athletics, before retiring from the game*

July 17, 1961: *Dies in Atlanta, Georgia*

One of baseball's greatest icons, Tyrus Raymond Cobb is perhaps best known for his 892 stolen bases – a record that remained unbeaten until 1979. Other accomplishments include 4,191 hits, 2,245 runs and a lifetime batting average of .367. Affectionately called the Georgia Peach, in 1936 he became the first player to be elected to baseball's Hall of Fame. His plaque celebrates him as the one who "created or equalled more major league records than any other player."

Babe Ruth

302 Babe Ruth
[1895 - 1948]

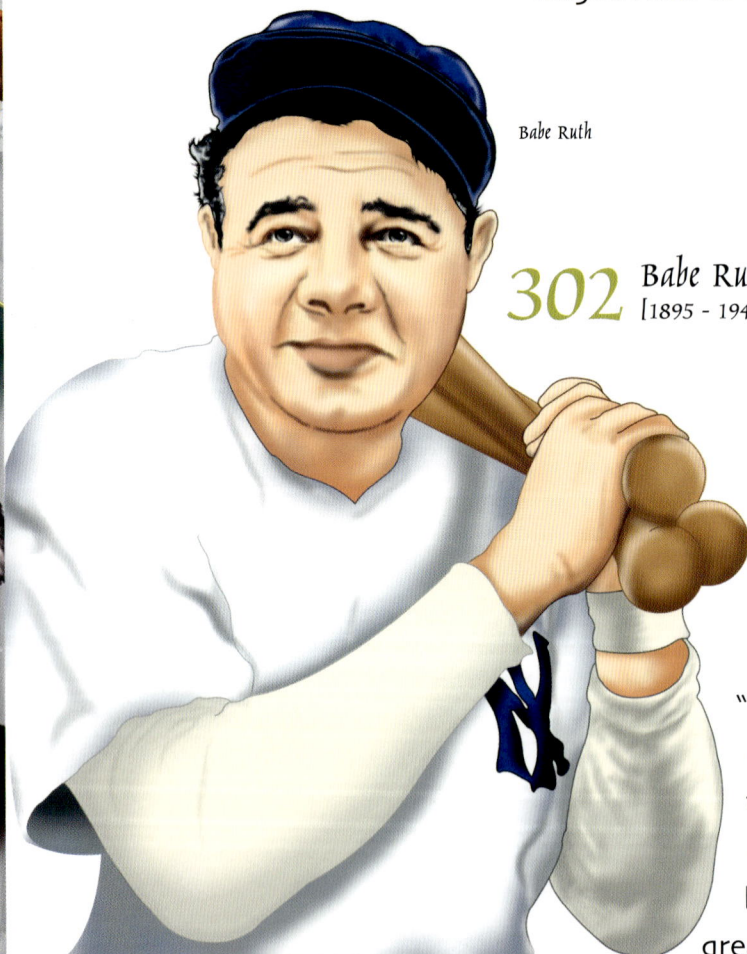

February 6, 1895: *Born in Baltimore, Maryland, U.S.*

1913: *Joins Baltimore Orioles*

1914: *Moves to Boston Red Sox*

1919: *Breaks Gabby Kraveth's record with 29 home runs*

December 1919: *Boston Red Sox sells him to New York Yankees*

1920: *Shatters his own home run record with 54 home runs – double his earlier record*

1935: *Retires from professional baseball*

August 16, 1948: *Dies at the Memorial Hospital, New York City, U.S.*

"The Sultan of Swat", "The Great Bambino", "The Colossus of Clout" – these are just a few of the names given to George Herman, popularly known as Babe Ruth. Perhaps the greatest baseball legend ever, Babe Ruth started his career as a pitcher. He set new records during the 1918 World Series when he pitched 29 innings without giving away runs – a record that stood strong for 43 years! But it was with the New York Yankees that he grew into the legend that is Babe Ruth. He is also credited with the invention of the modern baseball bat.

Lou Gehrig

303 Lou Gehrig
[1903 - 1941]

The first baseball player to have his uniform number retired, Henry Louis Gehrig was a baseball manager's dream. He stood out for his absolute reliability and his ability to deliver at all times.

June 13, 1903: Born in New York City, New York, U.S.

June 15, 1923: Begins his baseball career with the New York Yankees

1931: Makes American League history with 184 RBIs

1934: Wins the Triple Crown

1939: Elected to the Baseball Hall of Fame

June 2, 1941: Dies in Riverdale, New York, U.S.

Teamed with Babe Ruth, "The Iron Horse", as he was popularly called, formed a formidable hitting side. The only player in history to have driven in more than 500 runs in three years (1930-32), Gehrig's total of 184 RBI's in a single season (1931) was also a first in American League history. With a total of 23, he also holds the record for the most career grand slams.

304 Joe DiMaggio
[1914 - 1999]

American baseball all-rounder, Joseph Paul DiMaggio was a hitter and fielder par excellence. He holds the distinction of hitting safely in 56 successive major league games. Between 1936 and 1951, DiMaggio helped his team, the New York Yankees, win nine World Series titles. In 13 seasons, the star performer scored 361 home runs and ended with a lifetime average of .325. In 1969, on the occasion of baseball's 100th anniversary, DiMaggio was chosen by a nationwide poll as the game's "greatest living player".

November 25, 1914: Born in Martinez, California, U.S.

1932: Plays with the minor league San Francisco Seals

1936: Enters the major leagues by joining the New York Yankees

1939: Marries film actress Dorothy Arnold; is married again in 1954, to actress Marilyn Monroe

1951: Retires from the game

1955: Elected to the Baseball Hall of Fame

March 8, 1999: Dies in Hollywood, Florida, U.S.

305 Hank Aaron
[1934 -]

A baseball bat autographed by Hank Aaron

February 5, 1934: Born in Mobile, Alabama, U.S.

April 13, 1954: Makes his major league debut

1957: Leads the National League to victory in the World Series; declared the league's most valuable player

1976: Retires from play

1982: Elected to the Baseball Hall of Fame

Over a 23-year career, Henry Louis Aaron set some 13 records for the sport of baseball. His 755 home runs broke previous records by such greats as Babe Ruth and Ty Cobb and remains unbeaten by any other major-league player. Among other records set by "Hammerin' Hank," ones that still stand include those for the most runs batted in (2,297), total bases (6,856) and long hits (1,477).

100 GREATS
in sports

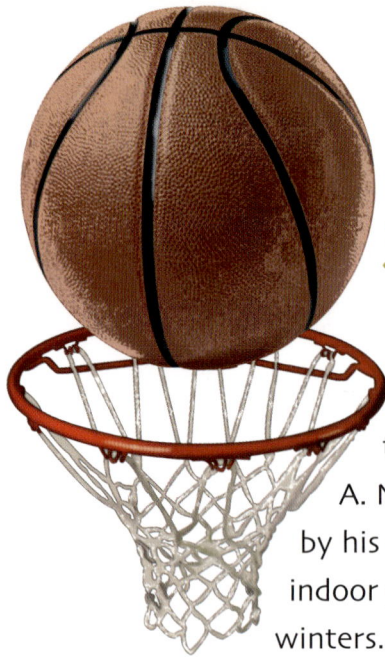

Basketball

306 James A. Naismith
[1861 - 1939]

At the International YMCA Training School, the instructor, James A. Naismith, was asked by his Head to devise an indoor game especially for the winters. What Naismith came up with was a game sprinkled with little bits from various outdoor sports, including soccer and field hockey. A soccer ball, a couple of peach baskets and 18 players starred in the new game. That was how, in 1891, the ever-popular game of basketball came into existence!

November 6, 1861: Born in Almonte, Ontario, Canada

1891: Invents basketball and develops the original 13 rules of the game

1936: Introduces basketball to the 1936 Berlin Olympics

November 28, 1939: Dies in Lawrence, Kansas, U.S.

1959: Enshrined as a contributor in the Naismith Memorial Basketball Hall of Fame, Springfield, Massachusetts

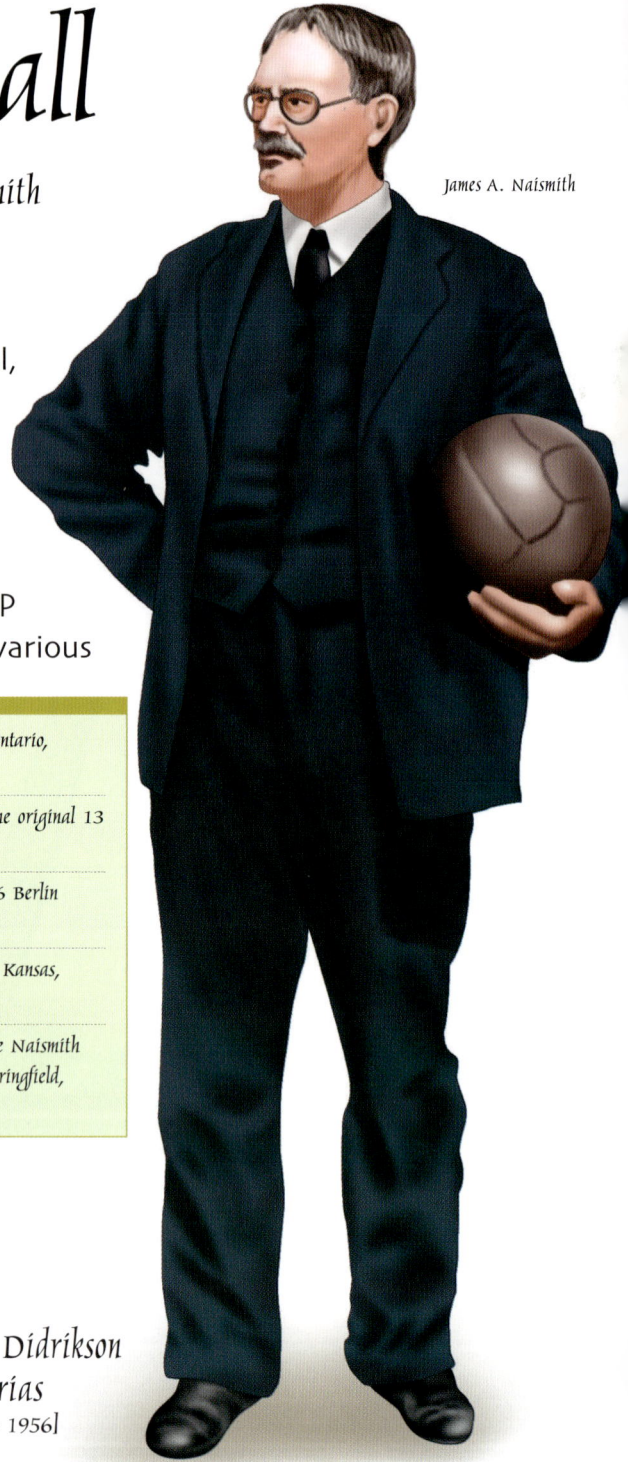

James A. Naismith

307 Babe Didrikson Zaharias
[1911 - 1956]

June 26, 1911 (although she wrote herself that she was born in 1914): Born in Port Arthur, Texas, U.S.

1930-32: Gets selected thrice as the All-American women's basketball player

1932: Sets world records and wins gold and silver medals for various track and field events at the Olympic Games

1933: Begins her tours of rural U.S. with professional basketball team called 'Babe Didrikson's All-Americans'

1938: Marries professional wrestler George Zaharias

1946-47: Wins 17 straight golf tournaments; also becomes the first American to win the British Women's Amateur

1953: Diagnosed with cancer

1955: Publishes her autobiography, This Life I've Led

September 27, 1956: Dies in Galveston, Texas, U.S.

In a 1950 poll conducted by the Associated Press, Mildred "Babe" Didrikson Zaharias was voted the greatest woman athlete of the first half of the 20th century – a feat she accomplished six times between 1931 and 1954! It was the fulfillment of a childhood dream for Didrikson, who always wanted to be nothing but the greatest! Apart from being an excellent performer in a range of sports – such as basketball, track and field and golf – Babe also excelled in swimming, figure skating, baseball, tennis and billiards.

308 Wilt Chamberlain
[1936 - 1999]

At over seven feet, Wilton Norman Chamberlain took to the basketball court like a natural. His talent brought him fame even while he was in high-school. As a player with the National Basketball Association, he became one of its leading scorers. Scoring over 4,000 points in the 1961-62 season alone, by 1968 he had scored a record 25,000 career points. He was named NBA's most valuable player (MVP) four times and was a two-time NBA Champion.

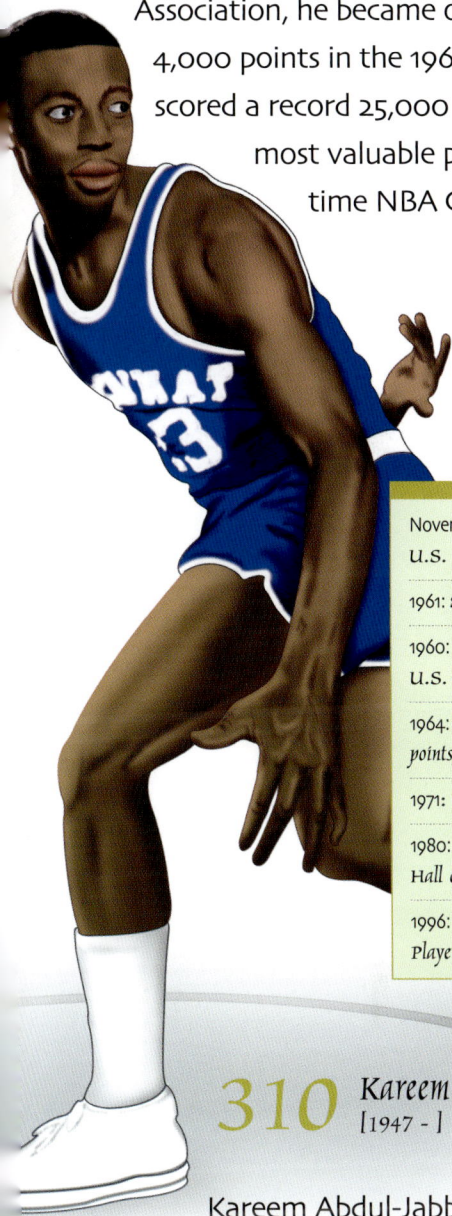

August 21, 1936: Born in Philadelphia, Pennsylvania, U.S.

1959-65: Joins the Philadelphia Warriors of the National Basketball Association (NBA)

1960, 1966-68: Selected as the most valuable player for four years

1962: Scores 100 points against the New York Knicks

1978: Enshrined in the Naismith Memorial Basketball Hall of Fame

October 12, 1999: Dies in Los Angeles, California, U.S.

Oscar Palmer Robertson

November 24, 1938: Born in Charlotte, Tennessee, U.S.

1961: Selected Rookie of the Year

1960: Wins Olympic gold medal as co-captain of U.S. basketball team

1964: NBA Most Valuable Player; averaged 31.4 points, 9.9 rebounds and 11 assists for each game

1971: NBA Champion

1980: Elected to the Naismith Memorial Basketball Hall of Fame

1996: Is recognised as one of the 50 Greatest Players in NBA History

309 Oscar Palmer Robertson
[1938 -]

One of the great all-rounders in basketball history, Oscar Palmer Robertson was already a high-school and college star before moving on to the National Basketball Association (NBA). In a 14-year career with the Cincinnati Royals and the Milwaukee Bucks, "Big O" Robertson scored 26,710 points, 7,804 rebounds and 9,887 assists. His 1961-62 season numbers remain an NBA record – a double-figure average in points (30.8), rebounds (12.5) and assists (11.4) per game!

310 Kareem Abdul-Jabbar
[1947 -]

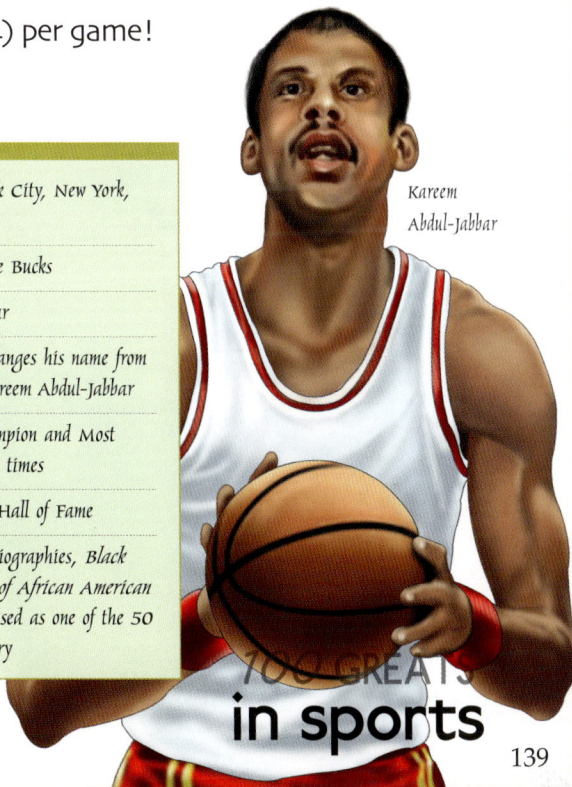

Kareem Abdul-Jabbar had a brilliant and unusually long basketball career. Before his debut at the NBA, he had led the University of California to three national titles. His spells with the Milwaukee Bucks and the Los Angeles Lakers was marked by six NBA titles. At the time of his retirement in 1989, Abdul-Jabbar held NBA records for most points (38, 387), most field goals (15,837) and most blocked shots (3,189).

April 16, 1947: Born in New York City, New York, U.S.

1969: Joins the NBA Milwaukee Bucks

1970: Selected Rookie of the Year

1971: Having adopted Islam, changes his name from Ferdinand Lewis Alcindor to Kareem Abdul-Jabbar

1971-88: Selected as NBA Champion and Most Valuable Player for a record six times

1995: Elected to the Basketball Hall of Fame

1996: Publishes a collection of biographies, Black Profiles in Courage: A Legacy of African American Achievement and is also recognised as one of the 50 Greatest Players in NBA History

Kareem Abdul-Jabbar

311 Larry Bird
[1956 -]

Widely considered one of the greatest players of all time, Larry Joe Bird was a complete player. He was confident and hardworking and had a passion for the game that spurred him on – even when he was badly injured. He not only helped rebuild an average Celtics team but also led them to three NBA titles. He was only the third player to win the NBA Most Valuable Player award thrice in a row. A member of the original "Dream Team" that won the gold medal at the Barcelona Olympics, Larry retired in 1992 due to an injured back.

December 7, 1956: Born in West Baden, Indiana, U.S.

1979: Makes his NBA debut with Boston Celtics against Houston Rockets

1980: Named NBA Rookie of the Year

1981: Leads the Celtics to the first of the three NBA Championships

1984-1986: Selected thrice as the NBA Most Valuable Player

1992: Wins Olympic gold medal for U.S. basketball team and also announces retirement

1996: Is recognised as one of the 50 Greatest Players in NBA History

1998: Named NBA Coach of the Year and also inducted into the Basketball Hall of Fame

312 Magic Johnson
[1959 -]

Magic Johnson

One of basketball's most successful stars, Earvin Johnson, Jr. won nearly every competition – be it the state championship for his high-school team, the national collegiate for Michigan State University, or leading the U.S. basketball "Dream Team" to a gold at the 1992 Olympics . He also helped the Los Angeles Lakers win five NBA championships.

August 14, 1959: Born in Lansing, Michigan, U.S.

1979: Joins the Los Angeles Lakers

1980-88: Five-time NBA Champion

1987-90: Three-time winner of NBA's Most Valuable Player

1992: Wins Olympic gold medal for U.S. basketball team and also receives the J. Walter Kennedy Citizenship Award

1993: Publishes his autobiography, My Life

1996: Retires from the game and is also chosen as one of the 50 Greatest Players in NBA History

2002: Elected to the Naismith Memorial Basketball Hall of Fame

313 Dennis Rodman
[1961 -]

May 13, 1961: Born in Trenton, New Jersey, U.S.

1986: Makes his debut at the NBA with Detroit Pistons

1989-90: Helps Detroit Pistons win their first NBA Championship. Also wins the first of his three Defensive Player of the Year awards

1992: Becomes the first forward to win seven straight rebounding titles. Only Wilt Chamberlain has more titles at 11

1995: Joins Chicago Bulls

2000: Retires from the NBA

2003: Announces plans for a comeback

A fantastic rebounder and defender, Dennis Rodman was the "bad boy" of basketball. Despite his playing record, he is equally as famous for his coloured hair and his several suspensions for bad behaviour on-court. However, he has to his credit the most number of rebounds after the legendary Wilt Chamberlain. Seven-time rebounding champion, Rodman helped the Chicago Bulls to win three championships. He also helped Detroit Pistons to two championship titles.

Michael Jeffrey Jordan

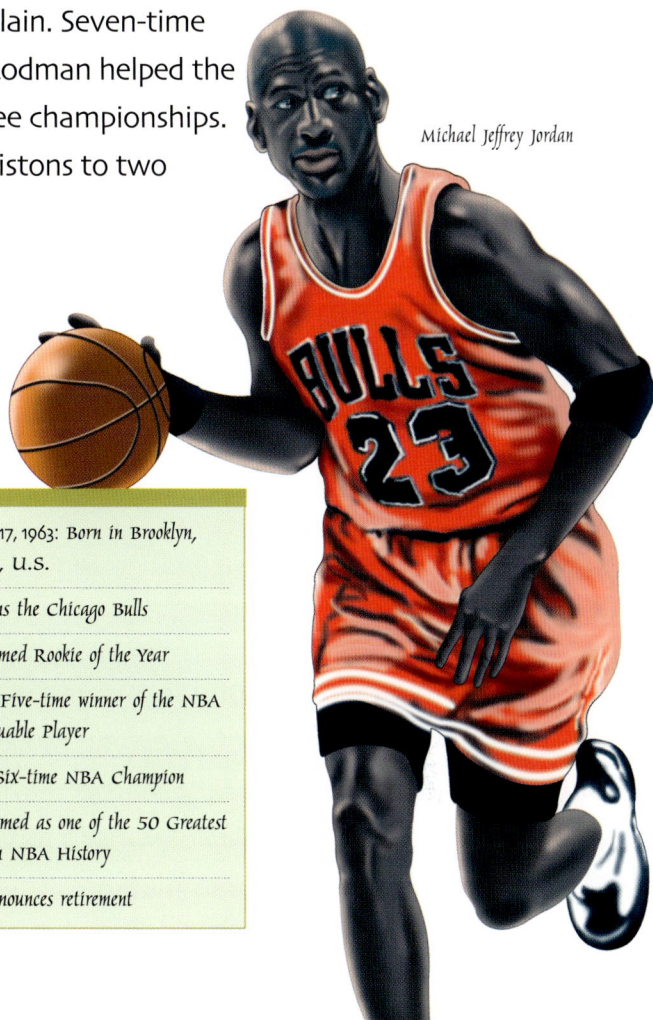

314 Michael Jeffrey Jordan
[1963 -]

A living legend, Michael Jeffrey Jordan had one of the most celebrated careers in basketball. Over 15 seasons with the NBA, the American player led the Chicago Bulls to six championships (1991-93, 1996-98). His career totals included 32,292 points and the best points-per-game average in NBA history – 30.12. "Air Jordan" was also a member of the U.S. basketball team that won Olympic gold medals in the 1984 and the 1992 Olympic Games.

February 17, 1963: Born in Brooklyn, New York, U.S.

1984: Joins the Chicago Bulls

1985: Named Rookie of the Year

1988-98: Five-time winner of the NBA Most Valuable Player

1991-98: Six-time NBA Champion

1996: Named as one of the 50 Greatest Players in NBA History

2003: Announces retirement

Shaquille O'Neal's jersey

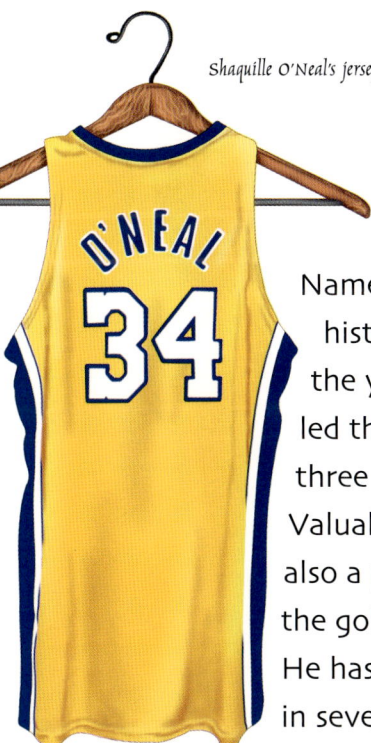

315 Shaquille O'Neal
[1972 -]

Named one of the 50 greatest players in NBA history, Shaquille Rashaun O'Neal became the youngest player to earn the honour. He led the LA Lakers to the NBA Championships three times in a row and was judged the Most Valuable Player during this period. He was also a part of the U.S. Olympic team that won the gold medal at the 1996 Atlanta Olympics. He has also released many rap albums and acted in several movies.

March 6, 1972: Born in Newark, New Jersey, U.S.

1992-93: Makes his NBA debut with Orlando Magic and is named NBA Rookie of the Year

1994: Appears in the movie, Blue Chips, alongside actor Nick Nolte

1996: Wins the gold medal at Atlanta Olympics and also leaves Orlando Magic to join LA Lakers. Becomes the youngest player to get selected as one of the 50 greatest players in NBA history

2000-02: Named the Most Valuable Player at the NBA Finals for the first time after he helps LA Lakers to win the NBA Championship. Repeats the feat for the next two years

100 GREATS
in sports

Boxing and Wrestling

316 George Hackenschmidt
[1878 - 1968]

The epithet "Russian Lion" aptly describes one of the all-time wrestling greats – George Hackenschmidt. In freestyle wrestling, his strength, skill and courage had no match for a long time. Intelligent and confident, Hackenschmidt shunned the savage methods used by many wrestlers. His later rivalry with Frank Gotch – to whom he finally lost in a 1908 match in Chicago – is legendary.

August 2, 1878: Born in Tartu, Estonia, Russia

1898: Wins the Greco-Roman amateur wrestling championship in Vienna, Austria

1936: Publishes *Man and Cosmic Antagonism to Mind and Spirit*

February 19, 1968: Dies in London, England

George Hackenschmidt

317 Frank Gotch
[1878 - 1917]

Coming from a humble farming background, Gotch got his first shot at wrestling fame under the guidance of the legendary Martin "Farmer" Burns. He followed up a series of wins in Iowa with a tremendous performance in Alaska, earning him the title, "Champion of the Klondike". But his moment of glory came in 1908, when he overcame Hackenschmidt to become the world heavyweight champion. This made Gotch an overnight superstar. He was considered unbeatable and he lived up to his reputation until his retirement in 1914.

April 27, 1878: Born in Humboldt, Iowa, U.S.

June 18, 1899: Meets former American heavyweight champion Dan McLeod who introduces him to his future trainer Martin "Farmer" Burns

April 3, 1908: Defeats Hackenschmidt in a two-hour long match at the Dexter Park Pavilion in Chicago, U.S. to become the new world heavyweight wrestling champion

September 4, 1911: Defeats Hackenschmidt once again at the Comiskey Park in Chicago

April 1, 1913: Defeats George Lurich at Kansas City in, what is now termed as, his retirement match

1914: Retires from professional wrestling

December, 1917: Dies due to kidney failure at the age of 39

318 Jack Dempsey
[1895 - 1983]

World heavyweight boxing champion from 1919 to 1926, William Harrison "Jack" Dempsey was variously called the "Manassa Mauler" and "Jack the Giant Killer". He was known for the knockouts that he delivered, often in the first round. In all, Dempsey won 62 of the 84 bouts he participated in. He was inducted to the Boxing Hall of Fame in 1954.

June 24, 1895: Born in Manassa, Colorado, U.S.

1914: Becomes a professional boxer under the name "Kid Blackie"

1919: Becomes the world heavyweight champion by defeating Jess Willard in a three-round duel in Toledo, Ohio, U.S.

1926: Loses his title to Gene Tunney in a 10-round bout in Philadelphia, U.S.

1940: Publishes his first autobiography, Round by Round

1960: Publishes his second autobiography, Dempsey

1977: Publishes third aotubiography, The Autobiography of Jack Dempsey

May 31, 1983: Dies in New York City, New York, U.S.

319 Sugar Ray Robinson
[1921 - 1989]

Walker Smith, Jr., got the name "Ray Robinson" after he used the amateur certificate of another player to qualify for a match! As a professional in the boxing ring, Robinson remained undefeated in his first 40 bouts. He was a six-time world champion – once in the welterweight category (1946) and five times as a middleweight, between 1951 and 1960. Widely regarded as one of the best fighters ever, "Sugar Ray" lost only 19 times in a total of 202 bouts.

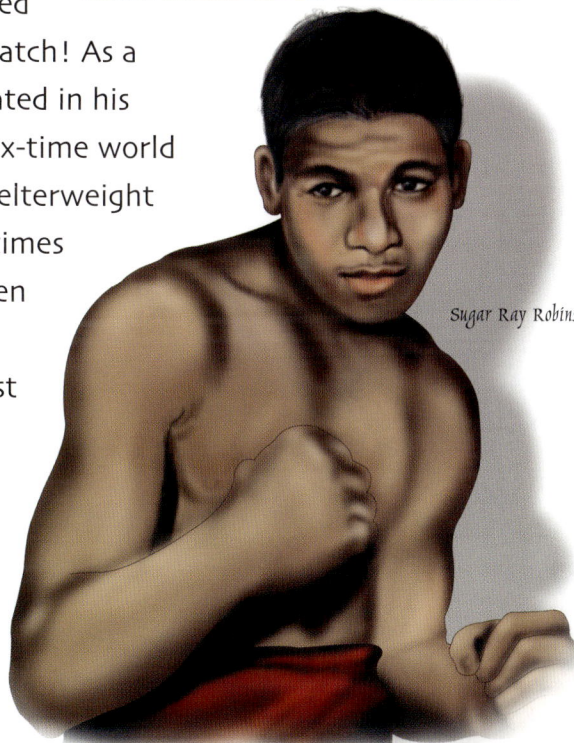

May 3, 1921: Born in Detroit, Michigan, U.S.

1940: Turns professional

1946: Defeats Tommy Bell to win the world welterweight title

1951: Wins the middleweight championship by defeating Jake LaMotta

1965: Retires from the game

April 12, 1989: Dies in Culver City, Los Angeles, U.S.

Sugar Ray Robinson

320 Joe Louis
[1914 - 1981]

For 12 years – from June 22, 1937, to March 1, 1949 – American Joseph Louis Barrow ruled the boxing arena as the world heavyweight champion. During this record term, he successfully defended his title 25 times. In his entire career, Louis fought 71 bouts and lost only three! After announcing his retirement in 1949, he made a couple of attempts to regain his title. Both, however, were unsuccessful.

Joe Louis

May 13, 1914: Born in Lexington, Alabama, U.S.

1934: Becomes a professional boxer; wins 12 contests the same year

1942: Enrols in the U.S. Army during the Second World War

April 12, 1981: Dies in Las Vegas, Nevada, U.S.

100 GREATS
in sports

321 Aleksandr Vasilyevich Medved
[1937 -]

Considered to be one of the greatest freestyle wrestlers of all time, Medved won gold medals in three consecutive Olympics – a record that remains unequalled. He ruled the world of wrestling ever since he won his first national title in 1961. After winning his first Olympic gold medal in the light-heavyweight category, Medved went on to win gold medals in heavyweight and super-heavyweight categories too.

September 16, 1937: Born in Belaya Tserkov, Ukraine, U.S.S.R. (now Bila Tserkva, Ukraine)

1961: Wins the first of his eight national championship titles

1964: Wins his first gold medal at the Tokyo Olympics

1968: Wins the heavyweight gold medal at the Mexico Olympics

1972: Retires after winning the super-heavyweight gold medal at the Munich Olympics

322 Muhammad Ali
[1942 -]

Muhammad Ali

A living legend and, arguably, the greatest boxer ever, Muhammad Ali's bout with the sport began at the age of 12. Winning national championships while still at high school, he went on to claim the gold in the light heavyweight category at the 1960 Olympics in Rome. The same year he began his professional career. The world championship honour came four years later. Ali successfully defended the title 19 times! He was also the first boxer to win the world heavyweight title thrice. In 1999, Ali was crowned "Sportsman of the Century" by American magazine, Sports Illustrated.

January 17, 1942: Born in Louisville, Kentucky, U.S.

1964: Defeats defending champion Sonny Liston to claim the world heavyweight championship, held in Miami, U.S.; changes his name from Cassius Marcellus Clay to Muhammad Ali

1967-71: Suspended from the sport for refusal to join the U.S. Army during the Vietnam War

1974: Defeats reigning champion, George Foreman, to regain the world heavyweight title

1975: Defeats Joe Frazier in a fiercely fought contest

1981: Announces retirement

323 George Foreman
[1949 -]

George Foreman

The American boxer was a two-time world heavyweight champion. In 1973, he defeated Joe Frazier in just two rounds at Kingston, Jamaica. But a year later, he lost the title to Muhammad Ali in the famous "Rumble in the Jungle" duel in Kinshasa, Zaire. After retiring in 1977, Foreman made a remarkable comeback a decade later. In 1994, 45-year-old Foreman defeated Michael Moorer to become the oldest-ever world heavyweight champion!

January 10, 1949: Born in Marshall, Texas, U.S.

1968: Wins the heavyweight boxing gold at the Mexico Olympics

1969: Turns professional

1977: Becomes an ordained minister of the church

2003: Inducted into the International Boxing Hall of Fame

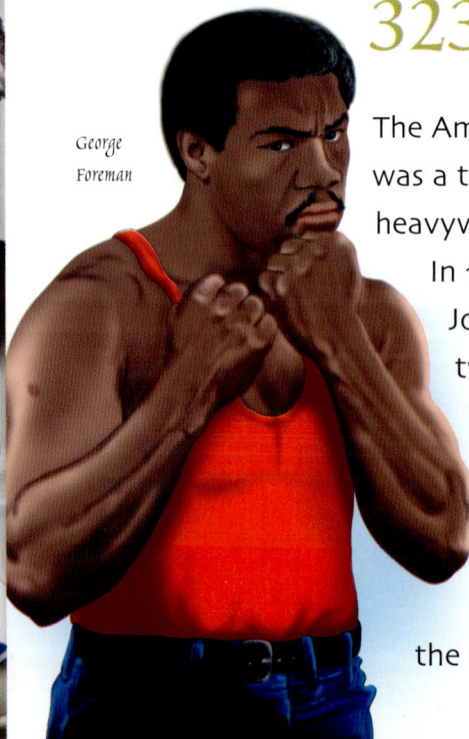

324 Mike Tyson
[1966 -]

The youngest heavyweight champion ever, Michael Gerard Tyson showed promise as a boxer from a very young age. But his talent has been over-shadowed by his recklessness and repeated trouble with the law. During his incredible career, Tyson won most of his bouts in the very first round. It did not take him long to become the "undisputed heavyweight champion". However, by 1990 Tyson's career witnessed a downhill trend while his personal problems mounted. In 1992, his career was put on hold when he was imprisoned on charges of assault. He returned to the ring three years later. However, the infamous bout in which he bit off part of Evander Holyfield's ear proved he had not changed his ways.

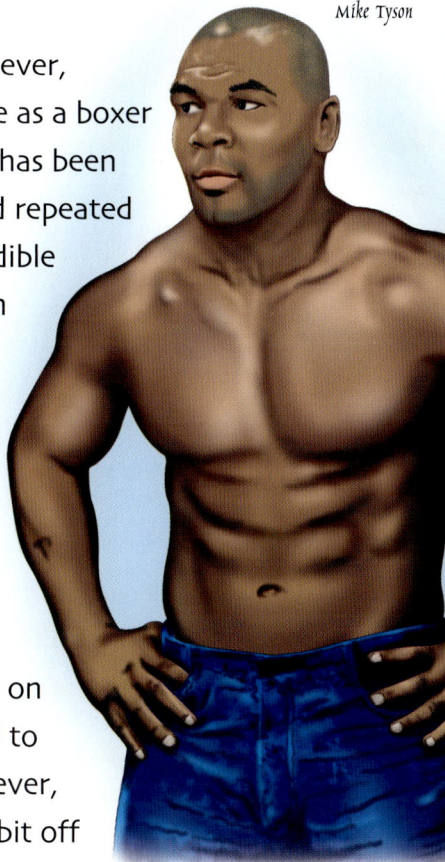

Mike Tyson

June 30, 1966: *Born in New York City, New York, U.S.*

1980: *Meets his future trainer Cus D'Amato*

March 6, 1985: *Makes his professional debut in Albany, New York, U.S.*

November 22, 1986: *Becomes the youngest heavyweight champion after knocking out Trevor Berbick in just two rounds*

August 1, 1987: *Wins the International Boxing Federation (IBF) title from Tony Tucker*

February 11, 1990: *Loses to a lesser-known James 'Buster' Douglas in a tenth round knockout*

January 27, 1992: *Accused of assaulting Desiree Washington, a beauty contestant*

June 28, 1997: *Takes on Evander Holyfield for the WBA heavyweight title but is disqualified in the third round. An angry Tyson attacks Holyfield and bites a chunk off his ear*

July 9, 1997: *Banned from boxing for a year and fined $3 million*

August 31, 1998: *Attacks two people after a car accident*

February 5, 1999: *Sentenced to one year imprisonment and fined $5,000 for the act*

June 2002: *Fights Lennox Lewis in Memphis, Tennessee, U.S. Loses in an eighth-round knockout*

Oscar De La Hoya's championship belt

325 Oscar De La Hoya
[1973 -]

February 4, 1973: *Born in East Los Angeles, California, U.S.*

1990: *Wins the U.S. National Championship and a gold medal at the Goodwill Games*

1991: *Named Boxer of the Year by USA Boxing*

1992: *Wins Olympic gold medal by defeating Marco Rudolph of Germany*

November 23, 1992: *Wins his debut fight as a professional boxer by knocking out Lamar Williams*

May 6, 1995: *Wins the International Boxing Federation (IBF) lightweight title*

October 10, 2000: *Releases his first music album, which was nominated for the Grammy Awards*

2001: *Wins the WBC junior middleweight title from Javier Castillejo to become the youngest boxer to win world titles in five different weight classes*

Though he began boxing at the age of six, Oscar de la Hoya never gave professional boxing a serious thought. He hated fights and preferred non-violent sports like skateboarding and baseball. But since boxing was a family tradition, young Oscar was pushed into the sport. Gradually, he discovered his talent, especially his powerful left hand that was to make him a star in the world of boxing. He shot to fame by winning the gold medal at the 1992 Barcelona Olympics. The "Golden Boy" then went on to become one of the best middleweight boxers ever with a record of 36 wins, of which 31 were knockouts.

100 GREATS
in sports

Chess

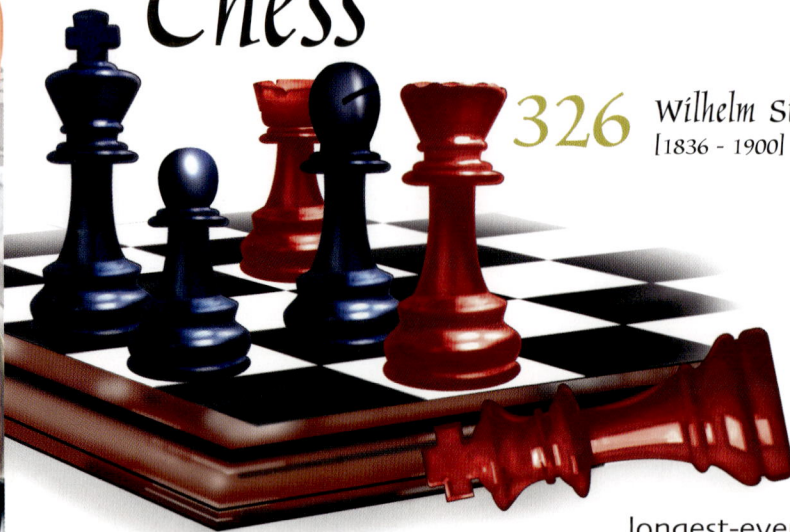

326 Wilhelm Steinitz
[1836 - 1900]

For close to three decades, Wilhelm Steinitz reigned as the world chess champion. It is considered to be the longest-ever stay at the top. In 1866, the Austrian-American chess master defeated Adolf Anderssen to become the unofficial world champion (the official title came into existence in 1886). He remained practically unchallenged until 1894, when the German Emanuel Lasker finally claimed the world championship.

327 Emanuel Lasker
[1868 - 1941]

For 26 years and 337 days, Emanuel Lasker was the chess world's official champion. His retirement from the game in 1925 could not last long. Being a Jew, he was forced out of Germany in 1933, during Hitler's rule. Left with no property, Lasker, then in his 60s, had to get back into competitive chess. And he did

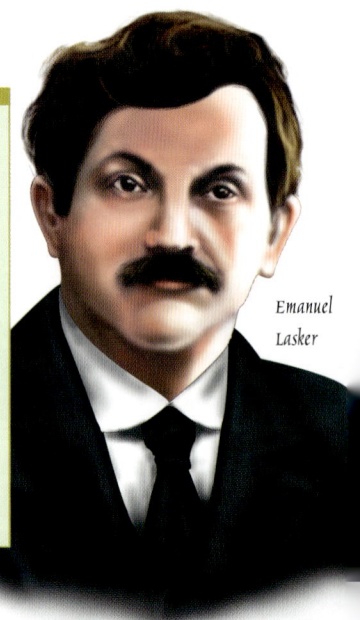

Emanuel Lasker

remarkably well, competing at the highest levels. He is regarded as one of the greatest chess players ever!

328 Bobby Fisher
[1943 -]

He was the little six-year-old boy who said, "All I want to do, ever, is play chess." At the age of 15, Robert James Fischer became the world's youngest grandmaster! Between 1957 and 1966, he was the U.S. champion eight times, winning all his eight attempts. The grand triumph – that of the world championship – came in 1972, when he defeated Boris Spassky of the Soviet Union in Reykjavik, Iceland.

329 Anatoly Yevgenyevich Karpov
[1951 -]

The youngest player to be awarded the title of Soviet Master, Anatoly Karpov became a grandmaster in 1970. He won the 1975 world championship title under unusual circumstances – defending champion Bobby Fischer had refused to follow the official match conditions set by the International Chess Federation (FIDE)! Subsequently, Karpov won the title against countryman Viktor Korchnoi, in 1978 and 1981. In 1985, he lost the FIDE world championship to fellow countryman Garry Kasparov. However, he regained it in 1993 and also successfully defended it in 1998.

Garry Kasparov

Anatoly Yevgenyevich Karpov

May 23, 1951: *Born in Zlatoust, Russia, U.S.S.R.*

1969: *Wins the World Junior Chess Championship at Stockholm, Sweden*

1976: *Becomes U.S.S.R. champion; retains the title in 1982 and 1988*

330 Garry Kasparov
[1963 -]

At 22 years, Russian chess master Garry Kimovich Kasparov became the youngest world champion ever. He defeated reigning title-holder and fellow countryman Anatoly Karpov, in a 72-game series through 1984-85. Kasparov retained his title until November 2000, when he lost to another Russian, Vladimir Kramnik. One of Kasparov's most celebrated contests took place in 1996 – when he took on a machine, the powerful IBM computer called Deep Blue! He won the contest, but lost a rematch the following year.

April 13, 1963: *Born in Baku, Azerbaijan, U.S.S.R.*

1980: *Becomes international grandmaster; wins World Junior Championship*

1981: *Wins U.S.S.R. championship*

1985: *Becomes the youngest world champion*

1993: *Leaves FIDE and forms the Professional Chess Association (PCA) with the English grandmaster Nigel Short*

100 GREATS
in sports

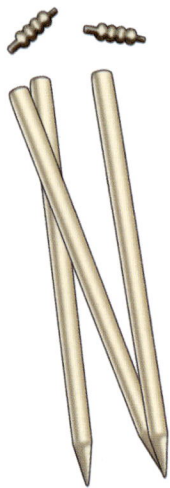

Cricket

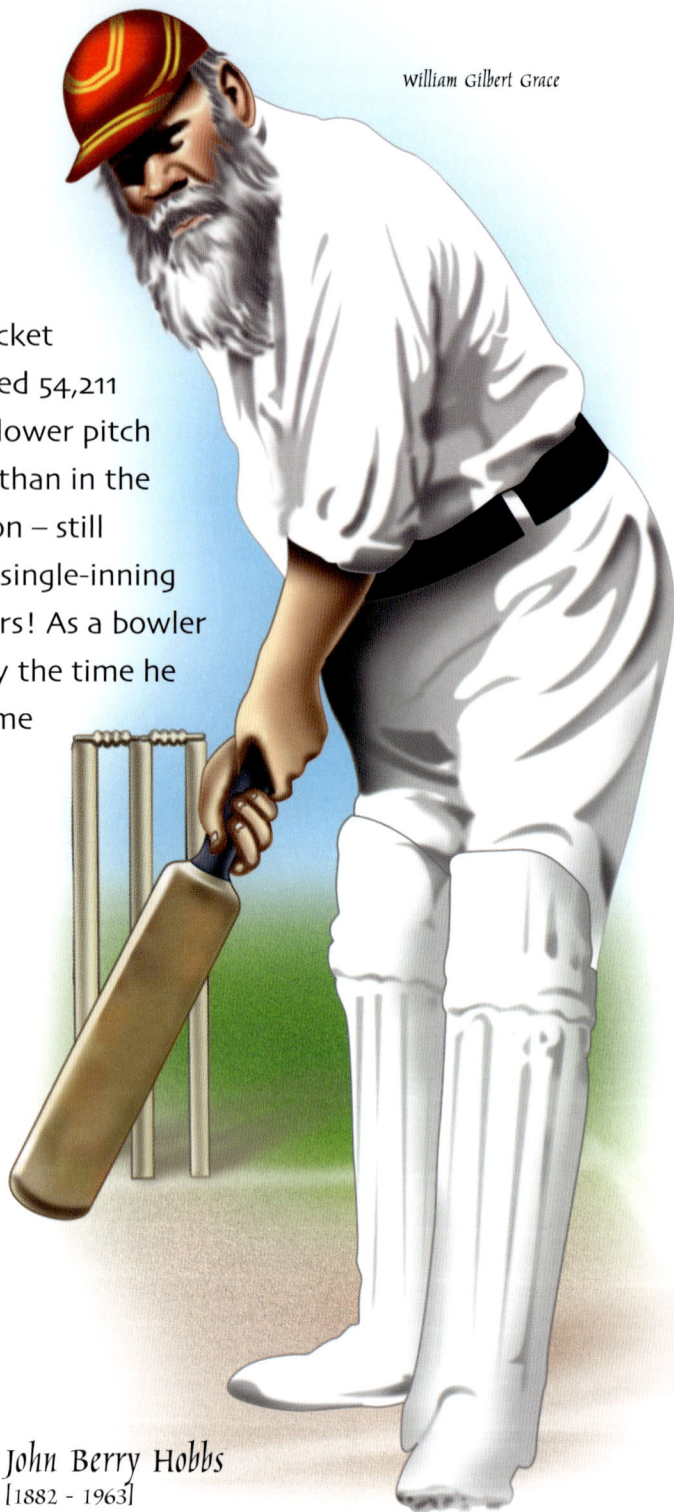

331 William Gilbert Grace
[1848 - 1915]

In 44 seasons of first-class cricket (1865-1908), W.G. Grace scored 54,211 runs. Playing at a time when lower pitch quality typically led to lower scoring than in the modern game, Grace – a doctor by profession – still managed to make 124 centuries. His record single-inning score of 344, made in 1876, stood for 19 years! As a bowler he claimed 2,809 wickets. Unfortunately, by the time he made his Test debut, Grace was past his prime on the cricket field.

July 18, 1848: Born in Downend, Gloucestershire, England

1880: Member of the English team that played the first Test match against Australia in England

1896: Named Wisden Cricketer of the Year

1899: Plays his last Test against Australia in the first match of the Ashes series

July 25, 1914: Plays his last match for Eltham

October 23, 1915: Dies in Mottingham, Kent, England

332 John Berry Hobbs
[1882 - 1963]

December 16, 1882: Born in Cambridge, England

1905: Makes his first-class debut on the Surrey cricket team

1928-29: Scores a Test century to become, at the age of 46, the oldest person to do so

1953: Becomes the first professional English cricketer to be knighted

December 21, 1963: Dies in Hove, Sussex, England

2000: Voted one of the five Wisden Cricketers of the Century

In first-class cricket history, John Berry Hobbs is the man with the most number of runs (61,760) as well as centuries (199). This he achieved despite the break-out of World War I (1914-18), which suspended play for four summers. Hobbs still went on to have an unusually long cricketing career (1905-34). Regarded as one of the finest batsman of his time, he made his Test-match debut in 1907, against Australia in Melbourne. He made 5,410 runs over 61 test matches.

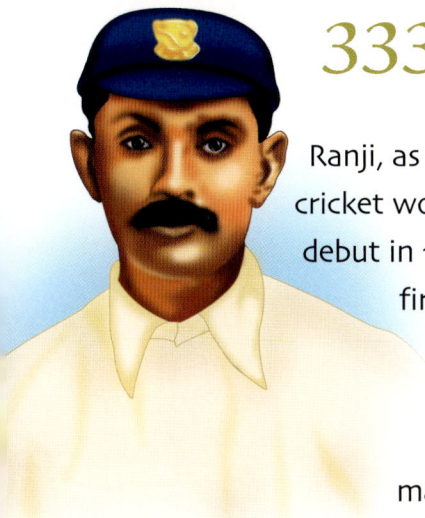

333 Ranjitsinhji Vibhaji
[1872 - 1933]

Ranji, as Ranjitsinhji was fondly called, took the cricket world by surprise when he made a forceful debut in 1895. Scoring 77 not out and 150 in his first match for Sussex, he followed it up with 62 and 154 not out in his first Test the very next year (1896). Then, in 1899, he became the world's first batsman to score over 3,000 runs in a season. He is remembered, chiefly, for his back-foot strokes - shots that were practically unheard of before.

Ranjitsinhji Vibhaji

September 10, 1872: Born an Indian prince in Sarodar, Kathiawar, India

1890-93: Attends Trinity College, Cambridge, England

1895: Plays his first match at the Lord's Ground

1896: Makes Test debut in England's second match against Australia held at Manchester, England

1897: Named Wisden Cricketer of the Year

March 1907: Becomes ruler of Nawanagar

1920: Plays his last match for Sussex

1932: Elected chancellor of the Indian Chamber of Princes

April 2, 1933: Dies in Jamnagar Palace, India

334 Donald Bradman
[1908 - 2001]

Donald Bradman

August 27, 1908: Born in Cootamundra, New South Wales, Australia

November 30, 1928: Makes his test debut against England, at Brisbane

January 3, 1929: Scores his first century in the match against England at the Melbourne Cricket Ground

1931: Adjudged Wisden Cricketer of the Year

1936-48: Captains the Australian cricket team

1949: Plays his last innings in first-class cricket. Also conferred with knighthood

1950: Publishes his memoirs, Farewell to Cricket; The Art of Cricket, comes out in 1958

2000: Voted (overwhelmingly) one of the five Wisden Cricketers of the Century

February 25, 2001: Dies in Adelaide, Australia

The best batsman of all time, Donald Bradman's batting achievements will never be matched. On his very first tour of England, in 1930, he made 334 runs in one innings. By the time he retired, Bradman had to his name 6,996 runs in international Test matches (at an average of 99.94 - a statistic now infamous because, out for a duck in his final test innings, he needed only to score four runs for an average of exactly 100).

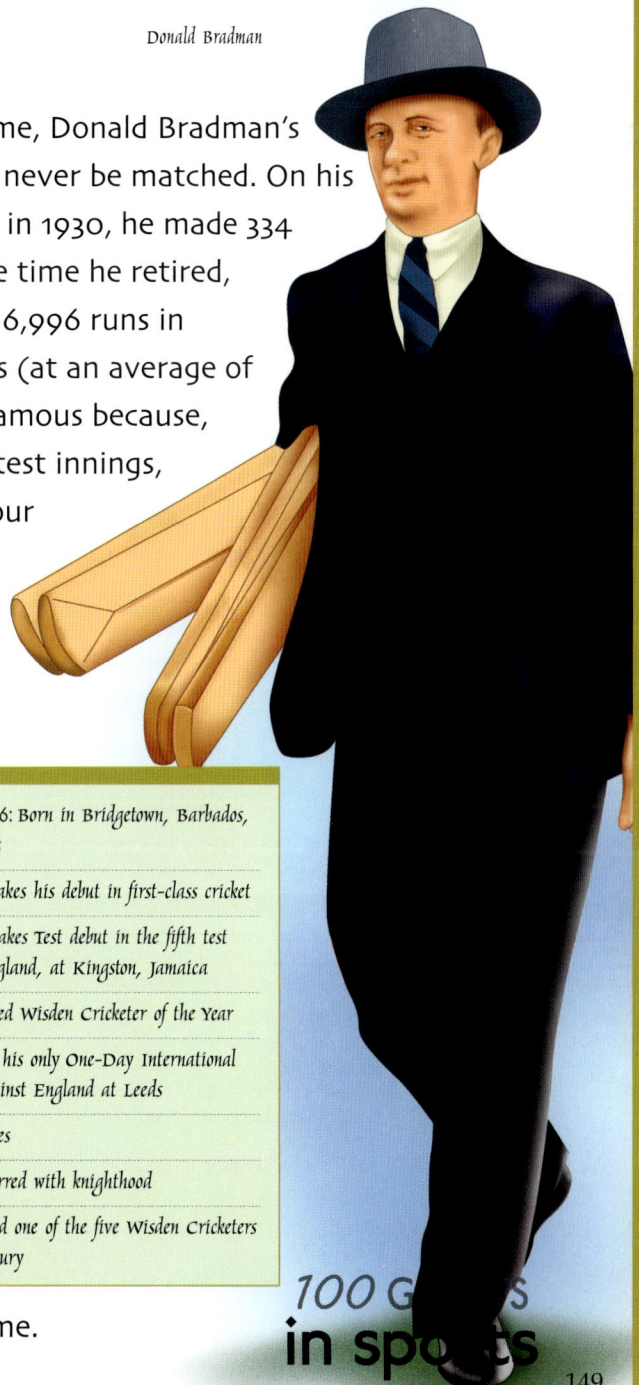

335 Garfield Sobers
[1936 -]

It is almost impossible to decide whether Garfield St. Aubrun Sobers was a greater batsman or bowler! He continues to be regarded as the greatest all-rounder in modern cricket. In 1958, the self-taught cricket whiz scored 365 not out against Pakistan – a Test batting record that stood for 36 years. He also scored six consecutive sixes off one over from the Australian bowler Malcolm Nash. Between 1965 and 1972, Sobers served as captain of the West Indies team for 39 Tests. He retired with 8,032 Test runs, 235 wickets and 109 catches to his name.

July 28, 1936: Born in Bridgetown, Barbados, West Indies

1952-53: Makes his debut in first-class cricket

1953-54: Makes Test debut in the fifth test against England, at Kingston, Jamaica

1964: Named Wisden Cricketer of the Year

1973: Plays his only One-Day International (ODI) against England at Leeds

1974: Retires

1975: Conferred with knighthood

2000: Voted one of the five Wisden Cricketers of the Century

100 GREATS in sports

336 Courtney Walsh
[1962 -]

Quiet by nature, Courtney Walsh took time to step out of the shadows of other greats like Joel Garner and Malcolm Marshall. However, by the 90s he had formed one of the most successful bowling partnerships with Curtly Ambrose. Previously holding the record for the most number of test wickets, Walsh still holds the record for the most economical spell (5 wickets for one run) in one-day cricket. He also has the dubious record of the most number of Test ducks (43 in 128 tests). But the "Gentle Giant" will always be remembered for his sporting spirit – a true gentleman in a gentleman's sport.

October 30, 1962: Born in Kingston, Jamaica, West Indies

1984: Makes his Test debut for West Indies against Australia, in Perth, Australia

1985: Makes his ODI debut against Sri Lanka

1986: Takes 5 wickets for one run against Sri Lanka, at Sharjah

1995: Gets his career best in Tests (7-37) against New Zealand in Wellington, New Zealand

March 19, 2001: Becomes the first player to take 500 wickets in Test history

April 23, 2001: Retires after helping West Indies win their final test match against South Africa at his home-ground in Sabina Park, Jamaica

Courtney Walsh

337 Allan Border
[1955 -]

Allan Border's autograph

One of the toughest Australian players ever, Allan Border was also a tough captain. When he took over the reigns, Australia was struggling to regain its lost glory. Not only did Border rise up to the challenge but he also set an example for future captains by excelling in his individual records. Holder of the record for the most Test runs (11,174), Border also holds the record for most Tests as captain (93)! During a decade-long captaincy (1984-94), he also helped his team bring the 1987 World Cup home by defeating England.

July 27, 1955: Born in Cremorne, Sydney, Australia

1978-79: Makes his Test debut in the third Test against England, in Melbourne, Australia

January 13, 1979: Plays his first One-Day International (ODI) against England in Sydney, Australlia

1982: Named Wisden Cricketer of the Year

1994: Retires from international cricket

November 24, 1955: Born in Oldfield, Heswall, Cheshire, England

1976: Makes ODI debut against West Indies, in Scarborough, England

1977: Makes Test debut in the third Test against Australia, in Nottingham, England

1993: Retires from the game

338 Ian Botham
[1955 -]

A popular sports personality and affectionately nicknamed "Beefy", his exceptional skills with the bat and the ball made Ian Terence Botham the English cricket team's match-winner. He got his 1,000 runs and 100 wickets from his first 21 matches and his 2,000 runs and 200 wickets from 42 – all of which were record-breaking feats! Botham's career total of 5,200 runs and 383 wickets came from just 102 Tests.

339 Steve Waugh
[1965 -]

Steve Waugh

The most successful captain ever, Steve Waugh will be remembered for his ruthlessness and loyalty to his team. A gritty captain, Steve was an equally determined player. His 10,927 Test runs is second only to his mentor Allan Border. But Steve's contribution as a captain surpasses all his other achievements. He has a tremendous record of 41 wins out of the 57 Tests he has led Australia in. And in his last Test match against India, Steve played a captain's innings by helping Australia draw a match that was almost lost.

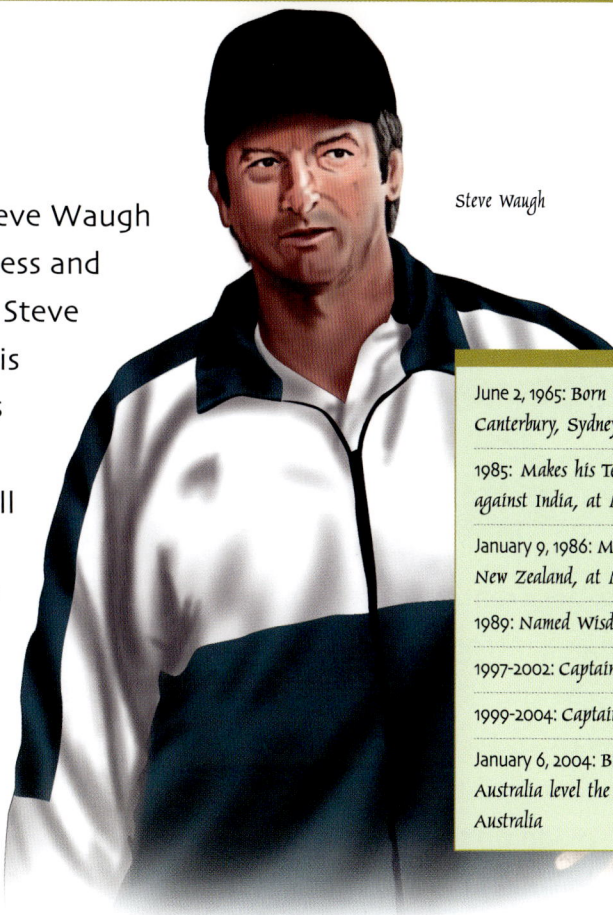

June 2, 1965: Born Stephen Rodger Waugh in Canterbury, Sydney, Australia

1985: Makes his Test debut in the 2nd match against India, at Melbourne, Australia

January 9, 1986: Makes his one-day debut against New Zealand, at Melbourne

1989: Named Wisden Cricketer of the Year

1997-2002: Captains the Australian one-day team

1999-2004: Captains the Australian Test team

January 6, 2004: Bids farewell to cricket after helping Australia level the series with India at Sydney, Australia

340 Sachin Tendulkar
[1973 -]

Sachin Tendulkar

Arguably the greatest batsman after Don Bradman, Sachin Tendulkar is a class apart. Ever since his debut at the tender age of 16, Tendulkar has shown a hunger for runs that remains unsatisfied. The first to score over 50 centuries at the international level, the highest number of Test centuries, the highest number of one-day hundreds, the only batsman to pass the 14,000-run mark in One Day Internationals – his list of records goes on. A fluid stroke-play, confident drives and perfect timing is the secret of his success.

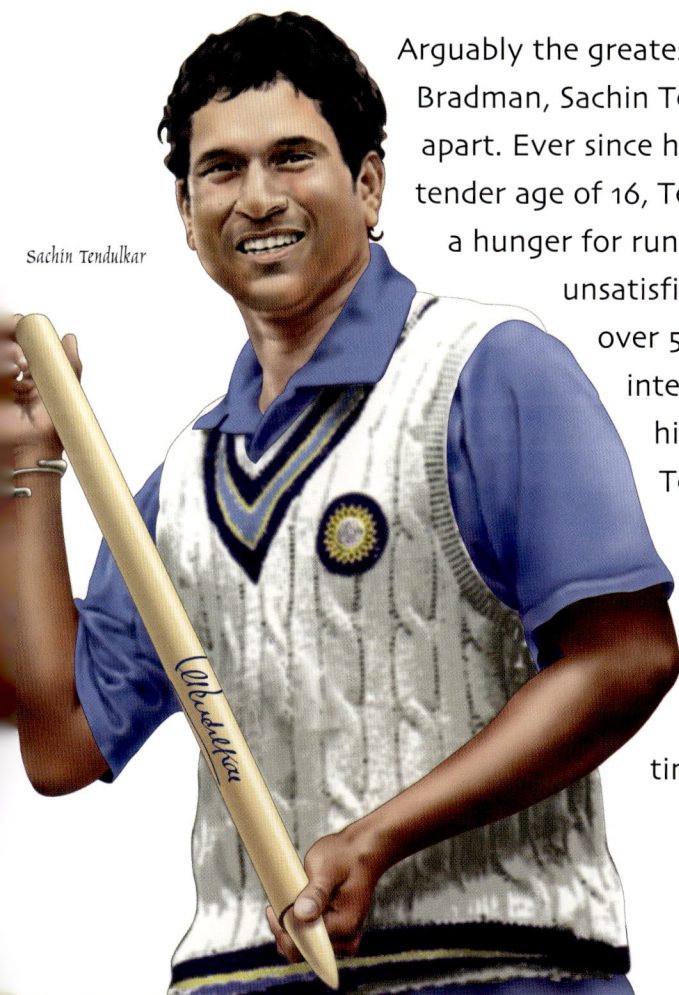

April 24, 1973: Born in Mumbai, India

November 15, 1989: Makes his international debut against Pakistan in Karachi

August 14, 1990: Scores his first Test hundred

1992: Makes his World Cup debut

September 9, 1994: Scores his first century in one-day cricket against Australia in Colombo, Sri Lanka

1997: Named Widen Cricketer of the Year

March 31, 2001: Becomes the first batsman to score 10,000 runs in one-day cricket

2003: Captures the record for the most number of runs at the World Cup

December 10, 2005: Scores a record 35th Test century against Sri Lanka, overtaking Sunivil Gavaskar's record

100 GREATS
in sports

Figure Skating

341 Jackson Haines
[1840 -1876]

A pioneering American skater, Jackson Haines is regarded as the father of figure skating. A ballet dancer, Haines created graceful dance steps especially for the ice and introduced accompanying music. He is thought to be the first to have screwed his figure skates directly to the boot. Haines brought both grace and charm to the stiff movements that had until then made up the sport of skating. His teachings became known as the International Style of Skating.

1840: Born in New York, U.S.

1863: Sets up a skating school in Vienna, Austria

1876: Dies in Gamla-Karleby, Finland

342 Sonja Henie
[1912 - 1969]

For 10 years in a row (1927-36), Sonja Henie was the world figure skating champion. The record remains unbroken. The Norwegian-born American took to skating as a six-year-old and competed in the Winter Olympics even before she had turned 12! Her three successive Olympic gold medals (1928, 1932, 1936) came before she was 24! Henie toured extensively to stage grand ice shows, thereby greatly adding to the popularity of the sport.

April 8, 1912: Born in Kristiania (now Oslo), Norway

1922: Wins the Norwegian national figure skating championship

1927: Wins the first of her ten consecutive world championships

1936: Turns professional skater; also stars in her first film, One in a Million

1940: Publishes her autobiography, Wings on My Feet

October 12, 1969: Dies en route from Paris to Oslo

Sonja Henie

343 Carol Heiss
[1940 -]

A competitive winner at the age of nine, Carol Elizabeth Heiss went on to become a five-time world champion in figure skating. From 1953 to 1956, she won four successive silver medals in the U.S. figure skating championships and from 1957 to 1960, four straight gold medals! She took her Olympic gold at the 1960 Winter games in Squaw Valley, California.

January 20, 1940: Born in New York, U.S.

1956: Wins a silver at the Olympic Winter Games in Cortina d'Ampezzo, Italy

1956-60: Wins five world championships in a row

1960: Marries Hayes Jenkins, another champion figure skater

1976: Elected to the World Figure Skating Hall of Fame

Carol Heiss

344 Irina Rodnina
[1949 -]

Irina Konstantinovna Rodnina was in two of the most successful figure skating pairs in the sport's history. With Aleksey Ulanov, she won the gold in the 1972 Winter Olympic Games in Sapporo, Japan. The pair also took four world championships (1969-72). Rodnina's partnership with her husband Aleksandr Zaytsev was even more successful – two Olympic gold medals (1976, in Innsbruck, Austria and 1980, in Lake Placid, New York) and six world championships (1973-78).

September 12, 1949: Born in Moscow, Russia, U.S.S.R.

1969-78: Wins 10 consecutive European pairs championships; wins again in 1980

1975: Marries Aleksandr Zaytsev

1980: Retires from skating

345 Scott Hamilton
[1958 -]

August 28, 1958: Born in Toledo, Ohio, U.S.

1986: Helps form a touring figure skating company, Stars on Ice

1990: Inducted into the International Figure Skating Hall of Fame

1999: Publishes his autobiography, Landing It: My Life on and off the Ice

Scott Hamilton

In his childhood, Scott Hamilton suffered from a disease that stopped his growth for nearly six years. Later, he grew to only 5 feet 2.5 inches. Thankfully, at the age of nine, he took to skating like a natural and in two years he was competing in regional competitions. Then, from 1981 to 1984, Hamilton won four consecutive world championships as well as four U.S. national titles. He capped it all with a gold medal at the 1984 Winter Olympics in Sarajevo, Yugoslavia (now in Bosnia and Herzegovina).

100 GREATS
in sports

Football

346 Stanley Matthews
[1915 - 2000]

Nicknamed the "wizard of dribble", Sir Stanley Matthews was known for his speed and accurate passes. Son of a feather-weight boxer, Sir Stanley's talent for football became clear at a young age. Just two years after he turned professional, Sir Stanley was in the English team. Famous for his sportsmanship, Sir Stanley was often referred to as "the first gentleman of soccer". True to his character, Sir Stanley was never once booked for foul play in his 34-year career!

Stanley Matthews

February 1, 1915: Born in Stoke-on-Trent, England

1932: Debuts for Stoke City

1934: Makes his debut for England against Wales

1947: Joins Blackpool

1948: Named Football Player of the Year

1953: Helps Blackpool defeat Bolton Wanderers in the FA Cup final. The match is popularly known as the "Matthews Final"

1956: Awarded the first European Football Player of the Year

1957: Made a Commander of the Order of the British Empire

1964: Becomes the first football player to be knighted

1965: Retires after a long career that lasted more than three decades

February 23, 2000: Dies at the age of 85

October 11, 1937: Born in Ashington, Northumberland, England

October 6, 1956: Scores two goals for Manchester United in his debut against Charlton Athletic

February 6, 1958: Survives the Munich air disaster in which eight of his team mates from Manchester United die

April 19, 1958: Makes his international debut for England against Scotland

1963: Stars in the Manchester United win at the FA Cup

1966: England defeat West Germany to win their first World Cup. Sir Bobby is named European Footballer of the Year for his performance during the tournament

1968: Manchester United becomes the first English team to win the European Cup

1973: Retires from international football

1984: Becomes a director of Manchester United club

1994: Conferred knighthood

347 Robert Charlton
[1937 -]

Born into a family of football players, it was Sir Bobby's mother who first taught him how to play. A professional from the start, he keenly studied the various styles of great players of the time. His idol was Sir Stanley Matthews from whom young Charlton learned the importance of speed. Sir Bobby was still in school when he joined Manchester United Football Club. He was greatly involved in rebuilding the club and turning it into the football giant it is today. He played a major role in England's Word Cup triumph in 1966.

348 *Pelé*
[1940 -]

According to a popular story, Edson Arantes do Nascimento was playing with some Turkish children when he tried to stop the ball with his hands. This earned him the name "Pelé", ("pe" meaning foot and "lé" meaning fool). Whatever the reasons, among all modern sports heroes, his is easily one of the most famous names! Pelé's status can be measured by the fact that in 1967, the Nigerian civil war was stopped for two days so that he could play an exhibition match at Lagos!

October 23, 1940: *Born in Três Corações, Brazil*

1958: *Leads Brazil in its first World Cup triumph. Helps the team to win it again in 1962 and 1970*

1956: *Joins the Santos Football Club, which wins the first world club championship in 1962*

1974: *Retires from international football. At the time he held a tremendous record of 1220 international goals – an average of one goal per match*

1975: *Comes out of retirement to play for the New York Cosmos*

1978: *Conferred with the International Peace Award*

1980: *Named Athlete of the Century*

Pelé

349 *Franz Beckenbauer*
[1945 -]

Franz Beckenbauer

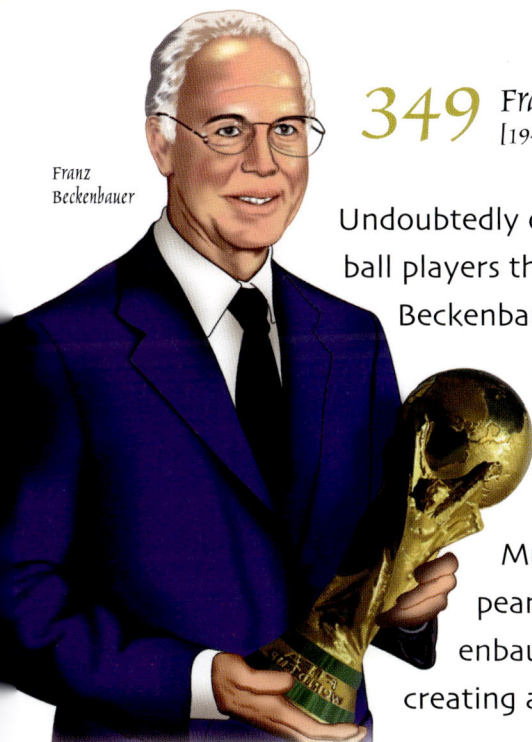

Undoubtedly one of the greatest German football players the world has ever known, Franz Beckenbauer changed the way football was played. He is the only person to have won the World Cup both as a player and as a manager. He also led his club, Bayern Munich, to three successive European Cups. Called the "Kaiser", Beckenbauer revolutionised football by creating an attacking role for the sweeper.

September 11, 1945: *Born in Munich, Germany*

June 6, 1964: *Debuts for Bayern Munich*

September 26, 1965: *Makes his international debut for West Germany*

1966: *Plays in his first World Cup final against England. West Germany lost that match*

1972: *Wins European Championship. Named the European Footballer of the Year*

1974: *Wins the Munich World Cup and the European Cup*

1976: *Bayern Munich wins the European Cup for the third time under his captaincy. He is once again named the European Footballer of the Year*

1984: *Announces his retirement. Becomes the manager of the West German team*

1990: *As the manager of a united German team, he plays a major role in its World Cup triumph in Italy*

April 25, 1947: *Born in Amsterdam, Netherlands*

c. 1960: *Drops out of school to concentrate on football*

1963: *Makes his debut for Ajax*

1966: *Debuts for Netherlands against Hungary*

1971: *Wins the first of the three European Cup and the first of the three European Footballer of the Year awards*

1974: *Makes his only World Cup appearance in Munich.*

1978: *Retires from international football as a political protest after helping Netherlands qualify for the World Cup in Argentina*

350. *Johan Cruyff*
[1947 -]

Despite a short international career, Cruyff is regarded as one of the all-time football greats. He achieved international fame with his elegance, technique and his well-timed passes. His brilliance was most evident during the 1974 World Cup at Munich. He led an average Netherlands team into the finals where, despite a promising start, Netherlands was defeated by West Germany. However, Cruyff was named the Player of the Tournament.

100 GREATS
in sports

351 Michel Platini
[1955 -]

One of the greatest midfielders the game has ever known, Platini was creative and aggressive. He is the all-time top scorer for the French and is the only player to have won the European Footballer of the Year award thrice in a row. Though Platini achieved most of what the game had to offer, he failed to add the World Cup to his trophies. However, he led France in many of its memorable victories and helped in making it a powerful team.

FIFA World Cup

June 21, 1955: Born in Joeuf, France

1976: Plays at the Olympics and makes his international debut against Czechoslovakia

1978: Makes his World Cup debut

1982: Leads France to the semi-finals of the World Cup in Spain

1983: Wins the first of his three European Footballer of the Year awards

1984: Leads France to its first European Championship

May 29, 1985: Platini helps Juventus, the Italian club to win their first European Cup

1988: Retires from professional football and becomes the manager of the French team

January 26, 2007: Elected President of the Union of European Football Associations (UEFA)

352 Diego Maradona
[1960 -]

Diego Maradona

October 30, 1960: Born in Villa Fiorito, Buenos Aires, Argentina

February 27, 1977: Makes his international debut for Argentina against Hungary

1993: Named the Best Argentine Footballer ever

1994: Banned for failing a drug test during the World Cup

1995: Receives the Golden Ball for his achievements

October 30, 1997: Retires from professional football

Considered the Pelé of Argentina, Diego Maradona is one of the most talented and controversial players to ever grace the game. Known for his technique and magical left foot, Maradona is best remembered for helping Argentina win the 1986 World Cup. The tournament is also famous for two of his most memorable goals. Apart from the infamous "Hand of God", the quarter-finals against England also witnessed a classic Maradona act, in which he outwitted seven English players to score what is regarded as one of the best goals in World Cup history.

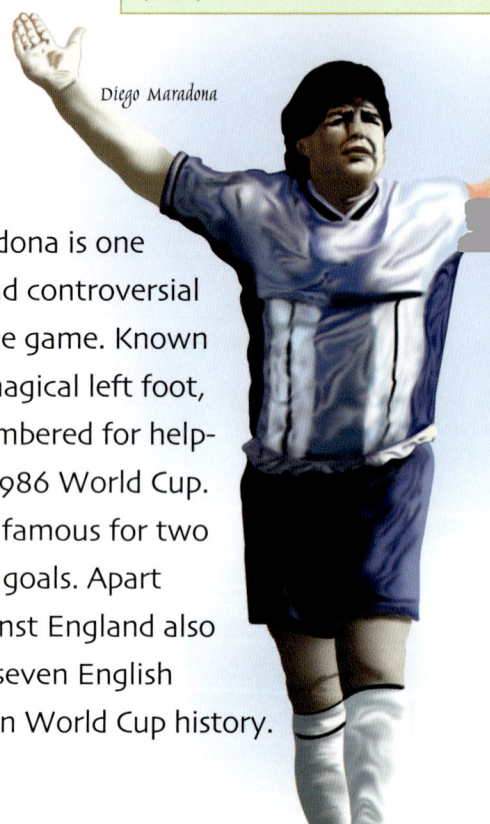

353 Marco Van Basten
[1964 -]

October 31, 1964: Born in Utrecht, Netherlands

1982: Debuts for Ajax

September 7, 1983: Plays his first match for Netherlands against Iceland

1987: Moves to the Italian club, AC Milan

1992: Becomes the first Dutch player to be named the FIFA World Player of the Year

July, 2004: Named as manager of the Dutch national team

Regarded as the most dangerous striker the game ever produced, Marco van Basten was known for his cool and calm nature. Never one to give into pressure, Marco has scored several memorable goals. Aptly named "Marco Goalo", he was feared by all international defenders of the time. He joined other great names in Dutch football like Rudd Gullit and Frank Rijkaard to bring lost glory back to the Netherlands. Marco's greatness is clear from the fact that he won three European Footballer of the Year awards and was the World Soccer Player of the Year twice.

354 Zinedine Zidane
[1972 -]

The best French player after Platini, Zidane is regarded as one of the best-ever midfielders. He shot to fame in 1994, when he scored two goals as a substitute in a match between France and the Czech Republic. An integral part of the French team ever since, Zidane also starred in his country's World Cup triumph in 1998. He became the most expensive footballer ever when the Spanish club Real Madrid acquired him for a whopping £46 million!

June 23, 1972: Born in Marseille, France

1994: Debuts for France as a substitute

1996: Wins European Super Cup and World Club Cup with Juventus

July 12, 1998: Helps France defeat Brazil in the World Cup final by scoring two spectacular goals

1998: Becomes European footballer of the Year and FIFA World Player of the Year in the same year

2000: Wins Euro 2000 Championship with France and is named the World Player of the Year again

2001: Real Madrid pays the largest amount in football history to acquire him from Juventus

2002: Helps Real Madrid win the European Champions League

2006: Retires from football after the 2006 World Cup Final, which France lost to Italy on penalties after extra-time

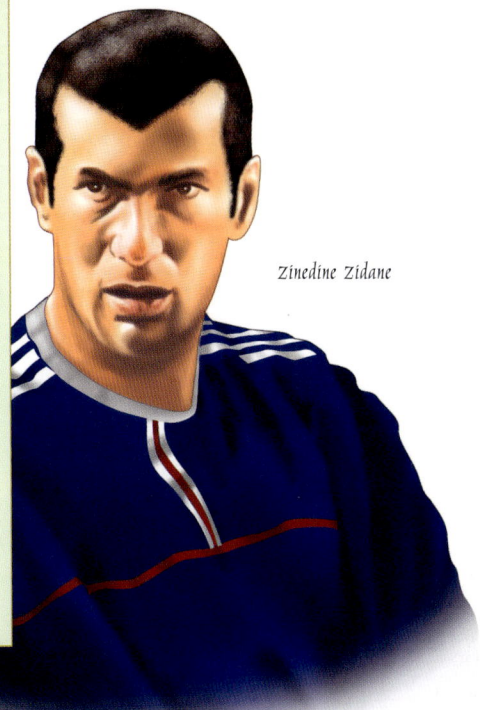

Zinedine Zidane

355 Ronaldo
[1976 -]

Ronaldo

One of the most talented football players of all time, Ronaldo is second only to Pelé in his football-crazy country. Regarded as one of the best forwards in the game, Ronaldo's career has also had its downside. Troubled by injuries, Ronaldo has been in and out of the international scene. His biggest disappointment came during the 1998 World Cup, when Brazil (the favourites to win the Cup) lost to France in the final. However, Ronaldo had the chance to make up for his earlier disappointment when he helped Brazil to win the 2002 World Cup.

September 22, 1976: Born in Bento Ribero, Brazil

1994: World Cup winner

1996: Named the FIFA World Player of the Year

1997: Becomes the European Footballer of the Year and wins the World Player of the Year award again

2002: Wins the Golden Boot for becoming the top scorer at the World Cup as Brazil wins the cup. Also becomes the FIFA World Player of the Year for a record equaling third time

100 GREATS
in sports

Formula 1

356 Bernd Rosemeyer
[1909 - 1938]

October 14, 1909: Born in Lingen, Germany

1935: Wins his first important race – the Masark Grand Prix, in Czechoslovakia

January 28, 1938: Dies near Mörfelden, Germany

In just three seasons of car racing (1935-37), Bernd Rosemeyer stamped his name among the sport's most memorable icons. The year 1936 saw Rosemeyer become European champion, as he raced to victory in the German, Swiss and Italian Grand Prix. His trophies in 1937 included the German Grand Prix, the Vanderbilt Cup (U.S.), the Acerbo Cup (Italy) and the Donnington Grand Prix in England. In 1938, while participating in a contest to set new speed records, the fearless Rosemeyer ignored warnings of strong winds and crashed to his death on the Frankfurt-Darmstadt track.

357 Juan Manuel Fangio
[1911 - 1995]

Juan Manuel Fangio

Juan Manuel Fangio dominated the first decade of Formula 1, winning his first World Championship in 1951. He won five World Championships in total - a record which stood for 46 years - with four different teams, a feat that has never been repeated. He is a true icon and is considered by many to be the greatest racing driver of all time. He won 24 Grand Prix in 51 starts, the best winning percentage in the sport's history.

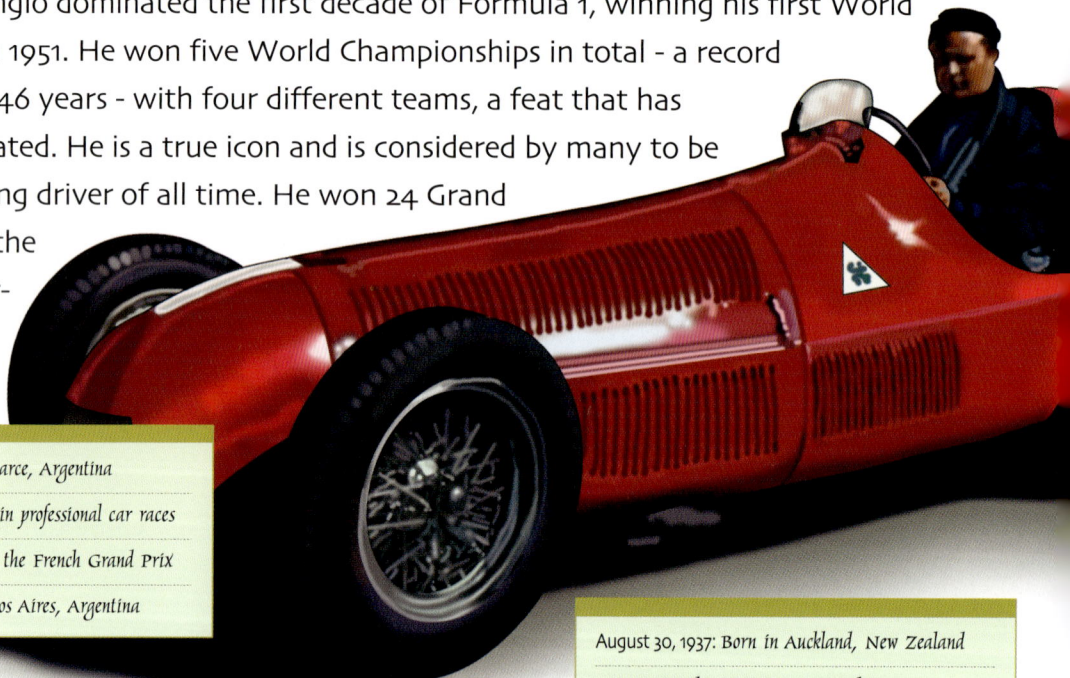

June 24, 1911: Born in Balcarce, Argentina

1936: Starts participating in professional car races

1958: Drives his last race, the French Grand Prix

July 17, 1995: Dies in Buenos Aires, Argentina

358 Bruce McLaren
[1937 - 1970]

August 30, 1937: Born in Auckland, New Zealand

1960: Wins the Argentinean Grand Prix

1962: Wins the Monaco Grand Prix

1964: Starts designing racing cars

June 2, 1970: Dies in a testing accident at the Goodwood circuit near Chichester, Sussex, England

In 1959, Bruce McLaren won the U.S. Grand Prix at Sebring to become the youngest winner in Formula 1 history. In 1966, McLaren put together his own F1 team. It was to become one of the most successful racing teams in the world. Besides four Grand Prix championships, McLaren's other major wins were the Le Mans 24-hour race (1966), the Canadian-American Challenge Cup series (1967, 1969) and the Belgian Grand Prix (1968). Most of these wins came in cars designed by the champion himself!

359 Ayrton Senna
[1960 - 1994]

It all started with the go-kart that he got from his father as a four-year-old. The little Ayrton Senna da Silva was to become a car-racing legend and Brazil's national hero. Senna earned a total of 41 Grand Prix wins and 3 World Championships (1988, 1990, 1991). Known for his fast and fearsome driving, he had records for the fastest qualifying times. He sped to his tragic, premature death driving at the San Marino Grand Prix.

Ayrton Senna

March 21, 1960: Born in São Paulo, Brazil

1973: Wins his first karting race

1984: Makes his Formula 1 debut

May 1, 1994: Dies in a car crash in Imola, Italy

Michael Schumacher

360 Michael Schumacher
[1969 -]

Michael Schumacher is the most successful F1 racing driver ever. A record 7 World Championship titles, of which four were consecutive, and the most number of wins in Grand Prix top the long list of F1 records. From karting, to king of the Formula 1 circuit, "Schumi" has come a long way. He won his first World Championship title in 1994. He went on to retain it in 1995. This led to his alliance with Ferrari, one that was to go down in F1 history as the most successful racing partnership ever. Schumacher's driving career was not without controversy - he was disqualified from the 1997 World Championship. Despite this, his brilliance is without question. A devoted family man, Schumacher is also known for generous charitable donations from his great wealth.

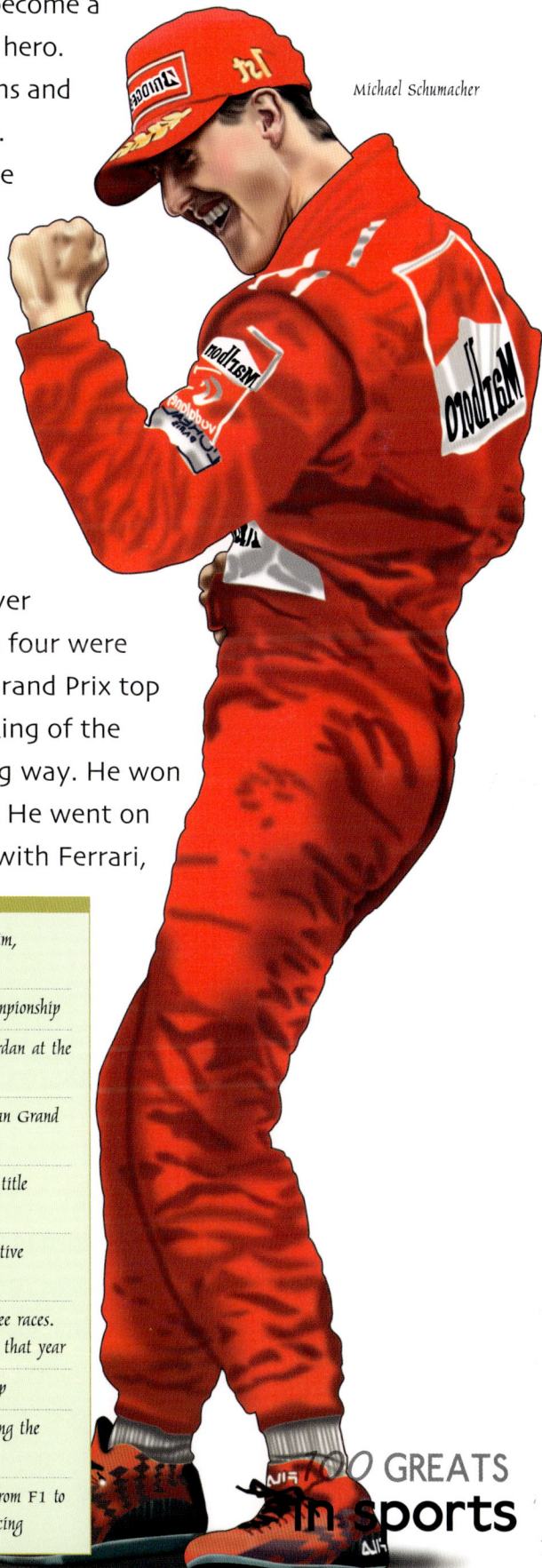

January 3, 1969: Born in Hurth-Hermulheim, Germany

1984: Wins the German Junior Kart Championship

1991: Makes his Formula 1 debut with Jordan at the Belgian Grand Prix

1992: Wins his first F1 race at the Belgian Grand Prix

1994: Wins his first World Championship title driving for Benetton

1995: Becomes the youngest to win consecutive championship titles

1996: Moves to Ferrari, but wins only three races. Damon Hill becomes the World Champion that year

2000: Wins his third World Championship

2003: Overtakes Fangio's record by becoming the World Champion for the sixth time

September 10, 2006: Retires as a driver from F1 to take up executive position with Ferrari racing

700 GREATS in sports

Golf

361 James Braid [1870 - 1950]

February 6, 1870: Born in Earlsferry, Fife, Scotland

1893: Goes to London to work as a club-maker

1896: Becomes a professional player

November 27, 1950: Dies in London, England

Along with the Englishmen Harry Vardon and John Henry Taylor, Scotsman James Braid dominated the game of golf in the early part of the 20th century, Together they became famous as the "great triumvirate". Braid had his first success in 1901, when he won the British Open. By the close of the decade, he had become the first man to win the event five times. Braid also secured four British PGA Championships and the 1910 French Open.

362 Joyce Wethered [1901 - 1997]

November 17, 1901: Born in Brook, Surrey, England

1937: Marries Sir John Heathcoat-Amory

1951: Becomes the first president of the English Ladies' Golf Association

1975: Inducted into the Professional Golfers' Association (PGA) World Golf Hall of Fame

November 18, 1997: Dies in London, England

Joyce Wethered is regarded as one of the greatest woman golfers. She made her mark in a career that lasted barely a decade! Wethered first caught the public eye as a 19-year old, when she won the English Ladies' Championship. She went on to win four British Women's Amateur Championships (1922, 1924, 1925 and 1929) and five English Ladies' Championship titles in a row (1920-24).

363 Bobby Jones [1902 - 1971]

March 17, 1902: Born in Atlanta, Georgia, U.S.

1923: Wins the U.S. Open, his first major championship

1930: Retires from competitive golf at the age of 28

1931: Produces the famous 12-part educational golf film titled, How I Play Golf

1933: Opening of the Augusta National golf course designed by him. The course plays host to the Masters, one of the four major tournaments today

December 18, 1971: Dies, in Atlanta, Georgia, U.S.

Bobby Jones

A child prodigy, Bobby Jones won the Atlanta Athletic Club junior title at the age of nine! However, success in the major championships took longer. As a youth he struggled with his temperament and his performances were mixed. The tide turned when he finally won the 1923 U.S. Open in New York. Within the next seven years, Jones won the U.S. Open 4 times, the U.S. Amateur 5 times, the British Open 3 times and the British Amateur once. In 1930, he became the first man to achieve the grand slam by winning the British and U.S. Opens and Amateur Championships in a single year!

364 Sam Snead
[1912 - 2002]

Sam Snead

Samuel Jackson Snead's name brings to mind the image of an ever-smiling man wearing a straw hat and walking barefoot on the golf course. "Slammin" Sam was an exceptionally successful golfer – his 81 PGA victories remain unmatched. He also won around 185 tournaments! The only championship that eluded him was the U.S. Open. By winning the 1965 Greater Greensboro Open title at the age of 52, he became the oldest golfer to win a PGA event.

May 27, 1912: Born in Hot Springs, Virginia, U.S.

1934: Becomes a professional golfer

1937: Wins five events including the Oakland Open in his first year on the PGA Tour

1938: Wins the first of his eight Greater Greensboro Open titles

1942: Wins his first major, the PGA Championship

1950: Wins 11 tournaments which continues to be the most number of wins in a year

1953: Elected to the PGA Hall of Fame

1962: Publishes his autobiography, The Education of a Golfer

May 23, 2002: Dies in Hot Springs, Virginia, U.S.

365 Patty Berg
[1918 - 2006]

In many ways, Patricia Jane Berg was an unusual woman. In her early teens, she played in the local boys' football team. During World War II, she served as a lieutenant in the Marine Corps. In 1950, she was a founding member and the first president of the Ladies Professional Golf Association (LPGA). Berg's career victories stand at an impressive 60, which includes 15 major championships – an LPGA record.

February 13, 1918: Born in Minneapolis, Minnesota, U.S.

1938: Wins the national women's amateur title

1940: Becomes a professional golf player

1941: Survives a car crash

1967: One of the original inductees into the LPGA Tour Hall of Fame

1978: The LPGA institutes the annual Patty Berg Award for outstanding contributions to women's golf; Berg herself won it in 1990

1980: Inducted into the International Women's Sports Hall of Fame

September 12, 2006: Dies aged 88 after a long struggle with Alzheimer's disease

Patricia Jane Berg

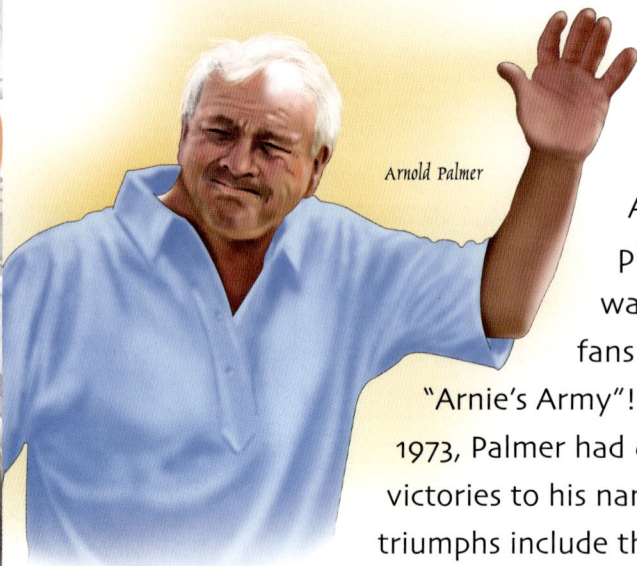

366 Arnold Palmer
[1929 -]

Arnold Palmer

As a leading golf player, Arnold Palmer was so popular that his fans became known as "Arnie's Army"! Between 1955 and 1973, Palmer had 62 U.S. PGA Tour victories to his name. His major triumphs include the U.S. Open (1960), the British Open (1961, 1962) and the four titles in the Masters Tournament (1958, 1960, 1962, 1964). As president of Arnold Palmer Enterprises, the golf champ greatly contributed towards the growth and popularity of the sport.

September 10, 1929: Born in Latrobe, Pennsylvania, U.S.

1954: Turns golf professional after winning the U.S. Amateur Championship

1964: Becomes first player to win the Masters Tournament four times

1967: Becomes the first golf professional to win $1,000,000 in prize money

1981: Wins the PGA Senior Open

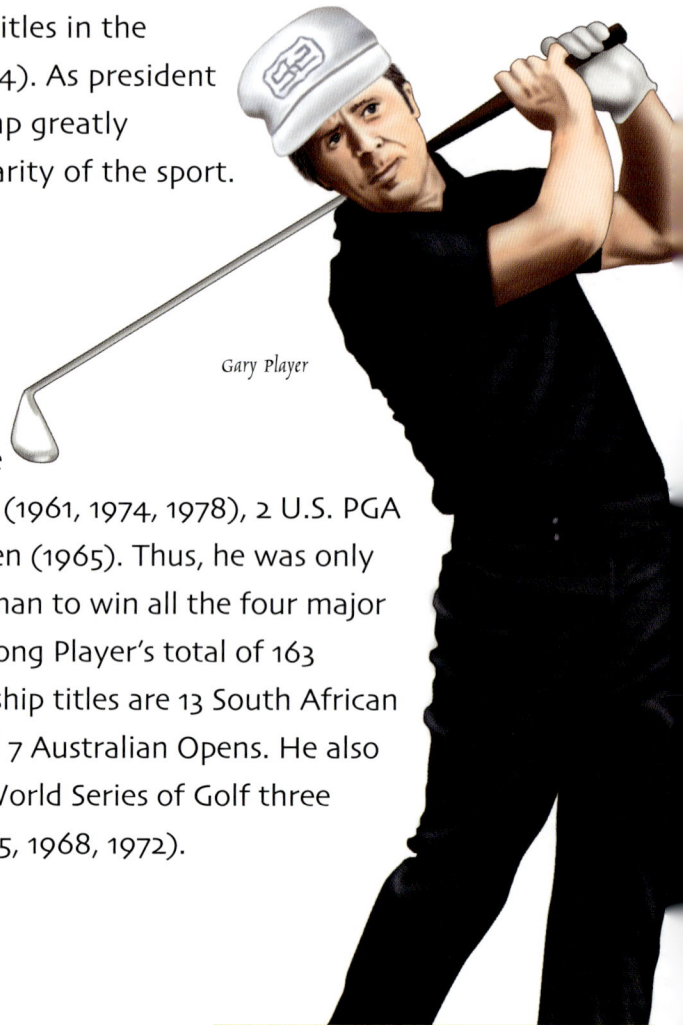

367 Gary Player
[1935 -]

Gary Player

Regarded as one of the all-time golfing greats, Gary Player's nine major titles include 3 British Opens (1959, 1968, 1974), 3 Masters (1961, 1974, 1978), 2 U.S. PGA Championships (1962, 1972) and the U.S. Open (1965). Thus, he was only the third man to win all the four major titles! Among Player's total of 163 championship titles are 13 South African Opens and 7 Australian Opens. He also won the World Series of Golf three times (1965, 1968, 1972).

November 1, 1935: Born in Johannesburg, South Africa

1953: Turns professional

1957: Joins the U.S. PGA circuit

1974: Inducted into the World Golf Hall of Fame

368 Kathy Whitworth
[1939 -]

Kathrynne Ann Whitworth was the foremost LPGA player for nearly a decade. Her 88 tournament titles are more than any other professional golfer, male or female, has ever achieved. She was LPGA Player of the Year seven times (1966-69; 1971-73). She was also a recipient of the Vare Trophy seven times (1965-67; 1969-72) for best average in the LPGA tour. The only tour title that Whitworth failed to win was the U.S. Open.

September 27, 1939: Born in Monahans, Texas, U.S.

1958: Turns professional, joins the LPGA Tour

1967: Becomes president of the LPGA

1975: Inducted into the LPGA Hall of Fame

1981: Becomes the first woman to reach career earnings of $1 million on the LPGA Tour

1984: Inducted into the International Women's Sports Hall of Fame

1990: Leads the victorious U.S. team in the first Solheim Cup

369 Jack Nicklaus
[1940 -]

Nicknamed the "Golden Bear", Jack William Nicklaus was one of golf's super-achievers. Despite the brilliance of Tiger Woods, for the time being he is generally considered to be the greatest player the game has ever produced. Between 1962 and 1986, he won a record 18 major titles – six Masters Tournament, four U.S. Open, three British Open and five PGA championship titles. Besides winning the Players Championship a record three times, Nicklaus also represented the U.S. team in six Ryder Cup victories.

Jack Nicklaus

> January 21, 1940: Born in Columbus, Ohio, U.S.
>
> 1959: Wins the U.S. Amateur championship
>
> 1962: Turns professional
>
> 1967: Named PGA Player of the Year; earns the honour again in 1972, 1973, 1975 and 1976
>
> 1974: Inducted into the World Golf Hall of Fame

370 Tiger Woods
[1975 -]

Eldrick "Tiger" Woods has taken golf to new heights. His talent, teamed with his personality, have succeeded in making him one of the most recognisable sports personalities in the world. His rise to fame reads like a fairytale. Woods began playing golf from the time he learnt to walk. Such was his passion that he dropped out of college to pursue a career in golf. He created history for the first time in 1990, when he became the youngest player to win the U.S. Junior Amateur Championship. Ever since, Woods has been re-writing the record books.

Tiger Woods

> December 30, 1975: Born in Cypress, California, U.S.
>
> 1978: Appears on "The Mike Douglas Show" in a putting contest with Bob Hope, the comedian
>
> 1994: Becomes the youngest golfer ever to win the U.S. Amateur championship at the age of 18
>
> 1996: Turns professional
>
> 1997: Becomes the youngest and the first person of African or Asian origin to win the Masters Tournament
>
> 2000: Wins the PGA Championship, the U.S. and British Open
>
> April 2001: Wins his second Masters title becoming the first player in the history of golf to hold all four major golf titles at the same time. Also wins his third consecutive PGA Player of the Year award
>
> 2005: Is the highest paid professional athlete of the year with earnings of $87 million!

100 GREATS
in sports

Rugby

371 Gareth Edwards [1947 -]

Former Welsh captain Gareth Edwards is considered by many to be the greatest player in the history of the game. The best scrum-half ever to have graced the sport, Edwards made 53 consecutive appearances for Wales and was captain for 13 of them. His most glorious moment was helping the British Lions Team to post its first-ever victory over New Zealand in 1973. Since his retirement in 1978, Edwards has been seen in many roles including those of a commentator and writer.

372 John Peter Rhys Williams [1949 -]

One of the greatest names in rugby, Dr. JPR Williams was a key player during the golden age of Welsh rugby. A surgeon by profession, his first passion, however, was tennis. Despite winning the 1966 Junior Wimbledon Championship, JPR had to give up tennis in favour of his studies. Later he started to play rugby as a full back. What tennis lost, rugby gained! The most capped Welsh player, JPR made a total of 55 appearances for his country, including five as captain.

Philippe Sella

373 Philippe Sella [1962 -]

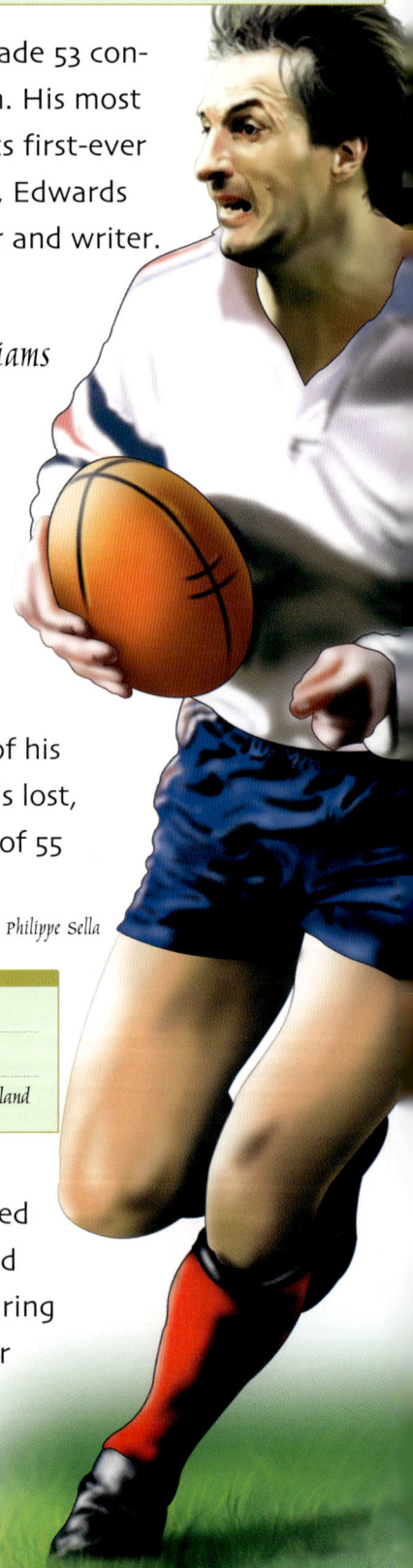

Known for his speed and grace, Sella held the record for the highest number of international caps (and has since been overtaken by only two men). He joined with French rugby giants like Serge Blanco, Pierre Berbizier and Laurent Rodriguez to make France the best European team during the 1980s. Sella is considered the best centre the sport has ever known. Despite his big build, Sella was very quick on the field. He also helped France win the Five Nations Tournament five times and reach the world cup final in 1987. He accumulated a total of 111 caps in 13 years.

374 David Campese
[1962 -]

Fondly called "Campo", David Ian Campese is one of the most prolific try scorers in the history of rugby. His debut in 1982 came about when the Queensland players pulled out of the national team the day before the New Zealand tour. Young Campo grabbed this opportunity with both hands and the rest is history. Talented and powerful, Campese is famous for his "goose-step" move – a technique that fooled his rivals into thinking that he was slowing down when he was in fact speeding up. He was largely responsible for Australia winning the 1991 World Cup; an event that made him a rugby giant.

October 21, 1962: Born in Queanbeyan, Australia

1982: Debuts against New Zealand

1991: Helps Australia win the World Cup and is named Player of the Tournament

1996: Plays his 100th test against Italy and makes his final appearance against Wales

2002: Awarded the Order of Australia Medal for his contributions to the sport

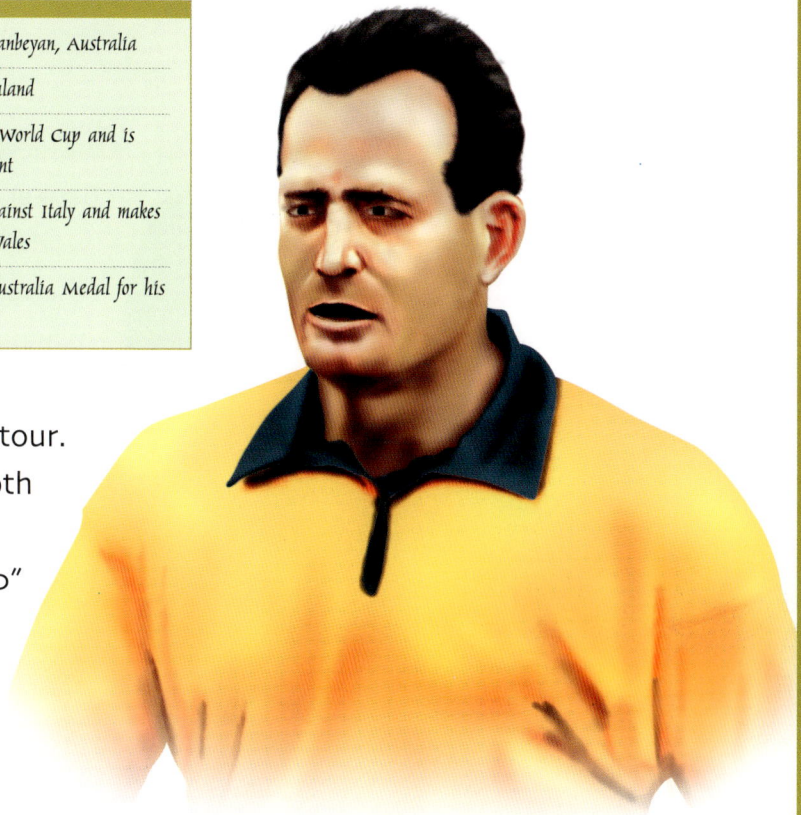

David Campese

375 Sean Fitzpatrick
[1963 -]

One of the greatest players that New Zealand ever produced, Sean Fitzpatrick had rugby in his blood. Son of Brian Fitzpatrick, a former New Zealand player, Sean went on to become a bigger legend than his father. The hooker played in 63 consecutive tests, which is a world record, and captained his team 51 times! Having amassed 92 caps, the main force behind New Zealand's glorious run had to retire following a knee injury.

Sean Fitzpatrick

January 4, 1963: Born in Auckland, New Zealand

1986: Makes his debut against France

1987: Helps New Zealand win the World Cup

1992: Becomes the captain of the New Zealand team

1997: Makes his final appearance against Wales

100 GREATS
in sports

376 Michael Jones [1965 -]

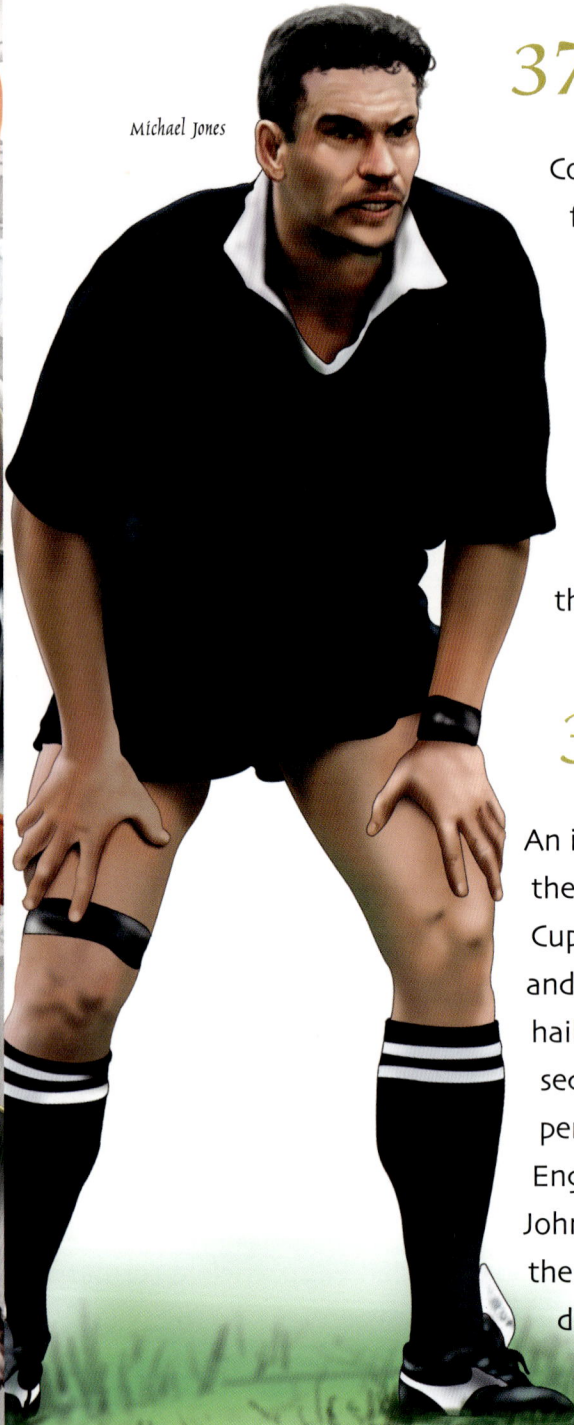

Michael Jones

April 8, 1965: Born in Auckland, New Zealand

1987: Makes his debut against Italy in the World Cup

1998: Makes his final appearance against Australia

2003: Inducted into the International Rugby Hall of Fame

Considered the best flanker in the rugby world, Michael Jones first made his mark during the 1987 World Cup. With his speed, talent and planning skills, he engineered New Zealand's win in the tournament, becoming an integral part of the team – so much so that he was selected despite his refusal to play on Sundays due to religious reasons. He also has the distinction of scoring the opening try in the 1987 and 1991 World Cups.

377 Martin Johnson [1970 -]

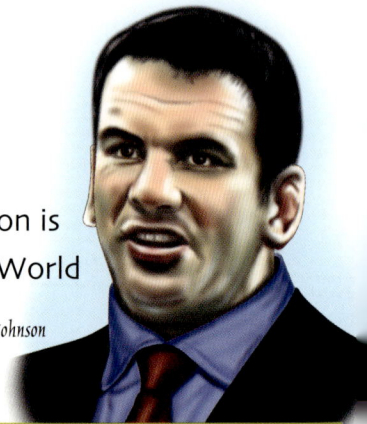

Martin Johnson

An inspiring captain, Martin Johnson is the man who brought the Rugby World Cup to England. Aggressive and powerful, Johnson is hailed as the world's best second-row forward. A permanent member of the English team since 1994, Johnson's strength is that he is the most dependable person during tight situations. He

March 9, 1970: Born in Solihull, England

1993: Makes his debut against France

1997: Becomes the captain of Leicester Tigers

1999: Takes over from Lawrence Dallaglio as the captain of England

2003: Retires from international rugby

proved it by leading his team to an historic win against Australia in the 2003 World Cup final.

378 John Eales [1970 -]

June 27, 1970: Born in Brisbane, Queensland, Australia

1991: Makes his debut against Wales

1991: Australia wins the World Cup

1999: Australia becomes the first country to win the World Cup twice

2001: Plays his last international against New Zealand

Former Australian captain, John Eales, made his mark in the world of rugby at the 1991 World Cup. He dominated the entire tournament, despite having made his debut only a few months before. He deservedly won the World Cup winner's medal. He also became one of the five players to have won the World Cup twice, when he led Australia to its second World Cup victory in 1999.

Summer Olympics

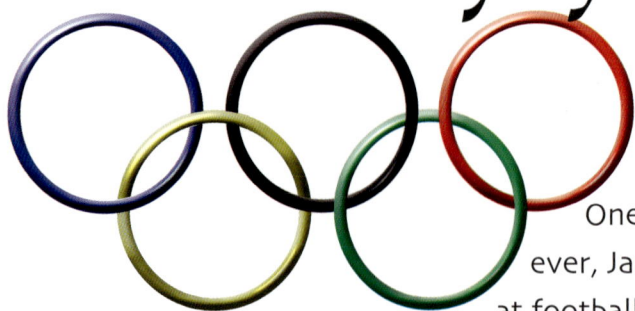

381 Jim Thorpe
[1887 - 1953]

One of the greatest all-round athletes ever, James Francis Thorpe excelled at football, baseball, basketball, boxing, lacrosse, swimming and hockey. In 1912, besides leading his college football team to a national championship, Thorpe or Wathahuck-Brightpath (his Indian name) won the decathlon and pentathlon athletic events at the Olympic Games in Stockholm. Later, he played major-league baseball (1913-19) and had considerable success in his favourite sport, American football; of which he became one of the game's early popularisers and stars.

Jim Thorpe

May 28, 1887: Born on the Sac and Fox Indian Reservation, Prague, Oklahoma, U.S.

1912: Wins the decathlon and pentathlon athletic events at the Stockholm Olympics

1913: His Olympic gold medals are withdrawn on the basis of his having played semi-professional baseball during 1909-10

1950: Voted by the Associated Press as the "Greatest Male Athlete of the First Half-Century"

March 28, 1953: Dies in Lomita, California, U.S.

1982: The Olympic medals are restored to his family

January 30, 1998: Oklahoma Governor proclaims the day as "Jim Thorpe Day" in the State

382 Jesse Owens
[1913 - 1980]

On May 25, 1935, Jesse Owens created three world records and tied a fourth at the Big Ten track-and-field meet in Ann Arbor - all in a matter of little over an hour! The American athlete turned in another record-breaking spell at the 1936 Berlin Olympics. There, he set new world records in the 200m (20.7 sec) and the long jump (8.06 m). In the 100m, he tied the Olympic record at 10.3 seconds. To cap it all, he was also in the winning U.S. team for the 4x100 relay, breaking the world record with 39.8 seconds. His long-jump record stood for 25 years!

September 12, 1913: Born in Oakville, Alabama, U.S.

1933: Ties the world record for the 100-yard dash (9.4 sec), at the National Scholastics Championships in Chicago, U.S.

1936: Wins four gold medals in the 100m, 200m, long jump and 4x100m relay – the first American to win four Olympic gold medals in a single day

1976: Receives the nation's highest civilian honour, the Medal of Freedom

March 31, 1980: Dies in Tuscon, Arizona, U.S.

383 Mark Andrew Spitz
[1950 -]

At the 1968 Olympics in Mexico City, swimmer Mark Spitz announced beforehand that he was going to take six gold medals! He won only two in the relay events. However, at the next Games in Munich, he went a mark higher to capture seven golds! Not only that, he set world records too – in the 100m (51.22 sec) and 200m (1 min 52.78 sec) freestyle, as well as the 100m (54.27 sec) and 200m (2 min 0.7 sec) butterfly. The other three medals were for relay events, all again at world-record times. Spitz remains the only person ever to win seven gold medals in a single Olympics.

Edwin Moses

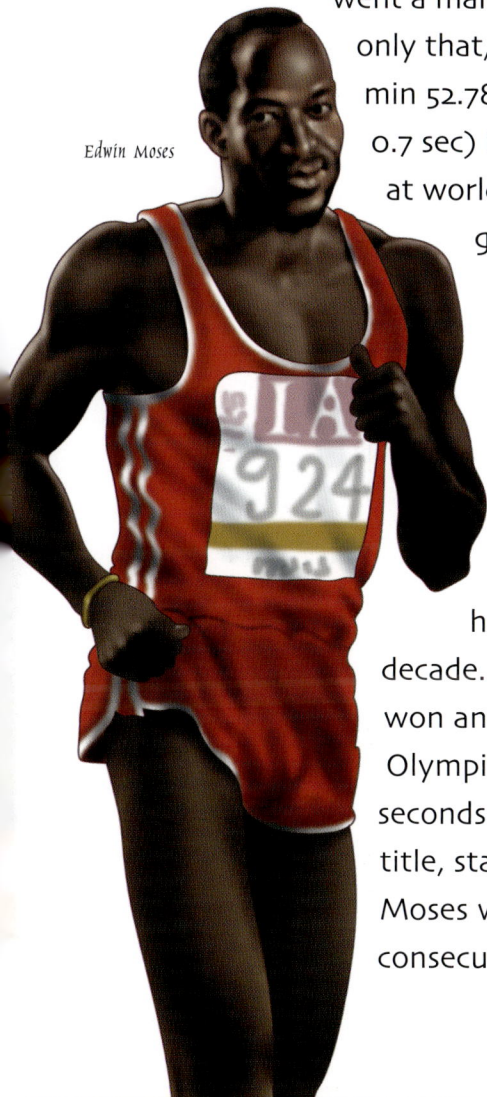

384 Edwin Moses
[1955 -]

One of the greatest athletes the world has ever known, Edwin Moses dominated the 400m hurdles event for more than a decade. He first made his mark when he won an Olympic gold at the Montreal Olympics, setting a world record at 47.64 seconds. The next year, he broke his own record to win the U.S. title, starting an incredible winning streak. Over nearly a decade, Moses won 122 hurdles events in a row – the highest number of consecutive victories ever by an athlete!

385 Greg Louganis
[1960 -]

Greg Louganis

The American Olympian, Gregory Efthimios Louganis, is regarded as one of the greatest divers ever. In two consecutive Olympic Games (1984, Los Angeles; 1988, Seoul), he took two gold medals for the springboard and platform events. It was the first time that a male diver had won double medals in two Olympics in a row. Louganis went on to win the same two titles at the 1982 and 1986 World Championships.

100 GREATS
in sports

386 Carl Lewis
[1961 -]

For King Carl, the sky was the limit. One of the most dominant athletes in recent years, Carl Lewis has nine Olympic gold medals to his name – a record that he shares with just three others: Mark Spitz, Paavo Nurmi and gymnast Larysa Latynina. In 1984, he equalled his hero Jesse Owen's record of four gold medals in a single Olympics. He reigned the long jump event for ten years with 65 consecutive victories! The only record to elude the great athlete was the long jump record set by Bob Beamon; a feat eventually achieved by Mike Powell.

Carl Lewis

July 1, 1961: Born as Frederick Carlton Lewis in Birmingham, Alabama, U.S.

1983: Wins the 100m, 200m and long jump titles at the U.S. National Championships.

1984: Wins four gold medals at the Los Angeles Olympics

1988: Wins the long jump and 100m gold medal for a second time at the Olympics

1991: Loses the long jump event for the first time in ten years. Mike Powell beats him to the title at the World Championships in Tokyo with a record-breaking jump

1992: Beats Powell to his third Olympic gold medal in long jump

1996: Wins the Olympic gold medal in long jump for a fourth time to share with Al Oerter the record of winning four gold medals in the same event

1997: Announces his retirement

Nadia Comaneci

387 Nadia Comaneci
[1961 -]

November 12, 1961: Born in Gheorghe Gheorghiu-Dej, Romania

1970: Wins the national junior championships

1972: Wins three gold medals in her first international competition

1975: Wins four gold medals in the European Championships

1976: Wins five medals at the Montreal Olympics

1980: Wins four gold medals at Moscow Olympics

1984: Retires from competitive sport

1989: Defects to the United States

2003: Publishes autobiography, Letters to a Young Gymnast

The Romanian teenager accomplished something that nobody had managed previously – a perfect score of 10 in a gymnastic event at the Olympics! At the 1976 Games in Montreal, she received seven perfect 10's as well as three golds, one silver and a bronze. At the 1980 Olympics in Moscow, Comaneci took two gold and two silver medals. In 1981, participating in her last major contest – the World University Games held in Bucharest, Romania – she won all five gold medals.

388 Jackie Joyner-Kersee
[1962 -]

At the Goodwill Games in Moscow, in 1986, Jacqueline Joyner-Kersee became the first athlete to earn more than 7,000 points in the heptathlon, with 7,148 points. This was followed by two gold medals in two consecutive Olympics – in the 1988 Seoul Olympics and in 1992 at Barcelona. Her 1988 record of 7,291 in the heptathlon still stands. At Seoul, Joyner won a gold medal in long jump as well. Not for nothing is she regarded by many as the first lady of heptathlon!

March 3, 1962: Born in East St. Louis, Illinois, U.S.

1984: Wins the heptathlon silver at the Olympic Games in Los Angeles

1987: Wins both long jump and heptathlon events at the Rome World Championships

1988: Wins Olympic gold medal in heptathlon

1992: Wins heptathlon gold and a bronze in the long jump

1993: Wins the heptathlon gold at the World Championships in Stuttgart, Germany

1996: Wins Olympic bronze in the long jump event at Atlanta, U.S.

Jackie Joyner-Kersee

Sergei Bubka

December 4, 1963: Born in Voroshilovgrad, Ukraine, U.S.S.R. (now Lugansk, Ukraine)

1983: Wins the first of his six straight World Championships at Helsinki, Finland

1984: Sets the first of his many world records. Breaks his own records setting a total of nine records in one year

1993: Sets an indoor world record that is yet to be surpassed

1994: Sets an outdoor world record of 6.14 metres, which remains unbroken

2000: Makes a final effort to win an Olympic medal in Sydney, Australia

February 4, 2001: Formally bids farewell to pole vaulting

389 Sergei Bubka
[1963 -]

The best pole-vaulter ever, Sergei Bubka dominated the sport from his first World Championship in 1983. The first to cross the six-metre mark, Bubka had only one person to beat – himself. His feat of 35 world records remains unsurpassed. But for a man who has left his mark on every major competition, Bubka was unlucky where Olympics were concerned. He was denied a golden opportunity when the Soviet Union boycotted the Los Angeles Olympics. He won his only Olympic gold medal at Seoul.

September 13, 1967: Born in Dallas, Texas, U.S.

1991: Wins his first World Championship in the 200m

1993: Wins the 400m World Championship

1996: Wins the gold medal for 400m and the 200m gold in a record time of 19.32 seconds

1999: Breaks the 11-year-old world record in 400m by clocking 43.18 seconds

2001: Runs his final event in a major tournament at the Goodwill Games in Brisbane, Australia

390 Michael Johnson
[1967 -]

This famous American sprinter has been compared to Carl Lewis. And why not? Michael Johnson is the only man ever to win gold in both the 200m and 400m events at the same Olympics. He first burst onto the world field in 1990. However, it took him six years to win an Olympic gold in an individual event. At the 2000 Sydney Olympics he became the first to win the 400m gold medal twice.

100 GREATS
in sports

Tennis

Don Budge

391 Don Budge
[1915 - 2000]

John Donald Budge was the first tennis player to win all four Grand Slam events in a single year. The year 1938 saw him sweeping the singles titles in the Australian, French, British (Wimbledon) and U.S. Open Championships. Just the previous year, Budge had clinched the Wimbledon Championships by winning the singles, the men's doubles (with Gene Mako) and the mixed doubles (with Alice Marble)!

June 13, 1915: Born in Oakland, California, U.S.

1937: Leads the U.S. team to a Davis Cup win – the first since 1926; becomes the first tennis player to receive the James E. Sullivan Memorial Trophy as the outstanding U.S. amateur athlete of the year

1938: Completes the tennis Grand Slam

1939: Turns professional. Also publishes *Budge on Tennis*

1964: Inducted into the International Tennis Hall of Fame

January 26, 2000: Dies in Scranton, Pennsylvania, U.S.

392 Maureen Catherine Connolly
[1934 - 1969]

"Little Mo", as Maureen Catherine Connolly was called affectionately, was the youngest girl to win the U.S. National Junior Championship. She was only 15 years old! Two years later, in 1951, she won the women's singles at the U.S. Open Championship. She retained the title in 1952 as well. In 1953, she became the first woman to win all the four Grand Slam events – the British (Wimbledon), U.S., Australian and French Open – in the same year!

September 17, 1934: Born in San Diego, California, U.S.

1951: Wins her first U.S. Championship

1952: Wins her first Wimbledon title; wins again in 1953 and 1954

1954: Wins her second French Open title; a horseback-riding accident forces her to retire from the game, at the age of just 19

1968: Inducted into the International Tennis Hall of Fame

June 21, 1969: Dies in Dallas, Texas, U.S.

393 Rod Laver
[1938 -]

Australia's Rod Laver was one of the all-time greatest winners on the tennis court. Only the second player in the history of men's tennis to win the Grand Slam, he is also the only player to have done it twice! In 1969, Laver also achieved an incredible 17 victories in 32 singles tournaments. At the time of retiring, he had 47 singles titles to his name.

August 9, 1938: Born in Queensland, Australia

1960: Wins his first Australian Open singles title

1961: Wins the Wimbledon singles; again in 1962, 1968 and 1969

1963: Turns professional but does not play at any of the major events until the start of the Open Era in 1968

1981: Inducted into the International Tennis Hall of Fame

394 Margaret Smith Court
[1942 -]

Margaret Smith Court's 62 Grand Slam wins in both singles and doubles tennis tournaments place her in a class of her own. The record remains unbroken! In 1970, the Australian player became only the second woman to win the sport's Grand Slam. Earlier, in 1963, she had claimed the Grand Slam in mixed doubles too. Her co-player was fellow Australian Kenneth Fletcher. Court's list of singles titles includes 11 Australian Open, five French and U.S. Open and three Wimbledon titles!

July 16, 1942: *Born in Albury, New South Wales, Australia*

1960: *Wins her first Grand Slam event, the Australian Open singles (the first of six Australian Opens in a row)*

1963: *Becomes the first Australian woman to win the Wimbledon title*

1966: *Retires from professional tennis to marry Barry Court and start a family*

1970: *Returns to the tennis court and proves she has not lost her touch by completing the Grand Slam*

1975: *Retires for good*

1979: *Inducted into the International Tennis Hall of Fame*

Margaret Smith Court

395 Martina Navratilova
[1956 -]

Martina Navratilova

One of the greatest tennis legends ever, the achievements of Martina Navratilova are numerous. No other player has won as many as her 167 singles titles! Of her 20 Wimbledon crowns, a record-breaking nine wins came in the singles. She won the singles titles at the U.S. Open four times, the Australian Open thrice and the French Open twice. Navratilova also holds 173 doubles titles, with 40 of them at Grand Slam events, in both doubles and mixed doubles.

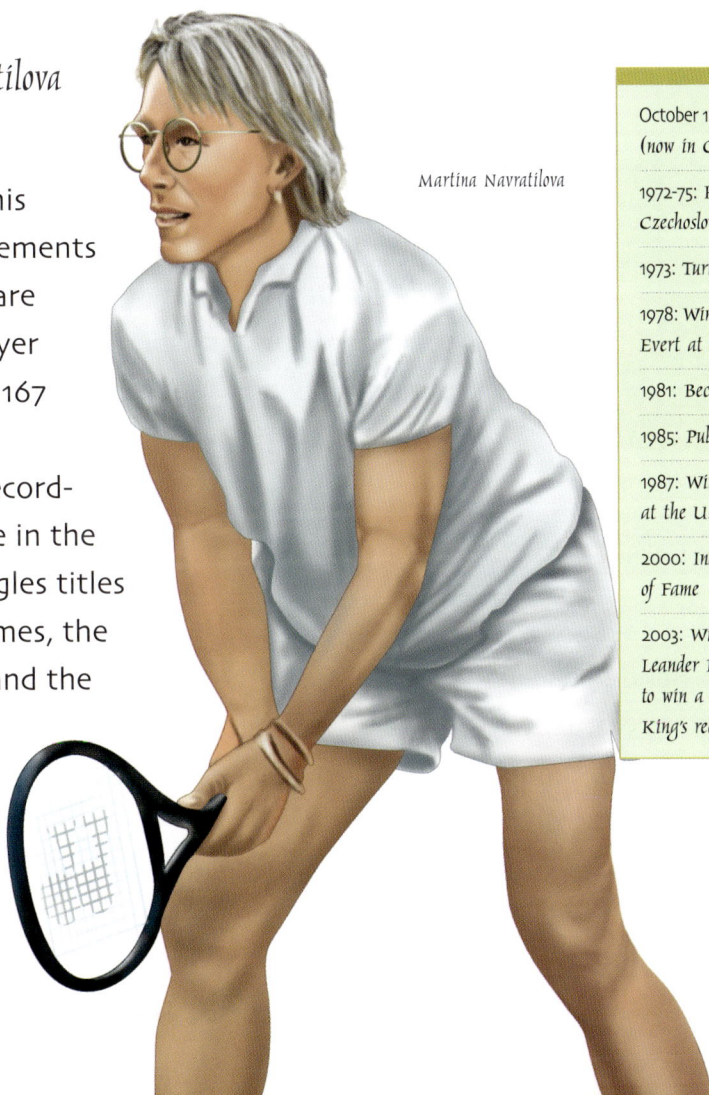

October 18, 1956: *Born in Prague, Czechoslovakia (now in Czech Republic)*

1972-75: *Ranked the No. 1 tennis player in Czechoslovakia*

1973: *Turns professional*

1978: *Wins her first Grand Slam by defeating Chris Evert at the Wimbledon finals*

1981: *Becomes a U.S. citizen*

1985: *Publishes her autobiography, Martina*

1987: *Wins the singles, doubles and mixed doubles at the U.S. Open*

2000: *Inducted into the International Tennis Hall of Fame*

2003: *Wins Australian Open mixed doubles (with Leander Paes of India) to become the oldest person to win a Grand Slam title. Also equals Billie Jean King's record of most number of Wimbledon titles*

100 GREATS
in sports

396 Björn Borg
[1956 -]

In 1975, Björn Borg, then a teenager, helped Sweden win its first Davis Cup. From 1976 to 1980, he won the Wimbledon singles title consecutively. After winning the French Open singles in 1974 and 1975, he became the first to win it for four successive years (1978-81). The U.S. Open title somehow eluded the tennis great, who was a runner-up on four occasions.

June 6, 1956: Born in Södertälje, Sweden

1974: Wins the Italian National

1983: Retires from professional tennis at the age of 26

1987: Inducted into the International Tennis Hall of Fame

Björn Borg

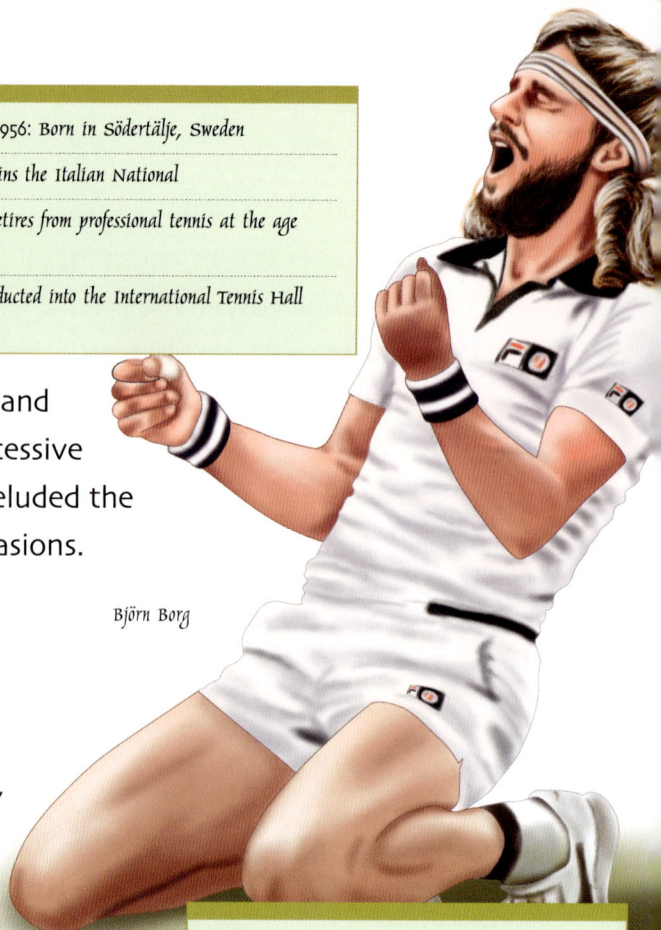

397 John Patrick McEnroe
[1959 -]

American tennis player John Patrick McEnroe, Jr., won 154 tournament titles in his career – 77 singles and an equal number of doubles! His 17 Grand Slam titles included four singles and doubles titles at the U.S. Open and three singles and five doubles at Wimbledon. McEnroe also helped the U.S. team to five Davis Cup victories. Known for his fiery temper, he was disqualified from the 1990 Australian Open for misconduct on the court.

Davis Cup

February 16, 1959: Born in Wiesbaden, West Germany

1977: Reaches the semi-finals at Wimbledon while still an amateur

1978: Wins the National Collegiate Athletic Association singles title; turns professional; member of the winning U.S. team in the Davis Cup

1979: Wins his first U.S. Open singles; wins again in 1980, 1981 and 1984

1981: Wins his first Wimbledon singles; also wins in 1983 and 1984

1999: Inducted into the International Tennis Hall of Fame

398 Jimmy Connors
[1952 -]

A powerful two-handed backhand, aggressive shot-making and a fiery temperament – that was Jimmy "the brat" Connors! The American tennis player was renowned for getting into all kinds of troubles, but his track record is impressive – two Wimbledon singles (1974, 1982) and five U.S. Open singles (1974, 1976, 1978, 1982, 1983). His 109th win, in 1989, made him the leading male tennis player in tournament victories. He was ranked No.1 in the world for 160 consecutive weeks.

September 2, 1952: Born in East St. Louis, Illinois, U.S.

1972: Turns professional

1973: Wins Wimbledon doubles title

1974: Wins Australian Open singles title

1975: Wins U.S. Open doubles title

1998: Inducted into the International Tennis Hall of Fame

399 Steffi Graf
[1969 -]

One of the greatest women tennis players ever, Steffi Graf stormed onto the tennis circuit by winning all four Grand Slam events in 1988. That year she also won a gold medal at the Seoul Olympics. She has a total of 107 singles titles to her credit of which 22 are Grand Slam titles. Known for her powerful serve and an even more powerful forehand, she was nicknamed "Fraulein Forehand". She retired from professional tennis in 1999, a few months after winning her sixth French Open title.

Steffi Graf

June 14, 1969: *Born in Mannheim, Germany*

1982: *Turns professional*

1987: *Wins her first Grand Slam title by defeating Martina Navratilova at the French Open*

1988: *Wins all the four Grand Slam titles and Olympic gold*

1999: *Retires from professional tennis*

October 22, 2001: *Marries André Agassi*

400 Pete Sampras
[1971 -]

With 14 Grand Slam singles titles to his name, Pete Sampras was the greatest player on the men's circuit in his time. He won his first Grand Slam title at the U.S. Open, when he defeated the likes of Ivan Lendl, John McEnroe and Andre Agassi to become the youngest-ever to win the title. He has seven Wimbledon, two Australian and five U.S. Open titles to his credit. Known for his powerful serves, he set a new record by serving over 1000 aces in a season, earning him the name "Pistol Pete".

August 12, 1971: *Born in Washington D.C., U.S.*

1988: *Enters the professional circuit at the age of 16*

1990: *Wins his first Grand Slam title*

1993-98: *Dominates the men's circuit by finishing number one for six consecutive years*

2003: *Announces retirement. Bids farewell to professional tennis at a formal ceremony during the U.S. Open*

Pete Sampras

100 GREATS
in sports

Great

Stage Performers

379 Jonah Lomu
[1975 -]

Jonah Tali Lomu burst onto the world stage with his incredible performance during the 1995 Rugby World Cup. He helped New Zealand sail through to the final, scoring some of the best tries ever seen in the game. He was deservedly named Player of the Tournament. However, the following year the winger was diagnosed as having a kidney disorder. This kept him out of action for a year. But 1997 saw a recovered Lomu take to the rugby field once again.

Jonah Lomu

Rugby World Cup

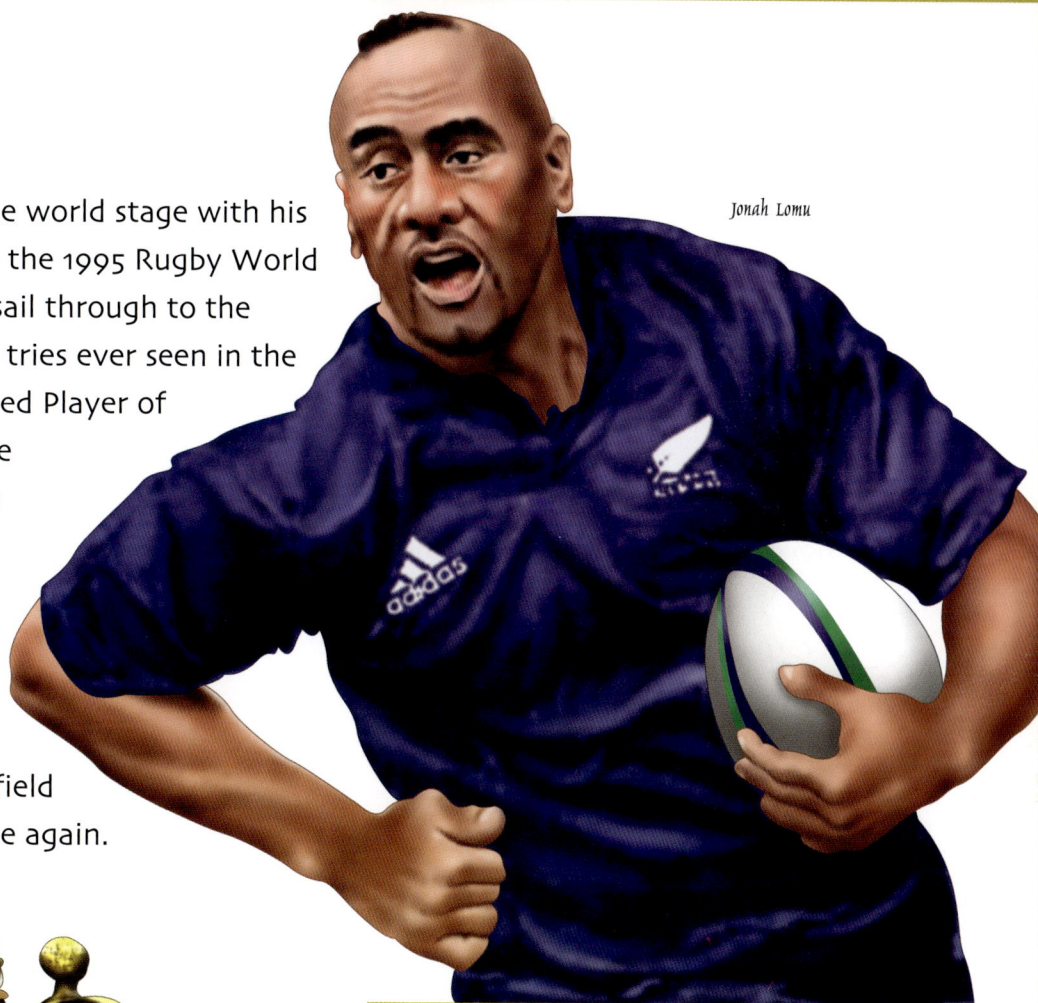

May 12, 1975: Born in Auckland, New Zealand

1994: Debuts against France

1995: New Zealand wins World Cup. He is voted Player of the Tournament

1997: Returns to the field after almost a year away

1998: Wins gold medal in the Commonwealth Games at Kuala Lumpur

380 Jonny Wilkinson
[1979 -]

Born into a family of rugby players, Jonny Wilkinson took to the sport at the age of four. His unending hunger for points attracted the attention of England's selectors and soon he found himself in the national team as a replacement. After a disappointing start to his career, Jonny pulled himself together in time to prove himself. Today he is considered one of the best fly-halfs in the world. He is England's highest point scorer and the youngest ever to score more than 500 points in internationals. But the highpoint in his career was his last-minute drop goal that clinched the 2003 World Cup for England and made him a rugby legend.

May 25, 1979: Born in Frimley, Surrey, England

1998: Makes his international debut against Ireland

1999: Selected to play for England at the World Cup

2001: Breaks Rob Andrew's record to become the country's top point scorer

2002: Voted "International Rugby Player of the Year"

2003: Helps England to win the World Cup with a last-minute drop goal. Also receives the Member of Order of the British Empire from the Queen of England and becomes the first rugby player to receive the BBC Sports Personality of the Year award

100 GREATS
in sports

Classical Composers

401 Antonio Vivaldi
[1678 - 1741]

March 4, 1678: Born in Venice, Italy
1703: Is ordained a priest
c. 1725: Publishes Four Seasons
July 28, 1741: Dies in Vienna, Austria

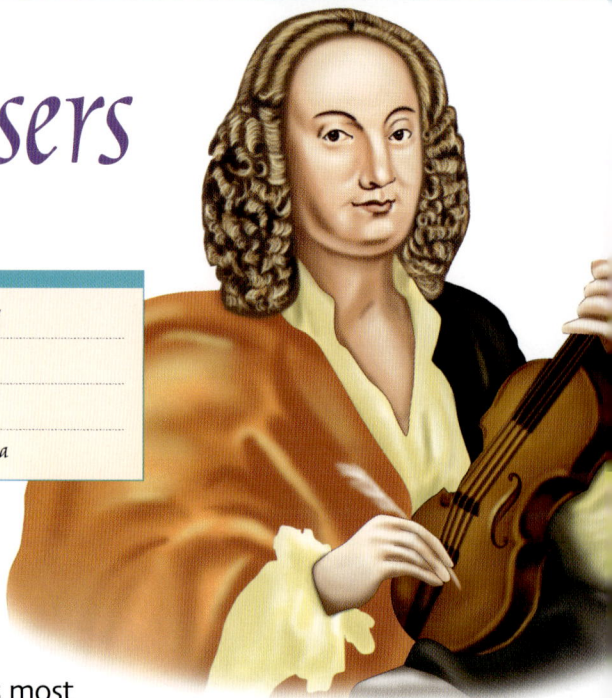

Vivaldi was an Italian music composer and violinist from the Baroque period of Western music. He is credited with more than 500 compositions. Vivaldi lived most of his life in Venice, Italy, where he taught music at a girls' orphanage. *Four Seasons*, an opera, is one of his most renowned works. He also composed concertos for a wide variety of instruments like the cello, violin, flute, lute, mandolin, recorder and oboe.

Antonio Vivaldi

402 Johann Sebastian Bach
[1685 - 1750]

Renowned German organist and composer, Johann Sebastian Bach came from a musical family that boasted of several generations of musicians. After intensive training in playing the organ,

March 21, 1685: Born in Eisenach, Germany
1703: Gets his first job as an organist in Neuekirche, Arnstadt
1723: Is appointed 'Thomaskantor' in Leipzig, Germany
July 28, 1750: Dies in Leipzig, Germany

Bach performed in a succession of churches and also for royal patrons. Though most of his works were religious organ compositions, he also composed pieces for almost all instruments and occasions.

Signature of Johann Sebastian Bach

403 George Frideric Handel
[1685 - 1759]

February 23, 1685: Born in Halle, Thuringia, Germany
1705: Almira, his first operatic composition is performed
1717: Writes the famous Water Music
1727: Composes the anthem, Zadok the Priest, for the coronation of George II, which has been sung at every British coronation since then
1742: Messiah premiers in Dublin, Ireland
April 14, 1759: Dies in London, England

The German organist and composer, Handel, is best known for his development of the English oratorio style. He has also written several operas and concertos in Italian and English. Handel's most famous work is the *Messiah*, a rare religious composition. Though Handel began his career in an opera house in Germany, it was after his travels to Italy and England that he published his best compositions. On his death, he was buried at Westminster Abbey.

404 Joseph Haydn
[1732 - 1809]

Haydn began his illustrious musical career as a choirboy at St Stephen's Cathedral in Vienna, Austria. Though he was trained in vocal music, he soon mastered the violin and keyboard instruments. He also began composing church, theatre and even chamber music (a form of classical music, written for a small group of instruments which traditionally could be accommodated in a palace chamber). His compositions include piano sonatas and trios, choral pieces, operas and songs, but he is best known as the father of symphony and string quartet.

March 31, 1732: Born in Rohrau, Austria

1766: Is appointed 'Kapellmeister' by the Esterházy household, a leading Hungarian aristocratic family

1791: Recieves the honorary degree of Doctor of Music from the Oxford University, England

May 31, 1809: Dies in Vienna, Austria

Joseph Haydn

405 Wolfgang Amadeus Mozart
[1756 - 1791]

January 27, 1756: Born in Salzburg, Austria

1762: Performs before the Austrian empress at the age of six

1787: Is appointed 'Kammerkompositor' by the Austrian emperor

1791: Stages the premier of his last opera, La Clemenza di Tito, in Prague

December 5, 1791: Dies in Vienna, Austria

An Austrian composer of great eminence, Mozart spent most of his life in Salzburg, Austria, where he served in the royal court. He also travelled to Italy, Germany and France for his work. He composed a wide variety of compositions, which included masses, symphonies, concertos, sonatas, dramatic music, serenades and operas. Inspired by Haydn, he also composed string quartets. He spent the last 11 years of his life in Vienna, where he tragically died due to a mysterious illness.

*Jupiter Symphony 1
by Wolfgang Amadeus Mozart*

100 GREATS
of the **stage**

406 Ludwig van Beethoven
[1770 - 1827]

One of the most renowned classical composers of all time, Ludwig van Beethoven was an outstanding pianist of the Romantic period. This extraordinary German musician began composing at the age of 12, which was also when he began publishing his compositions! He went on to compose a number of great piano sonatas, symphonies and string quartets. His exceptional output is remarkable, especially considering he was almost totally deaf from his late twenties onwards!

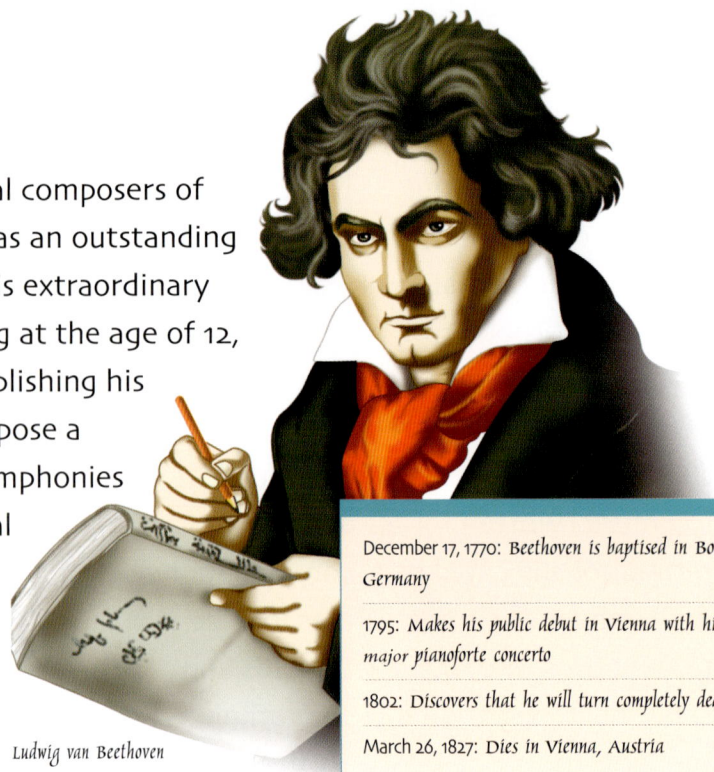

Ludwig van Beethoven

December 17, 1770: Beethoven is baptised in Bonn, Germany

1795: Makes his public debut in Vienna with his Bb major pianoforte concerto

1802: Discovers that he will turn completely deaf

March 26, 1827: Dies in Vienna, Austria

407 Frederic Chopin
[1810 - 1849]

March 1, 1810: Born Zelazowa Wola, Poland

1831: Moves to Paris, France

October 17, 1849: Dies in Paris, France

Chopin was born to a French father and Polish mother.

He grew up in Warsaw, Poland, where he received his early training in music. He was a brilliant pianist and composed almost exclusively for the piano. He eventually moved to Paris, the centre of art and culture at that time. Here he taught piano and composed a number of nocturnes, waltzes, preludes, mazurkas and impromptus. His innovative style was copied by many of his contemporaries.

Frederic Chopin

408 Richard Wagner
[1813 - 1883]

May 22, 1813: Born in Leipzig, Germany

1836: His opera, Das Liebesverbot, based on Shakespeare's Measure for Measure , is staged

August 1876: The Ring is performed at Bayreuth, Germany

February 13, 1883: Dies in Venice, Italy

German composer, conductor and author, Wagner was one of the most important musicians of the 19th century. As a conductor, Wagner led productions of several masterpieces by Beethoven, Mozart and other classical composers.
Inspired by legends, he wrote and composed several grand operas. His most outstanding composition is *The Ring*, which consisted of four operas that last for more than 15 hours!

409 Pytor Ilych Tchaikovsky
[1840 - 1893]

Pytor Ilych Tchaikovsky

This 19th century Russian composer and conductor is the creator of popular operas like *Queen of Spades* and *Eugene Onegin*, and ballets like *Swan Lake* and *The Nutcracker*. He also composed several original and grand symphonies, songs and orchestra pieces – many of them inspired by Russian folk tunes. Till 1880, Tchaikovsky was successful only in Russia, but by the 1890's his compositions were being performed in other countries as well.

410 Richard Strauss
[1864 - 1949]

Strauss is one of the most well-known, late 19th- early 20th-century composers. Born in Germany, Strauss began composing when he was just a boy of six. During his career he conducted the Berlin Royal Opera for 20 years and was also the Joint Director of the Vienna Opera. He travelled all over Europe and America to conduct his compositions. His works range from operas and tone poems to symphonies.

Richard Strauss

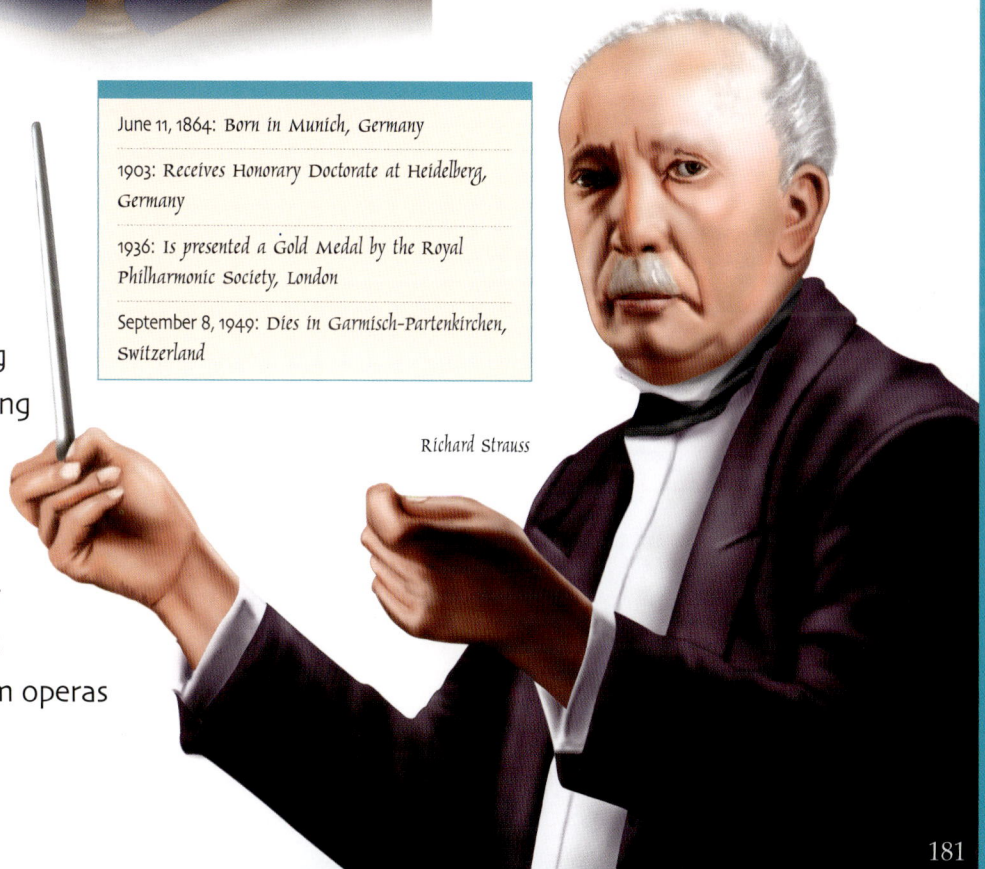

More Composers

411 William Schwenck Gilbert & Arthur Seymour Sullivan
[1836 - 1911]   [1842 - 1900]

November 18, 1836: William Schwenck Gilbert is born in London, England

May 13, 1842: Arthur Seymour Sullivan is born in London, England

May 28, 1878: Their first great hit, HMS Pinafore, is staged

1896: Their last play, The Grand Duke, is performed

November 22, 1900: Sullivan dies in London, England

May 29, 1911: Gilbert dies in Harrow Weald, Middlesex, England

Gilbert and Sullivan were the famous pair who gave English theatre such outstanding comic operas as the *Pirates of Penzance* and *The Mikado*. Gilbert was an "operetta librettist", who began his career writing burlesques and pantomimes. Sullivan, on the other hand, composed opera. It was in 1871 that the two met and began composing the comic operas they are famous for. Their successful partnership lasted for around 25 years, after which they parted ways.

July 12, 1895: Hammerstein born in New York, U.S.

June 18, 1902: Rodgers born in New York, U.S.

1943: Produce their first musical together, Oklahoma!

1959: Write their last musical together, The Sound of Music (released as a film in 1965 after Hammerstein's death)

August 23, 1960: Hammerstein dies in Pasadena, U.S.

December 30, 1979: Rodgers dies in New York, U.S.

412 Oscar Hammerstein II & Richard Rodgers
[1895 - 1960]   [1902 - 1979]

American playwright and composer, Oscar Hammerstein II, helped revive the operetta and developed a new and popular form of theatre known as the "musical". Some of his most famous works are, *The Sound of Music*, *Show Boat* and *Oklahoma*. His best works were produced in collaboration with Richard Rodgers. He won many awards, including two Pulitzer Prizes, two Academy Awards and five Tony Awards. Richard Rodgers was one of the great composers of musical theatre. He wrote more than 900 published songs, and 40 Broadway musicals. Many of his compositions are still widely loved and have had a significant impact on the development of popular music.

Pulitzer Award

413 George Gershwin
[1898 - 1937]

September 26, 1898: Born in New York City, U.S.

1917: Composes Swanee, his first Broadway hit for the musical, Sinbad

1919: Composes music for the Broadway show, La, La, Lucille, his first full musical score

1932: Wins the Pulitzer Prize for Of Thee I Sing, the first musical to do so

June 11, 1937: Dies in Hollywood, Los Angeles, U.S.

Among America's most successful 20th century musicians, George Gershwin was a songwriter, composer and conductor. Born Jacob Gershovitz, of Russian immigrants, Gershwin became a professional musician as a teenager and began writing and composing for Broadway from the 1920s. Along with his brother Ira, Gershwin created many memorable songs and instrumental scores for the stage and cinema. He also wrote classical pieces.

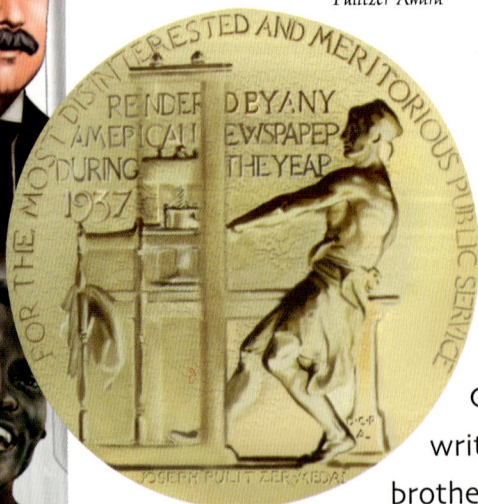

414 *Stephen Sondheim*
[1930 -]

Stephen Sondheim

Stephen Sondheim is one of the most famous contemporary American composer and lyricist of all time. Inspired by playwright and composer, Oscar Hammerstein II, an adolescent Sondheim began his training in music. He has composed over 14 musicals, written song lyrics, composed music and written screenplays for a variety of motion pictures. In 1956, he was chosen to write the lyrics for the famous Broadway musical, *West Side Story.* Some of Sondheim's best musicals include the light farce, *A Funny Thing Happened On The Way To The Forum,* and the more serious, *Passion.*

March 22, 1930: Born in New York, U.S.

1957: Premiers his first Broadway success, West Side Story

1985: Wins Pulitzer Prize for Sunday in the Park with George

1993: The Kennedy Center honours him

415 *Tim Rice & Andrew Lloyd Webber*
[1944 -]   [1948 -]

November 10, 1944: Rice born in Amersham, England

March 22, 1948: Lloyd Webber born in London, England

1971: Jesus Christ Superstar premiers

1978: Stage London premier of Evita

1992: Lloyd Webber knighted

1994: Rice knighted

1997: Lloyd Webber made life peer

2002: Rice inducted as Disney Legend

Andrew Lloyd Webber is a successful contemporary British musician. He has written, directed and produced several stage musicals. His compositions include *Joseph and the Amazing Technicolour Dreamcoat, Jesus Christ Superstar* and *Evita* (all working with Tim Rice), *Cats* and *Phantom of the Opera.* He has also produced one of the West End's latest hit musicals, *Bombay Dreams,* along with Indian musical genius, A.R. Rahman. Tim Rice is a musical theatre lyricist, author, radio presenter and gameshow panelist. He is particularly known for his collaborations with Andrew Lloyd Webber and his work with Disney on *The Lion King* (with Sir Elton John), *King David, Aladdin* and *Beauty and the Beast.* Indeed, the company made him a Disney Legend. Rice also wrote the lyrics to the musical *Chess,* for which the music was written by Benny Andersson and Björn Ulvaeus, formerly of Abba.

100 GREATS
of the **stage**

Musicians and Opera Singers

416 Enrico Caruso
[1873 - 1921]

With the natural beauty, range and power of his voice, Enrico Caruso, the Italian operatic tenor, is widely considered one of the greatest singers ever. He was also the most popular singer of any genre in the first 20 years of the 20th century and one of the pioneers of recorded music.

February 25, 1873: Born in Naples, Italy

1894: Operatic debut in Naples

1903: American debut as the duke in Rigoletto at the NY Metropolitan Opera is huge success

August 2, 1921: Dies in Naples

1951: Life highly fictionalised in Hollywood Movie The Great Caruso starring Mario Lanza

417 Marian Anderson
[1897 - 1993]

February 27, 1897: Born in Philadelphia, Pennsylvania, U.S.

1924: Gives her first recital in New York Town Hall

1939: Sings in the historic concert at the Lincoln Memorial in Washington DC

January 7, 1955: Debuts at the Metropolitan Opera Company with Verdi's The Masked Ball – the first African-American to do so

April 8, 1993: Dies in Portland, Oregon, U.S.

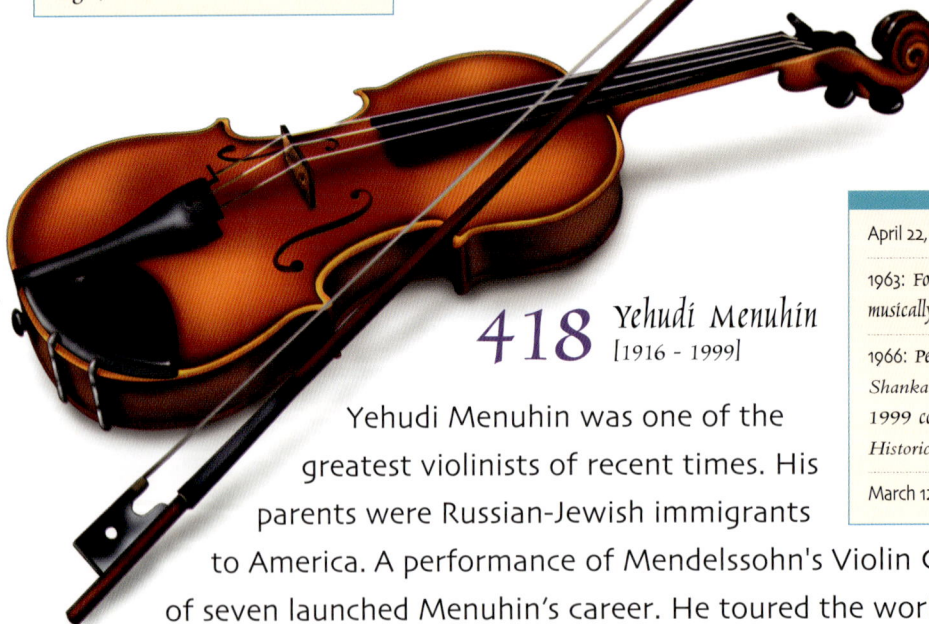

An outstanding opera singer, Marian Anderson was also a symbol of African-American liberation. She was a versatile contralto, whose voice range stretched from high soprano notes to low baritones. She overcame racial barriers and won a place in the hearts of opera and classical music lovers all over Europe and America. Her inspiring music and courageous life have encouraged generations of singers to follow her.

418 Yehudi Menuhin
[1916 - 1999]

April 22, 1916: Born in New York, U.S.

1963: Founds the Yehudi Menuhin School for musically gifted children in Stoke D'Abernon

1966: Performs at concert, Menuhin meets Ravi Shankar. This successful collaboration led to the 1999 compilation of West Meets East: The Historic Shankar/Menuhin Sessions

March 12, 1999: Dies in Berlin, Germany

Yehudi Menuhin was one of the greatest violinists of recent times. His parents were Russian-Jewish immigrants to America. A performance of Mendelssohn's Violin Concerto at the age of seven launched Menuhin's career. He toured the world as a teenager and was considered a maestro long before he was even 20 years old! Later in life he broke from his traditional roots to work outside of the classical genre – one of his most successful ventures was with the great Indian composer and sitarist, Ravi Shankar. During his career, he performed with almost all the great orchestras of the world and continued to conduct till he died at the age of 82.

419 *Marilyn Horne*
[1934 -]

The outstanding American mezzo-soprano Marilyn (Benice) Horne made her operatic debut at the age of twenty, but her first great career success occured at the inauguration of Gelsenkirchen's new opera house in 1960 as Marie in Berg's *Wozzeck*, a role she then resumed in the States. An international star, Marilyn performed regularly in the world's great opera houses, and was called by Opera News "probably the greatest singer in the world". She is, without doubt, one of the greatest mezzo-sopranos in opera history.

January 16, 1934: Born in Pennsylvania, USA

1954: Sings the voice of Carmen Jones in Oscar Hammerstein's recreation of Bizet's Carmen

1960: Performs as Marie in Berg's Wozzeck

1994: Launches the Marilyn Horne Foundation at Carnegie Hall, to support young singers

1999: Inducted into the American Classical Music Hall of Fame

420 *Luciano Pavarotti*
[1935 -]

Italian tenor, Luciano Pavarotti, is the most popular and recognisable face in contemporary opera. Since his stage debut in 1961, he has travelled all over the world performing in the greatest opera houses and at large public gatherings. He has entertained and attracted the attention of audiences everywhere. An extraordinary showman and attractive personality, he has done a great deal to popularise classical opera music.

Luciano Pavarotti

October 12, 1935: Born in Modena, Italy

1961: Makes his solo debut on stage as Rodolfo in La Boheme

February 1965: Makes American debut in a Miami Opera production of Lucia di Lammermoor with Joan Sutherland, beginning a historic partnership

421 *Yanni*
[1954 -]

Yanni Chrysomallis, composer and keyboardist, was born in Greece, but moved to the U.S. in 1972. He began by playing with a rock band, but soon left to start his own career in composing music. He uses classical and world-music influences to elevate pop-inclined compositions to more sophisticated levels. Yanni's musical works are very elaborate and are dominated by the keyboard.

Yanni

November 14, 1954: Born in Kalamata, Greece

September 1993: Performs live for the first time in his own country, and releases the recording as Live at The Acropolis, a double album that reaches platinum status several times over

1996: Composes music for Summer Olympic Games (his music had been used in previous years as well)

1997: Releases Tribute, a live album recorded at the Taj Mahal in India and the Forbidden City in China

100 GREATS
of the **stage**

Country and Folk Musicians

422 Jim Reeves
[1923 - 1964]

James Travis Reeves was one of the biggest singing stars from Nashville, the home of country music. He sang romantic ballads and was as comfortable with country music as he was with pop. Reeves was responsible for bringing audiences back from rock and roll to country music in the 1950s and 60s. Some of his most famous songs are *Blue Boy*, *Billy Bayou* and *Am I Losing You*.

August 20, 1923: Born in Panola County, Texas, U.S.

1953: Records *Mexican Joe*, a major country hit

1959-60: His *He'll Have to Go* tops country charts and comes #2 in the pop charts

July 31, 1964: Dies near Nashville, Tennessee, U.S.

1967: Is elected to the Country Music Hall of Fame

Jim Reeves

423 Hank Williams
[1923 - 1953]

The father of contemporary country music, Hiram King Williams was a superstar by the age of 25 and was dead at the age of 29. In those four short years, he paved the way for all the country performers that followed him. He was one of the most popular country singers and songwriters of the 1950s. Williams' childhood exposure to blues music is evident in most of his work. In the 1950s he also brought out a series of spiritual albums under the name of 'Luke the Drifter'. He wrote and sang several songs inspired by incidents and experiences from his personal life which was as troubled and restless, as depicted in his songs. Many have become popular classics, such as *I Saw the Light*, *Your Cheatin' Heart* and *Hey Good Lookin*.

September 17, 1923: Born in Mount Olive West, Alabama, U.S.

1947: His first single for MGM, *Move It On Over*, is also his first Billboard chart entry

August 7, 1948: Begins appearing on *Louisiana Hayride*, a radio program in Shreveport, Louisiana

January 1, 1953: Dies in Tennessee, U.S. in controversial circumstances

1961: Becomes one of the first artists to be inducted to the Country Music Hall of Fame

424 Doris Day
[1924 -]

Popular American singer and actress, Doris Day was born as Doris Von Kappelhoff. As a teenager Doris changed her surname when she began performing on radio. After singing for various bands, from 1947 she began singing solo. Her attractive singing style and clean good looks brought her popularity and offers for movie roles. Day acted in several successful musicals and comedies, singing some of her best-known songs, like *It's Magic* and *Que Será Será*.

Doris Day

April 3, 1924: Born in Cincinnati, Ohio, U.S.

1945: Sings her first world-wide hit, *Sentimental Journey*, with Les Brown's band

1948: Acts in her debut film, *Romance on the High Seas*

1959: *Pillow Talk* released, co-starring Rock Hudson

1968: Begins hosting *The Doris Day Show*, a TV sitcom on CBS

425 Chet Atkins
[1924 - 2001]

Guitarist and music producer, Chester Burton Atkins was a famous country music personality. Within five decades Atkins had recorded over 100 albums. He also sang for his first album (1947). From 1952 he doubled as a talent scout and produced the albums of several emerging artists like Elvis Presley and Jim Reeves. Both as an artist and as a producer, Atkins' contribution to music is inestimable.

June 20, 1924: Born in Luttrell, Tennessee, U.S.

1955: Scores his first hit with a cover version of *Mr Sandman*

1967-88: Wins the CMA's Instrumentalist of the Year honour 11 times

1973: Is inducted into the Country Music Hall of Fame

1993: Receives the Lifetime Achievement Award from the National Academy of Recording Arts and Sciences (NARAS)

June 30, 2001: Dies in Nashville, Tennessee, U.S.

Harry Belafonte

426 Harry Belafonte
[1927 -]

Renowned folk-singer, Harold George Belafonte, is an icon of African-American music of the 1950s and 60s. Though Belafonte is best known for popularising calypso music in the 1950s, he sang pop and jazz too. He also acted in several motion pictures. Throughout his career, "The King of Calypso", used his popularity to talk to people about human rights and equality. Some of his best-known songs are *Jamaica Farewell*, *Banana Boat Song* and *Day-O*.

March 1, 1927: Born in New York City, New York, U.S.

1955: Releases the million-selling album, *Calypso*

2001: Brings out *The Long Road To Freedom: An Anthology of Black Music*, a set of early African recordings

100 GREATS
of the **stage**

427 Kenny Rogers
[1938 -]

Country singer and songwriter, Kenneth David Rogers has recorded over 58 albums, which have sold over 100 million copies! He has toured all over the world giving live performances. Rogers received four Grammys and eight Academy of Country Music Awards, apart from many others. With over five decades of singing behind him, Kenny Rogers still continues to record and perform. Many of his songs having inspired television movies.

August 21, 1938: Born in Houston, Texas, U.S.

1975: *Lucille* establishes him as a country star

1985: Participates in the historical recording of *We Are The World*, for famine relief in Africa

1986: Rogers is voted Favorite Singer of All Time in a *PM Magazine/USA Today* poll

1990: Receives the Horatio Alger Award, for his personal achievements

Kenny Rogers

Connie Francis

428 Connie Francis
[1938 -]

Connie Francis, born Concetta Rosa Maria Franconero, was one of the most popular American singers of the 1950s and 60s. She was a country singer who also successfully sang rock and roll music. Francis is a multi-linguist, who has sung in Japanese, Spanish, French, Italian and many other languages! Francis also enjoyed a brief career in motion pictures, acting in a few light-hearted musicals like, *Where The Boys Are.* Francis is due to be immortalised in an upcoming feature film based around her life and times, written by the singer Gloria Estefan.

December 12, 1938: Born in Newark, New Jersey, U.S.

May 1955: Records her first song, *Freddy*, for MGM

March 1958: Reaches #1 spot on the American Bandstand with *Who's Sorry Now*

1961: Acts in *Where The Boys Are*, her first role in a motion picture

188

429 Joan Baez
[1941 -]

Joan Baez

Joan Chandos Baez is one of America's most outstanding folk singers. Her most productive period was during the 1960s, when she sang several traditional American and British songs. During this period, many of her songs were also strongly political. She has always openly opposed war and spoken in favour of non-violence and peace. She has continued to sing and write, both solos and duets with other artists – besides being involved in social activism and humanitarian aid work.

January 9, 1941: *Born Staten Island, New York, U.S.*

1960: *Records first album, Joan Baez, for Vanguard Records*

1992: *Releases Play Me Backwards, a universally acclaimed country rock album*

1995: *Collaborates on Ring Them Bells with other modern female folk artists*

430 Bob Dylan
[1941 -]

Bob Dylan, born Robert Allen Zimmerman, was one of the most influential songwriters of the 20th century. He inspired an entire generation during the 1960s. A renowned American folk singer, Dylan's participation in the civil rights movement is evident in many of his songs. He also sang rock and roll, folk rock and evangelical songs – eventually returning to his own brand of blues-based folk music. A prolific artist, he has recorded numerous albums and continues to perform all over the world.

May 24, 1941: *Born in Duluth, Minnesota, U.S.*

March 1962: *Releases Bob Dylan, his first album*

1965: *Reinvents himself as a folk rocker at the Newport Folk Festival*

1979: *Wins his first Grammy in the Best Rock Vocal performance for Gotta Serve Somebody*

1991: *Receives the Lifetime Achievement Grammy Award*

2000: *Wins the Best Original Song Academy Award for the song Things Have Changed, on the soundtrack of the film The Wonder Boys*

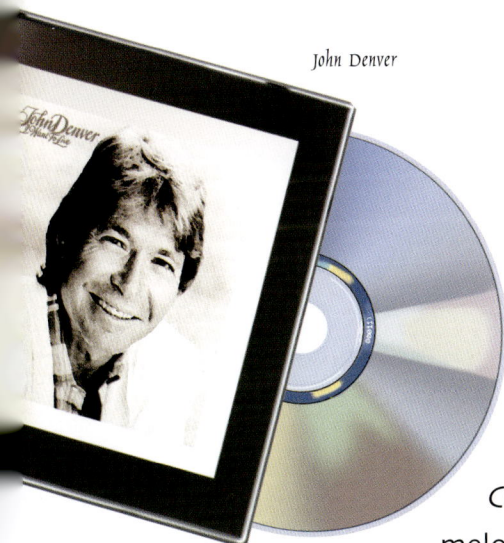

John Denver

431 John Denver
[1943 - 1997]

December 31, 1943: *Born in Roswell, New Mexico, U.S.*

1969: *Records his debut song, Rhymes and Reasons*

1971: *Releases his third solo album, the first to bring him success, Poems, Prayers and Promises*

October 12, 1997: *Dies in a plane crash at Monterey Bay, California, U.S.*

Born Henry John Deutschendorf, Jr., John Denver was one of the biggest selling artists in the 1970s and one of the most significant personalities in country music of all time. He composed and sang many country hits like, *Take Me Home, Country Road* and *Sunshine on My Shoulders*. His simple lyrics and melodious tunes appealed to people all over the world, making him a popular and highly successful artist. He also worked for environmental and humanitarian causes.

100 GREATS
of the **stage**

Dancers

432 Anna Pavlova
[1881 - 1931]

Russian ballerina, Anna Pavlova, is considered among the most famous of all classical ballet dancers. With her slim frame, ethereal grace and expressive style she re-defined conventional ballet dancing. She is credited with inventing the modern pointed shoe, an essential accessory for every ballerina today. Pavlova began dancing at the age of ten and travelled all over the world, giving performances till she died at the age of 49.

January 31, 1881: Born in St Petersburg, Russia

September 19, 1899: Debuts at the Maryinsky Theatre

1907: Performs the Dying Swan, her signature piece

January 23, 1931: Dies in The Hague, Netherlands

433 Martha Graham
[1894 - 1991]

Martha Graham

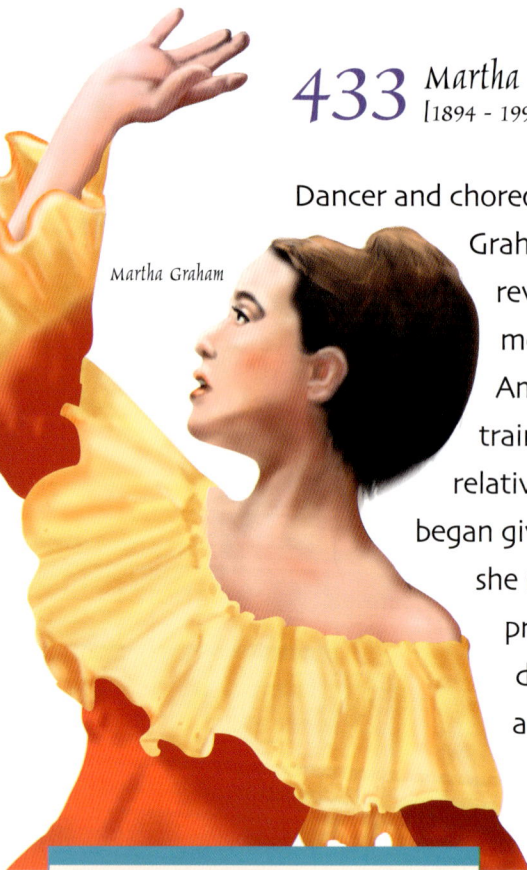

Dancer and choreographer, Martha Graham is credited with revolutionising and modernising dance in America. Graham trained in dance from the relatively late age of 22 and began giving solo performances only when she was 32. However, she made up for lost time by performing over 150 presentations in the next 50 years. Her dancing style was defined by angular movements. Her sets were plain, stark and minimal, and her costumes were simple.

May 11, 1894: Born in Allegheny County, Pennsylvania, U.S.

1926: Makes New York debut at 48th Street Theatre

1930: Founds the Dance Repertory Theater, New York

1944: Performs her most famous dance, Appalachian Spring

1970: Receives a Distinguished Service to Arts Award from the National Institute of Arts and Letters; retires as a dancer

April 1, 1991: Dies in New York City, New York, U.S.

434 Fred Astaire
[1899 - 1987]

May 10, 1899: Born in Omaha, Nebraska, U.S.

1933: Makes his film debut in Dancing Lady with Joan Crawford

1950: The Academy of Motion Picture Arts and Sciences presents Astaire with an honorary Oscar

1981: The American Film Institute presents Astaire with a Lifetime Achievement Award

June 22, 1987: Dies in Los Angeles, California, U.S.

1989: Is posthumously awarded the Grammy Lifetime Achievement Award

Fred Astaire, born Frederick Austerlitz, is one of America's most famous dancers. Astaire began by dancing in vaudevilles with his sister Adele. In 1917 they made their debut on Broadway, and in 1932 Fred struck out on his own. Soon Astaire gained fame as a tap dancer and choreograph in movies. Together with his partner, Ginger Rogers, Astair transformed the way musical films were made.

435 Ginger Rogers
[1911 - 1995]

Ginger Rogers, born Virginia Katherine McMath, was a well-known American movie actress and dancer of the 1930s and 40s. Rogers began as a child artist, performing in vaudevilles, on Broadway and eventually in motion pictures. One of the highest paid actresses of her time, Rogers is famous for her dancing roles with Fred Astaire. She acted in 70 motion pictures, of which ten were musicals co-starring Astaire.

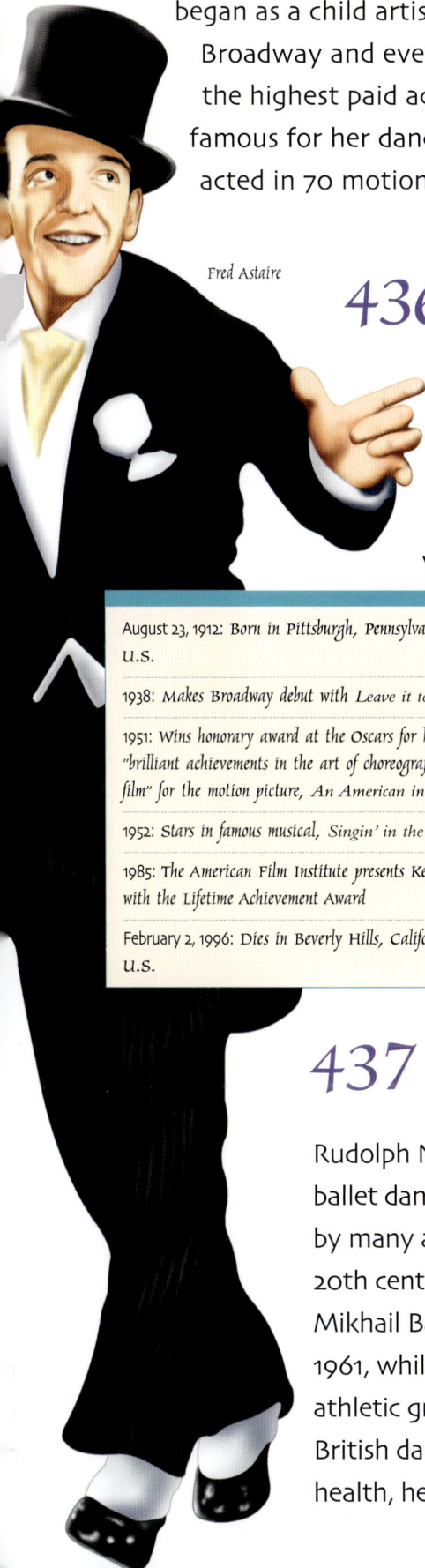

July 16, 1911: Born in Independence, Missouri, U.S.

1929: Makes her debut on Broadway in Top Speed

1940: Wins an Academy Award for her leading role in Kitty Foyle

April 25, 1995: Dies in Rancho Mirage, California, U.S.

1992: Is honoured with a Lifetime Achievement Award by the Kennedy Center

Fred Astaire

Gene Kelly

436 Gene Kelly
[1912 - 1996]

Gene Kelly, born Eugene Curran Kelly, is an outstanding Hollywood dancing star. Kelly, like many of his contemporaries, began dancing in vaudeville. After a spell as a dance instructor, he moved to Broadway in 1932. His first movie role was in 1941. The first film in which he choreographed dances was *Cover Girl*, in 1944. In this film he created the "alter ego" dance, where he danced with himself. He has also presented some memorable dance specials on television.

August 23, 1912: Born in Pittsburgh, Pennsylvania, U.S.

1938: Makes Broadway debut with Leave it to Me

1951: Wins honorary award at the Oscars for his "brilliant achievements in the art of choreography on film" for the motion picture, An American in Paris

1952: Stars in famous musical, Singin' in the Rain

1985: The American Film Institute presents Kelly with the Lifetime Achievement Award

February 2, 1996: Dies in Beverly Hills, California, U.S.

437 Rudolph Nureyev
[1938 - 1993]

March 17, 1938: Born near Irkutsk, Siberian USSR

1958: Becomes soloist for the Kirov Ballet

1961: Defects from the Soviet Union while in Paris

1983: Revisits Russia at Mikhail Gorbachev's invitation

1992: Gives his last public performance in Paris to a standing ovation

1993: Dies of AIDS in Paris, France

Rudolph Nureyev was the leading classical ballet dancer of his generation, and is regarded by many as the greatest male dancer of the 20th century, alongside Vaslav Nijinsky and Mikhail Baryshnikov. He became a soloist with the Kirov Ballet in 1958 and, in 1961, while touring in Paris, defected from the Soviet Union. He was noted for his athletic grace, stage presence and partnership with Margot Fonteyn, the leading British dancer of her time. After many years of declining health, he died in Paris in 1993.

100 GREATS of the stage

Magicians and Showmen

438 Phineas Taylor Barnum
[1810 - 1891]

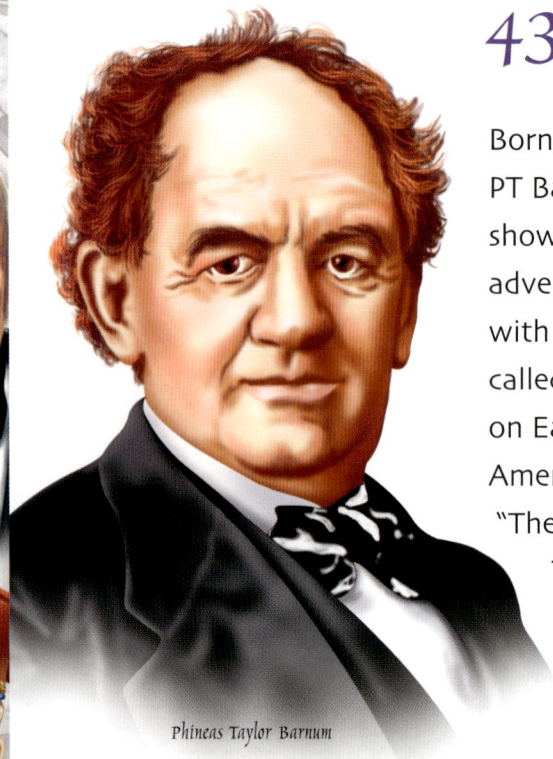

Born in Connecticut, U.S., PT Barnum was a great showman. The father of advertising, Barnum started with a travelling show called "The Greatest Show on Earth". At 60, he set up America's largest circus – "The PT Barnum's Grand Traveling Museum, Menagerie, Caravan and Circus" – a runaway success. Later, with partner James Bailey, the "Barnum and Bailey Circus" was formed. The show exists to this day!

Phineas Taylor Barnum

July 5, 1810: Born in Bethel, Connecticut, U.S.

1842: Barnum's first major success was the introduction of General Tom Thumb

1853: Starts New Yorks first illustrated newspaper

1854: Publishes autobiography, Struggles and Triumphs

1870: Forms "The PT Barnum's Grand Traveling Museum, Menagerie, Caravan and Circus"

1888: James Bailey joins him as equal partner to form the "Barnum and Bailey Circus"

April 7, 1891: Dies in Bridgeport, Connecticut, U.S.

439 Harry Houdini
[1874 - 1926]

Bob Hope has several Walk of Fame Stars to his name

One of the greatest magicians and escapologists, Harry Houdini was born as Ehrich Weisz to poor Hungarian parents. Houdini started his career by performing small magic acts in vaudevilles. When he teamed up with his wife, Wilhelmina Beatrice Rahner, he began performing more complex acts. But it was after 1899 that he began to establish himself as an escapologist. He performed daring and astonishing escape acts, such as escaping from straitjackets and from the Upside-Down Water Torture Cell!

March 24, 1874: Born Ehrich Weiss, in Budapest, Hungary

1878: Houdini's family emigrates to the United States of America

1894: Teams up with his wife and starts the act The Houdinis

1912: Houdini is lowered into New York's East River in a crate, wrapped in chains, from which he escapes in less than a minute!

October 31, 1926: Houdini dies in Detroit, U.S.

440   Julius Henry "Groucho" Marx
[1890 - 1977]

Popular American stand-up comedian, Groucho Marx is immortalised by his famous one-liners that are used by comedians even today. He started with small stage shows and, with his five brothers, performed slapstick comedies for at least 20 years in vaudeville. The Marx Brothers moved on to Broadway and later to the movies. Groucho always had the leading role and the best lines. He also worked in radio and television shows, hosting a popular and long running comedy quiz show.

October 2, 1890: Born in New York City, New York, U.S.

1947: Starts his show You Bet Your Life, which runs until 1961 on radio and, from 1950, on television

1972: Is honoured with the "Commandeur des Arts et Lettres" by the French government at the Cannes Film Festival

1973: Is presented an Academy Honorary Award in recognition of his creativity and the achievements of the Marx Brothers in the art of motion picture comedy

January 16, 1977: The Marx Brothers are inducted to the Motion Picture Hall of Fame

August 19, 1977: Groucho dies in Los Angeles, California, U.S.

441   Bob Hope
[1903 - 2003]

May 29, 1903: Born in Eltham, South London, England

1933: Stars in Broadway musical Roberta, which makes him famous

October 1997: Is made an Honorary Veteran by the US Congress – the first individual to be presented this honour

1998: Receives honorary knighthood – Knight Commander of the Most Excellent Order of the British Empire (KBE)

May 2000: Inaugurates the Bob Hope Gallery of American Entertainment at the Library of Congress, Washington

July 27, 2003: Dies at Toluca Lake, California

Leslie Townes Hope, or "Bob" Hope as he was better known, was one of America's most-loved comedians. In a career of over 80 years, he performed on the stage, in the movies, on radio and on television too! Hope started his career with a dancing vaudeville act but soon became one of the most popular entertainment personalities in the country. He received many awards for his contribution to the arts and his services to his nation.

David Copperfield

442   David Copperfield
[1956 -]

David Copperfield is one of the most well known magicians of our times. He was the youngest magician to be admitted to the Society of American Magicians and was teaching magic at New York University at the age of 16! He is famous for his wonderful magic acts, such as making the Statue of Liberty disappear, walking through the Great Wall of China, and making an aeroplane disappear! He also hosts a popular show on television and has co-authored two books.

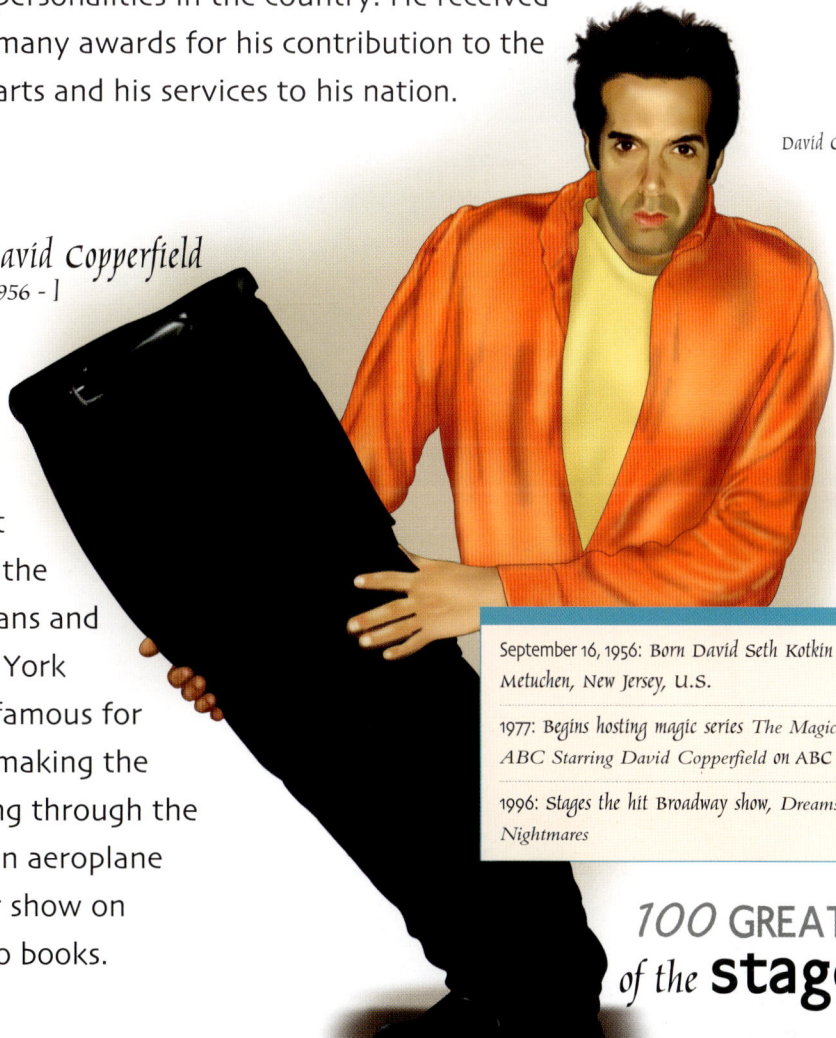

September 16, 1956: Born David Seth Kotkin in Metuchen, New Jersey, U.S.

1977: Begins hosting magic series The Magic of ABC Starring David Copperfield on ABC

1996: Stages the hit Broadway show, Dreams & Nightmares

100 GREATS
of the **stage**

Pop and Rock Musicians

443 Chuck Berry
[1926 -]

American guitarist, Charles Edward Anderson Berry is an icon of 20th century popular culture. Berry integrated rhythm and blues with more popular styles to produce rock and roll. This was the musical style that became very popular with the youth of the 1950s and 60s. He was a talented and lively performer and an inspiration to musicians like the Beatles, the Rolling Stones and the Beach Boys.

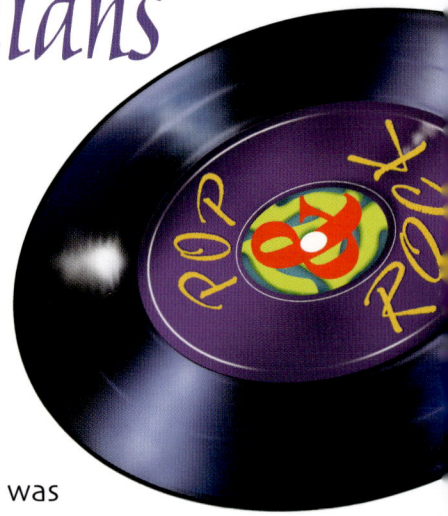

October 18, 1926: Born in St Louis, Missouri, U.S.

1955: Made rock and roll history with first single, Maybellene

1972: Sings My Ding-a-Ling, his only #1 hit

February 26, 1985: Berry is honoured with the Lifetime Achievement Grammy Award

January 23, 1986: Is inducted into the Rock and Roll Hall of Fame

1987: Publishes Chuck Berry: The Autobiography and releases rockumentary, Hail! Hail! Rock 'n' Roll

Jerry Lee Lewis

444 Little Richard
[1932 -]

Little Richard, born Richard Wayne Penniman, was one of the most popular and significant personalities of rock and roll music in the 1950s. In 1955, he recorded his first rock and roll song *Tutti Frutti*, one of the greatest hits of all time! Since then he has recorded numerous albums and performed live for huge audiences in the U.K. and U.S. His enthusiastic and lively performances have inspired many popular acts.

December 5, 1932: Born in Macon, Georgia, U.S.

1956: Sings biggest hit, "Long Tall Sally"

January 23, 1986: Is inducted into the Rock and Roll Hall of Fame

February 23, 1993: Receives the Grammy Lifetime Achievement Award

Little Richard

445 Quincy Jones
[1933 -]

Quincy Jones is one of America's most talented entertainment personalities. A multifaceted craftsman, he began as a trumpeter but is now a composer, conductor, arranger and music and television producer! Apart form recording and conducting his own compositions, Jones has written arrangements for leading musicians and produced successful albums for artists like Michael Jackson and Aretha Franklin. He has also composed scores for several motion pictures and television shows. His music is a mixture of pop, soul, jazz and African and Brazilian beats.

> March 14, 1933: Born in Chicago, Illino...
>
> 1948: Forms combo with Ray Charles
>
> 1957: Moves to Paris, where he studies compositio... with Nadia Boulanger and Olivier Messiaen
>
> 1964: Becomes vice-president of Mercury Records
>
> 1991: Wins Grammy Living Legend Award
>
> 1993: Together with David Salzman, stages the spectacular concert An American Reunion to celebrate the inauguration of President Bill Clinton
>
> 1995: Wins the Jean Hersholt Humanitarian Award at the Oscars

446 Elvis Presley
[1935 - 1977]

Elvis Aaron Presley is one of the most famous musicians of all time. Indeed, he is an icon of 20th century American culture. This great singer was partly responsible for the 1950s and 60s musical craze – rock and roll. As a child, Presley had heard a lot of blues and gospel music. He later combined these influences with country music to popularise rock and roll. "The King's" songs and stage persona continue to inspire his fans today!

> January 8, 1935: Born in Tupelo, Mississippi, U.S.
>
> January 1956: Records Heartbreak Hotel, the first of ten consecutive #1 hits
>
> 1968: Makes a comeback with NBC TV special, Elvis
>
> August 16, 1977: Dies in Memphis, Tennessee, U.S.
>
> January 23, 1986: Is inducted into the Rock and Roll Hall of Fame

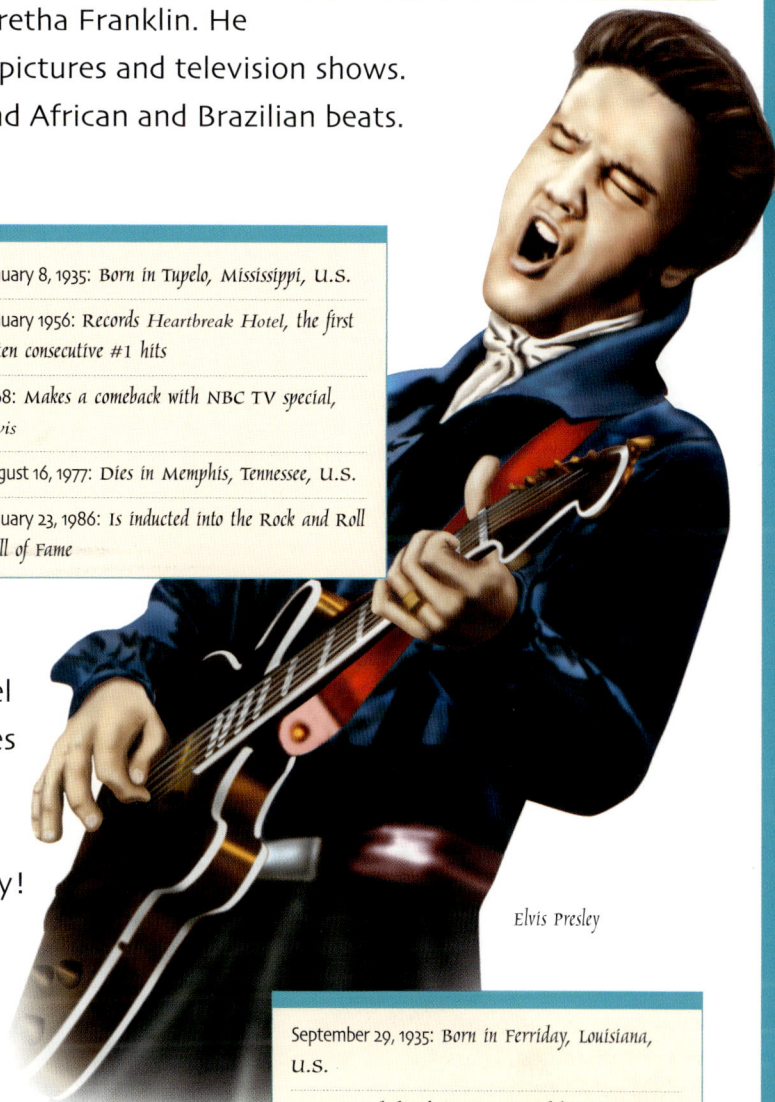

Elvis Presley

447 Jerry Lee Lewis
[1935 -]

Jerry Lee Lewis, pianist and singer, is a popular American rock and roll artist of the 1950s. His early exposure to music included gospel, blues and country – all of which influenced the musician in him. Though the "Killer" has recorded several successful albums over the years, it is at concerts and shows that he has given his best performances. His dynamic and energetic performances have always been enormously successful!

> September 29, 1935: Born in Ferriday, Louisiana, U.S.
>
> 1957: Records his first international hit, Whole Lotta Shakin' Goin' On, and his Great Balls of Fire becomes a huge best-seller
>
> 1973: The Session goes to the US Top 40, his only album to do so
>
> January 23, 1986: Is inducted into the Rock and Roll Hall of Fame

100 GREATS of the stage

195

448 Buddy Holly
[1936 - 1959]

...r and songwriter Charles Hardin Holley, ... known as Buddy Holly, is considered one of the founding fathers of rock and roll. His music was sophisticated for its day and, combined with his personal style, influenced youth culture and musicians for decades to come. His career was cut short by a tragic plane crash, immortalised in Don McLean's popular 1971 ballad *American Pie* as "The Day the Music Died".

September 7, 1936: Born in Lubbock, Texas, U.S.

1957: With his band, the Crickets, records *That'll Be the Day*, a top-selling record on both the pop and R&B charts

February 3, 1959: Dies in plane crash in Iowa, U.S., along with Ritchie Valens and JP Richardson ('The Big Bopper')

1971: *American Pie* by Don McLean released

1978: Hollywood biography released about his life

1986: Inducted into the Rock and Roll Hall of Fame

449 Neil Diamond
[1941 -]

Neil Leslie Diamond, one of America's most popular songwriters and singers, is among the Top 20 most successful artists of his country. His compositions are varied, including popular melodies, country style ballads, gospel and blues-influenced songs and progressive rock. He has also written for other artists and composed award winning music for movies such as *Jonathan Livingston Seagull* and *The Jazz Singer*. His album *Tennessee Moon*, recorded in 1996, is a country-style compilation.

Neil Diamond

January 24, 1941: Born in Brooklyn, New York, U.S.

1966: Records his first major hit, *Cherry Cherry*

1972: Releases landmark album, *Hot August Night*

1973: Wins Grammy for *Jonathan Livingston Seagull's* original soundtrack

450 Paul Simon & Art Garfunkel
[1941 -]   [1942 -]

Simon and Garfunkel were one of the most successful singing partnerships of the 1960s, a time when folk rock was in. After a couple of unsuccessful early recordings, in 1966 they finally found success with their hit single *Sound of Silence*. However, due to personal differences they did not stay together for long, and decided to break up in the early 70s. Both have since had careers as solo singers.

Simon and Garfunkel have won numerous Grammy Awards

October 13, 1941: Paul Simon is born in Newark, New Jersey, U.S.

November 5, 1942: Art Garfunkel is born in Forest Hills, New York, U.S.

1967: Compose score for the film, *The Graduate*

1970: Release best-selling album, *Bridge Over Troubled Waters*, and win four Grammys that year

2003: Win the Grammy Lifetime Achievement Award

451 Barbra Streisand
[1942 -]

Barbra Streisand, singer, composer, actress, producer and director, is one of the foremost entertainment personalities of America. By the time she was 21 years of age, Streisand had sung pop, show tunes, rock and classical music with equal ease. She remains one of the top four best selling artists of all time in her country. Her career on stage and in movies have been equally spectacular. A highly successful and popular artist, Streisand has won several awards and honours.

April 24, 1942: Born in Brooklyn, New York, U.S.

1962: Makes debut with Broadway show, I Can Get It For You Wholesale

1963: The Barbara Streisand Album wins two Grammy Awards

1968: Wins the Best Actress Oscar for Funny Girl

1976: She wins the Academy Award for composing Evergreen, from the film A Star Is Born, becoming the first female composer to win the award

1992: Wins Grammy Living Legend Award

January 2000: Receives the Cecil B. DeMille Award for lifetime achievement

Barbra Streisand

452 Jimi Hendrix
[1942 - 1970]

Johnny Allen Hendrix, or Jimi Hendrix, is one of the most outstanding instrumentalists and influential figures in rock history. Hendrix taught himself to play the electric guitar by listening to records of legendary blues musicians. After playing in various groups he formed a band called the Jimi Hendrix Experience, which produced ground breaking rock compositions till 1969. Hendrix was an instinctive performer who was shy offstage but a showman and live-wire while performing.

November 27, 1942: Born in Seattle, Washington, U.S.

September 1966: Forms the Jimi Hendrix Experience with Noel Redding (bass) and John Mitchell (drums)

October 1968: Electric Ladyland, the trio's last album, is released

September 18, 1970: Dies tragically young in London, England

453 Bob Marley
[1945 - 1981]

Robert Nesta Marley, or Bob Marley, is the most famous reggae musician of all time. Marley formed his first band, the Wailing Wailers, in 1962 in Kingston, Jamaica. The band composed and sang several popular songs of the time. In the late 60s, Marley moved towards more spiritual and rhythmic sounds that greatly influenced reggae music. Marley composed, performed and toured widely, popularising his Caribbean tunes, till he died of cancer at the age of 36.

February 6, 1945: Born in Nine Miles, St Ann, Jamaica

1972: Releases Catch A Fire, the first full-length reggae album

April 1981: Is awarded Jamaica's Order of Merit, for his outstanding contribution to the country's culture

May 11, 1981: Dies in Miami, Florida, U.S.

January 19, 1994: Is inducted into the Rock and Roll Hall of Fame

Bob Marley

100 GREATS
of the **stage**

454 Eric Clapton
[1945 -]

Eric Clapton

Eric Clapton is a very successful contemporary British musician. A guitarist, singer and songwriter, Clapton began performing professionally from 1962. Initially Clapton focused more on playing the guitar, but by the end of the 1970s he began to concentrate on singing and songwriting too. His music is typically tinted with blues melody and rhythm, harking back to his childhood influences. Over the years he has played with different bands and has also recorded and performed successfully as a solo artist.

March 30, 1945: Born in Ripley, Surrey, England

August 1974: Records *461 Ocean Boulevard*, which goes to the top of the U.S. charts

1992: Records *Unplugged*, his most successful album, that earned him the Album of the Year Grammy

1994: Records *From the Cradle*, which wins him Best Traditional Blues Album at the Grammys

March 6, 2000: Is inducted into the Rock and Roll Hall of Fame

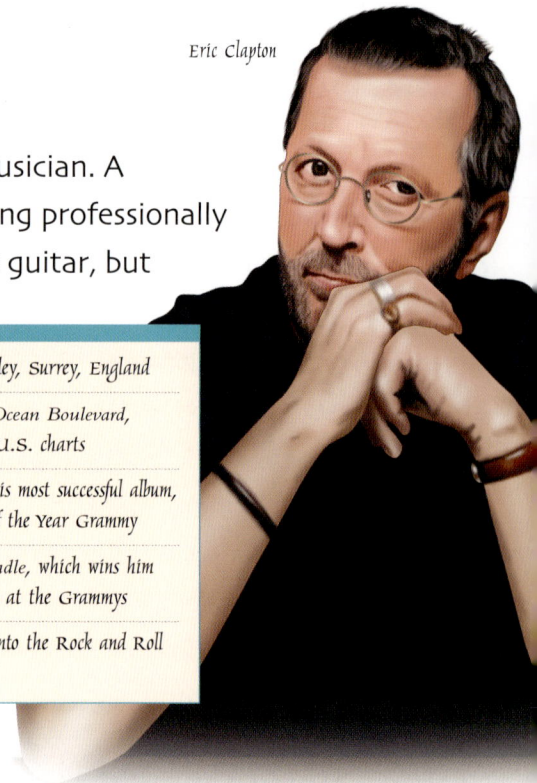

455 Elton John
[1947 -]

Elton John

Elton John is a very successful contemporary British musician. Born Reginald Kenneth Dwight, his childhood interest in music helped him to become a rock singer, pianist and songwriter. After playing for several small rock bands and an R&B band, John teamed up with lyricist Bernie Taupin in 1967 to begin a long and fruitful professional partnership. A great showman, he has attracted as much attention for his clothes and appearance as for his music!

March 25, 1947: Born in Pinner, Middlesex, England

1972: Records *Honky Chateau*, his first #1 album

1975: Makes *Captain Fantastic*, an album that opened at #1

January 19, 1994: Is inducted into the Rock and Roll Hall of Fame

February 12, 1997: Knighted

1999: Recieves Grammy Living Legend Award

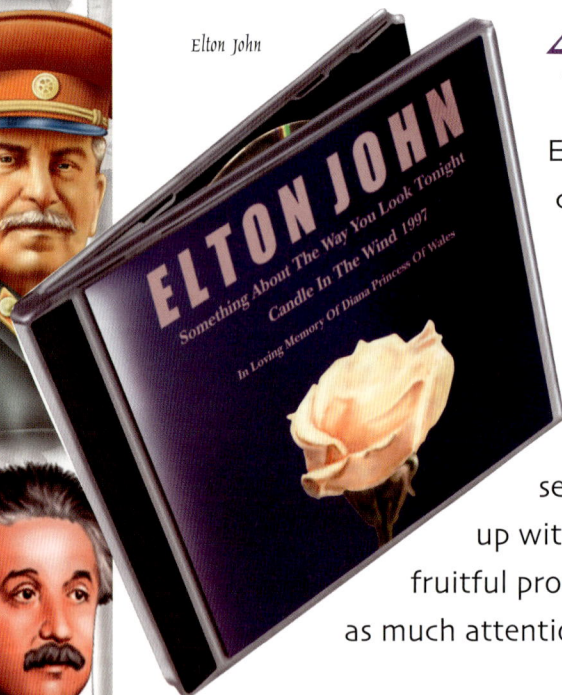

456 Billy Joel
[1949 -]

Billy Joel, born William Martin Joel, is one of America's most successful songwriters and singers. After starting his career with various bands, he struck out on his own in 1971. Joel's ascent as a rock star in the 1970s and 80s was greatly due to his image as a working class hero – narrating stories of family life. He has also sung pop songs and light-hearted numbers like *Uptown Girl* and *The Longest Time*.

May 9, 1949: Born in New York City, New York, U.S.

1978-80: Wins five Grammys for *Just the Way You Are*, *52nd Street* and *Glass Houses*

1991: Is honoured with the Grammy Living Legend Award

1992: Is inducted into the Songwriters Hall of Fame

March 15, 1999: Is inducted into the Rock and Roll Hall of Fame

2006: Play a record 12 sold-out shows at Madison Square Gardens, New York, U.S.

457 Bruce Springsteen
[1949 -]

Bruce Springsteen is a very famous American rock star. An icon of working class America, Springsteen wrote and sang in a language that everyone understood. His songs told the story of their life, love, joys and frustrations. The anger and moodiness of the early songs reflected Springsteen's own unhappy relationship with his father. His first album was released in 1973. Since then "The Boss" – as he is also known – has been recording and performing for audiences around the world.

September 23, 1949: Born in Freehold, New Jersey, U.S.

1975: Records Born To Run, a commercial and critical success

1984: Born in the USA is a major hit of the 1980s

March 15, 1999: Springsteen is inducted into the Rock and Roll Hall of Fame

Bruce Springsteen

Madonna

458 Madonna
[1958 -]

Madonna Louise Veronica Ciccone is probably the most successful female pop singer of the 20th century. Starting her musical career in 1980, Madonna has consistently come up with record breaking hit singles and albums. Her pop image, individualistic style and bold attitude found a large fan following among teenagers in the 1980s. Madonna has sung in many musical styles, such as R&B, hip-hop and pop. She has also co-written some of her own songs.

August 16, 1958: Born in Bay City, Michigan, U.S.

1984: Title track of second album, Like A Virgin, becomes her first #1 hit

1996: Acts as Eva Peron in the motion picture Evita

2007: Confirmed by the Guinness Book of Records as the highest earning female singer of all time

100 GREATS
of the **stage**

459 Michael Jackson
[1958 -]

Michael Joseph Jackson is one of the most famous names in the world of music and entertainment. America's biggest pop star, Jackson has been performing since the age of four! During this highly successful career, he has sung disco, funk, pop, rock and soul. A gifted dancer, he has also popularised a whole new style of dancing in his videos and stage shows. Michael Jackson's influence on pop and contemporary world music has been enormous.

August 29, 1958: Born in Gary, Indiana, U.S.

1963: Forms the Jackson Five, along with his four brothers

1979: Michael records Off The Wall, his first solo album as an adult

1982: Records Thriller, the biggest selling album of all time

1993: Wins Grammy Legend Award

March 19, 2001: Is inducted into the Rock and Roll Hall of Fame

2001: He celebrates his 30th anniversary as a solo artist by performing once again with the Jackson Five

Michael Jackson
invented the "moonwalk"

460 The Beatles
[1960 - 1970]

John Winston Lennon [1940 - 1980]   James Paul McCartney [1942 -]
George Harrison [1943 - 2001]   Richard Starkey (Ringo Starr) [1940 -]

The British rock and roll band, the Beatles, are probably the most popular band in the history of music. They achieved their final lineup in 1962, with John Lennon (guitar/vocals), Paul McCartney (guitar/vocals), George Harrison (guitar/vocals) and Ringo Starr (drums). Their songs continue to be popular today and their achievements have been an inspiration to many who have followed. The Beatles stayed together as a group until 1970. After this they broke up and followed solo careers. John Lennon was assassinated in New York in 1980.

August 1960: John Lennon's band, The Quarrymen, is renamed The Beatles

1962: Ringo Starr joins Lennon, McCartney and Harrison as the fourth member of the Beatles

October 1962: They record their first single, Love Me Do, which becomes a UK Top 20 hit

February 1963: They record their first album Please Please Me, which becomes an instant hit

1967: Sgt. Pepper's Lonely Hearts Club Band wins four Grammys

Beatles

461 The Beach Boys
[1961 -]

The epitome of the myth of American freedom and youthful dreams, the songs of the Beach Boys are etched into music culture. The early music, about surfing, cars and girls, was often bright and accessible, yet held sophisticated musical ideas. Their sometimes stormy career has seen many changes in musical style and lineup, and legal wrangles over the use of the name since the deaths of Carl and Dennis, yet their music has influenced many.

1961: Band formed in Hawthorne, California: Brian Wilson, his brothers Carl and Dennis, their cousin Mike Love and friend Alan Jardine

1966: Good Vibrations released — since acclaimed as one of the best rock singles of all time

1980: Play Fourth of July concert in Washinton on the National Mall, to become a regular event

1988: Inducted into the Rock and Roll Hall of Fame

462 The Rolling Stones
[1962 -]

The British band, The Rolling Stones, are one of the most successful rock bands of all time. First formed in 1962, at the height of its success the band included Bill Wyman (bass), Charlie Watts (drummer), Mick Jagger (lead vocals), Keith Richards (guitar and vocals) and Brian Jones (rhythm guitar and vocals). Their rebellious public image and bold new musical style made them very popular. Their clever mix of pop and R&B musical styles also contributed to their immense success.

1962: Make their debut at London's Marquee Club

1962: Bill Wyman joins Jagger, Jones and Richards

1963: Charlie Watts joins the act and completes the five-member band

1969: Brian Jones leaves the band

1969: Honky Tonk Women is their last single to become a UK chart topper

2002: They release 40 Licks

Jim Morrison, the lead singer of The Doors

463 The Doors
[1965 - 1973]

1965: Band formed with Jim Morrison (vocals), Ray Manzarek (keyboards), John Densmore (drums) and Robbie Krieger (guitar)

1967: The Doors, their first album is released

July 3, 1971: Jim Morrison dies at the age of 27

1978: American Prayer, an album with Morrison's poetry readings set to music, is released

1991: Oliver Stone makes the biographical film, The Doors

An American band of the 1970s, The Doors played a significant role in the development of rock music. The band was made famous by Jim Morrison's poetry, set to tunes influenced by blues, opera, classical and eastern music. Morrison's premature death was seen as one of the most tragic losses to music in recent times.

464 Pink Floyd
[1966 -]

1966: Band formed in Cambridge, England: Roger Waters (bass/ vocals), Nick Mason (drums), Rick Wright (keyboards) and Syd Barret (guitar/ vocals)

1967: Arnold Layne, their first single, entered at #2 on the UK charts

1968: David Gilmour replaces Barret

1973: Dark Side of the Moon becomes their most successful album, reaching the top of U.S. charts

1985: Roger Waters leaves the band

1994: Division Bell, their last album is released

A famous British rock band of the 1960s and 70s, Pink Floyd were renowned for cerebral lyrics, sweeping compositions, striking album art and performances accompanied by psychedelic lightings. The group recorded and performed several rock classics before breaking up in the early 80s. The members pursue solo careers today, but occasionally get together to perform and record as a group.

100 GREATS
of the stage

BEE GEES

The Bee Gees Insignia

465 The Bee Gees
[1967 - 2003]

The English band Bee Gees – with brothers Barry, Maurice and Robin Gibb – were one of the most successful acts of the 1970s. They are also one of the best selling bands of all times, having sold over 110 million albums! The Bee Gees were popular for disco and funk, sung in a falsetto style. The Bee Gees have also written songs for several leading artists of the 1970s, 80s and 90s.

1967: *Spicks and Specks* is their first #1 hit

1977-78: Soundtrack of *Saturday Night Fever* is all time disco hit

1987: They record *E-S-P*, their last album

March 1988: Youngest brother, Andy Gibb, dies

May 6, 1997: They are inducted into the Rock and Roll Hall of Fame

2003: Maurice dies and the band's name is retired

466 ABBA
[1972 - 1982]

Björn Ulvaeus, Benny Andersson, Agnetha Fältskog and Anni-Frid Lyngstad formed the hugely popular 1970s Swedish pop band, ABBA. The four were collaborating from 1968 but didn't release their first song as a group until 1972. For the next ten years they toured all over the world and recorded lively pop songs and disco music. The group broke up in 1982, but their music is still immensely popular and several compilations of their hits have been released in the past decade. Indeed, the group have sold over 370 million records worldwide!

April 6, 1974: ABBA wins the Eurovision Song Contest held in London with *Waterloo*

April 1977: *Dancing Queen* becomes US #1, their only song to do so

1978: *ABBA–The Movie* and *ABBA–The Album* are released in the same year

1981: They release their eighth and last album, *The Visitors*

467 Led Zeppelin
[1968 - 1980]

A hugely influential British rock band of the 70s and 80s and one of the most successful groups in music history, Led Zeppelin played a crucial part in the development of heavy metal. The band formed in 1968 with Jimmy Page (guitar), Robert Plant (vocals), John Paul Jones (bass/ keyboards) and John Bonham (drums). The group has experimented with blues, funk, folk music and slow ballads apart from their typical rock compositions. They recorded eight albums and toured extensively till their break up in 1980, following the death of their drummer, John Bonham.

October 1968: Jimmy Page forms Led Zeppelin

1969: Their debut album, Led Zeppelin, is released

November 1971: Led Zeppelin IV, their biggest selling album is released

1974: The group forms their own record label, Swan Song

September 25, 1980: John Bonham dies

January 12, 1995: Band inducted into the Rock and Roll Hall of Fame

468 Deep Purple
[1968 -]

British hard rock band, Deep Purple, has been one of the most successful hard rock bands over the past 30 years. Initially formed in 1968, the band has gone through several changes in group members. They were one of the first heavy metal groups. One of their most famous songs – *Smoke on the Water* – has gained the status of a rock anthem.

1968: They record Shades of Deep Purple, their first album

1970: The group records, Concerto for Group and Orchestra, with the Royal Philharmonic Orchestra

1972: They release Machine Head, one of their most successful albums

2003: Bananas, their latest album, is released

469 Queen
[1971 - 1995]

Queen, the successful British band of the 1970s, included Brian May (guitar), Roger Taylor (drums), Freddie Mercury (lead vocal/ piano) and John Deacon (bass). They played a combination of pop, rock, disco and rock and roll music. Lead singer Freddy Mercury's showmanship on stage and his powerful voice, combined with Brian May on the guitar, made the band living legends. Posthumously, Mercury is considered perhaps the most gifted and compelling front-man in music history.

ABBA

The Queen Insignia

1971: John Decon joins May, Taylor and Mercury to complete the band

1975: They record Bohemian Rhapsody, their most outstanding single

November 24, 1991: Freddie Mercury dies

1995: They release Made in Heaven, their last album

March 19, 2001: Band inducted into the Rock and Roll Hall of Fame

May 14, 2002: Queen's musical, We Will Rock You, opens at London's Dominion Theatre

100 GREATS
of the **stage**

Jazz and R&B Musicians

470 Scott Joplin
[1868 - 1917]

American songwriter and composer, Scott Joplin was an outstanding ragtime musician. During his childhood he was trained in classical music and his initial compositions were waltzes and other dance music. Later, he began composing "rag", a musical style that blended European classical music with African-American rhythm. "The King of Ragtime", as he is also known, also wrote an opera, *Treemonisha*, but was unable to see it staged during his lifetime. Joplin wrote and published nearly sixty compositions.

Saxaphone

November 24, 1868: Born in Texas, U.S.

1899: Publishes Maple Leaf Rag, his most popular composition

April 1, 1917: Dies in New York City, New York, U.S.

1973: Film score featuring his music in the motion picture, The Sting, wins Oscar Award

1976: Posthumously awarded the Pulitzer Prize for his opera Treemonisha

471 Bessie Smith
[1892 - 1937]

A very successful classic blues singer of the 1920s, Elizabeth "Bessie" Smith is also known as the "Empress of Blues". She started out as a street singer in Chattanooga, Tennessee, and moved on to a travelling vaudeville. In 1923, she recorded her first song, *Down Hearted Blues*. It was a huge hit, selling two million copies in the first year alone! Smith's legacy was her massive influence on the shape and progress of blues music and the singers she inspired along the way.

July, 1892: Born in Chattanooga, Tennessee, U.S.

1923: Her first recording, Down Hearted Blues, is released

September 26, 1937: Dies in an automobile accident near Clarksdale, Mississippi

1980: Is inducted into the Blues Foundation's Hall of Fame

1989: Receives the Grammy Lifetime Achievement Award posthumously

Louis Armstrong

472 Louis Armstrong
[1901 - 1971]

Louis Armstrong was one of America's greatest jazz players. He was a natural musician who did not have any formal training. Armstrong started playing the cornet and bugle, before taking up the trumpet in the 1920s. In his later years, he also became a successful singer. Armstrong was an innovative and flamboyant player who set new trends in jazz music. He is an inspiration to many jazz musicians even to this day.

473 Peggy Lou Snyder
[1909 - 1994]

American singer and actress Peggy Snyder was better known by her show business name, Harriet Nelson (née Hilliard). Born in a family of professional actors, she took naturally to vaudeville. By the 1930s, she was singing popular dance numbers and romantic duets in nightclubs and on radio with her husband and bandleader, Ozzie Nelson. In the 1940s, moving away from music, the couple launched a popular radio comedy series, *The Adventures of Ozzie and Harriet.*

Peggy Lou Snyder

July 18, 1909: *Born in Des Moines, Iowa, U.S.*

1932: *Snyder joins Ozzie Nelson's orchestra as Harriet Hilliard*

1944: *Starts popular radio series, The Adventures of Ozzie and Harriet, with husband Ozzie Nelson*

October 2, 1994: *Dies in Laguna Beach, California, U.S.*

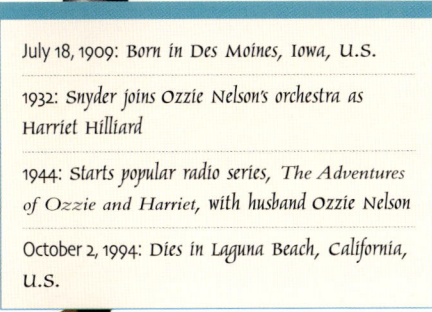

Frank Sinatra

474 Frank Sinatra
[1915 - 1998]

American singer, Francis Albert Sinatra, is one of the most famous singers of the 20th century. During his career, he sang in the musical styles of blues, jazz and the newly emerging pop music. He began singing in the early 1930s and after a few years of singing in various bands, he began on his own. But it was in the 1950s that he recorded his most memorable works. Sinatra has also acted in over 20 motion pictures.

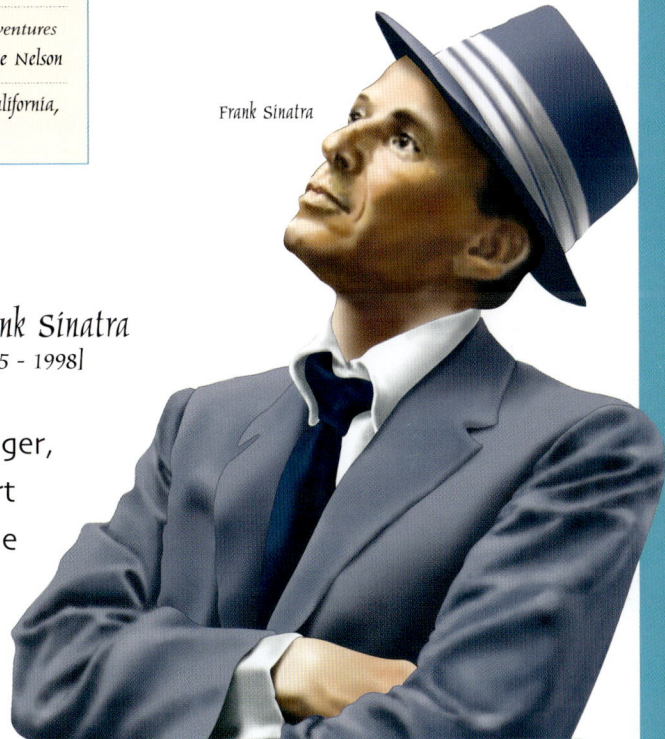

December 12, 1915: *Born in Hoboken, New Jersey, U.S.*

1953: *Wins the Best Supporting Actor Oscar Award for the film From Here to Eternity*

1953: *Signs up with Capitol Records, with whom he produces his best music*

May 14, 1998: *Dies in Los Angeles, California, U.S.*

1999: *Is inducted into the Grammy Hall of Fame for his album, Frank Sinatra Sings For Only the Lonely*

August 4, 1901: *Born in New Orleans, Louisiana, U.S.*

1917: *Armstrong becomes a student of trumpeter "King" Oliver*

1924: *Marries Lillian Hardin, and she encourages him to leave Oliver and start his own career in New York*

July 6, 1971: *Dies in New York City, New York, U.S.*

1972: *Receives the Grammy Lifetime Achievement Award posthumously*

100 GREATS
of the **stage**

475 Nat "King" Cole
[1917 - 1965]

An American jazz singer and pianist, Nathaniel Adams Cole was a widely popular and successful musician. He learnt to play the piano from his mother. Cole played as a member of a jazz band in clubs. When he was 20, at the request of his audience, he began singing too. Soon Nat "King" Cole established himself as a very popular jazz singer. He has sold over 50 million records during his career! Cole was a pioneer and figurehead for racial equality, being the first African American to host his own radio programme in the U.S.

March 17, 1917: Born in Montgomery, Alabama, U.S.

1946: (I Love You) For Sentimental Reasons becomes his first pop hit

1947: Nature Boy is another huge hit, becoming a gold record

1959: Wins Grammy for Best Performance for Midnight Flyer

February 15, 1965: Dies in Santa Monica, California, U.S.

1990: Is honoured with the Grammy Lifetime Achievement Award

Nat "King" Cole

476 Ella Fitzgerald
[1917 - 1996]

American jazz singer, Ella Jane Fitzgerald, was also known as "The First Lady of Song". She started out by performing on various talent shows before she was noticed and invited to join a band. But her solo career did not take off until after 1942. Her wonderful voice stood by her for over 50 years. During this time she recorded several solo albums and collaborations – winning 13 Grammy Awards and selling over 40 million albums! She also recorded the *Songbook Series*, an outstanding work on *The American Popular Song Book*.

Ella Fitzgerald

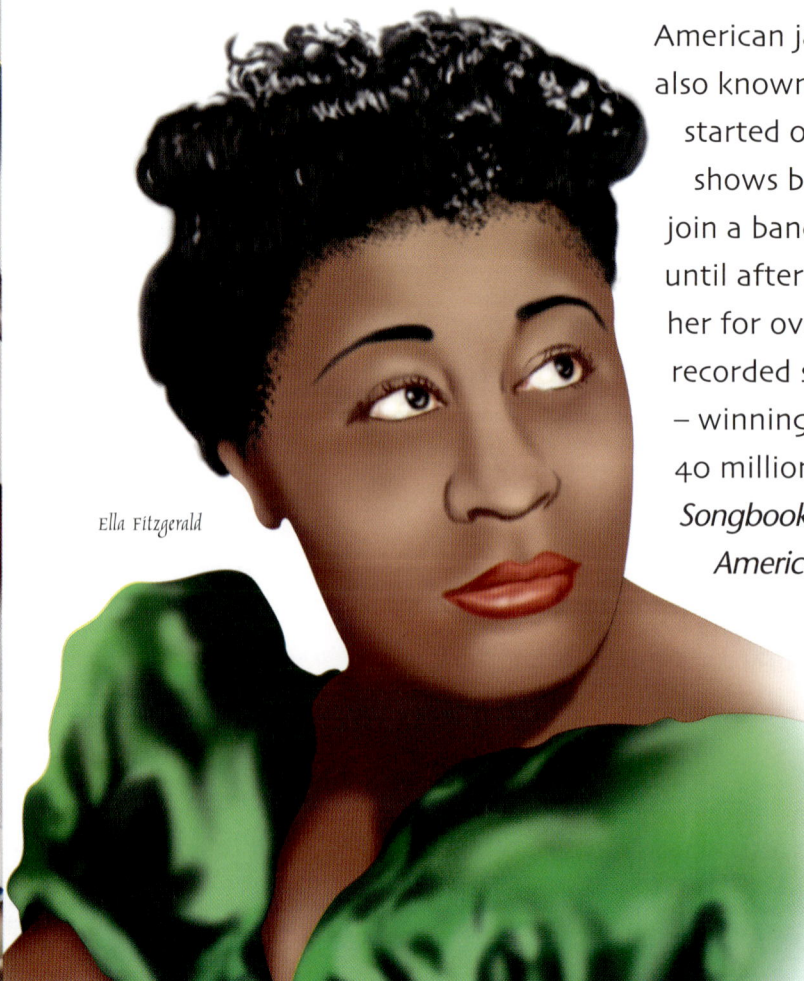

April 25, 1917: Born in Newport News, Virginia, U.S.

1959: Wins her first two Grammys for Best Female Vocal and Best Individual Jazz performances

1987: Is inducted into the Grammy Hall of Fame for album, A-Tisket, A-Tasket

June 15, 1996: Dies in Beverly Hills, California, U.S.

477 BB King
[1925 -]

Riley B King, or BB King, is a hugely popular American rhythm and blues musician. The "King of Blues" is a versatile and charismatic artist known by his famous trademark "Lucille", the name he has lovingly given to every guitar he's ever used! His style is influenced by rhythm and blues, jazz, swing and popular music. Though he has recorded many award-winning songs and hit albums, it is his live performances that he is most loved for.

September 16, 1925: Born in Indianola, Mississippi, U.S.

1951: Records his first big hit, *Three O'Clock Blues*

1966: Writes *The Thrill Is Gone*, his biggest and most popular hit

1987: BB King is inducted into the Rock and Roll Hall of Fame and receives the Grammy Lifetime Achievement Award too

478 Miles Davis
[1926 - 1991]

Jazz musician Miles Davis was an extraordinary trumpeter, composer and bandleader. He had a style that could easily adapt to shifting musical trends: in 1949 he was playing cool jazz, by the mid-50s it was modal jazz, then Spanish flamenco in the late 50s, and by the late 60s it had become a jazz fusion. As a bandleader, he recognised and nurtured the talents of many great musicians and future bandleaders such as saxophonist John Coltrane and pianist Herbie Hancock.

Miles Davis was a very famous jazz trumpeter

May 25, 1926: Born in Alton, Illinois, U.S.

1949: Records the classic, *Birth of the Cool*

1969-70: Records *Bitches Brew*, a revolutionary jazz fusion album

1990: Receives the Grammy Lifetime Achievement Award

September 28, 1991: Dies in Santa Monica, California, U.S.

479 John Coltrane
[1926 - 1967]

Tenor saxophonist John William Coltrane was a major contributor to the development and popularisation of jazz in America. The musical roots of Coltrane lay in ethnic African-American and swing music. Between 1949 and 1951, he took to playing tenor. By 1957, Coltrane was the most popular hard bop tenor in New York. During his career he gave many solo performances and also appeared as an accompanist to great jazz singers of the 50s and 60s. John Coltrane remains a key figurehead of jazz, despite his early death.

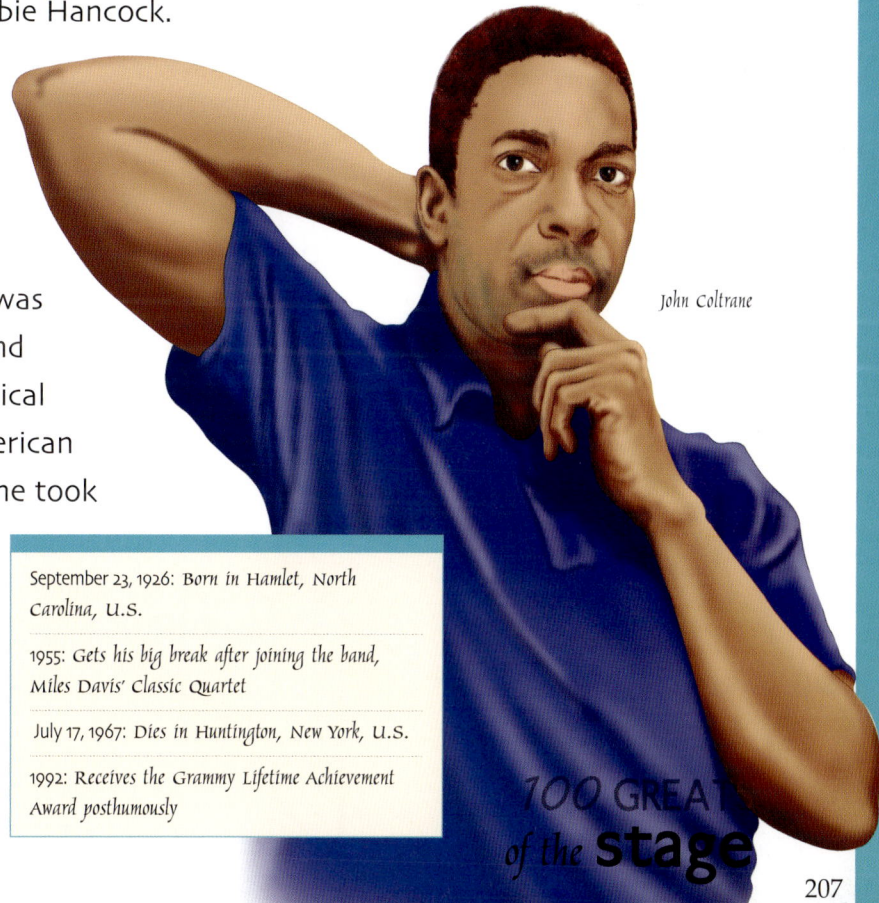

John Coltrane

September 23, 1926: Born in Hamlet, North Carolina, U.S.

1955: Gets his big break after joining the band, *Miles Davis' Classic Quartet*

July 17, 1967: Dies in Huntington, New York, U.S.

1992: Receives the Grammy Lifetime Achievement Award posthumously

100 GREAT
of the **stage**

480 Ray Charles
[1930 - 2004]

American soul musician, Ray Charles Robinson, was a pioneering singer, pianist, composer and musical arranger. In his musical journey, which spanned over 50 years, he played rhythm and blues, jazz and even rock and country music. Having lost his sight at the age of seven, Charles learnt to read and write music in Braille. Despite this, he is considered one of the finest songwriters to have lived and was imortalised in the Oscar-winning biopic of his life, *Ray* (2004).

Ray Charles

September 23, 1930: *Born in Albany, Georgia, U.S.*

1956: *Drown in My Own Tears becomes his first R&B chart hit*

1960: *The Genius Hits the Road is his first Top Ten Album*

January 23, 1986: *Is inducted into the Rock and Roll Hall of Fame*

1987: *Is awarded the Grammy Lifetime Achievement Award*

June 10, 2004: *Dies in Beverly Hills, California, U.S., just months before the release of Ray (2004), the film he helped make*

481 James Brown
[1933 - 2006]

May 3, 1933: *Born in Macon, Georgia, U.S.*

1956: *Please, Please, Please reaches #5 on the Billboard R&B chart*

1963: *Releases Live At The Apollo, which becomes the first live R&B album to reach #2 on the Billboard chart*

1992: *Is awarded a Grammy for his lifetime achievements*

1998: *Releases I'm Back, his latest album*

December 25, 2006: *Dies, Atlanta, Georgia, U.S.*

American singer James Brown is one of the most famous musicians to have lived. Despite coming from a poor and underprivileged background, James Brown rose to become one of the most influential singers of all time. The self-styled "Godfather of Soul" has sold more than 100 million albums, and has had 98 entries on the Billboards Top 40 – 17 of which were Number One hits! His innovative singing style has contributed widely to the development of funk, rock, disco and rap music.

482 Aretha Franklin
[1942 -]

Aretha Franklin, the "Queen of Soul", is a top American singer. As her father was a Baptist preacher, her musical training began with church music. In fact, all through her career she has moved between gospel and soul music – equally adept at both. She has also recorded several hits with leading musicians such as Elton John, Whitney Houston and James Brown. Franklin's career has spanned almost five decades, and she still continues to sing and record!

March 25, 1942: Born in Memphis, Tennessee, U.S.

January 1967: Records I Never Loved A Man (The Way I Love You), her first song to reach the US Top 10

January 3, 1987: First woman to be inducted into the Rock and Roll Hall of Fame

1994: Receives the Grammy Lifetime Achievement Award

2003: Releases her latest album, So Damn Happy

483 Stevie Wonder
[1950 -]

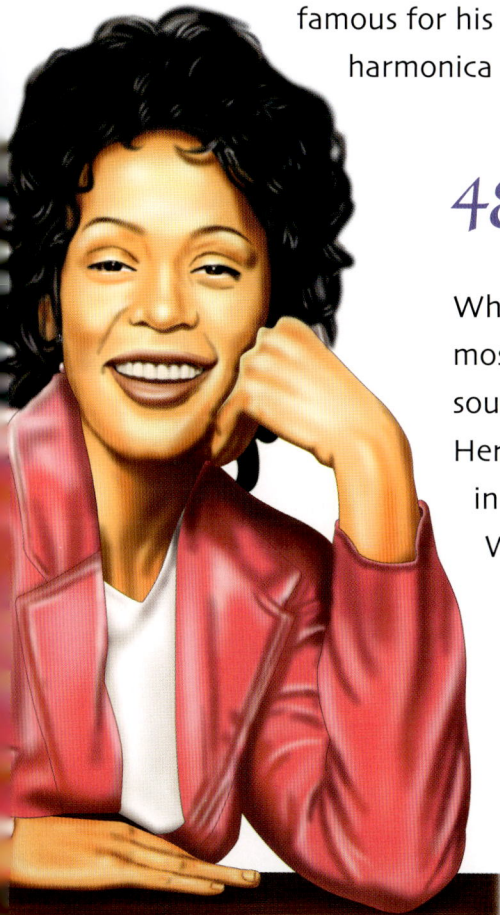

Stevie Wonder, born Steveland Hardaway Judkins, is one of the most gifted songwriter and composer of soul, funk and pop music to have lived. Wonder lost his sight as an infant, but went on to learn to play the piano, the drums and the harmonica by the age of nine! In his illustrious career, Stevie Wonder has won many accolades, including a record 21 Grammy Awards! Selling over 100 million records worldwide, Wonder is famous for his talented piano playing and energetic harmonica solos.

May 13, 1950: Born in Saginaw, Michigan, U.S.

1963: Fingertips (Part II), a live recording, becomes Wonder's first commercial success

1983: Records his biggest-selling single, I Just Called To Say I Love You, for the motion picture The Woman In Red

1989: Inducted to the Rock and Roll Hall of Fame

1996: Receives the Grammy Lifetime Achievement Award

2005: Records A Time to Love, his latest album

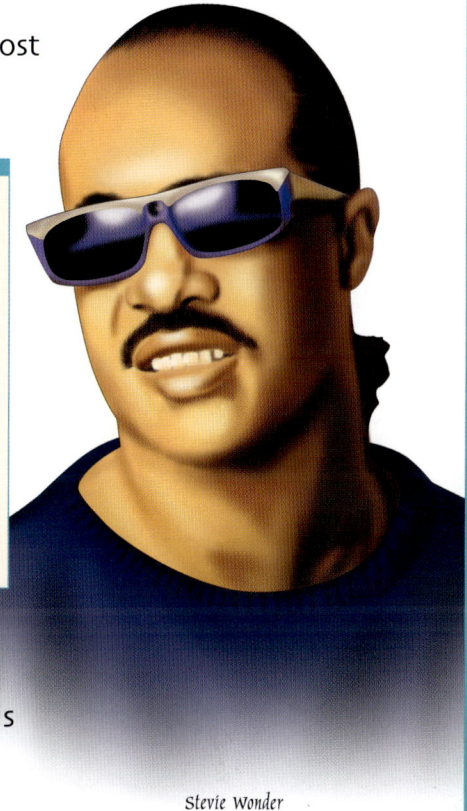

Stevie Wonder

484 Whitney Houston
[1963 -]

Whitney Houston is one of America's most famous rhythm and blues and soul singers of the 1980s and 90s. Her powerful voice helped her to sing in a gospel choir as a child. Initially, Whitney sang as a backup for senior artists. But in 1984 she presented her own album, *Whitney Houston*. This was a huge hit all over America. Successive albums, released during the next few years, were all very popular. Whitney has won an Emmy Award, several Grammy awards and has also acted in films.

August 9, 1963: Born in Newark, New Jersey, U.S.

1985: Arista Records releases her first hit album, Whitney Houston

1987: Whitney, her second album, becomes the first by a female artist to debut at the top of the charts

1992: Makes her acting debut with the film, The Bodyguard, the single for which – I Will Always Love You – tops the US charts for 14 weeks

Whitney Houston

100 GREATS
of the **stage**

Playwrights

485 Euripides
[c. 480 BC - c. 406 BC]

Euripides was a great Greek playwright, who mainly wrote tragedy. Though there is not much known about his life, it is believed that he wrote over 90 plays. He wrote about personal and social problems and his heroes usually had to make difficult choices. Though his plays were moderately successful, he was ridiculed for his liberal views. Some of his famous plays are *Medea*, *The Bacchae* and *Hippolytus*.

c. 480 BC: Born at Salamis near Athens, Greece

441 BC: Wins honours at the Athenian Dramatic Festival

c. 406 BC: Dies in Macedonia, Greece

Euripides

486 William Shakespeare
[1564 - 1616]

Shakespeare is widely considered to be the greatest playwright to have ever lived. 37 plays and 154 sonnets are credited to him, and it is believed that about 15 of his plays had been written and performed before he was 33. "The Bard" was immensely successful as a playwright and actor during his lifetime and often performed before royal audiences. His comedies, tragedies and historical dramas have been translated into many languages and are peformed all over the world.

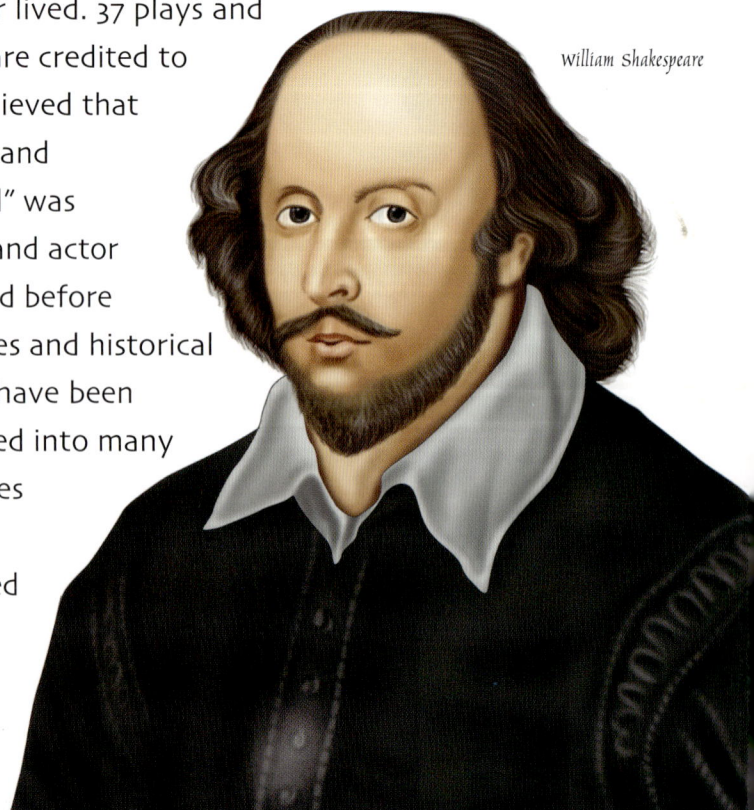

William Shakespeare

April 23, 1564: Born at Stratford-upon-Avon, England

1582: Marries Anne Hathaway

1599: Builds The Globe Theatre along with his troupe members

1603: Shakespeare's troupe is appointed as "The King's Men" by King James I

April 23, 1616: Dies in Stratford-upon-Avon, England

487 John Dryden
[1631 - 1700]

An important figure of 17th century literature, John Dryden was a dramatist, poet, translator and critic. His works included heroic dramas, political satires and comedies. In fact, he is famous as the author of some of the best Restoration-era comedies. John Dryden also translated Greek classics by Virgil, Homer and Horace.

August 9, 1631: Born in Aldwinkle, Northamptonshire, England

1663: Dryden becomes a member of the Royal Society

1668: King Charles II appoints him Poet Laureat

May 1, 1700: Dies in London, England

488 Jean Baptiste Poquelin "Molière"
[1662 - 1673]

Jean Baptiste Poquelin
"Molière"

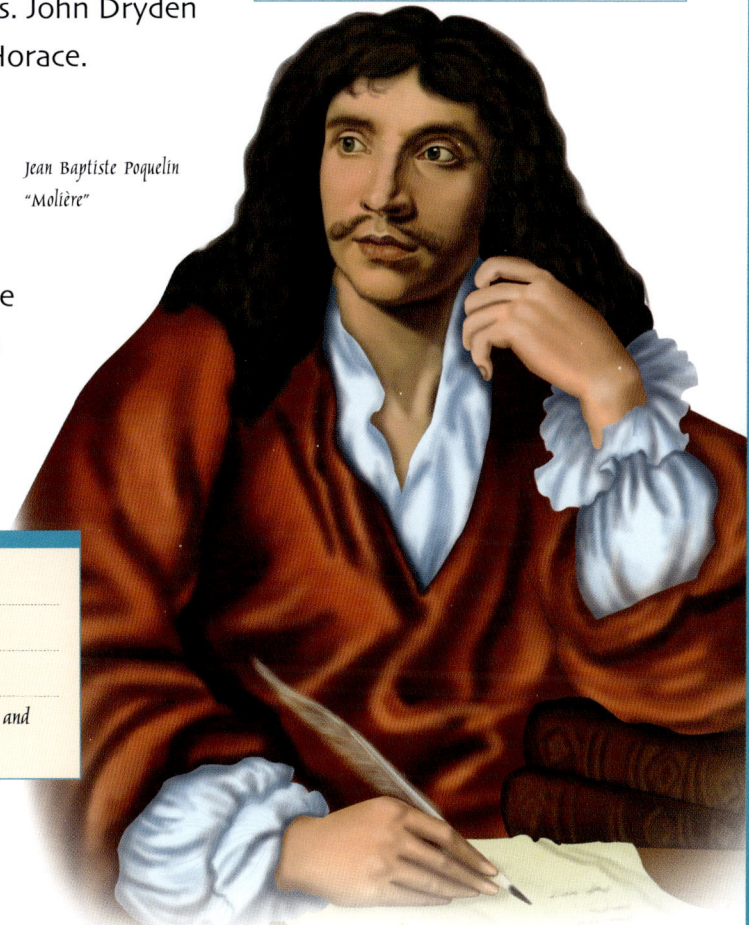

The 17th century French playwright, Molière, wrote comedies and satires. He began his career on stage with a group of travelling performers, but soon began writing his own plays and performing in the best theatres in Paris. Despite the adulation of the royal court, his comedies often satirised religious hypocrisy, bringing him round condemnation from the Church.

January 15, 1622: Born in Paris, France

1664: Stages Tartuffe, his most famous play

1666: Stages The Misanthrope

February 17, 1673: Suffers brain haemorrhage and dies in Paris, France

Oscar Wilde

489 Oscar Wilde
[1854 - 1900]

Oscar Fingal O'Flahertie Wills Wilde, Irish author and play-wright, lived during the late 19th century. He supported "Aestheticism", a 19th century art movement. In 1892 he wrote his first play, *Lady Windermere's Fan*, which was a great success. This inspired him to write more plays – all of which are as popular today as when first performed. Wilde also wrote fairy-tales for children.

October 16, 1854: Born in Dublin, Ireland

1888: Publishes The Happy Prince and Other Tales, fairy tales for children

1890: Publishes his first and only novel, The Picture of Dorian Grey

1895: Writes The Importance of Being Earnest, one of his most popular plays

November 30, 1900: Dies in Paris, France

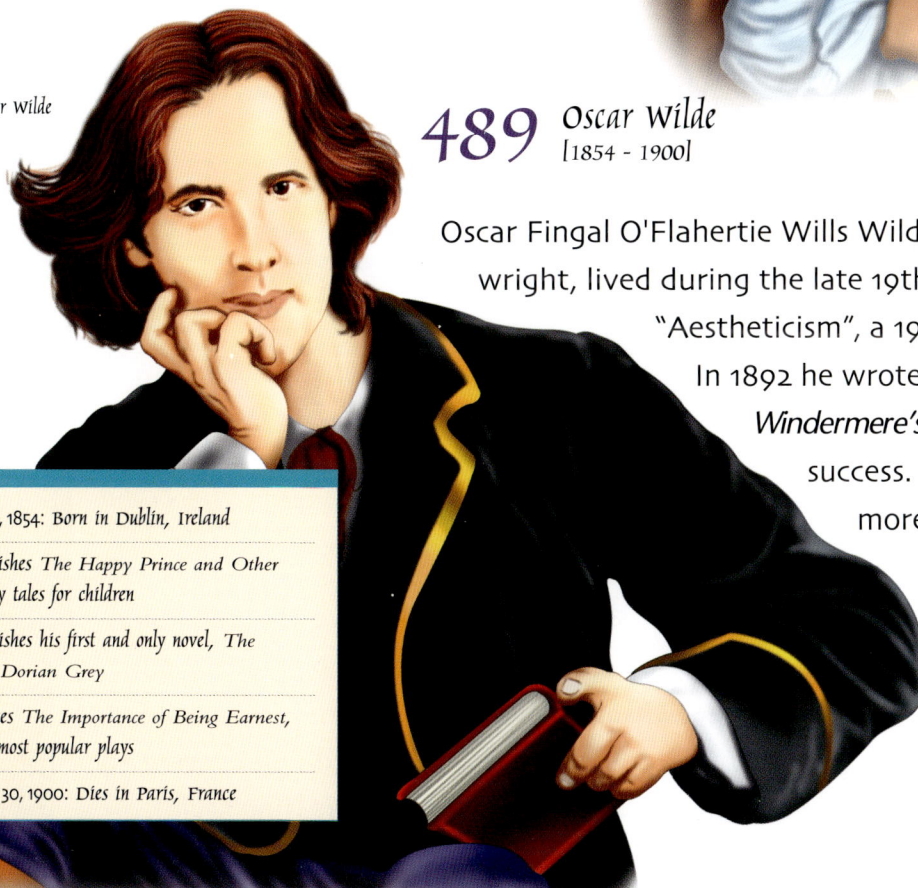

100 GREATS
of the **stage**

490 George Bernard Shaw
[1856 - 1950]

One of the 20th century's leading literary figures, Shaw was an Irish playwright and critic. From the age of 20, he began to write about art, literature and music. Shaw's books, plays and essays mostly deal with social and political issues. He has written over 50 plays, some of which have also been made into films. *Candida, Caesar and Cleopatra, Arms and the Man* and *Pygmalion* are some of his most famous plays.

George Bernard Shaw

July 26, 1856: Born in Dublin, Ireland

1924: Writes *Saint Joan*, one of his best plays

1925: Shaw is awarded the Nobel Prize for Literature

November 2, 1950: Dies in Ayot St. Lawrence, Hertfordshire, England

491 Anton Pavlovich Chekhov
[1860 - 1904]

Russia's most popular playwright, Chekhov, is the author of master-pieces like *Uncle Vanya, The Cherry Orchard* and *The Three Sisters*. Yet he was a practising doctor and a journalist too! Chekhov was greatly inspired by vaudeville and French farces, and has written comedies in this style. Unfortunately, Chekhov died at the age of 44. Chekhov's plays are now widely revered the world over as being as equally challenging as rewarding.

January 29, 1860: Born in Taganrog, Russia

1887: Stages first play, *Ivanov*, a success in St Petersburg

March 1897: Suffers lung haemorrhage

July 14, 1904: Dies of tuberculosis

December 19, 1899: Born in Teddington, England

1917: Acts in his first motion picture, DW Griffith's *Hearts of the World*

1920: Presents *I Leave it to You*, his first play in the West End

1970: Is knighted by Her Majesty, the Queen of England

March 29, 1973: Dies in Jamaica, West Indies

492 Noël Pierce Coward
[1899 - 1973]

Coward is a famous 20th century British playwright. He gave his first stage performance at the age of six and wrote his first full length play at 16! He was also a good painter and singer. Inspired by Broadway productions, he began writing similar plays for the London audience. Coward's plays were so popular that people started imitating his mannerisms and dressing style!

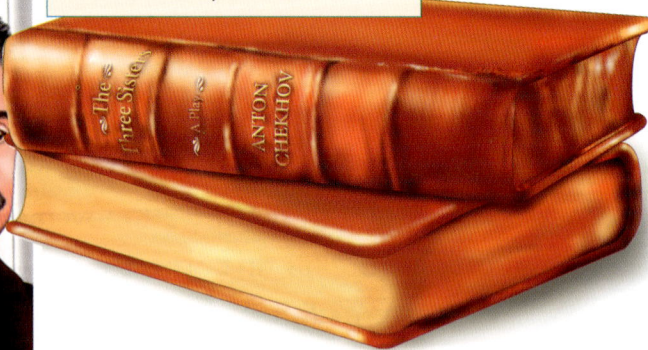

493 Arthur Miller
[1915 - 2005]

Arthur Miller is one of the most famous American playwrights of all time. Inspired by Greek classics and the Russian author, Dostoevsky, Miller began writing for the stage while he was still a university student. *The Crucible* and *Death of a Salesman* are among his most famous plays. He also wrote screenplays for movies, two travelogues and an autobiography. His liberal views found him embroiled in the McCarthy anti-communist witch-hunt. He was held in contempt of Congress when he refused to name friends and colleagues who might have been communists. He was also famous for his short-lived marriage to Hollywood legend, Marilyn Monroe.

Arthur Miller

October 17, 1915: *Born in New York, U.S.*

1944: *The Broadway premier of his first play,* The Man Who Had All The Luck, *is staged*

1949: *Writes* Death of a Salesman, *winner of the Drama Critics Circle Award, three Tonys and the Pulitzer Prize – the first play ever to win all three*

1953: *Writes the Tony Award-winning,* The Crucible

February 11, 2005: *Dies in Roxbury, Connecticut, U.S.*

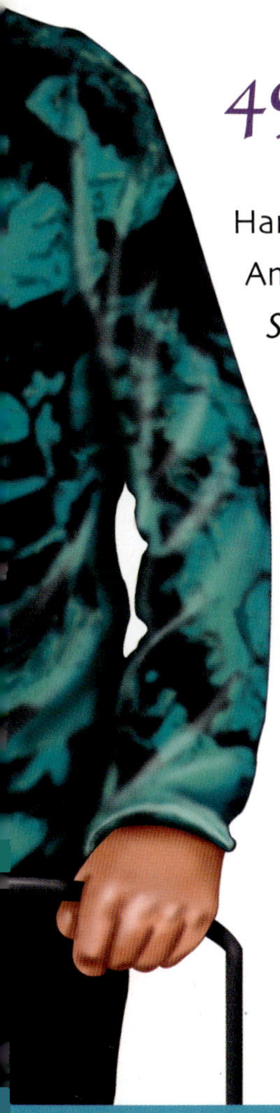

Noël Pierce Coward

494 Lorraine Hansberry
[1930 - 1965]

Hansberry was a 20th century American playwright. *A Raisin in the Sun*, her most famous work, was the first play by an African-American woman to be staged on Broadway. It was performed 530 times in New York! Her characters were ordinary people fighting for their rights and for others around them. She died of cancer at the age of only 34, cutting short a promising career.

Lorraine Hansberry

May 19, 1930: *Born in Chicago, Illinois, U.S.*

1959: *A Raisin in the Sun is staged on Broadway*

1964: *The Sign in Sidney Brustien's Window, is her second play*

January 12, 1965: *Dies in New York, U.S.*

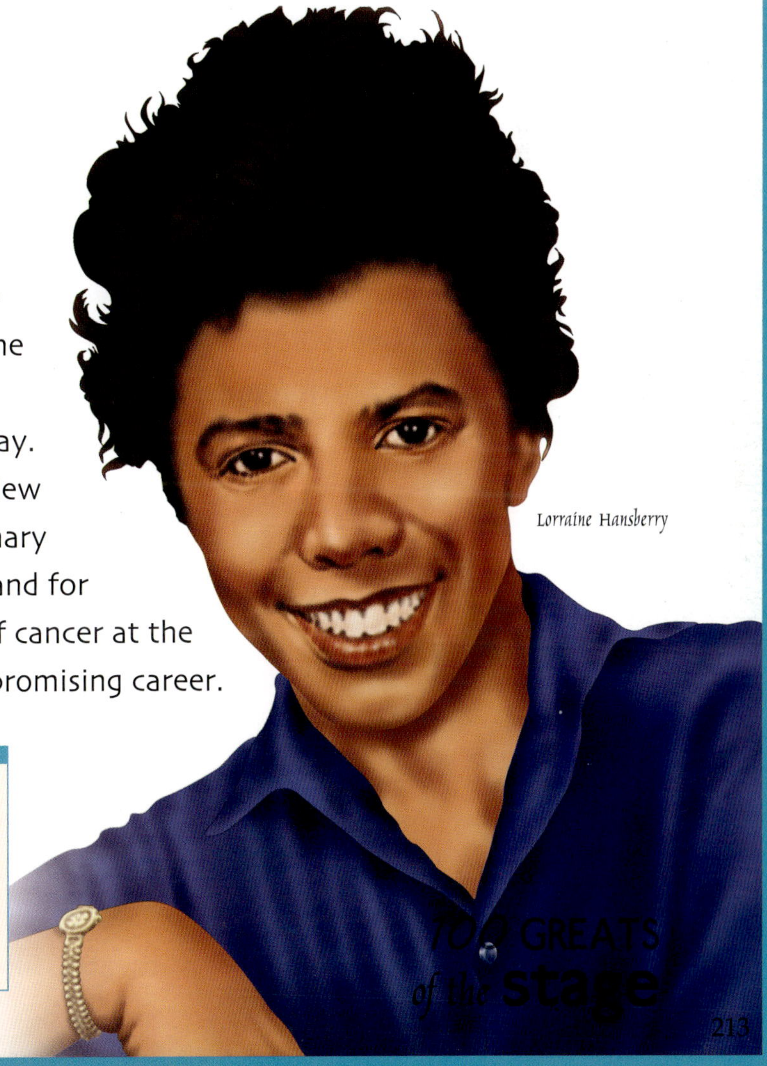

Stage Actors

Sarah Bernhardt

495 Sarah Bernhardt
[1844 - 1923]

Sarah Bernhardt was a very famous actress of the latter part of the 19th century. She was also a talented artist, writer, model and producer of plays. She started by acting in comedies and burlesques, and became famous all over Europe and the U.S. Later she took more serious roles too. She also acted in eight movies and was one of the first actresses of the age of silent films. At the age of 71, her right leg was removed – but the great actress continued to act with a wooden limb!

October 23, 1844: Born as Henriette Rosine Bernard in Paris, France

1862: Starts her stage career as a student at the Comedie Francaise, a prestigious French acting academy

1899: Founds the Theatre Sarah Bernhardt in Paris

1914: Is made member of France's Legion of Honour

March 26, 1923: Dies in Paris, France

496 Konstantin Sergeyevich Stanislavsky
[1863 - 1938]

January 17, 1863: Born in Moscow, Russia

1898: Co-founds the Moscow Art Theatre with Vladimir Nemirovich-Danchenko

August 7, 1938: Dies in Moscow, Russia

Stanislavsky was a Russian actor and director, who began performing on stage from the age of 14. Over the next 40 years, in an attempt to find a style of acting more appropriate to the realism of 20th century drama, he developed the acting style called the "Stanislavsky System" from which "method acting" was derived. Stanislavsky co-founded the Moscow Art Theatre and travelled widely, producing and performing the plays of some of Russia's greatest artistes – such as Chekov and Tolstoy. He gained great fame for his acting, directorial and coaching skills.

497 Helen Hayes
[1900 - 1993]

October 10, 1900: Born in Washington D.C., U.S.

1980: Wins Tony Award for her career achievements

1986: Wins Presidential Medal of Freedom, highest U.S. civilian honour

March 17, 1993: Dies in Nyack, New York, U.S.

Helen Hayes, also known as "the First Lady of American theatre", was a famous American stage actress. She began performing professionally at the age of six and by the time she was nine, she had already made her Broadway debut! At 30, she acted in her first Hollywood film, *The Sin Of Madelon Claudet*, which won her an Academy Award. During her 80-year career, she made outstanding contributions to the fields of theatre, films and television.

The tiny footprints of Helen Hayes grace the sidewalk outside the Broadway theatre named in her honour

498 Stella Adler
[1901 - 1992]

February 10, 1901: Born in New York, U.S.

1906: Makes her stage debut

1931: Joins the Group Theatre

December 21, 1992: Dies in Los Angeles, California, U.S.

Stella Adler was an American stage actress, and for decades was regarded as America's foremost acting teacher - indeed, Adler was the first influential acting teacher of the great Marlon Brando, one of the most celebrated actors of all time. Through her association with the Group Theatre, she was introduced to Stanislavsky's "method acting". This was to have an effect on her acting style and on her decision to begin dramatic teaching. Other famous students included Robert De Niro and Warren Beatty.

Laurence Olivier

499 Laurence Kerr Olivier
[1907 - 1989]

May 22, 1907: Born in Dorking, England

1947: Is knighted

1949: Wins Best Film and Best Actor Academy Awards for Hamlet

1979: Is awarded the Lifetime Achievement Academy Award

July 11, 1989: Dies in Steyning, West Sussex, England

Sir Laurence Olivier is one of Britain's most outstanding stage actors. At the age of 15, while still in school, he began playing classical and Shakespearean roles! In 1926, he joined the Birmingham Repertory. Later, he also performed on Broadway and acted in about 60 motion pictures. Olivier also directed, produced and acted in many films, such as *Henry V* and *Hamlet*. Lord Olivier is interred in Poets' Corner in Westminster Abbey, London.

March 20, 1908: Born in Bristol, England

1934: Briefly becomes a school teacher before turning to acting full-time

1959: He is knighted for his services to theatre

March 21, 1985: Dies in London, England

500 Michael Scudamore Redgrave
[1908 - 1985]

Sir Michael Redgrave - father of actors Corin, Lynn and Vanessa Redgrave, and grandfather of actors Natasha Richardson, Joely Richardson, Jemma Redgrave and Carlo Gabriel Nero - was a British stage and screen actor, and a director. He began his stage career at the Old Vic in London, after which he also performed at the Queen's Theatre. His impressive career included working with the Shakespeare Memorial Theatre Company, performing at the Haymarket, on Broadway and in films such as Hitchcock's *The Lady Vanishes*. Sir Redgrave also wrote several books and a play.

100 GREATS
of the **stage**

501 Betty Comden
[1919 - 2006]

Famous American stage actress, Betty Comden, was also a singer and songwriter. In collaboration with Adolph Green, she wrote books and lyrics for several Broadway musicals and librettos. In 1944, Comden and Green staged their first big Broadway show, *On The Town*. They went on to collaborate on all-time hits like *Singin' in the Rain*, *Its Always Fair Weather* and *Bells are Ringing*. Betty Comden won six Tony Awards, three Screenwriters' Guild Awards and several other honours.

May 3, 1919: Born in Brooklyn, New York, U.S.

1944: Comden and Green write and perform their first Broadway hit, On The Town

1956: Stages Bells are Ringing, with Judy Holliday in the leading role

1991: The Kennedy Center honours Comden

Nov. 23, 2006: Dies in Nw York, U.S

Judi Dench

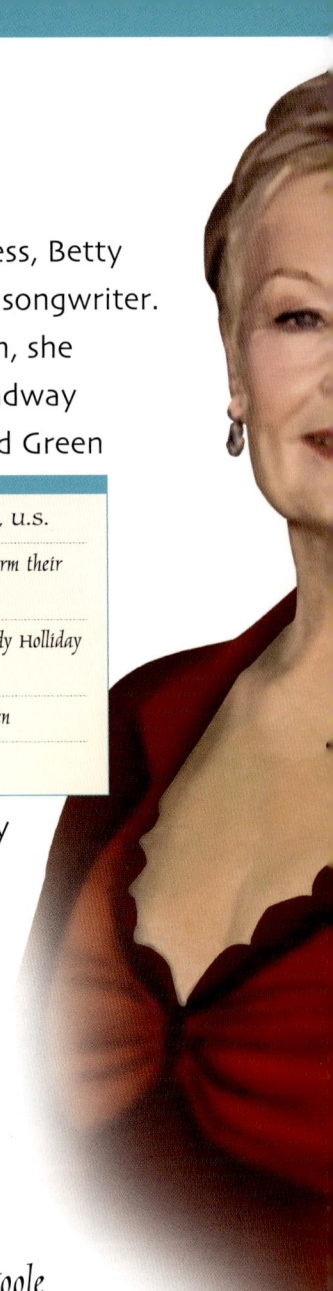

502 Peter O'Toole
[1932 -]

Peter O'Toole is one of Britain's finest actors. He began his career on stage, in 1954, and has since acted in numerous plays, motion pictures and television films. His career, spanning over 40 years, includes performances at the Old Vic in Bristol and London, The Royal Court Theatre and with the Royal Shakespeare Company.

August 2, 1932: Born in Connemara, Ireland

1954: Makes his stage debut with A Midsummer Night's Dream, in Brighton

1962: Acts in Lawrence of Arabia, the film that made him an international star

1963: Wins the BAFTA Best British Actor award for Lawrence of Arabia

2002: Awarded the Oscar Lifetime Achievement Award

503 Judi Dench
[1934 -]

Noted British stage actress, Dame Judith Olivia Dench, won international acclaim after turning 60. She was a member of the Royal Shakespeare Company for several years and later worked with the National Theatre as well. After numerous stage performances, she acted in her first film in 1964 with *The Third Secret*. She has won one Oscar, nine BAFTA Awards and one Golden Globe Award. Some of her most famous roles on the silver screen include *Room With a View*, *Mrs. Brown*, *84 Charing Cross Road*, *Iris*, *Chocolat*, *Shakespeare in Love*, *Golden Eye* and *Die Another Day*.

December 9, 1934: Born in York, England

1957: Makes her stage debut as Ophelia, in the Liverpool Old Vic's production of *Hamlet*

1961: Joins the Royal Shakespeare Company

1970: Is awarded the Order of the British Empire

1988: Is made Dame Commander of the British Empire (DBE)

504 Margaret Natalie Smith
[1934 -]

British stage actress, Dame Maggie Smith, took to theatre as a teenager. She made her mark as a vaudevillian – singing and dancing – in England as well as on Broadway. She then joined the Royal National Theatre Company in London, and went on to act in numerous plays – ranging from the classics and Shakespearean plays to modern drama – acting out comic as well as serious roles. Maggie Smith has also portrayed several memorable roles in films.

December 28, 1934: Born in Ilford, Essex, England

1956: Makes professional stage debut as Viola in *Twelfth Night*

1969: Wins first Academy Award for *The Prime of Miss Jean Brodie*

1970: Is awarded Commander of the British Empire (CBE)

1990: Is made Dame Commander of the British Empire (DBE)

Diana Rigg

505 Diana Rigg
[1938 -]

Dame Diana Rigg, the English actress, is equally famous for her stage and television roles. A noted Shakespearean, she has worked in several stage, film and television versions of Shakespeare's plays. Her work has been greatly admired in both England and the U.S. One of her most popular and memorable roles is that of "Emma Peel" in the television series, *The Avengers*. Diana Rigg also starred as a Bond girl in *On Her Majesty's Secret Service*.

July 20, 1938: Born in Doncaster, Yorkshire, England

1957: Makes professional debut with *The Caucasian Chalk Circle*

1994: Wins Tony Award for *Medea*

1994: Is made Dame Commander of the British Empire (DBE)

100 GREATS of the stage

Glossary

American Civil War: War between the U.S. federal government (Union) and 11 Southern states that fought to break away from the union

American Revolution: Also called the American Revolutionary War or American War of Independence, it freed 13 North American colonies of Britain, to form the United States of America

Alter ego: A person's secondary or alternative personality

Ace: In tennis, a serve where the receiver fails to return or even touch the ball. The point is won by the server

Ashes Series: The test match series played between Australia and England once every two years

Assist: In rugby, the final pass that directly results in a try. Only one assist is possible per try

Archimedes' Principle: The volume of fluid displaced when an object is immersed in it is equal to the weight of the object

Bay of Pigs invasion: Unsuccessful attempt by 1,500 Cuban exiles opposed to Fidel Castro to invade Cuba. It was supported by the United States

Barometer: An instrument used for measuring atmospheric pressure. It is widely used to predict the weather

Blasting gelatine: An explosive containing mostly nitro-glycerine and a little collodion, a solution containing alcohol usually used as an adhesive

Big-bang theory: The theory that proposes that the universe was formed 20 billion years ago, following a violent explosion

Black hole: A cosmic body with gravity so intense that even light cannot escape it. It is normally formed following the death of a star at least three times bigger than the Sun

Battle of Issus: The battle between Alexander the Great and Darius III on the Issus plain near the Gulf of Iskenderun (now in southern Turkey)

Baroque: Highly ornate and complex style of European architecture, art and music of the 17th and 18th centuries

Century: A hundred runs scored by a single batsman in a test or a one-day match

Christopher Columbus: A famous explorer who discovered the continent of America

Cold War: An open but weapon-less enmity between the U.S and the U.S.S.R and their allies

Czar: Also spelt Tsar, it is the title given to the Russian or Byzantine emperor. The title is derived from Caesar

Concerto: A musical composition for an orchestra and one or more solo instruments

Cholera: A highly infectious disease of the digestive system that causes severe vomiting and diarrhoea. It is normally spread through water. It has almost been eradicated

CAT scanner: A machine that produces 3-D photographs of the internal body structure

Disarmament: Reduction of a country's military forces and weapons

Dutch Wars: Four naval wars fought between England and the Netherlands in the 17th and 18th centuries

Dynamo: A device that converts mechanical energy into electrical energy (like in a bicycle). It especially produces direct current

DNA: A complex compound that carries genetic information and is capable of making exact copies of itself

Duet: A musical composition for two singers

Dictator: An absolute ruler, who uses force to suppress his opponents

Dream Team: Name given by the American media to its team that won the gold medal at the 1992 Olympic Games in Barcelona, Spain. For the first time, the team consisted of non-amateur players

Dribble: In sports like football and basketball, the twists, turns, tricks and general ball artistry by which the player who has the ball tries to outmanoeuvre a defending player to get past or away from him

Epithet: A term used as a descriptive substitute for the name or title of a person

Evangelical: Related to Christianity and Biblical sources

218

Electromagnetic radiation: Radiation containing both electric and magnetic fields

Epidemic: An outbreak of a highly infectious disease (like cholera) that spreads fast and among a huge population of people

Eskimo: A group of people found in extremely cold regions like Alaska, North Canada, Greenland and East Siberia

Electric transformers: A device that transfers an alternating current from one circuit to another with changes in the voltage and other electric characteristics

Easter Rising: Attempt by Irish Republicans to forcibly free Ireland from Britain

Exile: To be banished from one's land

Fascism: Rule using military force, which existed in Italy during the early 1900s

French Revolution: The period between 1789 and 1799 in which Louis XVI, the King of France was overthrown by the people

Fossil: The remains of an organism (like the skeleton of an animal or a leaf imprint) embedded and preserved in the earth's crust

Falsetto: A method of singing used by male singers, especially tenors, to sing notes higher than their normal range

Farce: A comic or dramatic work that has silly and idiotic characters and depicts ridiculous situations

FA Cup: The championship tournament played by members of the English Football Association - formed of English football teams, founded in 1863 to standardise rules

FIFA: *Federation Internationale de Football Association,* the world governing body of football; founded in 1904

Geneva Protocol: A treaty created by the League of Nations for peaceful settlement of disagreements between nations

Genghis Khan: Founder and ruler of the Mongol Empire

Gettysburg Address: The famous speech made by President Abraham Lincoln at the dedication of a cemetery at Gettysburg, Pennsylvania, for those killed at the Battle of Gettysburg during the American Civil War

Glasnost: Russian term meaning openness, it allowed open criticism of the government and encouraged public discussion of political and social issues

Gospel: An intense, devout style of African-American religious music

Grand Prix: Any of several competitive international road races for sports cars of specific engine size over an exacting, usually risky course

Greco-Roman: An international style of wrestling in which the legs cannot be attacked, nor used for offence. This places a great emphasis on throws

Geophysicist: A person who studies earth and its physical properties, including seismology, ocean-ography and meteorology

Holy League: An association of Roman Catholics during the French Wars of Religion

Hungarian Revolution: Popular uprising to free Hungary from the control of the Soviet Union

Heavyweight: There are 12 weight classes in Olympic competition, where grouping is determined by weight. The boxer/wrestler must be exactly on or below the specified weight to qualify for the weight class. The heavyweight specification is 201 pounds.

Heptathlon: An athletic contest in which each contestant participates in the following seven track and field events: 200-metre and 800-metre runs, 100-metre hurdles, shot put, javelin throw, high jump, and long jump

Home run: In baseball, when the batter goes around all the bases and reaches the home plate safely and without stopping

Heavy metal: Loud sounding rock music with strong beats

Hybrid: Something made by combining two different elements

Irish Free State: The state comprising 26 of the 32 counties of Ireland, which have been separated from the United Kingdom under the Anglo-Irish treaty

International grandmaster: An international chess player regarded as having the highest level of ability

Illustrious: Leading, famous and highly thought of person

Immortalise: To glorify, honour or pay tribute to

Impromptu: Spontaneous and unplanned

Influential: A thing or person, that is important, dominating or controlling

Innovative: New, unusual and modern

505 GREATS

Jazz: A type of African-American music that is lively and rhythmic

Korean War: Fought between South and North Korea (1950-53) over division of territories

King Ptolemy: Ptolemy XIII, King of Egypt and Cleopatra's brother

King Philip of Macedon: Eighteenth King of Macedonia (located in south-eastern Europe) and Father of Alexander the Great

Knockout: A victory in boxing in which one's opponent is unable to rise from the canvas within a specified time after being knocked down or is judged too injured to continue

League of Nations: An organisation, like the United Nations, created to promote international peace. It was established by the Allies at the end of World War I

Locarno Pact: An agreement signed between Germany and the Allied powers that determined the borders and normalised relations between the two parties

Lacrosse: A game played on a rectangular field by two teams of ten players each, in which participants use a long-handled stick with a webbed pouch on one end to manoeuvre a ball into the opposing team's goal

Lightweight: One of the weight classes in Olympic boxing/wrestling competition. The lightweight specification is 132 pounds

Legacy: An inheritance or something handed down by an older and more experienced person

Liberal: Someone who is broad minded and easy going

Librettist: Person who writes the text of an opera or other long vocal works

Lute: Stringed instrument with a round body, long neck and flat front, which is played by plucking the strings

Lyricist: Songwriter

MRI scanner: A machine that uses nuclear magnetic resonance to produce electronic images of human cells, tissues and organs

Magnetic force: The force between two poles of a magnet or an electric charge that attracts substances like iron

Mammals: Warm-blooded animals with vertebrae (backbone) and a four-chambered heart. The females suckle their young ones

Mapping: To locate a gene sequence in a specific region of a chromosome

Mesozoic Era: From 63 million to 230 million years ago

Maestro: An expert and well-respected male conductor of classical music

Mandolin: An instrument similar to the lute, which has paired strings that are plucked with a plectrum (a thin flat piece of plastic or tortoise shell)

Mazurka: A lively Polish dance

Novgorod: An ancient city in north-western Russia

Naturalist: One who specialises in natural history (zoology or botany)

Nebula: A cloud of particles or gas (usually hydrogen), or both, that is visible as a hazy patch of light or areas of darkness between the stars

Neuron: Nerve cell

Nuclear disarmament: Reduce or stop production of nuclear weapons

Ottoman Empire: Founded by Osman I, a Turkish tribal prince, the empire is named after him. It included Turkey, part of the Middle East and Africa and south-eastern Europe

Orbit: The path in which a planet or a satellite moves around another planet or star. It can also refer to the path of the electron around the atomic nucleus

ODI: One Day International, a game of cricket consisting of 50 overs an innings played on a single day, between two sides representing one of the official test nations, or other national sides, in recognised tournaments such as the World Cup

Oboe: A wind instrument made of a pair of reeds, which has three pitches and emits a sharp and loud sound

Oddities: Strange or weird persons or things

Opera: Drama set to music for instrumentalists and singers

Operetta: A shorter version of an opera, which is light or funny

Oratorio: An elaborate religious musical composition for orchestras and singers

Palestine Liberation Organization: Political organisation formed in 1964 to fight for a Palestinian State

Palestinian Authority: Also called the Palestinian National Authority, is the governing body of the Palestinian regions of the West Bank and Gaza Strip

Pathan: A native of Afghanistan

Protestants: Those who follow Christian religious groups that broke away from the Roman Catholic Church

Peloponnesian War: War fought between the ancient Greek cities of Athens and Sparta that destroyed Athens

Plague: A fatal disease that is spread through rats

Pathologist: A person who studies the nature of disease, its causes and development

Pythagorean Theorem: A popular theorem relating to the field of geometry

Pentathlon: A modern athletic contest in which each participant competes in five track and field events, usually the 200-metre and 1,500-metre runs, the long jump and the discus and javelin throws

Pitch: The rectangular batting area in the centre of a cricket field, which has a wicket at each end and along which the bowler bowls the ball to the batsman

Pantomime: Stage show that includes music, slapstick comedy and jokes on contemporary issues

Pop music: A type of music that is modern, popular, and has a catchy melody and beat

Quartet: A group of four members

Quintet: A group of five members

Rh factor: A substance found on the surface of red blood cells. It gets its name from the Rhesus monkey, in which it was first discovered

Rap: Musical style with African-American roots, involving fast and rhythmic recitation of words with instrumental music in the background

Reggae: A popular Jamaican musical style, with a strong beat

Rendition: Performance of a musical, artistic or dramatic composition

Rhythm and Blues: A popular African-American music that is a mixture of blues and jazz music

Rock and roll: 1950s dance music that has strong beats and catchy tunes

Romantic period: Late 18th century art and literary movement in which the creator's inspiration, views and feelings were given importance

Roman Catholicism: Refers to the Roman Catholic Church. The members of this church accept the Pope's (Bishop of Rome) authority in matters of faith

Soviet bloc nations: Communist countries of the time like Czechoslovakia, Romania, and Hungary, which had political and military ties with the U.S.S.R.

Sonata: Musical composition for a solo instrumentalist, often played with an accompanist on the piano

Symphony: Long and complex musical composition - usually in four parts - that is performed by an orchestra

Travelogue: Book or film describing a person's travel experiences

Tennis Grand Slam: When you win all four of tennis' major tournaments (Australian Open, French Open, Wimbledon and US Open) in one season, you are said to have won the Grand Slam. Therefore, the four major tournaments are also known as Grand Slam events

Test match: A five-day first class cricket match between sides representing one of the official test nations

Track and Field events: All sporting events involving races like 100 m sprint, 400 m, 800 m, relay, marathon, hurdles etc., and hammer throw, discus throw, javelin throw, high jump, long jump, pole vault and such

URL: An Internet address

Vietnam War: Attempt by the U.S. backed South Vietnam to prevent the unification of North and South Vietnam under communist leadership

Vaudeville: A type of stage show that features music, dance and comic acts

Vocalist: Singer

WBA: The abbreviation for World Boxing Association

Waltz: A dance for a couple, which involves turning about as they move around the dance floor

Yuri Gagarin: The first person to travel into space

Zoologist: A scientist who studies animals and their structure, development and classification

505 GREATS

Index

Pete Sampras 175
Peter I 22
Peter O'Toole 216
Philip II 20
Phil Knight 131
Philippe Sella 164
Phineas Taylor Barnum 192
Pierre-Simon Laplace, Marquis de 64
Pink Floyd 201
Pompey the Great 12
Pythagoras 52
Pytor Ilych Tchaikovsky 181

Q

Queen 203
Quincy Jones 195

R

Ranjitsinhji Vibhaji 149
Ramses II 10
Ray Charles 208
Ray Tomlinson 131
Raymond V. Damadian 130
Rene Laennec 100
Richard Rogers 182
Richard Strauss 181
Richard Wagner 180
Robert Alexander Watson-Watt, Sir 119
Robert Boyle 58, 95
Robert Charlton 154
Robert Dennard 129
Robert Fulton 99
Robert Goddard 118
Robert Hooke 95
Robert James Fischer 146
Robert Koch 72, 75
Robert Patch 133
Robert S. Ledley 128
Robert Wolpole, 1st Earl of Orford 22
Rod Laver 172
Rolling Stones, The 194, 201
Ronaldo 157
Ronald Reagan 42
Ronald Ross 77
Rudolf (Carl) Virchow 68
Rudolf Diesel 113

Rudolph Nureyev 191
Rufus Stokes 127
Ruth Handler 124

S

Sachin Tendulkar 151
Sam Snead 161
Samuel Colt 104
Samuel Morse 101
Sarah Bernhardt 214
Schuyler Wheeler 114
Scott Hamilton 153
Scott Joplin 204
Sean Fitzpatrick 165
Sergei Bubka 171
Seymour Cray 128, 129
Shaquille Rashaun O'Neal 141
Sigmund Freud 75
Simon Bolivar 27
Sirimavo Bandaranaike 43
Sonja Henie 152
Srinivasa Ramanujan 83
Stanley Matthews 154
Steffi Graf 175
Stella Adler 215
Stephen Hawking 91
Stephen Sondheim 183
Steve Waugh 151
Stevie Wonder 209
Sugar Ray Robinson 143
Susruta 55

T

Theodora 15
Theodore Roosevelt 30
Thomas Adams 104
Thomas Alva Edison 110, 113, 125
Thomas Hunt Morgan 79
Thomas Jefferson 25
Tiger Woods 163
Tim Berners-Lee 133
Tim Rice 183
Timur 18
Tycho Brahe 57
Ty Cobb 136, 137

V

Valdemar Poulsen 116
Victoria - Queen Of England 29
Vladimir Ilyich Lenin 33, 34, 35

W

Wallace Hume Carothers 120
Walter Hunt 110
Werner Heisenberg 87
Whitney Houston 209
Wilbur and Orville Wright 116
Wilhelm Conrad Roentgen 72
Wilhelm Steinitz 146
Wilhelm Wundt 71
Willem Kolff 123
William Gilbert Grace 148
William Harvey 58, 59
William Herschel 63
William I 16, 23
William Lear 121
William Pitt, the Elder (1st Earl of Chatham) 23
William Schwenck Gilbert 182
William Shakespeare 210
William Sturgeon 100
Willis Carrier 117
Wilt Chamberlain 139
Winston Churchill 34
Wolfgang Amadeus Mozart 179
Woodrow Wilson 30

Y

Yanni 185
Yasser Arafat 44, 46
Yehudi Menuhin 184
Yitzhak Rabin 44

Z

Zenobia 14
Zinedine Zidane 157

505 GREATS

225

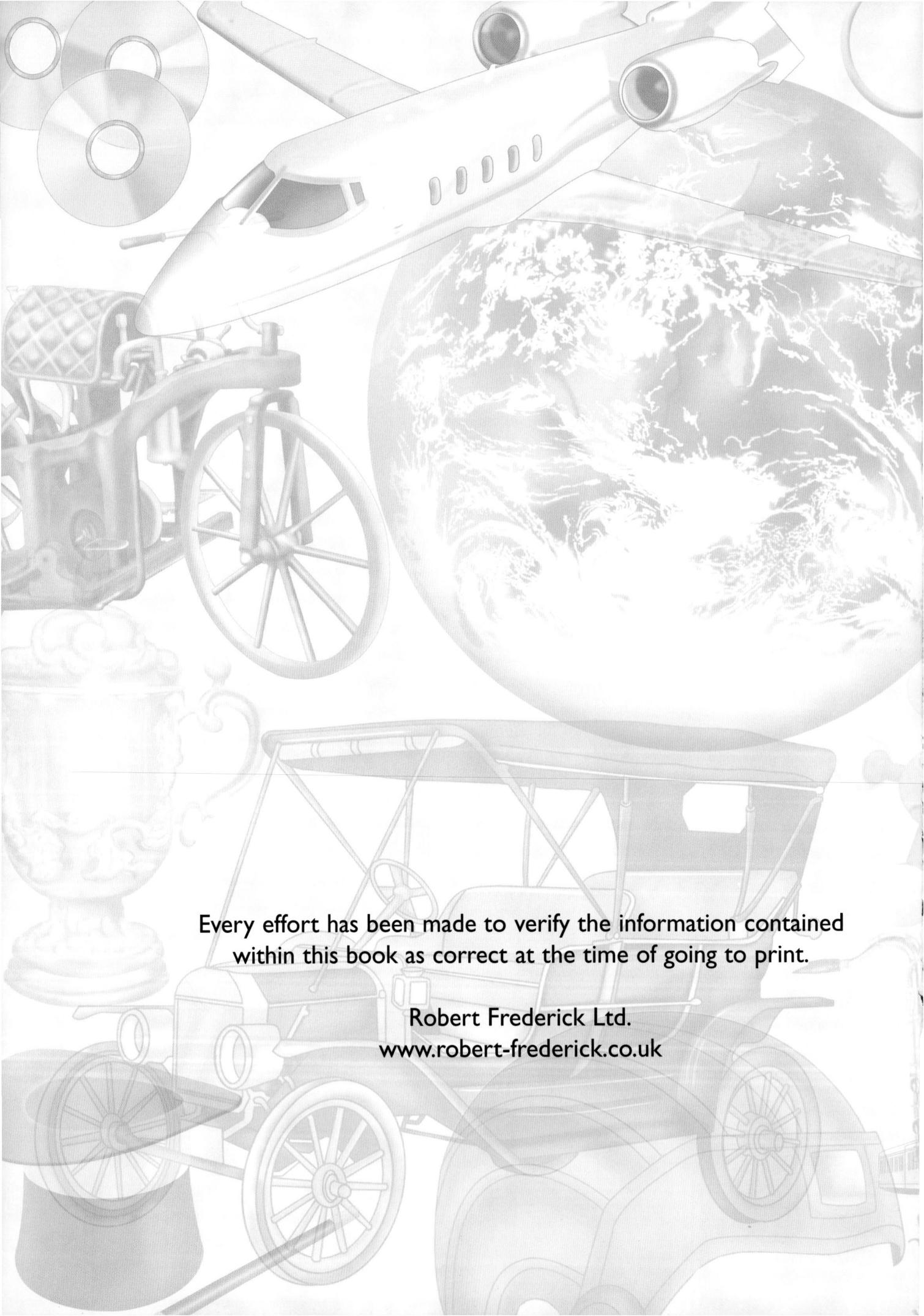

Every effort has been made to verify the information contained within this book as correct at the time of going to print.

Robert Frederick Ltd.
www.robert-frederick.co.uk